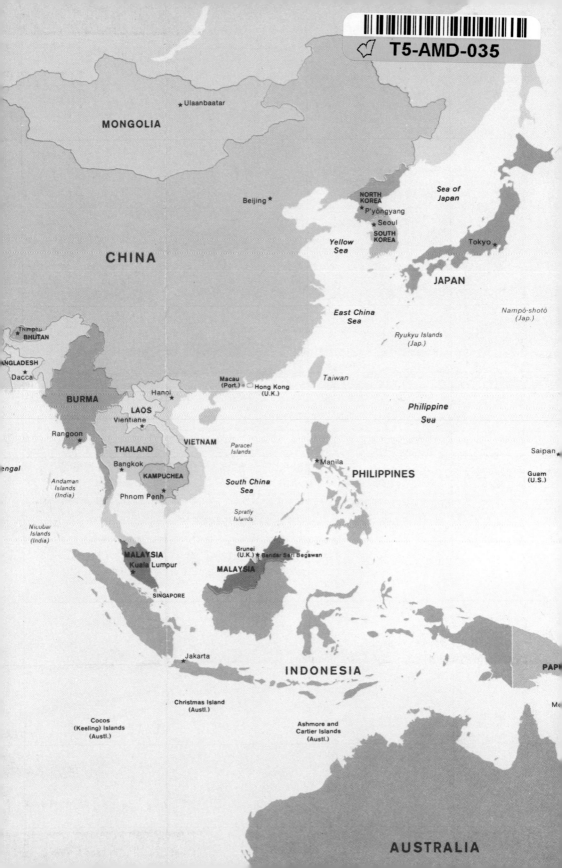

MONGOLIA

★ Ulaanbaatar

CHINA

Beijing ★

NORTH
KOREA
★ P'yŏngyang
★ Seoul
SOUTH
KOREA

Sea of
Japan

Yellow
Sea

Tokyo ★

JAPAN

East China
Sea

Nampō-shotō
(Jap.)

Ryukyu Islands
(Jap.)

Thimphu
★ BHUTAN

ANGLADESH
★
Dacca

BURMA

Hanoi
★

LAOS
Vientiane
★

Rangoon
★

THAILAND

VIETNAM

Bangkok
★

KAMPUCHEA
★
Phnom Penh

Macau
(Port.)   ▯ Hong Kong
          (U.K.)

Taiwan

Paracel
Islands

South China
Sea

Spratly
Islands

★ Manila

Philippine
Sea

PHILIPPINES

Saipan
★

Guam
(U.S.)

engal

Andaman
Islands
(India)

Nicobar
Islands
(India)

MALAYSIA
Kuala Lumpur

SINGAPORE

Brunei
(U.K.) ★ Bandar Seri Begawan

MALAYSIA

Jakarta
★

Christmas Island
(Austl.)

INDONESIA

PAP

Me

Cocos
(Keeling) Islands
(Austl.)

Ashmore and
Cartier Islands
(Austl.)

AUSTRALIA

# SUICIDE IN ASIA AND THE NEAR EAST

# SUICIDE IN ASIA AND THE NEAR EAST

*Edited by*
**Lee A. Headley**

*With a foreword by*
**Norman L. Farberow**

University of California Press
Berkeley    Los Angeles    London

University of California Press
Berkeley and Los Angeles, California

University of California Press, Ltd.
London, England

**Library of Congress Cataloging in Publication Data**

Main entry under title:

Suicide in Asia and the Near East.

   Includes index.
   1. Suicide—Asia—Addresses, essays, lectures.
2. Suicide—Near East—Addresses, essays, lectures.
I. Headley, Lee A.
HV6548.A78S94   1983      362.2      82-45913
ISBN 0-520-04811-3

Printed in the United States of America

1   2   3   4   5   6   7   8   9

# Contents

# Foreword

When Dr. Headley first discussed with me her plans to compile this book I asked a number of colleagues whether they knew anything about suicide in Asia and in countries like Kuwait, or Pakistan, or Syria. Their answers generally were consistent on three points: (1) they knew practically nothing about suicide in that part of the world; (2) they would be very interested in knowing what suicide was like in those countries and in other parts of Asia and the Near East; and (3) they felt that the task of collecting information about suicide in many of the countries in Asia was virtually impossible. They considered the preparation of such a book impossible because (1) some of the Asian and Near Eastern cultures strongly oppose the idea of suicide so that any evidence of it would be denied or disguised or rejected; (2) some of the Asian and Near Eastern religions forcefully condemn suicide, adding to the denial of its occurrence and resistance to its study; (3) official government records in such countries would be highly suspect and probably both inaccurate and incomplete; (4) studies of suicide in such countries would likely be few, if any, and would also be suspect in view of the inherent resistances; (5) outsiders wishing to encourage studies or to initiate studies of their own would not be welcome, and cooperation would be minimal; (6) political conditions in some countries would be inhospitable both to a study and to any investigator; (7) physical conditions in some countries are so primitive that they would present insuperable difficulties in visiting the countries or in communicating regularly with any prospective contributors.

Despite all the above objections, this "impossible" book now exists. Such a task could have been accomplished only through the exercise of much persistence, adaptability, and resourcefulness. These qualities Dr. Headley fortunately possesses in abundant degree. Early in the planning stage, she approached me as then president of the International Association for Suicide Prevention (IASP) for help in finding contributors, as the association has national representatives in a number of countries scattered throughout the world. Unfortunately, since there are few Asian IASP members, we were able to suggest only five national representatives who might serve as contributors. These were Professors Tatai in Japan, Rin in Taiwan, Rao in India, and Okasha in Egypt, and the Reverend Mr. Tu in Hong Kong, who subsequently provided all or part of the chapters for their respective countries. The IASP could provide only "official" support to Dr. Headley in her efforts to get information from other countries not represented in the IASP.

It was therefore an enormously difficult problem to find contributing researchers in Asia and especially in the Middle Eastern countries where almost nothing was known about Muslim suicides. Repeated visits to these countries were necessary to locate interested professionals and to encourage them in the task of gathering material, often from handwritten police and hospital records. Frequently the persons Dr. Headley queried in the Middle East felt that there were no Muslim suicides and that statistics would be impossible to obtain. Some of those she approached displayed an understandable reluctance to identify themselves as investigators in this area, perhaps feeling they would risk their professional status. Thus the fact that the final version of this book contains descriptions of fourteen countries of Asia and the Near East is all the more impressive and must stand as evidence of the persuasive powers of Dr. Headley.

This volume presents for the first time anywhere a collection of clinical and statistical data on completed and attempted suicides in most of Asia and the Near East. The statistical data present rates of completed suicide and basic demographic information, such as age, sex, marital status, occupation, and so on, for all the countries. The same information is supplied for attempted suicide, but usually in less detail than for completed suicide, for attempts were often not recorded in official files and are concealed by families. Methods of suicide and the precipitating or contributing causes are discussed in relation to the culture and religion of the countries. Special features or distinctive aspects are sometimes discussed, such as student suicide in Japan, multiple suicide pacts in India, and suicide among prisoners in Syria. Clinical examples are included in a number of the papers. The individual contributors are frank and explicit in telling us when the data are limited by unreliability and incompleteness. Better still, they also explain why the data are unreliable. So long as we are aware of these limitations we can adjust the level of confidence in the interpretations and still find the data meaningful.

Dr. Headley found that suicide occurred in all the countries reported on, despite the fact that, as the contributors from Islamic countries point out, suicide is strictly forbidden in the Koran. Undoubtedly the religious proscriptions in those countries have served to lessen the probability that self-destruction would be used as a resolution for personal problems. Apparently self-destructive impulses, when they did appear, would be suppressed, and if suicidal acts occurred, they would be denied by the family. It is of considerable interest, therefore, that suicides still could be found in these cultures, most often as an escape from unbearable psychological pain and unacceptable personal circumstances. Such motivations are the same as those found in Western countries, and one cannot help but be impressed not only by the universality of human needs and desires but also by the similarity of human behavior in response to them.

For me, relatively unfamiliar with the Asian part of the world, the most interesting part of each contribution lies in the descriptions in depth of the culture of each country, with its historical, social, and religious development, and in the relationships of these cultures to attitudes and feelings about suicide. One cannot understand, for example, the high or low rates found, the methods used, the attitudes toward survivors, the age and sex distributions in such Middle East countries as Pakistan, Syria, Iraq, Iran (pre-Khomeini), Kuwait, or Jordan without knowing what the attitude of the Islamic religion is toward suicide (severely condemnatory), toward age (elderly are respected; young boys are the responsibility of the mother until age seven to nine and thereafter are the father's, and toward women (inferior and insignificant). Women, especially young women, in many of the countries have relatively few options for expressing their depression and frustration other than to hurt or kill themselves. It is not surprising, therefore, to find that they outnumber males in attempted suicide. Of course, females in Western countries also outnumber males in attempted suicide, but it is mostly for different reasons. The fact that young women also outnumber young males in committed suicide in many countries is a startling finding which points up the difference in status, socially and culturally, of women in Asian countries. Since suicide by any member is seen by the family as a great shame and dishonor, a woman experiencing overwhelming problems and difficulties may feel she has only the single, powerful, retaliatory weapon available to her—suicide.

The chapters have been arranged in a consistent format so that the information on different countries can be compared. The conclusion pulls together statistical patterns, notes, similarities and differences among countries, and makes suggestions for government and volunteer action to understand and prevent suicidal behavior in Asia.

Dr. Headley made many trips to Asia over a period of eleven years in the search for and encouragement of contributors to this book, coping with differing languages, poor transportation and communication facilities, and occasional hostilities between countries. A woman traveling alone in a masculine-dominated, feudalistic, autocratic country is perhaps greeted with curiosity and interest, but with little gallantry. Perhaps in the future Dr. Headley can be persuaded to write about her kidnapping in India, her travels from bombed-out Beirut with refugees in a group taxi to Damascus, Syria, and on to Jordan, or her crossing the Khyber Pass by local transportation when Afghanistan closed its regular routes to Pakistan, and other experiences. They would make a fascinating supplement to this volume.

Our understanding of suicide has been greatly enriched by this book.

Norman L. Farberow

Los Angeles, California
January 1983

# Editor's Preface

It is very hard to convey to the Western reader, and possibly to his Asian counterpart, the difficulties in getting the information to create this book. Many edited books are compilations of papers given at national and international meetings where participants from various countries come to attend a conference. The International Association for Suicide Prevention (IASP) meetings had very few Asian representatives and the papers were widely divergent. Some Western edited books are formed by an editor writing to well-known institutions or personalities specializing in specific subjects such as social studies. This procedure was not possible in Asia, and most of the contributors to this book were unknown to the IASP or other organizations or agencies in the West. Suicide investigations in Asia and the Near East were either in their infancy or nonexistent, with extremely few reports in the suicide literature.

Consequently it was necessary to go to the countries to locate persons who could or would obtain the information. It would seldom be found in agencies such as the census or medicolegal departments, as their figures were often obviously inadequate, as in Iran and Afghanistan. Also, an acceptable report would require more than just suicide numbers—preferably a knowledge of contributing factors and of the human element. The amount of time and effort required to find these contributors cannot be gauged by Western standards. Logistical problems were legion, adding to the frustrations and difficulties.

Communication by letter to Asia is poor. Many letters to me from these colleagues never arrived; nor did my letters, even though sent by registered mail, reach them. The United States Post Office returned a long-awaited report to Iraq without my knowledge with the notation "no such person at this address," although I have lived at the same address for years. Telephone service in most of the countries past the South Pacific coast ranges from poor to deplorable owing to primitive equipment, frequent breakdowns of service, and frustrations of language, even with interpreters. It required three days in Tehran to reach a professor at Tehran University by telephone. When the appointment was made I went to the university and was told the professor was not there. I walked down endless halls saying the professor's name at each door and after forty-five minutes of queries found him waiting as agreed. A telephone call from Amman, Jordan, to Baghdad was attempted for two days and I was ready to abandon the effort when luckily a student of the chapter contributor, working at the telephone bureau, was able to arrange the call. Cairo communications are so impossible that one employs a messenger or goes personally.

Asian attitudes toward time are quite different from Western attitudes. An agreement to do something is regarded as almost the same as having done it. Time is fluidly interpreted, as explained by Dr. Al-Hakim in the chapter on Syria. This attitude does not facilitate meeting deadlines.

Unexpected problems arose which prevented completion of projects. A number of Asian countries—Malaysia, Indonesia, Korea, Turkey, Israel, Afghanistan, China, and Bangladesh—are not included in this book although I spent several years working with possible contributors and had gathered varying amounts of information. Some had changes in their personal lives which made participation impossible; others faced political situations that became unsafe. Bangladesh became chaotic with opposing military forces and guerrilla attacks on police posts. Under the President Park regime in South Korea almost any article or statement could be disapproved and could lead to imprisonment: scores of priests, professionals, and intellectuals were jailed. Afghanistan suffered a revolution followed by invasion. Although I had considerable information on Israel, Muslim contributors were adverse to the inclusion of Israel and felt it would prevent their participation.

The physical difficulties of travel in Asia were also more severe than in the West, particularly as it was necessary from the uncertainties of my work to travel without reservations and to move every four or five days on the average from country to country. Political frictions occurred between countries which sometimes required my traveling by native bus or group taxi from one country to another as air communications halted. Unfortunately, I developed a life-threatening illness during the middle portions of this study which created further difficulties.

There have been problems of translation of Asian language materials given to me, and of course some contributors have had a limited command of English. Some suicide prevention centers have given me raw statistics to analyze and put in a narrative text because they lacked time or language facility. This has been time consuming.

In spite of all the above problems, I found this pioneering task to be an exciting and satisfying endeavor. It was work well worth doing. It has been educational and rewarding to me to have had close contact with the peoples of these many countries. Working with the authors of these chapters has been enjoyable and stimulating, and I value them as colleagues and friends.

# Acknowledgments

I feel immensely grateful to Dr. Norman L. Farberow, of the Institute for Studies of Destructive Behaviors and the Los Angeles Suicide Prevention Center, for his moral support, his suggestions, and his encouragement throughout this project and its tribulations. He has been a strong force toward the completion of this book.

I am also indebted to Dr. Y. B. Motamed of Iran who translated and interpreted for me on my visits there, and for his kind encouragement and continued friendship.

Dr. Mohammad I. Barhoum of Jordan has given me significant assistance from his wide-ranging knowledge of the Middle East. I appreciate his warm support. It has been a pleasure to work with him and his wife, Amal.

Dr. Masaaki Kato, Director of the Institute for Mental Health of Japan, gave of his interest and support to this project.

William Weatherall, doctoral candidate at the University of California, Berkeley, and resident of Tokyo, kindly contributed information about suicide cases in Tokyo.

I appreciate the cooperation and detailed information of the staff and volunteers of the suicide prevention centers of Japan, Taiwan, Singapore, and Hong Kong.

Dr. Abdel Karim Al Yafi of Damascus University Sociology Department was very helpful to me in finding a suicide researcher for the chapter on Syria.

I deeply appreciate the contribution of information by Dr. K. Sathyavathi of the National Institute of Mental Health and Neurosciences, Bangalore, India.

The Reverend Wallace Brownlee of Tokyo kindly translated Japanese materials for me.

Most important, I appreciate the hard work and dedication of those who contributed chapters on their respective countries.

L. A. H.

# Contributors

Syed Haroon Ahmed, M.D., Department of Neuropsychiatry, Jinnah Post Graduate Medical Center, Karachi, Pakistan

Maliha Awni Al-Kassir, LL.B., M.A., Department of Sociology, University of Baghdad, Baghdad, Iraq

Khaldoun Al-Hakim, Ph.D., University of Damascus, Syria

Mohammed Issa Barhoum, Ph.D., Department of Sociology, University of Jordan, Amman, Jordan

Somporn Bussaratid, M.D., Department of Psychiatry, Siriraj Hospital, Mahidol University, Bangkok 7, Thailand

Tuan Chen, B.A., Department of Psychiatry, National Taiwan University Hospital, Taipei, Taiwan

Hock Boon Chia, M.D., Singapore Medical Centre, Suites 6–46/47, 19 Tanglin Road, Singapore 1024

Padmal De Silva, B.A., M. Phil. (Clinical Psychology), Department of Psychiatry, University of Sri Lanka, Columbo, Sri Lanka (Ceylon). Now a lecturer at the Institute of Psychiatry, Maudsley Hospital, London.

S. A. W. Dissanayake, FRC Psych., FRCP(E), DPM (UK), Department of Psychiatry, University of Sri Lanka, Colombo, Sri Lanka

Dorry H. Ezzat, FRC Psych., Kuwait Psychological Medicine Hospital, Kuwait

Hassan Farzam, M.D., Mehr Hospital, Zartosht Avenue, Tehran, Iran

Lee A. Headley, Ph.D., private practice, 12210 Brookmill Road, Los Altos, California, U.S.A. 94022

Farouk Lotaief, M.D., Department of Psychiatry, Ain Shams University, Cairo, Egypt

Kalyani K. Mehta, B. Soc. Sc., Samaritans of Singapore, 591–A New Bridge Road, Singapore, 0208

Ahmed Okasha, M.D., Department of Psychiatry, Ain Shams University, Cairo, Egypt

A. Venkoba Rao, M.D., Department of Psychiatry, Madurai Medical College, Madurai, India

Hsien Rin, M.D., Department of Psychiatry, National Taiwan University Hospital, Taipei, Taiwan

Sompop Ruangtrakool, M.D., Department of Psychiatry, Siriraj Hospital, Mahidol University, Bangkok 7, Thailand

Kichinosuke Tatai, M.D., director, Japan Biorythm Laboratory, Tokyo, Japan

# INTRODUCTION

In the past two decades interest in suicide has markedly increased and, with it, the number of publications dealing with the subject. Suicide prevention centers have been established in the larger cities in the United States and in Europe. Staffing, training, and treatment services, more defined in the centers, have provided a pool of information for researchers. The increase in interest in suicide has stimulated those in academic circles to delve further into the complexities of life-threatening behavior.

A large majority of inquiries about suicide have concerned populations in the United States, Canada, Great Britain, central European countries, and South America. There is now a general awareness of the characteristics to be found in the Western suicide profile. For completed suicides, the characteristics are a preponderance of male suicides, an increasing incidence of mortalities with age, and a higher proportion of deaths among those who are single, divorced, or widowed. Persons considered to be alienated from self and society are thought to be the most serious risks. The profile of the suicide attempter is likely to be the reverse of that of the person who completes suicide. More females than males attempt suicide, and the attempts tend to peak in late adolescence and early youth.

Although much is known about suicide, and many studies are in progress concerning it, a great deal of research is still needed. What are the critical determinants that cause a person to make serious or irreversible suicide attempts? What are the reasons for the popularity in certain areas for particular means of self-destruction? Although the number of studies of subgroups within populations is increasing, there is little information on the effect of major populations on minority groups as to suicidal trends. Comparatively few cross-cultural reports on suicide have been made, and cultural data have not been heavily stressed in many investigations.

My interest in suicide in Asia was first aroused when I undertook a comparison of the phenomenon in Japan and Israel in order to investigate the frequent assertion in professional literature that the suicidal rate for the Japanese is very high and that for Jews is very low. The reasons for the discrepancy were alleged to lie in the prohibitions against suicide in the Jewish religion. Previous studies had been made on minority Jewish populations within surrounding majority populations, often of quite different cultural stamp. My study[1] revealed that the rate of suicide in Israel is not as

---

[1]Part of the study is published as "Suicide in Israel" in *Suicide in Different Cultures*, ed. N. L. Farberow (Baltimore: University Park Press, 1975).

low as is generally believed; it is slightly lower than that in the United States and higher than that in Norway, the Netherlands, and Italy.

One of the problems I encountered in working on that study, however, was that the data concerning Japan and Israel could be compared only with those for Western countries. Although Israel is considered Western in its outlook, its population is more than 65 percent Oriental Jewish, with non-Western orientations. Since no reports of suicidal research in Near Eastern countries existed, I could not relate Israel's statistics to those of any of the countries near it, although the bordering states are similar in terrain and cultural history, if not in religion.

Very few data on suicide in Japan are available. A few articles were written by Western researchers after World War II stimulated American interest in Japan and things Japanese. Articles by Japanese investigators published in Japanese journals were of little use to Westerners because of the language difficulty and journal unavailability. Although Westerners are generally aware of ritualized suicide in Japan, few of them have a clear picture of the rate or the causes of suicide in Japan.

Almost no data on suicide in other Asian countries are available to Westerners. The works of the very few researchers who have undertaken suicidology studies in the Pacific Asia area have been published in their own national journals, often in languages not comprehensible to Westerners. For central Asia there are no data at all. The few persons who are interested in suicidology are unknown to other professionals in neighboring Asian countries, and there is no organized exchange of data and residency in the West. Among the reasons for this lack are governmental restrictions on travel, based on political considerations, and the absence of funds for such traveling. Furthermore, professionals seeking additional training or contacts outside their own countries usually travel to the United States or Great Britain. Asians are as unaware of Asian suicide data as are Westerners.

Thus almost half the world's patterns of suicidal behavior are unknown, a circumstance I found very intriguing. Would suicides in Asia follow the Western profile, or would they be completely different? While the obvious course would be to collect data from as many Asian countries as possible, numerous problems immediately manifested themselves: the time and effort that would be required, language barriers, competency of investigators, reliability of statistics. The researcher in each country would need to be an indigenous national speaking the language and/or dialects and would have to be able to find and utilize resources and to relate the data to cultural determinants. Suicide statistics alone would not be enough; it would also be necessary to have background information about matters such as geography, which influences trade, climate, and degree of interchange with other countries. Historical data, economic status, and religion also enter into an assessment of suicide data.

The task of finding qualified professionals in each country was difficult, as there were almost no persons who belonged to the International Association for Suicide Prevention. In consequence, it has taken eleven years to complete this project. It was not funded by any private or public grant. The trips across Asia, which usually required two or three months a year, had to be made while I suspended my private practice. Traveling independently in Asia on a tight schedule is very difficult, and unreliable telephone and cable services increase the difficulty. To accomplish my goal, I had to be determined and persistent in the face of constant obstacles.

On my many trips to Asia I went to the psychiatry, psychology, and sociology departments of universities, to psychiatric and general hospitals, ministries of justice, legal medicine departments of cities and countries, public health departments, and statistical agencies. As would be expected, the persons most interested were psychiatrists and psychologists working in hospitals and mental health centers and sociologists attached to universities. Through my inquiries I developed a substantial list of highly qualified persons who agreed to contribute data to the book.

It is evident that the quality of such a group of research reports would be uneven. The statistical resources in each country would vary considerably: some reports would be representative of the country as a whole, whereas others could be gathered only from the largest city of a country, where police and hospital reports might be adequate. The usual questions about the reliability of the data would arise. In the United States, it is estimated that there may be six to ten times as many suicides as are reported and a far higher percentage of unreported attempted suicides. Since some religions in Asia, especially Islam, have strict prohibitions against suicidal behavior, families would be likely to conceal suicide deaths and attempts. This factor would need to be evaluated as fully as possible in order to assess the reliability of figures obtained. Such prohibitions are present in Christian, or westernized, countries as well, and, as we know, they account for the concealment of many suicide attempts. Such factors affect suicide data in all Western countries as well as in Asia, and they should not be taken as a reason to discount the reports.

There would be differences in the time span covered in the research, for it depends on factors such as the scope of governmental statistical reporting and of the data available to the researcher. Some reports might cover many decades; others might have a span of three or four years. These inevitable differences would make comparisons among countries difficult, but at least the period under study could be related to general historical and economic movements in a particular country and in similar countries.

The qualifications of those doing the research are similar in general. Psychiatrists from the Pacific to India have often been trained in universities in the United States. Some individuals have taken postgraduate courses in the United States or have been exposed to Western psychiatry by means of exchange programs which enabled American psychiatrists to do a tour of duty in Asian countries. From India to Jordan, the educational slant has been toward Britain and France. In particular, Iranian professionals have gone to France for training. A number of psychiatrists and psychologists, as well as sociologists, from the Near East have gone to Britain for professional training, earning degrees that reflect the British system. Most psychiatrists and psychologists who have contributed to this volume are attached to universities, hospitals, or teaching hospitals.

Suicide is usually considered to be the act of a person desperately trying to cope with unbearable stresses, both internal and external. Consequently, certain kinds of background data are desirable in order to achieve a balanced perspective. Each contributor was requested to include geographical and political descriptions of his country so as to present an accurate picture of the composition of the population, political stability, and economic conditions, both past and present. Obviously, these factors would influence an individual's attitudes toward problems of living and determine the alternatives available to him for alleviation of difficulties and stress.

Cultural attitudes are of special importance in this discussion, particularly religious attitudes and the strictness of their application. Religious conformity may differ from the official position of religious spokesmen. In Israel, which is often called a theocratic state, religious forms are widely observed, but it is generally agreed that Israelis are not very religious in the usual meaning of the term. Although Italy is regarded as a solidly Catholic country, recent surveys suggest that the average Italian is less religious than the average American. Certainly the recent passage of laws in Italy regarding divorce and the legalizing of abortion are in direct defiance of the Vatican. Recent political elections in Italy have installed members of liberal groups bitterly opposed by the Catholic hierarchy. Religious rules are definitely contributory to cultural attitudes, but the degree of acceptance of and adherence to such rules is difficult to assess. Probably it can be estimated only by one born into a particular culture.

Legal attitudes toward suicide are usually a distillation of overall cultural attitudes, although in some countries, as in Sri Lanka and India, legal systems have been imported. Also, adherence to the law varies from country to country: some countries vigorously investigate suicide attempts; others take no action despite the existence of laws penalizing those who attempt suicide.

The social structure of a country depends partly on family patterns—hierarchical or individualistic, nuclear or extended, rigidly enforced or disintegrating. Value systems affect the family and individual thinking and behavior. In countries whose established values are being affected by Western ideas and Western industrial processes, there may be considerable turbulence for those attempting to adjust to conflicting values. The chapters in this volume include such data as a further background to the statistical findings. Social and cultural values influence both the response of families toward the suicide attempter and the attitudes of larger social groups toward the family of the suicide or the survivors.

Contributors do not describe the religions of their countries in detail except for the cultural derivatives from those religions. Buddhism, Taoism, and Confucianism have a strong influence in Japan, Taiwan, Singapore, and Thailand. Buddhism is the main belief in Sri Lanka, with some Muslim and Hindu subgroups. India is Hindu with a Muslim minority. Iran, Pakistan, and all the Near Eastern countries are Islamic.

Buddhism grew out of Hindu beliefs, primarily the doctrine of reincarnation. Buddhist self-discipline is to free oneself from the passions of the world and the self in order to achieve Nirvana, which is a state of balance and peace, free of further reincarnations. The emphasis is on control and submission of human strivings and passions in order to know and to unite with the cosmic reality. Like other great religions, Buddhism has various schools of thought and differing emphases. The large divisions of the religion are the Mahayana and the Hinyana Buddhists, the greater and lesser "vehicles" and the middle way. Their interpretations vary widely, from Tibetan Tantric observances to practices of the different sects of Buddhism in Japan.

Hindus believe in a pantheon of gods and goddesses who represent forces such as creation and life giving, death and destruction, or who embody moral values. The central theme is reincarnation and the necessary struggle that each individual must go through in his behavior in life to determine his level of existence in future reincarnations.

The most ancient ethical system from China is Confucianism which arose in the sixth century B.C. The Confucian ethic of moral principles and right behavior is based on the *Analects*, a compilation of Confucius' sayings and actions by his students after his death. Kung Ch'iu (Confucius' Chinese name) was born in 551 B.C. of an impoverished noble line. He greatly admired the feudal values and systems of the ancient Chou dynasty which was then disintegrating. In his capacity as the teacher of young nobles, he advocated a return to those earlier values; his students came to have an important influence on the government. Confucius sought a high government post for himself so that he could put his ideas about a proper society into action, but he failed in that endeavor and was largely unknown in China when he died. His ideas about education, proper values and behavior, and moral attitudes, however, have deeply affected Chinese life and all countries touched by Chinese culture. Although Confucius believed in humanitarian and just behavior, he viewed it within the feudal framework, which for him primarily concerned the nobility and the upper classes. He was contemptuous and intolerant of women and peasants.[2]

The major value in Confucianism is carefully controlled and respectful behavior to parents, elders, and superiors. Confucius described the superior man as one who is always calm and at ease; an inferior man is full of worry and stress. (This attitude is reflected in some comments on suicide in the Taiwan chapter.) A superior man is one who merits that designation by being responsible, "human-hearted," correct and observant in filial piety, enlightened by education, honest, and just. These values, which Confucius taught to young nobles, were later transmuted to general principles applicable to anyone. Rulers of China fostered and supported Confucian ideas because they contributed to respect for authority, submission to the upper classes, and maintenance of order.

Taoism followed Confucianism by two hundred years, and many of its views are opposed to those of Confucius. Confucianism teaches discipline, ceremonial observance, duty to superiors, and public service. Taoist philosophy is personal and individualistic. Taoism is a philosophy, but it also developed a coexisting organized religion which is prevalent today in Taiwan, Thailand, and Singapore. Taoism has roots in early Chinese folk religion and continues some aspects of it in mysticism. Tao is the Way, the Absolute, the true Reality that underlies all existence and experience. Man and nature are one and are part of a continuing interchange between the divine cosmos and man in society. Man is the microcosm of the universe, reflected from the universe's larger plan. The rhythm of the universe arises from the opposite faces of reality, Yin and Yang. Yin and Yang are interrelated opposites, such as dark and light, winter and summer, male and female, constantly changing and transforming. To live in harmony and to follow Tao is to be accepting, realizing the inevitable flow of the cosmos, and to become attuned within oneself to the primordial life-force. Since life and death are natural, rhythmically reoccurring facets of reality, one should neither fear nor desire death. If one does not achieve the goals of complete acceptance of and harmony with the divine forces it is because one has not made enough progress within oneself in self-realization.

The Taoist religion in the South Pacific has priesthoods, texts, and rituals. Taoist priests conduct purification rites, often through mediums, and officiate at festivals that establish communication between the community and the heavens. As in Chinese folk religion, a shaman or magician acts as intercessor between the individual and the gods via prayer, exorcism, sacrifice, ritual, meditation, and mystical rites.

[2]Liu Wu-chi, *Confucius: His Life and Time* (New York: Philosophical Library, 1955), pp. 151–152.

As seven Muslim countries are included in this study, information on Islam may be helpful to the Western reader. Muhammad rose to prominence in A.D. 622, the time of the hegira or flight from hostile Mecca to Medina. He proclaimed the existence of one God, in contrast with the polytheistic idol-worshiping Meccans. His group was victorious over the Meccans, and from that time on his beliefs and his leadership were acclaimed. The basis of Muhammadanism is the Koran, a collection of the Prophet's sayings while he was in a trancelike state which are said to be messages from God. The religion has elements of Judaism and Christianity, probably gained through contact with Jewish and Christian traders in Mecca, and of the Bedouin nomad culture. Muhammad declared himself a prophet and spokesman for God but said that he was only one of the prophets whom God had sent at various times, including Abraham and Jesus. He described himself as a simple man through whom God was again trying to bring people back to such values as humanitarianism and egalitarianism. The majority of Islam views Muhammad as the last prophet, although various sects disagree on the number of prophets and some give allegiance to other prophets.

It is estimated that there are 500 to 750 million members of Islam. The majority group is the Sunnites, who follow the Sunna, or traditions about and commentaries on Muhammad's actions and sayings. The conservative branch of Islam is the Shia; the Shiites are comparable to Catholics in the Christian religion. There are various subsects of the Shiite branch. The Ismaelis recognize another imam or leader, Muhammad's son-in-law Ali, and venerate him for his death by violence. Observances of Ali's death are marked by fervent emotional behavior, beating oneself with chains or cutting oneself with knives. Members of the Ismaeli sect are found mostly in East Africa, Pakistan, India, Iran, and Yemen. Other Shia subsects are the Nusayris, the Yazidis, and the Ikwan, a puritanical group in Saudi Arabia. The Druze sect and the Sufis appeared in the eleventh century. The latter combined mysticism, asceticism, and emotionalism. They emphasized moral motivation, personal communion with God, and an intuitive understanding of God, rather than relating to God through Muhammad's prophethood. In achieving a state of ecstasy they reject worldliness and seek intuitive knowledge and experience of God.

In the early 1900s Mirza Gulam Ahmad claimed to be a prophet in Punjab India, now Pakistan. The sect, called the Ahmadis after the leader or Quadianis after his native city, has been opposed by other sects which hold that Muhammad was the last prophet. The Bahai movement grew into a separate non-Islam religion, an 1850 sect, which stressed humanitarian pacifism and universalism.

Islam has no appointed clergy. Its imams become leaders through religious scholarship, piety, or personal religious observance, which is then recognized by a substantial following. Women cannot be imams. The "five pillars" of belief are a profession of faith ("There is no God but Allah and Muhammad is his prophet"); prayer five times a day for the faithful; tithing; keeping the fast of Ramadan, the ninth month of the Muslim calendar when the Koran was revealed; and the hajj or pilgrimage to Mecca which the faithful must make once in a lifetime. The latter has become a giant migration each year of 1.5 to 2 million persons traveling to Saudi Arabia. Trains, planes, buses, and cars are full, and pilgrims stay in huge tent cities. Making the pilgrimage confers lifelong distinction on an individual.

Islam is not only a religion; it is a community of which one feels a part. Muslims from divergent social classes or different countries feel that they are all members of a close-knit group; they are brothers together. Since social action is linked to religious belief, political action such as the jihad (the holy war), when territories and peoples were won for Islam, has been encouraged. The sweeping annexations and subjugation of territory in earlier periods came to an end when the power of Western nations increased. Muslims tend to focus on past centuries of splendor and glory, unquestionably great in many fields, for the past and the present are in considerable contrast in some Islamic countries. Church and state are one in the religion—social action field. Turkey has varied from this standard in its separation of state and church, but the present Pakistani and Iranian governments have notably based the identity of their countries on religion.

The Koran stresses attitudes and recommends patterns of behavior which originated in Muhammad's Bedouin culture but are now found in many Islamic countries that are Arab, but not Bedouin, and perhaps also in some non-Arab countries. These Bedouin cultural factors are male superiority, female inferiority, the automatic superiority of age, and endogenous marriages. Male children are greatly desired and pampered. A female birth, greeted as a misfortune, means a loss of status for the mother in traditional cultures. Girls are given less attention than boys and are trained to serve men and to be submissive. A boy is catered to in his early years and, as he grows older, the stern and strict father teaches him subservience to the father's will and that of all male elders. Severe physical punishment is the means to achieve ego submission for both boys and girls. In time a boy gains precedence over all women and younger males.[3]

Since women in the Bedouin culture are viewed as inclined to unbridled sexuality if not strictly guarded at all times, the taboo on sexual misconduct is severe and punishment is extreme. Loss of virginity is a calamity that tarnishes the girl's entire paternal line, and the traditional punishment for her is death. If she is guilty of marital infidelity, she may be killed by her father or brothers. The male partner in infidelity may be given a set number

---

[3]The discussion of Islam and family life is drawn from Wilfred C. Smith's *Islam in Modern History* (Princeton: Princeton University Press, 1977); T. Prothro and L. Diab, *Changing Family Pattern in the Arab East* (Beirut: American University of Beirut, 1974).

of lashes, but in Bedouin cultures the woman's husband is expected to kill him to avenge the dishonor.[4] The result of such extreme attitudes toward containment of sexual thoughts and impulses is to oversexualize attitudes and perhaps to divert many natural impulses into aggressiveness. The proscriptions may also contribute to the establishment of homosexual relationships among males. Sex becomes almost sinful, and attitudes toward it are anxious and guilt-ridden.

Child-rearing practices include threats to ensure good behavior, although the threats are often not carried through. Praise and rewards are not emphasized. Children are taught to value kinship ties, to be loyal to family and tribe, to extend hospitality to strangers and guests, and to be courageous. Honor and "face" are paramount values which must be maintained for the repute of the kinship group and the individual family.

The numerous repressions in this system may lead to emotional outbursts of temper, unrestrained invective, and shouting matches that flare and then subside. Such expressions of anger are not regarded as permanent or damaging, and relations largely go on as before. At times, however, inflamed tempers lead to extreme violence, especially if groups are involved.[5]

A basic concept of Islam is predestination. Allah has already set the pattern of events and each person inevitably meets his destiny. Submission to the will of God is seen as a virtue, but it may extend to submission also to the will of others of higher rank. An important conclusion inherent in this system is that the individual is other-directed. One's clan and family are the judges of whether one's conduct is to be admired or condemned. Innovation, self-determination, or individuality can therefore be dangerous.

Criticism of Islam has focused on its tendency to look backward to historical roots for its stance today, on its subjugation and demeaning of women, its feudal and hierarchical relationships, its harsh treatment of those who break the law, and its intolerance of religious minority views. For example, in the formation of Pakistan at India's partition, Muslims exhibited extreme ferocity and barbarism toward the Ahmadi sect.

A study of the status of women and of divorce in Jordan[6] reveals a discrepancy between Islamic law and actual practice. The report states that

[4]In August 1980, Jacqueline Thibaut of the Minority Rights group in London reported to the United Nations Human Rights Committee that murders of young women for suspicion of sexual intimacy took place daily in Egypt, Iraq, Syria, Jordan, and other Arab countries. The offenses may have been extramarital relations, even during rape, or may have been merely exchanging words with a young man. Thibaut stated that the young women's throats were cut, they were buried alive, or they were poisoned by the father, an elder brother, a cousin, or a paid killer. The chapter on Syria reports similar incidents.

[5]Raphael Patai, *The Arab Mind* (New York: Charles Scribners's Sons, 1976).

[6]Muhammad Barhoum, "Divorce and the Status of Women in Jordan," *Journal of Social Sciences* (Kuwait University), May 1977.

the historical and social bias against women means that in most instances they have no voice in divorce. Although Islamic law provides for mediation by parents to avoid divorce, Jordanese women receive divorce notices without prior notice that such action is impending. Furthermore, a woman is entitled to a return of part of her dowry if she is divorced, as well as to child support, but she seldom receives these benefits. Under certain circumstances a woman may ask for a divorce, but if she does so the husband often withholds the dowry portion and the child support. The wife may keep the children until age seven for a boy and nine for a girl, but then the husband automatically has custody. Women are usually blamed for divorces and thus suffer devaluation in the society, although in 63 percent of the cases the reason for divorce is given as interference by the husband's family. Wives stated that the two most prevalent reasons for divorce were lack of feeling and understanding by the husband and his affairs with other women. Whereas men may obtain divorces easily, merely by saying "I divorce you" three times in tribal settings, women have much more difficulty in winning freedom from a marriage partner. After a divorce a man may remarry at once without loss of status, but a woman has little chance for remarriage because of the bias against divorced women. These data may be useful in evaluating suicides of females and of divorced and widowed women in Muslim countries.

Each contributor to this volume discusses his methods of data collection and estimates the reliability of the data. The latter is a complicated problem in all countries and for all researchers. Many Western reports have been criticized for insufficient scope, unreliable or biased sources, and so on, and no doubt these Asian reports could be similarly criticized. If, however, they include adequate discussions of sources and of the methods of collection, a fair estimate of their reliability can be made.

Statistics, insofar as they are available, have been gathered for completed and attempted suicides. In some situations no data on attempts could be determined. Conversely, in some countries the prevalence of attempted suicide could be determined, but not that of completed suicide: Age, sex, education, and urban-rural differences are included to whatever degree possible. A discussion of the most frequent means is reported as accurately as possible. Some countries, such as Taiwan and Japan, now have suicide prevention services, which are described in this volume.

I introduce each chapter with an editor's note so as to orient the reader to the particular country and to add whatever data from an overall viewpoint I feel may be helpful. In some instances I present a political summary which may help the reader to understand the current situation in a country. Sometimes additional data from other sources are included to assist the reader in gaining an overall picture. A brief summary of the professional situation and the background of the contributor is sometimes included.

The authors of these chapters are notable for their scientific curiosity and their dedication to research. The favorable circumstances existing in the West—grants, research teams, and government task forces—are seldom found in Asia. The individuals who have gathered the statistical material for this book have done so out of interest in the subject and in their limited personal time. It is a frequent practice in Asia for psychiatrists and psychologists to work for a government hospital or agency from morning to early afternoon. In the late afternoon and evening, psychiatrists attend to their private practice and work in clinics. Consequently it is understandable that a number of these researchers have taken a long time to gather their information. It has not been possible, in the absence of Western facilities, to cover as many sources of information as the authors would have liked. As it is, their contribution to the world's knowledge of suicide is a significant one, an impressive achievement under severe difficulties.

# 1 JAPAN

*Editor's Note*

Chapter 1 is a lengthy one because more material is available for Japan than for some other countries. Still, much of the information about Japanese suicides is in bits and pieces, owing to the particular focus of interest of most writers on the subject. The chapter is divided into two parts.

The author of Part I, Kichinosuke Tatai, is a graduate in medicine from Tokyo University and won a second degree in medical science after serving as a medical officer during World War II. After receiving a degree from the Harvard School of Public Health in 1952, he returned to Japan, serving at the National Institute of Public Health and as professor and lecturer at several universities. Dr. Tatai is presently affiliated with Tokyo University of Agriculture. With numerous publications on suicide, and with his continuing efforts to improve physical and psychological health in Japan, he is well qualified to discuss the subject of suicide. His work at the Institute of Public Health was helpful in stimulating the preparation in 1974, by himself and others, of a national survey entitled "Thinking of Suicide in Japan." Through the survey and other means, he brought suicide to the attention of the public and of professional groups. Dr. Tatai's aim, to create a suicide prevention service, has now been accomplished. Dr. Tatai has been the Japanese representative in the International Association for Suicide Prevention ever since its founding. In this chapter he has brought together all the material on suicide in Japan presently available. His observations on Japanese culture and personality are penetrating and realistic.

The staff members of Inochi no Denwa, a "lifeline" telephone service whose director is Yukio Saito, compiled the data for Part II of this chapter. The service had just completed a survey of its work when I visited its headquarters in Tokyo in 1980. This report, that I wrote, based on Inochi no Denwa's raw data, will help readers to understand the roots and the precipitating causes of suicidal behavior in Japan.

## PART I. KICHINOSUKE TATAI[1]

### INTRODUCTION

The nature of the Japanese islands and their distance from larger mainland countries have had a significant impact on the country's economy, political

---

[1] I wish to express my deep appreciation to Dr. Fusa Ueda of the Statistics and Information Department, Ministry of Health and Welfare, for her kind assistance in collecting data for this survey.

life, and value systems. Japan's location contributed to its early isolation, which was accentuated by the Tokugawa shogunate's closure of its shores in the 1600s to everybody except a few Portuguese traders. Since foreign ideas as well as traders were shut out, the shogunate was able to exercise complete control over the populace. The geographical character of the islands, mountainous with narrow strips of arable land along the seacoasts, made travel and communications difficult. Because of the limited land area, intensive farming was necessary and led to communal systems of production. Today Japan, with few natural resources and no petroleum, must rely on imported raw materials for industrial production. From an island nation closed to foreigners for 300 years, Japan has become a trading nation dependent upon commerce with numerous other nations, yet her values remain substantially the same.

The political events most significant to present-day Japanese life and culture began in the 1580s; in that decade Hideyoshi defeated the nobles of small states and began to centralize his government and solidify an empire. The later Tokugawa feudal empire was based upon hierarchical control of all phases of life. Occupation, behavior, and even possession of certain items were strictly regulated. Japanese feudalism was more detailed and more far-reaching than that of western Europe, although the main elements, especially rank, privilege, the exercise of power, and disdain for the lower classes, were similar. Like all repressive governments, the shogunate did not allow citizens to possess weapons. The helplessness of the populace was accentuated by the activities of a much feared, thorough, and pervasive police spy network.

An agricultural population, having almost no direct contact with other cultures and ideas, became a tightly regimented group responsible to distant lords and their military establishment. Their values were clan orientation, submissiveness to superiors, reliance on fellow villagers for help, tempered by suspiciousness, alertness to others in order to obtain favorable treatment and avoid negative reports to superiors, and a strong work ethic. Patterns of conduct were firmly established, with no deviations tolerated.

Today Japan, with an economy growing at an increasing pace, is one of the wealthiest countries in the world. Its industrial potential is based in large part on traditional elements of behavior. The strong urge of the Japanese to achieve status through work stimulates the young to obtain higher education. Once graduated from school or university, the young person enters a business firm for which his education and background qualify him, and he remains there for life. Because job transfers are looked upon with distrust, the work force remains stable and, in general, reliable. Businesses provide pensions, vacations, entertainment, supplementary classes, and other benefits for their employees. Seniority, with eventual retirement, is the goal of the worker. The work system is paternal, regimented, hierarchical, and fairly inflexible. Young people increasingly leave the farms for city jobs, while the elderly remain in rural areas. Western clothes, music, and patterns of speech suggest a changing order, but the basic Japanese personality and way of thinking seem to prevail. The increase of Western influences, however, is creating dissatisfaction with the status quo, which in turn leads to delinquency and violent acts, including suicides, among young persons.

## RELIGION

The indigenous religion of Japan is nature worship, Shinto, which is still observed today. Many of the best-known elements of Japanese culture are founded on Shinto beliefs and ethics. A torii gate marks the entrance to a sacred Shinto area, which may enshrine a natural wonder such as an enormous tree. The tea ceremony schools its participants in quiet, reverent appreciation of the peace of nature. Flower arranging, gardens, and nature motifs are part of the aesthetic enjoyment of nature's gift of life and sustenance. Festivals commemorating the different seasons, observed by most Japanese, provide colorful and happy occasions. Shinto teaches a cheerful and optimistic outlook, and its adherents believe in the nature gods' willingness to listen to prayer and accept offerings. Most weddings are celebrated with Shinto rites, whereas burials are usually conducted by Buddhist monks. In line with Shinto beliefs, the ancient Japanese, according to early classical literature, were optimistic and lighthearted. In *Manyoshu*, a collection of poetry compiled about 1,200 years ago, a well-known poem advises the reader: "Stop pondering in vain. Better to empty a cup of bold sake."

Chinese culture and Buddhism migrated to Japan around the sixth century. Chinese Buddhism had some elements of Confucianism, an ethical and cultural system stressing hierarchical authority. Shinto had become a state religion headed by the emperor, who was regarded as a direct descendant of the sun-goddess. Buddhism, in contrast, at first was more oriented toward the general population, as many of its precepts stress individual efforts, without intermediaries, toward self-enlightenment and self-improvement. Buddhist priests soon became powerful forces, however, and in later Tokugawa times Buddhism became the state religion and was closely allied with the ruling group. The samurai—bodyguards and highly trained warriors serving a lord—were especially attracted to Zen Buddhism. The question as to whether Buddhism actually permits suicide is controversial, for different sects have different views. Today Shinto and Buddhism are jointly observed by the Japanese in a seemingly harmonious synthesis or at least coexistence. For example, a household may have both a Buddhist altar and a Shinto shrine.

In ancient times Buddhism was a force used to foster and enforce feudal militarism through the doctrine of reincarnation. The suppressed and frustrated people could escape from the hopeless world they lived in and go to a better world of freedom and well-being. Rather than attempting to vent their anger toward an unyielding system, they could suppress their feelings and look forward to a happier life in the future. The warlords approved and encouraged the reincarnation doctrine as an aid to their demand that the defeated warrior commit suicide rather than be captured, probably with a view toward eliciting bravery based on desperation.

## CULTURE AND PERSONALITY ELEMENTS

The feudal regime of the past has left a deep imprint on the Japanese personality. The Tokugawa totalitarian government installed a system of social relationships which required a person to be attentive and sensitive to those above him while showing indifference and callousness to those of inferior status. There were no general standards of right or wrong irrespective of the individual's status. Western standards of generalized benevolence and fair play are not part of the heritage of the modern Japanese. Every action has to be considered as to whether or not it advances one within a competitive society; this tenet applies to friends, family, associates, employers and employees, politicians, teachers, and business associates. Japanese insecurity and sensitivity to the opinions of others are a constant concern, leading to carefully controlled behavior and attentive, pleasing, and deferential manners on the part of those whose status is uncertain. Individuals seek to avoid a sense of shame and guilt for unacceptable social behavior or for failure in school or work. The insecurity is exacerbated by the reluctance of the Japanese to confide in others for fear of betraying weakness or being put at a disadvantage. This overriding concern with self is based not only on insecurity about oneself and one's acceptability to others, but also on the accompanying feeling of helplessness and on inability to aid others in a rigid system. Although individuals do not openly dissent from others, they may join a group that will act for them; yet there are few who wish to stand out by self-assertive or vigorous behavior. Highly educated Japanese might be expected to be more expressive and communicative than less advantaged fellow countrymen, but they also tend to conform to social rules in order to protect their status in society. Even Japanese who are educated abroad soon mold themselves on the approved lines when they return home.

Under the Japanese hierarchical system, then, individuals cannot count on sympathy or help from others against authority or even against mistreatment, for justice is related to status. The Japanese are traditionally unwilling to help anyone in trouble for fear that they may become obligated to such individuals. Those who wield the least power are the ones most likely to suffer—the young, women, the poor, and outcast groups.

The unfortunate result of these attitudes is lack of concern for the social welfare of others. Politicians employ bloc voting through privilege systems and devote themselves to consolidating their position and deriving monetary benefit from it. In past times, military and nationalistic groups took no cognizance of the people's welfare. This history has led the Japanese to concentrate on enjoying the present and has made them resigned to death or to an ominous future—a combination of hedonism and nihilism.

A term often applied by foreigners to describe a Japanese attitude is *tereya* (shy or diffident). The origin of this attitude is *kenjo* (modesty or decorum), which was an important quality in traditional Japanese culture and which today still retains its force and significance, even among the supposedly westernized youth. In July 1973 the Japanese government made public the results of an international survey of the younger generation in ten countries: United States, United Kingdom, France, Switzerland, Sweden, Yugoslavia, India, Brazil, the Philippines, and West Germany (28). The survey revealed that Japanese young people are more solitary and more nihilistic than those in any of the other ten nations.

Other concepts used to describe the Japanese personality are *amae* and *sasshi*. *Amae*, as explained by Professor Takeo Doi of Tokyo University (1), is the pervasive wish for benevolent attention and treatment from others without personally exerting oneself. A Westerner might liken it to a return to indulged infantilism. *Sasshi*, which means a favorable attitude toward others, is probably based on the traditional sensitivity to the feelings of other people. The pursuit of *amae* and *sasshi* accustoms the Japanese individual to avoiding a definite yes or no by using vague and evasive speech, such as "more or less" (*mah mah* in Japanese). These two concepts provide a way to escape definite responsibility; they allow the individual to live in a world of romance and fantasy, leaving others to deal with problems. A Japanese finds it easier to endure adverse conditions if he has not exerted himself to make decisions, because the failure of one's own will is a great shame. The shame is harder to bear when an individual has taken a position and then is unable to follow it through successfully.

Humanity and nature fuse into one in Japan, based on an early Shinto belief that God or kami (spirits) are in everything—man, stones, rivers, other natural objects. Refined and delicate sentiments are expressed through admiration of nature. For example, the Japanese like wisterias. The flowers have been admired for more than a thousand years for their helplessly hanging nature. Weeping willows, weeping cherry trees, and other inclining trees and plants are purposefully cultivated for the same reason. This sentiment reflects the predilection of the Japanese to live passively, relying upon the power and authority of others in their vertically regimented semifeudal society. In a way, this high regard for nature leads to a kind of contempt for life. Shinto views death as part of the natural process of life; Buddhism teaches reincarnation and a new start through death. Yet the Japanese tend not to focus on death except as a romanticized outcome of struggle. Many dramas, poems, and other literary works express this attitude.

In a culture that discourages individuality and penalizes dissent, the individual must often deal with his aggression and his hostility toward others by turning those feelings against himself. Perhaps one of the reasons that so much attention has been directed at Mishima's[2] hara-kiri is that Mishima represented a Japanese personality type—narcissistic and arrogant, but dependent. From the foregoing it is clear that the culture may well produce these characteristics.

There are some factors that may alter Japanese attitudes toward life. After Japan's defeat in World War II, primogeniture was outlawed and women were given equal status (at least theoretically) and the vote. Education was stressed and made more easily available and certain judicial changes pointed in the direction of making the country more democratic. These factors may even out to some degree the possession of individual power. Material wealth has allowed more Japanese to travel and to learn about other people's ideas and ideals. For a time, at least, Japanese youth demonstrated a spirit of rebellion. Women, who have launched business careers and have entered the professions to an increasing degree, have formed political pressure groups of their own as well as consumer support organizations. Divorces have become more numerous through a breakdown of the older system, under which a wife could not initiate divorce, had no way to support herself, and lost custody of the children to her husband. Another sign of change is that some alimony support is now awarded to the wife in a divorce settlement. Although most marriages are still arranged, the wishes of individuals are now taken into account and the parents may be merely acceding to the couple's choice. Nuclear families are increasing as extended families are declining, a situation that will give the individual more responsibility for his or her own actions. Clearly, some system for support of and aid to older persons is urgently needed.

## FACTORS PREDISPOSING THE JAPANESE TO SUICIDE

Historically, Japan has a tradition of approved military and political suicides. Professor J. Hirayama of Rikkyo University has reported instances of suicide found in Japanese literature. Before A.D. 780, *junshi* or self-immola-

[2]Yukio Mishima was a famous novelist.

tion was popular. In the Kamakura era, 1185—1333, Buddhist stories related numerous suicides. In the middle period of military domination, 1333—1598, the country was incessantly at war, and there were many accounts of suicides in military ranks and in battles, including hara-kiri by defeated warriors. The Edo or Tokugawa era, 1598—1867, was marked by numerous single, double, and multiple suicides. Hara-kiri, beginning about 1,000 years ago, was originally committed to prevent capture. Later, some 400 years ago, it evolved into an act allowing members of the nobility to take their own lives whenever condemned by superiors, in contrast with the fate of ordinary persons, who were hanged in public squares.

Among traditional types of self-destruction in Japan is *junshi*, or suicide following the master's death. As in other ancient cultures, it was expected and often forced. Forced *junshi* was banned in A.D. 659, yet occasional examples are found in recent times. For instance, General Nogi and his wife committed suicide after the death of the Meiji emperor in 1912. *Gisei shi*, sacrificial suicide, has occupied a prominent place in Japanese history, although the self-sacrifice was often forced. Kamikaze pilots in World War II were not all voluntary suicides, and it may well be that all "human torpedo" suicides were not an individual choice. It is true, however, that many Japanese men, women, and children suicided when Japan was defeated in World War II. *Funshi* or *munenbara*, suicide based on resentment, hatred, or enmity, has its counterpart in ancient Indian practices. It is an outgrowth of a societal system providing few ways in which inferiors can express hostility to powerful superiors. Another term for a similar type of hostile message of remonstrance is *kanshi*.

The element of self-sacrifice is present in *shinju* suicides, which involve two or more persons. These include love-pact suicides (*joshi*) by frustrated lovers and parent-child suicides. Many of them are murder-suicide arrangements. Usually, in parent-child suicides, the parent kills the child or children and then commits suicide. The precipitating cause most often is economic or psychological distress and the lack of social institutions to relieve the distress. With few welfare agencies and Japanese unwillingness to take on the burdens of others, parents feel justified in killing their children rather than leaving them to shift for themselves. Since children are viewed as possessions of the parent, such action can be seen by the parent as protectiveness. More than one such group suicide occurs each day in Japan, arousing sympathetic attention as part of the romanticizing of death.

Historically, and in the literature of both past and present, suicide has been viewed as the sole resource of individuals caught in a rigid system. It is a means of clearing one's name, of washing away a sin or a disgrace. The Japanese still hold to this belief. Even today politicians proclaim their sincerity by saying, "If my political promise is not realized, I swear that I will commit hara-kiri." In short, to vow hara-kiri means to promise honorable behavior.

In summary, the factors that underlie Japanese suicides are as follows:

1. A historical tradition of suicide as an honorable solution to harsh and difficult personal situations.
2. A romanticizing of suicide as an escape from the stresses of life under a mantle of acceptability.
3. Inferences from the two religions of Shinto and Buddhism, observed by most Japanese, which formulate an idea of life after death. Shinto views death as an opportunity to become a kami, or spirit. Buddhism presents the idea of reincarnation and survival after death.
4. Lack of public institutions to help people suffering economic or psychological stress.
5. Absence of legal prohibition against and prosecutions for suicide.
6. Economic distress. Statistics indicate that the poor are more inclined to suicide than those in more secure status.
7. A rigid semifeudal society which demands conformity and success and prohibits failure and weakness.

## ATTITUDE TOWARD SUICIDE

A survey has shown that most students at a university in Kyoto regarded suicide as a personal problem; only 9 percent saw it as a social problem. Approximately 60 percent were either critical of or indifferent to the problems that suicidal individuals may have faced. Although suicide may have been an acceptable means of protest in Japan, at the present time the individual concerned arouses no helpful impulse in others. In ancient times suicide was viewed as a duty; today it may be regarded as a failure of will.

## SOURCES OF DATA

The Ministry of Health has reported the number of suicides and the rates per 100,000 population in Japan since the first decade of the twentieth century, but overall data on other aspects of suicide have not been available. Researchers have investigated limited numbers of cases or special groups of cases, such as students, psychiatric patients, and parent-child suicides. Then, in April–July 1974, for the first time, the Ministry of Health surveyed 4,925 cases of suicide, the largest number consistently investigated by one organization, to determine the characteristics of suicides. The inquiry covered marital status, personal living situation, occupation, employment status, methods, and precipitating causes (9).

Attempted suicides have not been widely studied owing to the concealment of attempts and the difficulty of obtaining all-Japan data. Two sources
deal with attempted suicides in Tokyo: the Tokyo Metropolitan Police
Board reports, 1951–1959 (24), and a study by M. Okamura of Tokyo
ambulance cases, published in 1974 (15). Other sources used here are
Japanese government suicide statistics; Ministry of Health reports; Japanese census data; Tokyo Institute for Education and Ministry of Education
information on attempted and completed student suicides; a review of
group suicides; and a brief review of suicide prevention activities.

## COMPLETED SUICIDES

It has long been known that suicide is less frequent during wartime and
more frequent in periods of economic depression. Statistics on suicide in
Japan clearly reveal this tendency (fig. 1-1). The suicide rate declined
during World War I, even in Japan, remote from the battle areas. In 1937,
when the invasion of China began, the rate per 100,000 immediately fell
from 22.2 in 1936 to a low of 17.5 in 1939. The decrease of suicide was,
however, far more striking during World War II. As the war continued,
until the day of surrender in 1945, the rate kept dropping until it reached
12.4 in 1944. The annual decline during eight years of wartime is estimated
at 10 percent, a rate slightly higher than that experienced during World
War I in England and Wales (8.3 percent) as well as in Germany (9.5
percent).

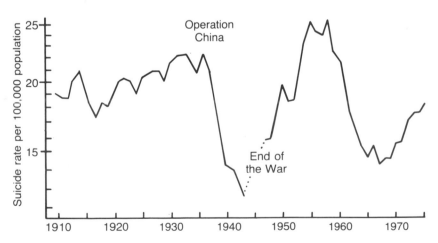

FIG. 1-1.     Trend of suicide rate per 100,000 population in Japan, 1910–1975.
Source of data: Ministry of Health and Welfare, Japan.

The economic prosperity that ordinarily accompanies war may cause this reduction in the suicide rate. According to reports, it even declined in France during intense political crises that involved no military action (5). Perhaps war and other national crises so centralize people's attention as to keep their minds off their own troubles and allow them to escape for a time from personal miseries. It is also possible that the suicide rate declines because national events arouse popular enthusiasm for a common purpose, which gives personal lives more meaning and makes the outlook for the future more optimistic. It is noteworthy that sex ratios in suicide differed only minimally before and during the war. Certainly national unity and Japanese hopes for world supremacy contributed largely to the remarkable decline of the suicide rate during wartime.

Reliable figures were unavailable in 1945 and 1946 because of disturbances and the necessity for readjustments in the country. Suicide rates steadily rose from 1947 to 1955 and reached the highest peak ever experienced in Japan in the period 1955–1958. The rapid increase, one might suppose, could be attributed to economic stresses, but in Japan the economic situation decidedly improved after the outbreak of the Korean conflict in 1949. Other possible causes, such as social disorganization, stemmed from policies of decentralization instituted for military purposes and accelerated by American bombing of larger cities. Japanese cities burned and destroyed by bombing obviously could not function as true urban areas in the immediate postwar years. Urbanization was further restricted because of food and housing shortages. Especially in Tokyo, administrative control of population movements was strict, and people were not allowed to move into the city until 1949. The Japanese postwar suicide rate for a six-year period was approximately 30 percent higher in urban than in rural areas.

According to census reports, the population in urban areas, estimated to be about 35 percent of the total population in 1947, rose to about 56 percent in 1955. The total population of Tokyo was 5,000,777 in 1947, 8,037,084 in 1955, and 11,500,000 in 1974. The city's population thus grew by an average of 380,000 a year between 1947 and 1955. Recent growth has not shown the same rapid acceleration. Government data indicate that the population movement to urban areas during the decade following World War II was really remarkable, with consequent pressures of adjustment.

The suicide rate steadily decreased after the peak period of 1955–1958 and sank to a low point between 1967 and 1969 (table 1-1). The explanations of so rapid a decline are marked migration to industrial areas and a notable increase of economic prosperity. After 1970, however, the suicide rate once again began to rise, reaching 17.6 per 100,000 in 1976, 17.8 in 1977, 17.6 in 1978, and 18.0 in 1979.

## TABLE 1-1
### SUICIDE RATES PER 100,000 POPULATION IN JAPAN BY SEX, FEMALE-MALE PERCENTAGE, AND AGE, 1955–1979

| Year | Total Male | Total Female | F/M percentage | 10–14 Male | 10–14 Female | 15–19 Male | 15–19 Female | 20–24 Male | 20–24 Female | Overall rate |
|---|---|---|---|---|---|---|---|---|---|---|
| 1955 | 31.6 | 19.0 | 60.1 | 1.1 | 0.7 | 37.6 | 26.4 | 84.8 | 47.2 | 25.2 |
| 1956 | 29.8 | 19.4 | 65.1 | 1.1 | 0.5 | 31.1 | 23.8 | 78.4 | 48.2 | 24.5 |
| 1957 | 29.7 | 19.1 | 64.3 | 1.1 | 0.5 | 31.8 | 23.2 | 74.5 | 48.3 | 24.3 |
| 1958 | 30.7 | 20.8 | 67.8 | 1.1 | 0.8 | 31.4 | 26.4 | 78.2 | 53.0 | 25.7 |
| 1959 | 26.6 | 18.9 | 71.1 | 0.9 | 0.5 | 23.9 | 22.9 | 61.6 | 43.7 | 22.7 |
| 1960 | 25.1 | 18.2 | 72.5 | 0.7 | 0.4 | 25.3 | 22.6 | 59.1 | 44.1 | 21.6 |
| 1961 | 22.3 | 16.9 | 75.8 | 1.1 | 0.4 | 22.2 | 20.1 | 47.0 | 37.0 | 19.6 |
| 1962 | 20.4 | 14.8 | 72.5 | 1.1 | 0.7 | 15.9 | 13.5 | 38.4 | 30.8 | 17.6 |
| 1963 | 18.9 | 13.4 | 70.9 | 1.3 | 0.4 | 11.0 | 9.3 | 31.4 | 26.1 | 16.1 |
| 1964 | 17.5 | 12.9 | 73.7 | 0.8 | 0.5 | 9.2 | 7.3 | 26.9 | 21.1 | 15.1 |
| 1965 | 17.3 | 12.2 | 70.5 | 0.7 | 0.3 | 8.8 | 6.1 | 23.3 | 18.3 | 14.7 |
| 1966 | 17.4 | 13.1 | 75.3 | 0.8 | 0.3 | 8.9 | 8.0 | 23.9 | 20.0 | 15.2 |
| 1967 | 16.2 | 12.2 | 75.4 | 0.9 | 0.3 | 8.3 | 7.2 | 20.4 | 19.4 | 14.2 |

| 1968 | 16.5 | 12.5 | 75.8 | 0.8 | 0.3 | 9.6 | 7.3 | 19.2 | 14.4 | 14.5 |
| 1969 | 16.4 | 12.7 | 77.4 | 0.8 | 0.4 | 8.9 | 6.3 | 18.2 | 15.0 | 14.5 |
| 1970 | 17.3 | 13.3 | 76.9 | 1.0 | 0.6 | 8.7 | 6.9 | 18.8 | 16.2 | 15.3 |
| 1971 | 17.9 | 13.3 | 74.3 | 1.0 | 0.4 | 10.4 | 6.3 | 20.3 | 16.9 | 15.6 |
| 1972 | 19.7 | 14.4 | 73.1 | 1.0 | 0.5 | 12.5 | 7.4 | 23.8 | 16.5 | 17.0 |
| 1973 | 20.2 | 14.7 | 72.7 | 1.7 | 0.7 | 12.5 | 7.5 | 26.1 | 17.6 | 17.4 |
| 1974 | 20.0 | 15.0 | 75.0 | 1.3 | 0.3 | 12.0 | 7.5 | 25.8 | 18.0 | 17.5 |
| 1975 | 21.4 | 14.5 | 67.8 | 1.5 | 0.6 | 12.6 | 6.8 | 25.9 | 16.8 | 18.0 |
| 1976 | 21.2 | 14.1 | 66.6 | 1.5 | 0.5 | 11.3 | 7.0 | 27.2 | 15.1 | 17.6 |
| 1977 | 22.0 | 13.8 | 62.7 | 1.5 | 0.6 | 11.6 | 6.5 | 26.6 | 13.4 | 17.8 |
| 1978 | 22.0 | 13.4 | 60.9 | 1.3 | 0.7 | 12.7 | 6.7 | 25.8 | 13.0 | 17.6 |
| 1979 | 22.6 | 13.6 | 60.1 | 1.4 | 0.6 | 13.9 | 6.3 | 25.8 | 13.3 | 18.0 |

Source: Ministry of Health and Welfare (8, 10). The ministry has supplied data to update the figures through 1979.

## FACTORS AFFECTING SUICIDE RATES

### Sex Ratios

At the beginning of the twentieth century the female suicide rate in Japan was 60 percent of the male rate. Age-specific female rates were, however, exceedingly high in the 15–19 group, where 1.2 to 1.5 suicides were female. The higher rate gradually declined after World War I, possibly because of the influences of Western civilization. Since World War II, however, the female-male ratio has been clearly increasing. After 1959 the female rate exceeded 70 percent and in 1966 it reached 75 percent of the rate for males, a percentage never before attained in Japan (see table 1-1). This gradual but steady rise may reflect, in part, a social change stemming from the fact that women have more social responsibilities while still carrying, in accordance with the traditional culture, a heavier family burden than men.

Female life expectancy in Japan is among the highest in the world. In 1974, for instance, it was 76.31 years for females and 71.16 for males; women tend to live longer in industrialized societies. The number of older women who commit suicide is increasing more rapidly than the number of older men and it is likely that the female-male suicide ratio will steadily increase. Older people in Japan are more apt to commit suicide than those in other countries, particularly because of their cultural attitude and the lack of institutions to care for them; their increase has been too rapid to permit the establishment of adequate programs. Moreover, as in most Western countries, children are less and less inclined to live with their parents, thus impairing the parents' traditional feeling of security.

Table 1-2 shows sex- and age-specific percentiles and rankings of suicide cases against total causes of death in Japan in 1974. Each percentile indicates the proportion of suicide among all causes of death in age-specific groups. The suicide death rate reached the top of all causes of death in the 15–24 age group in 1955. From 1958 on, the rate was continuously the highest until recently; in 1968 it paralleled the rate for auto accident deaths. Since then, accidents have ranked first. Among females alone, however, suicide still ranks highest among all causes of death in the 15–29 age bracket.

Table 1-2 shows the relative frequency of suicide between females and males for all deaths in each age group. Females between 15 and 24 commit suicide 30–50 percent more frequently than do males of the same ages. For the 25–44 age group, female and male suicide rates are practically the same. After the age of 45 females again clearly exceed males in suicide by 30–40 percent.

The sex- and age-specific suicide death rates after World War II are particularly impressive (fig. 1-2). Clearly the younger population, those up to 35 years of age, were more inclined to suicide after the war; the rate rapidly increased to the peak of 1955 and thereafter dropped rather quickly

TABLE 1-2
PERCENTAGES AND RANKINGS OF SUICIDE DEATHS COMPARED WITH ALL
DEATHS IN JAPAN IN 1974, BY AGE AND SEX

| Age | Male | | Female | | Total | | Ratio[b] |
|-----|------|------|--------|------|-------|------|-------|
| | Percentage | Ranking[a] | Percentage | Ranking[a] | Percentage | Ranking[a] | |
| 10−14 | 4.3 | 7 | − | − | 3.3 | 8 | − |
| 15−19 | 13.3 | 2 | 20.4 | 1 | 15.4 | 2 | 1.53 |
| 20−24 | 23.4 | 2 | 30.8 | 1 | 26.0 | 2 | 1.31 |
| 25−29 | 21.4 | 2 | 23.8 | 1 | 22.3 | 2 | 1.01 |
| 30−34 | 16.2 | 2 | 17.3 | 2 | 16.6 | 3 | 1.06 |
| 35−39 | 11.3 | 4 | 11.9 | 2 | 11.5 | 3 | 1.05 |
| 40−44 | 7.0 | 6 | 6.9 | 4 | 7.0 | 5 | 0.96 |
| 45−49 | 5.0 | 6 | 4.8 | 4 | 4.9 | 6 | 1.32 |
| 50−54 | 3.4 | 6 | 4.5 | 4 | 3.9 | 6 | 1.32 |
| 55−59 | 2.6 | 7 | 3.0 | 4 | 2.8 | 6 | 1.15 |
| 60−64 | 1.9 | 8 | 2.7 | 5 | 2.2 | 8 | 1.42 |
| 65−69 | − | − | 1.9 | 8 | 1.5 | 10 | − |

SOURCE: Ministry of Health and Welfare (9).
[a]Ranking of suicide among all causes of death.
[b]Ratio of female to male percentages.

to the level of 1947. In contrast, the older population showed the highest rate immediately after World War II, and the rate gradually decreased to a level lower than that of the prewar period. These data seem to reflect in part the traditional and nontraditional attitudes within Japanese culture.

## Marital Status

For the first time, the Japanese Ministry of Health and Welfare made a special survey of 4,925 suicides reported between April and July 1974. Among the aspects analyzed was marital status (see table 1-3). In general, the data are similar to Western suicide data. The suicide rate was lowest among the married, followed by the unmarried, and the highest rate was found among widowed and divorced persons. The rate for unmarried persons over 60 years of age, both male and female, was particularly high. Suicide was also frequent among widowed or divorced males between the ages of 30 and 49 and females aged 20 to 29.

## Householding

There was a sharp contrast between males and females among householders and nonhouseholders who committed suicide (table 1-3). Male nonhouseholders were more prone to suicide than householders; among females, however, householders were more likely to commit suicide. The contrast is attributable to the characteristics of Japanese culture. Indepen-

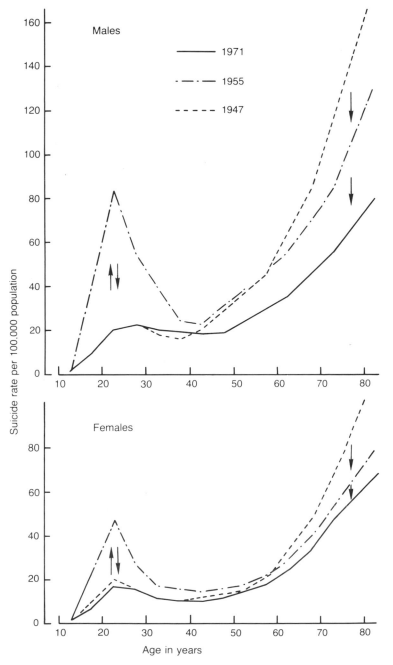

Fig. 1-2.      Suicide rate per 100,000 population in Japan, by sex, in 1947, 1955, and 1971. Source of data: Ministry of Health and Welfare, Japan.

TABLE 1-3
SUICIDE RATES PER 100,000 POPULATION IN JAPAN
BY SOCIAL STATUS, SEX, AND AGE, APRIL–JUNE 1974
(N = 4,925)

| Status | 20–29 | 30–49 | 50–59 | 60 and over | Total |
|---|---|---|---|---|---|
| | | Age group | | | |
| *Marital* | | MALE | | | |
| Unmarried | 8.3 | 31.6 | 30.0 | 52.0 | 11.5 |
| Married | 1.7 | 3.6 | 5.7 | 10.2 | 4.8 |
| Widower or divorced | 28.6 | 35.2 | 26.6 | 29.8 | 30.4 |
| | | FEMALE | | | |
| Unmarried | 6.3 | 13.0 | 10.3 | 28.0 | 7.7 |
| Married | 2.5 | 2.5 | 4.5 | 8.0 | 3.4 |
| Widow or divorced | 23.3 | 8.1 | 5.9 | 15.7 | 12.7 |
| *Householder or nonhouseholder* | | MALE | | | |
| Householder | 3.9 | 5.0 | 6.5 | 10.8 | 6.0 |
| Nonhouseholder | 7.7 | 7.1 | 6.5 | 23.6 | 9.6 |
| | | FEMALE | | | |
| Householder | 6.3 | 7.1 | 5.1 | 8.3 | 6.8 |
| Nonhouseholder | 4.1 | 3.0 | 4.8 | 13.3 | 5.2 |
| *Living alone or together* | | MALE | | | |
| Living alone | 7.8 | 34.4 | 38.6 | 34.0 | 15.4 |
| Living together | 5.9 | 4.9 | 6.0 | 12.9 | 6.6 |
| | | FEMALE | | | |
| Living alone | 7.6 | 13.0 | 7.4 | 12.5 | 10.0 |
| Living together | 4.1 | 3.1 | 4.8 | 12.7 | 5.2 |

SOURCE: Ministry of Health and Welfare (9).

dent life is usual and proper for males but unusual and improper for females. It is probable that a member of either sex living in a socially unapproved state suffers more stresses and faces more handicaps.

Solitary life is a predisposing cause of suicide in Western society, and Japan seems to share this characteristic (table 1-3). It is noteworthy that a higher suicide incidence is clearly shown among the middle-aged of both sexes who live alone.

Employment Status

The same Ministry of Health survey further revealed that the suicide rate among employed males was 4.6 per 100,000, whereas it was 15.5 for unemployed males. The rate for employed females was 2.5, but it was 7.4 among those without employment. It is significant that among both males and females without employment the incidence of suicide was about 2.5 times as high as among employed persons.

### Occupations

Differences in types of work also affect the suicide rate. The highest rate, 12.9 per 100,000, was found among miners and stonecutters. In decreasing order the rate for woodsmen and fishermen was 8.1; clerks, 6.8; servicemen, 4.9; men in transportation and communications, 4.0; skilled and unskilled workers, 3.8; salesmen, 3.1; professional and technical workers, 3.1; and administrators, 2.9. Those who do heavy work—miners, stonecutters, woodsmen, and fishermen—are accustomed to drink a great deal of sake, since consumption of alcohol is the easiest way to get the calories needed to maintain health and energy. The result is often addiction. Although the survey gives few data about alcoholism, it should not be disregarded as a predisposing factor in Japanese suicides. The rates given above reflect the social stresses of Japan's vertically structured semifeudalistic society. Those with least status and fewest options, such as laborers and fishermen, show the highest rate of suicide, whereas administrators, professional men, and technicians suicide much less frequently, probably because their lives are less stressful in such a society.

Among recently compiled data on suicide rates, the most marked feature is an increase in the male early teen group and among middle-aged males. The former may be affected by severe competition in school entrance examinations; the latter, by economic pressures.

### Area of Residence

Suicide rates are higher in areas of Japan undergoing rapid cultural change than in other areas. This is not to say that suicide is frequent only in the cities, for rural suicide rates may also be high. The determining factor seems to be to what extent traditionalism comes into conflict with Westernization and industrialization. Because the cities of Kyoto and Osaka have the sharpest culture conflict, they show the highest suicide rates. The same kind of conflict may also explain the high frequency of suicide among the aged, for, as the most tradition-oriented people in Japan, they fare the worst in its modernization. The Kinki Prefecture, in which Kyoto is located, represents the merchant culture, which stressed practicality and human feelings, and is in sharp contrast with the Tokyo samurai culture, which was the most authoritarian and nationalistic of Japan. Today Tokyo is more powerful in many ways, leading to anxiety and confusion in the Kyoto culture group.

Seasonal Fluctuation

Geographically Japan is composed of several islands which are narrow but long from north to south. The changing seasons—winter, spring, summer, autumn—are distinctly felt. Such climatic changes strongly affect the minds and attitudes of inhabitants. For example, the haiku, a short poem with a set number of lines, has been popular since ancient times. It is a strict rule that a haiku must contain some words about *ki* (the seasons). Even today most Japanese people tend to change their seasonal clothes according to the calendar rather than in response to the actual temperature or weather. Several studies on suicide show that spring coincides with a rise in suicide in the Western world. For this reason, I include data on seasonal change in suicide rates in Japan.

Data on seasonal fluctuations in the suicides in the period 1966–1972 show the peak incidence of male suicides came in April and May, and the peak for females often followed a month later. Western data suggest that social activity during the year may be the cause of such fluctuation. Stengel (19) believes that seasonal changes may account in part for the fact that depressive illness is highest in spring and early summer. His suggestion calls to mind the catecholamine hypothesis of depression, both neuro-pharmacologically and neuroendocrinologically. Since there is a clear seasonal change in the autonomic nervous and endocrinological stress systems, the biological interplay in the seasonal fluctuation of suicide cannot be overlooked. April and May in the northern hemisphere, and October and November in the southern, may be critical months in a zone where people are endogenously sensitized to depression and suicide.

There was a significant difference between seasonal suicide rates in two geographical regions in Japan, the north and the south, in the five-year period 1968–1972. The northern area, consisting of Hokkaido, Aomori, Akita, Yamagata, Iwate, and Miyagi, had 9,892 suicide cases, while the southern area, consisting of Kagoshima, Miyazaki, Ohita, Kumamoto, Saga, and Nagasaki, had 6,701 cases. Figure 1–3 shows the percentage of suicide deaths for each month. In the northern area the rate dropped in January and February, rose sharply in March and April, and maintained a high incidence in May and June, whereas in the southern area the variation was less distinct. After June, however, the rate per month declined steadily until December. During the second half of the year the differences between the areas were not significant. Neither area is highly urbanized and there is no known ethnic difference that might affect the suicide rate. Both areas have similar standards of education, economy, and means of mass communication.

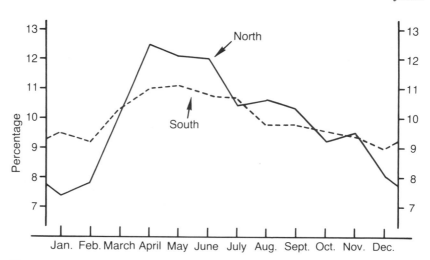

FIG. 1-3.    Monthly fluctuation in suicide in northern and southern areas of Japan, 1968–1972. Source of data: Ministry of Health and Welfare, Japan.

### Time of Day

In contrast with Western patterns, most suicides in Japan occur at night, between 8 P.M. and 4 A.M.

## METHODS

Choice of the method of committing suicide is limited by availability. Since in Japan, as in Great Britain, the possession of firearms is subject to strict licensing, suicide by gunshot is quite rare. Hanging, as in Europe in the nineteenth century or in Germany at present, is common. In 1974 it was the most frequent means (55.6 percent) of suicide among males of all ages and also among females (45.3 percent), especially after the age of 30 (table 1-4). Table 1-4 is based on 19,105 cases of completed suicide investigated by the Ministry of Health in 1974. Hanging was increasingly used by males from the age group 20–29 to those aged 60 or more, its incidence rising from 41.2 to 74.1 percent. Of the females in the 20–29 range who commited suicide, 22.1 percent used the method; the percentage rose to 64.6 for females aged 60 or more.

Gas was the second most important method of suicide, with 12.9 percent of total cases for men and 16.6 percent for women. The use of gas decreased with age: 21.2 percent for men in the 20–29 range, declining to 4.3 percent for those 60 and over; 32.3 percent for females aged 19 and under and 33.7 for the 20–29 group, dropping sharply to 4.1 percent for those 60 and over. Recently gas is being increasingly used by women. Gas and hanging

TABLE 1-4
COMPLETED SUICIDES IN JAPAN IN 1974
BY METHOD, AGE, AND SEX, IN PERCENTAGES
(N = 19,105)

| Method | 19 and under | 20–29 | 30–49 | 50–59 | 60 and over | Total |
|---|---|---|---|---|---|---|
| | | | Age group | | | |
| | | | MALE | | | |
| Drugs | 4.0 | 5.9 | 7.1 | 9.8 | 4.7 | 6.3 |
| Gas | 15.8 | 21.2 | 15.6 | 7.2 | 4.3 | 12.9 |
| Hanging | 50.7 | 41.2 | 49.8 | 64.1 | 74.1 | 55.6 |
| Drowning | 2.0 | 4.5 | 5.2 | 5.1 | 6.4 | 5.2 |
| Guns or explosives | 0.4 | 0.7 | 0.9 | 0.5 | 0.2 | 0.6 |
| Knives and stabbing | 1.3 | 2.4 | 4.1 | 2.9 | 1.7 | 2.9 |
| Jumping | 7.2 | 7.8 | 5.6 | 4.4 | 4.0 | 5.6 |
| Railroad | 5.3 | 8.6 | 8.0 | 3.8 | 3.6 | 6.6 |
| Other | 13.2 | 7.6 | 3.6 | 2.2 | 1.1 | 4.2 |
| | | | FEMALE | | | |
| Drugs | 9.7 | 9.3 | 11.4 | 9.0 | 5.3 | 8.3 |
| Gas | 32.3 | 33.7 | 22.6 | 10.9 | 4.1 | 16.6 |
| Hanging | 23.5 | 22.1 | 34.7 | 52.7 | 64.6 | 45.3 |
| Drowning | 8.1 | 12.3 | 12.8 | 13.9 | 19.0 | 15.0 |
| Guns or explosives | 0.3 | 0.2 | 0.1 | – | – | 0.1 |
| Knives and stabbing | | 1.9 | 2.4 | 2.8 | 0.8 | 1.7 |
| Jumping | 12.6 | 7.0 | 5.1 | 3.8 | 2.5 | 4.6 |
| Railroad | 9.7 | 9.7 | 7.1 | 4.8 | 2.5 | 5.7 |
| Other | 3.9 | 4.0 | 3.8 | 2.1 | 1.2 | 2.7 |

SOURCE: Ministry of Health and Welfare (9).

together accounted for 68.5 percent of male suicides and for 61.9 percent of female suicides in 1974.

The third most popular means was drowning, accounting for 15 percent of the total female deaths and for 5.2 percent of the male deaths. Hanging, gas, and drowning together represented 73.7 percent of total cases for men and 76.9 percent for women. Drowning was used by males in all age groups with very little percentage deviation. Women used the method at a slightly increasing rate (8.1 to 19.0 percent) with increasing age.

The use of drugs in completed suicides appeared as a minor method in the 1974 survey. Only 14.6 percent of the total cases used drugs, 6.3 percent male and 8.3 percent female. When the suicide rate was at its peak after World War II, drugs were used in 45 percent of the cases. Their use has diminished in completed suicide cases but not in attempted suicides. The highest percentage of use in 1974 was not large: 11.4 for females 30–49 years of age. Suicide by jumping in front of a train was almost as large a percentage of the total—12.3—as were drugs, but use of this method is decreasing. A recent method used by young people is jumping from a height, such as a modern high rise. Percentages of the total population were 1.4 per 100,000 in 1960, 2.5 in 1965, 3.6 in 1970, and 5.2 in 1974.

## REASONS FOR COMMITTING SUICIDE

In 1951—1959 the Tokyo Metropolitan Police Board attempted to itemize causes for completed suicides (24). The largest classification, 19.7 percent, was invalidism or serious illness; running a close second was depression, accounting for 19.4 percent. Mental derangement was third with 10.7 percent; family troubles caused 6.4 percent, with twice as many females in this category as males. Otherwise the male-female ratio within the categories was approximately the same. A very large proportion (38 percent) stemmed from unknown causes. The ranking of poverty at 2.5 percent seems to be at odds with the previous investigation of suicides by occupation, in which the largest number of suicides fell into the poor and marginal workingman groups.

The Health and Welfare Ministry's 1974 survey found a different ranking of causes for suicide, although invalidism and serious illness ranked first with 37.6 percent of all male cases and 43.5 percent of all female cases (table 1-5). This cause of suicide was particularly prevalent among the 50—59 and 60 and over groups of both sexes. Marital and other family problems accounted for 10.7 percent of total cases by males and for 19.9 percent by females. Two characteristics are noteworthy in the figures for females; they experienced the most serious difficulty in the age brackets 20—29 through 50—59; in general their percentages were two or three times as high as those for men. Family problems for males ranged from 7.9 to 12.2 percent and, for females, from 25.0 to 13.8 percent. Employment problems ranked third for men, at 9.1 percent, especially in the 20—29 age group. The third most important cause for women was unsatisfactory love affairs, 7 percent, with the highest incidence in the 19 and under group and an almost equal percentage in the 20—29 group.

School problems ranked high among both males and females aged 19 and under. Within this group school problems were listed as the cause of 27.4 percent of male suicides; the percentage dropped sharply to 3.5 in the 20—29 bracket. Females were less affected, rating 10.5 percent within the youngest age group and only 1.4 percent in the 20—29 group. These figures reflect the importance of entrance examinations for young men and to a lesser extent for girls.

TABLE 1-5
CAUSES OF SUICIDES IN JAPAN, APRIL—JUNE 1974,
BY AGE AND SEX, IN PERCENTAGES
(N = 4,925)

| Cause | Age group | | | | | |
|---|---|---|---|---|---|---|
| | 19 and under | 20—29 | 30—49 | 50—59 | 60 and over | Total |
| | MALE | | | | | |
| Invalidism | 10.8 | 18.2 | 29.0 | 43.9 | 66.4 | 37.6 |
| Marital problems | 0.6 | 3.1 | 6.8 | 5.3 | 4.1 | 4.8 |
| Other family members | 11.5 | 4.8 | 4.8 | 6.9 | 6.3 | 5.9 |
| Love affair | 8.9 | 12.3 | 3.2 | 0.3 | 0.3 | 4.3 |
| Money problems | 1.9 | 3.3 | 8.5 | 7.6 | 2.2 | 5.2 |
| Employment problems | 7.6 | 15.6 | 11.1 | 10.6 | 1.6 | 9.1 |
| School problems | 27.4 | 3.5 | – | – | – | 2.3 |
| Depression | 7.6 | 4.7 | 1.9 | 2.3 | 2.2 | 3.0 |
| Other | 3.8 | 3.1 | 4.4 | 4.0 | 3.6 | 3.8 |
| Unknown | 19.7 | 31.4 | 30.9 | 19.1 | 13.2 | 24.1 |
| | FEMALE | | | | | |
| Invalidism | 12.3 | 13.8 | 26.5 | 47.1 | 68.9 | 43.5 |
| Marital problems | 1.8 | 14.3 | 13.4 | 7.6 | 3.5 | 8.5 |
| Other family members | 12.3 | 10.7 | 12.1 | 14.1 | 10.3 | 11.4 |
| Love affair | 28.1 | 21.7 | 8.1 | 0.4 | 0.1 | 7.0 |
| Money problems | – | 0.7 | 3.1 | 2.2 | 0.3 | 1.3 |
| Employment problems | 1.8 | 4.5 | 2.0 | 2.9 | 0.2 | 1.9 |
| School problems | 10.5 | 1.4 | – | – | – | 0.5 |
| Depression | 1.8 | 1.0 | 0.9 | 1.4 | 1.7 | 1.3 |
| Other | 8.8 | 3.1 | 2.5 | 2.2 | 2.5 | 2.7 |
| Unknown | 22.8 | 28.7 | 31.4 | 22.1 | 12.4 | 21.8 |

SOURCE: Ministry of Health and Welfare (9).

## ATTEMPTED SUICIDES

### Prevalence

It has been more difficult to obtain data about attempted suicides in Japan than about completed suicides. The question of status and a desire to protect the attempter's family from unfavorable notice are reasons for concealment.

Okamura studied 21,562 cases of attempted suicide in Tokyo for the period 1967—1972 by checking records of emergency ambulance calls (15). The results of the survey, by age-specific groups, show that 52.8 percent of the cases fall into the 20—29 bracket and 63.9 percent, into the two groups, 15—19 and 20—29 (table 1-6). Female attempts were three times as frequent as male attempts in the 14 and under age group, 1.64 times, in the 15—19 group, 1.97, in the 20—29 group, and 1.49, in the 30—39 group.

The methods used in suicide attempts in 3,316 cases in Tokyo in 1974, based on ambulance calls, are shown in table 1-7. The chief methods were drugs (41.7 percent), gas (32.4 percent), and stabbing or jumping (20.3 percent). In Japan, as in other countries, females were less apt to use forceful methods such as stabbing and jumping, but their use of gas and drugs was not markedly higher than that of men. It is notable that hanging was seldom reported as a method—in only 3.4 percent of the cases—in contrast with its very frequent use in completed suicides. Hanging, therefore, appears to be a measure of lethality of intent. Most attempts were made in March—May and in midweek.

TABLE 1-6
ATTEMPTED SUICIDES IN TOKYO IN 1967—1972
BY AGE AND FEMALE—MALE RATIO, BASED
ON AMBULANCE CALLS

| | 14 and under | Age group | | | | | | 70 and over |
| | | 15—19 | 20—29 | 30—39 | 40—49 | 50—59 | 60—69 | |
| --- | --- | --- | --- | --- | --- | --- | --- | --- |
| Percentage | 1.4 | 11.1 | 52.8 | 17.8 | 8.0 | 4.1 | 2.9 | 2.1 |
| F/M ratio x 100 | 300 | 164 | 197 | 149 | 101 | 89 | 116 | 114 |

SOURCE: Okamura (15).

TABLE 1-7
METHODS USED IN ATTEMPTED SUICIDES IN
TOKYO IN 1974, BY SEX, IN PERCENTAGES, BASED ON
AMBULANCE CALLS
(N = 3,316)

| Method | Male | Female | Total |
| --- | --- | --- | --- |
| Drugs | 38.1 | 46.1 | 41.7 |
| Gas | 30.2 | 33.7 | 32.4 |
| Drugs plus gas | 1.5 | 2.7 | 2.2 |
| Hanging | 4.3 | 2.8 | 3.4 |
| Knives, jumping, etc. | 29.4 | 14.6 | 20.3 |

SOURCE: Okamura (15).

Motivating Factors

Two reports on motivations for suicide attempts are available. The Tokyo Metropolitan Police Board report for 1951—1959 (24) shows that love affairs and family troubles were the major cause of attempts by females, plus a rather vague classification of depression. Males attempted suicide primarily because of depression (table 1-8).

Okamura's report (15) on 3,316 emergency ambulance calls, 90 percent of which were cases of attempted suicide, again shows that the highest proportion of female attempts, 66.6 percent, were owing to love affairs and family troubles. These two categories together accounted for 38.0 percent of attempts by males. The category of neurosis, claiming 25.6 percent of attempts by males, seems too nebulous to be useful as an indicator. Invalidism, an important cause reported for completed suicides, accounted for only 15.3 percent of male attempts and 9.0 percent of female attempts (table 1-9).

# DISTINCTIVE FEATURES OF JAPANESE SUICIDES

Two aspects of suicide in Japan are particularly noteworthy: (1) the large number of student suicides, and (2) group suicides, of parent and child and of lovers, for example. A third distinctive feature is the high rate for young and older women.

Student Suicides

Mamoru Iga[3] has studied student suicides in great detail (11), for the number of Japanese students who kill themselves is striking. Some contrib-

TABLE 1-8
CAUSES OF SUICIDE ATTEMPTS AND
SUICIDES IN TOKYO, 1951—1959
(In percentages)

| Cause | Attempts | | | Suicides | | |
|---|---|---|---|---|---|---|
|  | Male | Female | Total | Male | Female | Total |
| Love affair | 9.1 | 18.4 | 13.1 | 2.8 | 6.6 | 4.1 |
| Family problems | 9.4 | 18.0 | 13.4 | 4.5 | 10.4 | 6.4 |
| Depression | 27.0 | 18.8 | 23.5 | 19.3 | 20.1 | 19.5 |
| Poverty | 3.3 | 2.6 | 3.0 | 2.5 | 2.1 | 2.5 |
| Mental derangement | 5.8 | 4.9 | 5.4 | 10.0 | 12.3 | 10.7 |
| Invalidism | 7.4 | 6.3 | 7.0 | 17.3 | 24.7 | 19.7 |
| Unknown | 38.1 | 30.3 | 34.8 | 43.5 | 24.0 | 37.3 |

SOURCE: Tokyo Metropolitan Police Board (24).

TABLE 1-9
REPORTED MOTIVATION FOR SUICIDE ATTEMPTS
IN TOKYO IN 1974, BY SEX, IN PERCENTAGES,
BASED ON AMBULANCE CALLS
(N = 3.316)

| Motivation | Male | Female |
|---|---|---|
| Love affair | 18.6 | 33.8 |
| Family problems | 19.4 | 32.8 |
| Neurosis | 25.6 | 12.8 |
| Invalidism | 15.3 | 9.0 |
| Depression | 10.2 | 6.9 |
| Poverty | 7.6 | 3.3 |
| Other | 3.2 | 1.1 |

SOURCE: Okamura (15).

uting factors are the critical importance of succeeding in examinations; the strain of studying for exams enabling a student to advance from grade school to college; the interdependence of Japanese mother and child in such efforts; status hierarchy; disregard for reason in the pursuit of success; the intensity of guilt and shame if a student fails in examinations.

There are seven suicides a month among Japanese students under 16 years of age. According to a Ministry of Education report, 341 junior and senior high school students (ages 12 – 17) suicided in Tokyo in 1973 (table 1-10). In 1974 the number of cases was slightly lower; the survey indicates that family problems were the main cause, with depression over future prospects and poor school performance ranking second. In 1978 there were 326 junior and senior high school student suicides. The superintendent of the Tokyo Institute for Education reported that from 1965 to 1972 the causes for suicides of high school students, in descending order, were depression about life, family problems, and unsuccessful love affairs.

In January 1979, 105 Japanese boys and girls killed themselves, until then the largest number of students to do so in one month. These young people had complained mainly about the harshness of school programs, the loneliness of their daily lives, and quarrels with friends and parents. In a particularly tragic case of unusual significance in reference to Japanese traditional culture, a high school boy with a fine scholastic record killed his grandmother and then himself with a knife. The grandmother had played an autocratic role in the family, demanding that the boy study constantly so that he could gain admission to a prestigious university. She forced the boy's mother to live separately from his father who, though a professor, was

[3]Mamoru Iga is a member of the Sociology Department of California State University, Northridge.

TABLE 1-10
STUDENT SUICIDES IN TOKYO, 1973—1978,
BY SEX AND SCHOOL LEVEL

| School level | Sex | 1973 | 1974 | 1975 | 1976 | 1977 | 1978 |
|---|---|---|---|---|---|---|---|
| Primary | M | | | | | 6 | 6 |
| school[a] | F | ? | ? | ? | ? | 4 | 3 |
| Total | | | | | | 10 | 9 |
| Junior | M | 73 | 46 | 51 | 47 | 63 | 64 |
| high school[b] | F | 35 | 23 | 28 | 25 | 26 | 27 |
| Total | | 108 | 69 | 79 | 72 | 89 | 91 |
| High | M | 158 | 133 | 140 | 145 | 150 | 157 |
| school[c] | F | 75 | 75 | 71 | 71 | 72 | 78 |
| Total | | 233 | 208 | 211 | 216 | 222 | 235 |

SOURCE: Ministry of Education.
[a]Ages 6—11.
[b]Ages 12—14.
[c]Ages 15—17.

not an effective head of family. The dominating behavior of a grandmother toward a whole family was customary before World War II, but nowadays it is infrequent. In this case the parents submitted to it because of their early training, but the boy could not bear it. His diary vividly described the mental and psychological pressures he suffered.

Students attending prefectural universities, which rank below governmental universities in prestige, have the highest suicide rate; those at governmental universities are second and those attending private universities are lowest. Although Tokyo University ranks highest in prestige, its students suicide at the national average for students, whereas Kyoto University has a very high rate, possibly because of the sharp culture conflict between traditional Kyoto culture and modern trends and because of the poorer economic situation of Kyoto.

Preparation for college entrance begins early, as mothers strive to get their children into the most prestigious kindergartens so that they can enter the best grade schools. The student's progression in school is a long and difficult one in which the mother is expected to inspire, discipline, and manage the child successfully. Since women have had few opportunities to succeed in their own right outside the home, they may enjoy vicarious success through that of their sons. The pressure is intense, and often households are arranged so that the student has a special place and good facilities for studying. Most students add one or two hours of homework a day to their regular classroom work in order to gain as much knowledge as possible for the coming college entrance examinations, which test learning by rote. The mother's expectation of and her responsibility for her child's success, plus the latter's gratitude for her extraordinary efforts, may result in catastrophic guilt and shame should the child fail.

Another stressful factor is the "once only" feature of college examinations. The student tries to enter the most prestigious school, usually a governmental one where the cost is much lower than in other schools; should he fail, he does not apply elsewhere. Instead he returns to his studying and tries to pass the exams the next year. As previously noted, his whole future, both economic and social, hangs upon entrance to the right university. His choice of a marriage partner and his lifetime employment are dependent on the outcome. Japan's status hierarchy does not allow for alternative means of meeting these crisis points, and this fact, combined with a duty owed to the mother by the student, brings despair to many young people. An additional factor is a disregard for reason: the student does not think of more reachable goals but must press on to achieve the highest rank possible.[4]

As high as the suicide rate among students is, it still does not surpass the rate among the unemployed. Since students are listed as unemployed, if their suicides are removed from the total for that category the unemployed rate would be even higher. Among the unemployed would be students who had failed several times to gain entrance to college and thus were unable to find suitable employment. In 1955 the student suicide rate was 31 per 100,000; for the unemployed it was 129.

### Group Suicides

Ohara and Reynolds, after studying parent-child and love-pact suicides, which occur daily in Japan, report that the latter accounted for 72 percent of all group suicides and the former, for 22 percent. Of the parent-child suicides, 73 percent were of mother and child. Of the mother-child suicides, 66 percent involved one child, 24 percent, two children, and 7.5 percent, three children. Since most cases concerned children in infancy, the mothers were young, whereas fathers in parent-child suicides were 35 to 44 years of age and the children were older. These cases might better be described as suicide-homicides. Investigation of ten cases in the Ohara-Reynolds study in which a parent survived showed that in five of them there were interpersonal difficulties with a spouse, in three, physically or mentally deficient children, and in one, poverty. As the Japanese view of these parental actions is lenient, the heaviest sentence was three years in prison.

---

[4]Paper given by Mamoru Iga at the International Association for Suicide Prevention Congress held in Ottawa, Canada, in 1979.

Dr. J. Koshinaga, director of the Tokyo medical examiner's office, reviewed group suicides for the period 1946—1972. Mother-child suicides were the most common, the leading causes being the father's infidelity and other family problems. Lovers' suicides have been decreasing since 1958, although there has been a slight increase in cases of the woman killing the man and then herself.

Parent-child suicides may reflect the Japanese view of death as a salvation, the emphasis on the family group, the romanticizing and dramatizing of death, and feelings of passing from a tragic life to the peaceful world of the kami. They may also indicate situations of dire economic distress with social helplessness and attendant shame. Young mother-child suicides are probably motivated by protest and hostility because of the father's infidelity or neglect. By killing her child and then herself, the mother removes the children from the husband's family and symbolically returns with them to her own family, thus depriving the husband of children who will continue his line and bring remembrance and reverence to his spirit after his death. Death can constitute a significant and final triumph for the mother in such situations.

Young Japanese Women

This group has the highest suicide rate in the world. It is the first cause of death for women in the 15—24 age group, and it is found particularly among single, widowed, and divorced women. In the period 1955—1975 the female-male suicide ratio increased steadily, until a decline set in 1975—1978. The data show that female deaths by suicide were 60 percent of male deaths in 1955, 77 percent in 1969, 75 percent in 1974, and 68 percent in 1975. Japanese women between the ages of 65 and 74 had the second highest suicide rate in the world; the highest rate was in Hungary. Divorced and widowed women in both the young age group and the over 60 group are most prone to suicide and reflect their disadvantaged economic and social position in Japan. The causes of young female suicides may be early conflicts over choosing between work and marriage, male-female stresses, and role conflicts of wives and mothers who are also working women. Older women often lose status and economic security because of divorce or widowhood; there is also less regard now for older women than in the traditional schema. The majority of women choose marriage, but in the event of divorce, poor marital relationships, or widowhood they have limited opportunities for self-support in spite of the liberalization of laws forced by American occupation after the war. Women, paid half as much as men for the same work, are often deprived of fringe, retirement, and other benefits. Many divorced women lacked work experience before marriage and therefore have no skills to sell. Education is less available to women than to men, and most of them go to two-year colleges. Preference in managerial positions and in the upper echelons of work goes to men; although women make up 40 percent of Japan's labor force, they are mostly in the lower economic scale. These conditions create severe disadvantages for divorced and widowed women, especially for those supporting several children.

The divorce rate in Japan has increased from 0.99 per 1,000 in 1971 to 1.14 per 1,000 in 1977. The Ministry of Public Health and Welfare reports that since 1965 more women are divorcing husbands, especially if there is only one child, than husbands are divorcing wives. Higher suicide rates for widowed and divorced males than for married males may be owing to the man's dependence on the wife. Japanese women are the financial managers, purchasers, and bookkeepers for the family. Since Japanese males rely on their wives not only for comforts at home but also for economic direction, the loss of a spouse may be an overwhelming disaster.

## CASE HISTORIES

### Case A

Yukio ———, a middle management employee of a large company, hanged himself, leaving a note of regret and apology to his wife and his employer. He had been an ambitious and competent man who worked diligently and faithfully. He was promoted to a higher position for which, unfortunately, his previous experience had not prepared him, and he found himself unable to function adequately in the job. As his standards for himself were high, he suffered severe feelings of self-criticism. The alternative of asking to be transferred did not seem possible to him because it would imply poor management on the part of his superior and would point to his own incompetence. He could think only of removing himself from the dilemma by killing himself.

### Case B

A 40-year-old widow with a son who was studying for university examinations pleaded with him not to take them, because she felt they were too difficult for him and he would surely fail, bringing them both serious problems of further tutoring expense, loss of face, and possibly another failure. When her request was unheeded she became very depressed and anxious. A week before the exams were to take place she turned on the gas at night and asphyxiated both herself and her son.

### Case C

A 21-year-old girl attempted suicide by taking a large number of tranquilizers at night, but she was found in time. When she recovered consciousness, she explained her plight as one that seemed insoluble. She was a restaurant employee who worked for low wages. Her mother suffered from recurrent and severe attacks of rheumatism which could not be alleviated. Her father, who worked as a guard, was also sickly and recently had been hospitalized because of an appendicitis attack. The hospital informed the girl that she would have to pay for his care, an enormous sum for one earning low wages. She felt that she would have to work and care for two invalids for the rest of her life and therefore would be unable to marry. The prospect was so gloomy that she attempted suicide.

After her recovery, and probably as a result of her attempt, her mother divorced the husband so she could get government aid (a necessary action in Japan) and thus relieved the girl of her burden of worry and responsibility.

### Case D

A young man slashed his wrists after discovering that his girl friend had been lying to him about her interest in a friend of his and that she had been seeing the other young man. When he accused her of being unfaithful she made derogatory remarks about him. These preyed on his mind and two days later he was discovered at home unconscious and bloody, as he had taken a number of pills before slashing his wrists.

## SUICIDE PREVENTION SERVICES

In 1970 thirty professional men and women joined together to form a group for suicide prevention (I was one of the founding members). The members met monthly to exchange information. The group also sponsored two symposia on suicide and its prevention and published the proceedings under the titles *Thinking of Suicide in Japan* (27) and *Suicide of Japanese Youth and Related Problems* (20). Both were influential in educating the public to these problems. There does not yet exist, however, a specific suicide prevention center or a telephone service solely for suicide calls.

With the advent of industrial development and increased prosperity after 1970, the number of telephone lines in Japan has sharply increased. Consequently, various kinds of telephone service have been developed, including counseling for personal problems. Some of them directly or indirectly include counseling regarding suicidal thoughts and intentions.

Ruth Hetcamp of the German Midnight Mission, a Christian organization, took the initial step in 1969 in organizing a lifeline telephone service in Tokyo, Inochi No Denwa, with financial aid from Germany. It opened on October 1, 1971, with a twenty-four-hour service. At present approximately eighty calls a day come from all parts of Japan; they concern interpersonal problems, sexual frustrations, family and marital conflicts, loneliness, and mental confusion—in fact, the whole gamut of problems in our modern society. Ten percent are suicide calls. Of the callers, 16 percent were 18 and under; 40 percent, 18—29; 17 percent, 30—39; 13 percent, 40—49; 9 percent, 50—59; and 4 percent, 60 and over. For whatever reason, older people apparently are less prone to make such calls. The male-female ratio of the callers is estimated to be 1:1.7. At present nearly 300 lay volunteers give time twice a month to the telephone service. In addition, professional persons serve in a volunteer capacity, training volunteers and serving as consultants in the review of cases. Psychiatric face-to-face inter-views with chronic callers, held every Saturday morning, started in Janu-ary 1973.

Inochi no Denwa was originally staffed by Christians but increasing numbers of Buddhist-Shintoists are among the volunteers. The present seven centers are supported by individual contributions, donations from various organizations, and industry grants. Crisis counseling, psychiatric counseling, and telephone medical consultations are part of the service. In 1977—78,[5] 26,372 calls were received, of which 15.5 percent concerned marital problems, 15.6 percent, the meaning of life (including loneliness, religion, and suicide), 12.4 percent, male-female relationships, and 10.6 percent, family problems. Thus problems that have to do with family and personal relationships accounted for 80.2 percent of the calls; the remaining 19.8 percent were calls related to medical, financial, legal, or informational matters. The increasing use of the service for help in personal matters is an important change in Japanese attitudes, for formerly one did not seek a confidant to whom to express one's feelings.

A new Inochi no Denwa opened in Osaka in 1973 and another in Okinawa in 1975. A telephone service for junior and senior high school students opened in Nagoya in 1974. Similar telephone services have been instituted by Buddhist groups that have recognized their importance in modern society. The best known is run by Superior Priest Nishirai, who opened a telephone service called "Dial a Friend" in March 1974. He receives about twenty calls a day. Local police bureaus manage young people's telephone services begun in 1976 with thirty-seven calls a day (19). One of my current projects is to coordinate these various telephone services with the aim of preventing suicides.

CONCLUSION

Influencing public attitudes toward suicide is an important goal. After Mishima's death at least eight youths killed themselves, and ten others attempted suicide in clear emulation of Mishima's suicide by hara-kiri. It is

[5] Annual report of Inochi no Denwa for 1978.

regrettable that on that occasion psychiatric specialists made only clinical remarks concerning Mishima's suicide and neglected the opportunity to disseminate constructive information that might influence people toward the prevention of suicide. The emphasis was upon admiration of Mishima's talent, omitting the negative aspects of his behavior. The response to Kawabata's[6] suicide was similar. No specialists at that time urged suicide prevention activities. Specialists and clinicians should emphasize the dignity of life, not death.

The situation in Japan requires clear thinking and strong efforts. As materialism increases, education seems oriented to obtaining higher degrees rather than to developing the whole person; physicians tend to be clinicians rather than diagnosticians who take into account the personal needs and problems of patients. The Japanese are less inclined toward strong family ties as the nuclear family becomes more widespread and family members become solitary individuals who lack social solidarity. Increasing leisure time, if not used constructively, may strengthen aggressive feelings and may cause an increase in suicidal behavior. The high rate of suicides and suicide attempts in young people and in the older generation is alarming and should lead the Japanese to cultivate *omoiyari*, sympathetic but rational thoughtfulness.

## SUMMARY

Japan's suicide profile is a U-curve with high rates of suicide in early youth and later age. The highest incidence is among females in the 15–24 age group and after age 45. Female and male rates are approximately the same in the 25–44 age group. Completed suicides are frequent among students of college age, owing to the entrance examinations upon which a student's whole economic future and status depend. The most frequent means of suicide is hanging, followed by the use of gas and then by drowning. The most common cause of suicide is severe illness and invalidism; family and marital problems come second; the third ranking cause is employment problems and depression.

Attempted suicides are most numerous among those in the 15–29 age group, accounting for 63.9 percent. Females attempted suicide three times as often as males in age group 0–14 and 1.64 times as often in the 15–19 age group. The chief method of attempters was drugs, 41.7 percent; gas accounted for 32.4 percent; stabbing and jumping followed.

Causes for attempts are chiefly unhappy love affairs, family problems, and depression. The latter cause is not specific enough to be helpful.

---

[6]Kawabata was a well-known novelist.

# BIBLIOGRAPHY

1. Doi, L. T. *Amae*, a key concept for understanding Japanese personality structure. In R. J. Smith and R. K. Beardsley, eds., *Japanese Culture: Its Development and Characteristics*. Chicago: Aldine Press, 1962.
2. Dublin, L. I. *Suicide: A Sociological and Statistical Study*. New York: Ronald Press, 1963.
3. Dublin, L. I., and B. Bunzel. *To Be or Not to Be*. New York: Smith and Haas, 1933.
4. Dubos, R. *Mirage of Health*. New York: Harper and Brothers, 1959.
5. Durkheim, E. *Suicide* (1897). Trans. J. A. Spauling and G. Simpson. Glencoe: Free Press, 1951.
6. Hasegawa, I. Writers and suicide. In K. Tatai and M. Kato, eds., *Thinking of Suicide in Japan*. In Japanese.
7. Hirayama, J. Japanese culture and suicide. In Tatai and Kato, eds., *Thinking of Suicide in Japan*. In Japanese.
8. Health and Welfare Statistics and Information Department. *Vital Statistics, Japan, 1974*. Tokyo: Ministry of Health and Welfare, 1976.
9. Health and Welfare Statistics and Information Department. Suicide in 1974: A Report on Survey of Socioeconomic Aspects of Vital Events. Tokyo: Ministry of Health and Welfare, 1976.
10. Health and Welfare Statistics and Information Department. *Provisional Report, 1975*. Tokyo: Ministry of Health and Welfare, 1976.
11. Iga, M., and K. Tatai. Characteristics of suicides and attitudes toward suicide in Japan. In N. L. Farberow, ed., *Suicide in Different Cultures*. Baltimore: University Park Press, 1975.
12. Kato, M. Effect of period and national traits. In Tatai and Kato, eds., *Thinking of Suicide in Japan*. In Japanese.
13. McFarland, R. A. *Human Factors in Air Transportation*. New York: McGraw-Hill, 1953.
14. Masuda, R. An investigation of self-destructive behavior in a district of Tokyo. In Tatai and Kato, eds., *Thinking of Suicide in Japan*. In Japanese.
15. Okamura, M. From emergency ambulance calls in Tokyo. In Tatai and Kato, eds., *Thinking of Suicide in Japan*. In Japanese.
16. Paulson, Joy. Evolution of the feminine ideal. In Joyce Lebra, ed., *Changing Women in Japan*. Stanford: Stanford University Press, 1978. Pp. 1–23.
17. Selye, H. *Stress of Life*. New York: McGraw-Hill, 1956.
18. Snyder, S. H. Biology. In S. Perlin, ed., *A Handbook for the Study of Suicide*. New York: Oxford University Press, 1975.
19. Stengel, E. *Suicide and Attempted Suicide*. Harmondsworth: Penguin Books, 1969.
20. Suicide Preventive Research Group. *Suicide of Japanese Youth and Related Problems*. Tokyo: Gakuji-Shuppan, 1976. In Japanese.
21. Takahashi, E. On suicide. *Japanese J. Public Health*, 11, 90 (1957). In Japanese.
22. Tatai, K. Recent trend of suicide in Japan. *Bull. Inst. Public Health*, 3, 6 (1952).
23. Tatai, K. A further study of suicide in Japan. *Bull. Inst. Public Health*, 7, 52 (1958).

24. Tatai, K. Recent trend of agents for suicide in Japan. *Bull. Inst. Public Health*, 12, 45 (1963).
25. Tatai, K. How to prevent suicide in public approaches. In Tatai and Kato, eds., *Thinking of Suicide in Japan*. In Japanese.
26. Tatai, K. Seasonal rhythmic fluctuation of suicide in Japan. *J. Interdisciplinary Cycle Research*. Forthcoming.
27. Tatai, K., and M. Kato, eds. *Thinking of Suicide in Japan*. Tokyo: Igaku-Shoiu, 1974.
28. Youth Bureau. *The Youth of the World: A World Survey Report*. Tokyo: Prime Minister's Office, 1973.

## PART II. INOCHI NO DENWA[7]

In October 1980, Inochi no Denwa (IND) completed nine years of a lifeline telephone service in Tokyo. Since the opening of the IND center in 1971, at least one new center has been added each year, and in 1979 four new centers were opened, in Hokkaido, Shimane, Nara, and Toronto, Canada. The latter, which started operations on May 1, 1979, was the first overseas Japanese-language counseling service for a group of Japanese adjusting to a new culture and new surroundings. It is probable that IND centers will soon be added in Yokohama, Asahigawa in Hokkaido, Utsonomiya, and Kobe. Increasing numbers of volunteers for the telephone service have applied, and the service has intentionally recruited its volunteers from a variety of backgrounds. Volunteers not only complete an initial training course but participate in a continuing series of educational and training programs.

There were 28,540 calls in 1979. IND handles all types of problems in taking calls, and as a consequence of its experience, two specialized programs have been added. The Psychiatric Counseling Service, which offers individual counseling, has been in existence for seven years. Severely disturbed and suicidal persons are given help there, often intensively. The General Counseling Service, launched in July 1975, offers individual and group therapy in less difficult cases. In addition, twelve volunteer attorneys are available for consultation with IND's clients.

The areas from which the clients telephone are primarily the twenty-three wards of Tokyo proper, but an increasing number of calls are coming from the suburbs and neighboring prefectures. Table 1-11 shows the area of residence of the clients who were seen for psychiatric and medical consultations from October 1978 through September 1979. These clients were the most seriously disturbed and therefore more likely to attempt suicide.

[7] I am grateful to Yukio Saito, director of Inochi no Denwa, for supplying me with the collected statistics on the service, and especially to the executive secretary, the Reverend R. Wallace Brownlee, for help in translating additional material.

Altogether volunteer medical personnel handled 478 medical consultations, and in 196 (41 percent) of them the problem was one of mental disorder. Table 1-12 gives the sex and age of the clients seen for psychiatric interviews and medical consultations during the same year. Of the 145 clients, the largest number (56) were in the 20−29 age group; the second largest (39), in the 10−19 group; and the third largest (30), in the 30−39 group. Thus more than half the clients (65.5 percent) were between the ages of 10 and 29; 86 percent were in the 10−39 age group. There were 83 females and 62 males.

The data in table 1-13 reveal the kinds of difficulties that impel Inochi no Denwa callers to ask for help. The table, covering the period October 1978 through September 1979, gives the number and percentage of callers within

TABLE 1-11

AREA OF RESIDENCE OF CLIENTS SEEN FOR PSYCHIATRIC AND MEDICAL
CONSULTATIONS, OCTOBER 1978−SEPTEMBER 1979

| Area of residence | Number of clients | | | Number of consultations | | |
|---|---|---|---|---|---|---|
| | Male | Female | Total | Male | Female | Total |
| Metropolitan Tokyo | 30 | 42 | 72 | 240 | 177 | 417 |
| Tokyo suburbs | 7 | 10 | 17 | 41 | 82 | 123 |
| Kanagawa Prefecture | 5 | 9 | 14 | 9 | 78 | 87 |
| Chiba Prefecture | 8 | 4 | 12 | 60 | 19 | 79 |
| Saitama Prefecture | 9 | 14 | 23 | 17 | 58 | 75 |
| Other | 3 | 4 | 7 | 17 | 9 | 26 |
| Total | 62 | 83 | 145 | 384 | 423 | 807 |

SOURCE: Inochi no Denwa, Tokyo.

TABLE 1-12

AGE AND SEX OF CLIENTS SEEN FOR PSYCHIATRIC AND MEDICAL CONSULTATIONS,
OCTOBER 1978−SEPTEMBER 1979

| | Sex | Age group | | | | | | Total |
|---|---|---|---|---|---|---|---|---|
| | | 10−19 | 20−29 | 30−39 | 40−49 | 50−59 | 60−69 | |
| Number of | Male | 18 | 22 | 12 | 7 | 3 | 0 | 62 |
| clients | Female | 21 | 34 | 18 | 5 | 3 | 2 | 83 |
| Total | | 39 | 56 | 30 | 12 | 6 | 2 | 145 |
| Number of | Male | 59 | 154 | 103 | 50 | 18 | 0 | 384 |
| consultations | Female | 74 | 213 | 53 | 24 | 41 | 18 | 423 |
| Total | | 133 | 367 | 156 | 74 | 59 | 18 | 807 |

SOURCE: Inochi no Denwa, Tokyo.

TABLE 1-13

STATISTICS OF INOCHI NO DENWA'S EIGHTH YEAR, OCTOBER 1978–SEPTEMBER 1979

| Problem | Male callers | | Female callers | | Total | |
|---|---|---|---|---|---|---|
| | Number | Percentage | Number | Percentage | Number | Percentage |
| *Philosophy of life* | | | | | | |
| 1. Meaninglessness | 500 | 4.8 | 1,340 | 7.4 | 1,840 | 6.4 |
| 2. Loneliness | 452 | 4.3 | 558 | 3.1 | 1,010 | 3.5 |
| 3. Personality problems | 193 | 1.8 | 464 | 2.6 | 657 | 2.3 |
| 4. Religion | 16 | 0.2 | 75 | 0.4 | 91 | 0.3 |
| 5. Occupation problems | 173 | 1.7 | 159 | 0.9 | 332 | 1.2 |
| 6. Suicide thoughts | 181 | 1.7 | 247 | 1.4 | 428 | 1.5 |
| 7. Other | 125 | 1.2 | 80 | 0.4 | 205 | 0.7 |
| Total | 1,640 | 15.7 | 2,923 | 16.2 | 4,563 | 16.0 |
| *Family problems* | | | | | | |
| 8. Dissatisfaction with family | 96 | 0.9 | 1,065 | 5.9 | 1,161 | 4.1 |
| 9. Anxiety about family | 109 | 1.0 | 953 | 5.2 | 1,062 | 3.7 |
| 10. Marriage of children | 3 | 0.02 | 167 | 0.9 | 170 | 0.6 |
| 11. Aging[a] | 5 | 0.04 | 50 | 0.3 | 55 | 1.2 |
| 12. Education at home | 15 | 0.1 | 501 | 2.8 | 516 | 1.8 |
| 13. Running away from home | 4 | 0.03 | 55 | 0.3 | 59 | 0.2 |
| 14. Other | 34 | 0.3 | 65 | 0.4 | 99 | 0.3 |
| Total | 266 | 2.5 | 2,856 | 15.8 | 3,122 | 10.9 |
| *Marital problems* | | | | | | |
| 15. Dissatisfaction with spouse | 121 | 1.2 | 1,335 | 7.4 | 1,456 | 5.1 |
| 16. Extramarital affair | 137 | 1.3 | 847 | 4.7 | 984 | 3.4 |

TABLE 1-13—*Continued*

| Problem | Male callers | | Female callers | | Total | |
|---|---|---|---|---|---|---|
| | Number | Percentage | Number | Percentage | Number | Percentage |
| 17. Personal sex life | 342 | 3.3 | 119 | 0.6 | 461 | 1.6 |
| 18. Sudden disappearance[b] | 25 | 0.2 | 35 | 0.2 | 60 | 0.2 |
| 19. Divorce | 80 | 0.8 | 481 | 2.7 | 561 | 2.0 |
| 20. Relationship with in-laws | 5 | 0.04 | 139 | 0.8 | 144 | 0.5 |
| 21. Other | 24 | 0.2 | 99 | 0.5 | 123 | 0.4 |
| Total | 734 | 7.0 | 3,055 | 16.9 | 3,789 | 13.3 |
| *Male-female relationship* | | | | | | |
| 22. Love uncertainties[c] | 574 | 5.5 | 831 | 4.6 | 1,405 | 4.9 |
| 23. Sexual relationships | 575 | 5.5 | 247 | 1.3 | 822 | 2.9 |
| 24. Problem pregnancy | 101 | 1.0 | 194 | 1.1 | 295 | 1.0 |
| 25. Marriage frictions | 233 | 2.2 | 378 | 2.1 | 611 | 2.1 |
| 26. Other | 141 | 1.3 | 252 | 1.4 | 393 | 1.4 |
| Total | 1,624 | 15.5 | 1,902 | 10.5 | 3,526 | 12.4 |
| *Human relationships* | | | | | | |
| 27. Friendships | 66 | 0.6 | 168 | 0.9 | 234 | 0.8 |
| 28. Relationships at work | 119 | 1.1 | 443 | 2.5 | 562 | 2.0 |
| 29. Relationships with neighbors | 29 | 0.3 | 767 | 4.3 | 796 | 2.8 |
| 30. Third party | 35 | 0.3 | 99 | 0.5 | 134 | 0.4 |
| 31. Other | 62 | 0.6 | 218 | 1.2 | 280 | 2.0 |
| Total | 311 | 3.0 | 1,695 | 9.4 | 2,006 | 7.0 |

| | | | | | |
|---|---|---|---|---|---|
| *Juvenile* | | | | | |
| 32. School life | 111 | 1.1 | 683 | 3.8 | 794 | 2.8 |
| 33. Studies | 123 | 1.2 | 260 | 1.4 | 383 | 1.3 |
| 34. Delinquent behavior | 41 | 0.4 | 90 | 0.5 | 131 | 0.4 |
| 35. Boy-girl relationships | 114 | 1.1 | 571 | 3.2 | 685 | 2.4 |
| 36. Other | 310 | 3.0 | 266 | 1.5 | 576 | 2.0 |
| Total | 699 | 6.7 | 1,870 | 10.4 | 2,569 | 9.0 |
| *Medical* | | | | | |
| 37. General medicine | 122 | 1.2 | 511 | 2.8 | 633 | 2.2 |
| 38. Mental illness | 398 | 3.8 | 1,008 | 5.6 | 1,406 | 4.9 |
| 39. Personal mental health | 170 | 1.6 | 486 | 2.7 | 656 | 2.3 |
| 40. Borderline cases between medical and other problems | 51 | 0.5 | 98 | 0.5 | 149 | 0.5 |
| 41. Other | 102 | 1.0 | 73 | 0.4 | 175 | 0.6 |
| Total | 843 | 8.0 | 2,176 | 12.0 | 3,019 | 10.6 |
| *Sex* | | | | | |
| 42. Anxieties (masturbation) | 843 | 8.0 | 36 | 0.2 | 879 | 3.1 |
| 43. Sex information | 373 | 3.6 | 13 | 0.07 | 386 | 1.3 |
| 44. Homosexuality | 140 | 1.3 | 26 | 0.1 | 166 | 0.6 |
| 45. Sexual deviation[d] | 423 | 4.0 | 129 | 0.7 | 552 | 1.9 |
| 46. Telephone sex[e] | 1,336 | 12.7 | 28 | 0.2 | 1,364 | 4.8 |
| 47. Other | 283 | 2.7 | 22 | 0.1 | 305 | 1.1 |
| Total | 3,398 | 32.4 | 254 | 1.4 | 3,652 | 12.8 |
| *Legal and financial* | | | | | |
| 48. Residency | 4 | 0.03 | 13 | 0.07 | 17 | 0.1 |
| 49. Marriage and divorce | 20 | 0.2 | 60 | 0.3 | 80 | 0.3 |
| 50. Inheritance | 5 | 0.04 | 38 | 0.3 | 43 | 0.2 |

TABLE 1-13—*Continued*

| Problem | Male callers | | Female callers | | Total | |
|---|---|---|---|---|---|---|
| | Number | Percentage | Number | Percentage | Number | Percentage |
| 51. Traffic accidents | 12 | 0.1 | 13 | 0.07 | 25 | 0.1 |
| 52. Crime | 17 | 0.2 | 25 | 0.1 | 42 | 0.1 |
| 53. Management | 4 | 0.03 | 6 | 0.03 | 10 | 0.03 |
| 54. Financial | 84 | 0.8 | 134 | 0.7 | 218 | 0.8 |
| 55. Housing and real estate | 9 | 0.1 | 82 | 0.5 | 91 | 0.3 |
| 56. Social welfare | 1 | 0.01 | 16 | 0.08 | 17 | 0.05 |
| 57. Other | 18 | 0.2 | 51 | 0.3 | 69 | 0.2 |
| Total | 174 | 1.7 | 438 | 2.4 | 612 | 2.1 |
| *Political and social* | | | | | | |
| 58. Political and social | 11 | 0.1 | 18 | 0.1 | 29 | 0.1 |
| *Information* | | | | | | |
| 59. Information and referrals | 192 | 1.8 | 458 | 2.5 | 650 | 2.3 |
| 60. Regarding IND | 188 | 1.8 | 289 | 1.6 | 477 | 1.7 |
| 61. Prank calls | 208 | 2.0 | 19 | 0.1 | 227 | 0.8 |
| 62. Other | 191 | 1.8 | 108 | 0.6 | 299 | 1.0 |
| Total | 779 | 7.4 | 874 | 4.8 | 1,653 | 5.8 |
| Grand total | 10,479 | | 18,061 | | 28,540 | |

[a]Status, health, and future.
[b]Desertion.
[c]Rejection, parental opposition, difference in class.
[d]Fetishism.
[e]Telephone masturbators.

each category and the number and percentages for each sex. Clearly, family
and personal problems predominated. Of the 28,540 callers, 63.3 percent
were female and 36.7 percent were male.

## SUICIDE TELEPHONE CALLS, 1975–1979

Inochi no Denwa has done a survey of the suicide cases it handled by
telephone in the four-year period, October 1975 through September 1979.
Of the total of 879 calls, 333 were made by males and 546 by females.
Statistics were gathered on the following variables: monthly incidence of
calls; time of day of calls; age and sex of callers; occupation of callers; related
family factors; number of suicide attempts; methods of suicide attempts;
medical treatment received; motivations and reasons for suicidal intent;
personality traits and characteristics; mood at time of calling.

### Monthly Incidence

About 41 percent of the total number of calls were received in April,
May, June, and July together; 10.7 percent were recorded in February and
8.6 percent in November. Males called most frequently in April and May,
with other high points in February, March, and November. Females called
most frequently in May, June, and July, with other high points in February, April, and November (see table 1-14).

TABLE 1-14
MONTHLY INCIDENCE OF CALLS RECEIVED BY
INOCHI NO DENWA, TOKYO, OCTOBER 1975–SEPTEMBER 1979

| Month | Calls from males | | Calls from females | | Total | |
|---|---|---|---|---|---|---|
| | Number | Percentage | Number | Percentage | Number | Percentage |
| January | 23 | 6.9 | 39 | 7.1 | 62 | 7.1 |
| February | 36 | 10.8 | 58 | 10.6 | 94 | 10.7 |
| March | 29 | 8.7 | 44 | 8.0 | 73 | 8.3 |
| April | 41 | 12.3 | 48 | 8.8 | 89 | 10.1 |
| May | 40 | 12.0 | 60 | 11.0 | 100 | 11.4 |
| June | 24 | 7.2 | 60 | 11.0 | 84 | 9.6 |
| July | 20 | 6.0 | 68 | 12.5 | 88 | 10.0 |
| August | 19 | 5.7 | 26 | 4.8 | 45 | 5.1 |
| September | 22 | 6.6 | 40 | 7.3 | 62 | 7.1 |
| October | 20 | 6.0 | 32 | 5.9 | 52 | 5.9 |
| November | 33 | 9.9 | 43 | 7.9 | 76 | 8.6 |
| December | 26 | 7.8 | 28 | 5.1 | 54 | 5.1 |
| Total | 333 | | 546 | | 879 | |

Daily Incidence

The largest number of calls were received between 11 A.M. and midnight. Peak periods were from 2 to 4 P.M. and from 9 P.M. to midnight.

Age and Sex of Callers

Of the 879 callers, 248 (28.2 percent) were in the 10–19 age group; 335 (38.1 percent), in the 20–29 group; 125 (14.2 percent), in the 30–39 group. More than three-fourths (80.5 percent) of the callers were thus between the ages of 10 and 39, with the largest number in the 20–29 range (table 1-15). In general, the same percentages were found for males and females, although 76.8 percent of the male callers of known age were in the 10–29 group, as against 59.9 percent of the female callers. About 40 percent of the females were 30 or over.

Occupations of Callers

It was possible to determine the occupations of only 463 of the 879 callers. The largest proportion (48 percent) were students (table 1-16). The second largest category was housewives. Only a small number of male callers (33) were jobless, suggesting that anxiety over employment was not a major reason for calling the service, a conclusion borne out by the statistics on motivation.

Related Family Factors

Of 148 responses in this category, 123 referred to deceased, separated, or divorced parents.

TABLE 1-15
SUICIDE CALLS RECEIVED BY INOCHI NO DENWA,
TOKYO, OCTOBER 1975–SEPTEMBER 1979, BY
AGE AND SEX OF CALLERS

| Age group | Male callers | | Female callers | | Total | |
|-----------|--------|------------|--------|------------|--------|------------|
|           | Number | Percentage | Number | Percentage | Number | Percentage |
| Under 10    | 0   | 0.0  | 1   | 0.2  | 1   | 0.1  |
| 10–19       | 98  | 29.4 | 150 | 27.5 | 248 | 28.2 |
| 20–29       | 158 | 47.4 | 177 | 32.4 | 335 | 38.1 |
| 30–39       | 37  | 11.1 | 88  | 16.1 | 125 | 14.2 |
| 40–49       | 16  | 4.8  | 34  | 6.2  | 50  | 5.7  |
| 50–59       | 1   | 0.3  | 15  | 2.7  | 16  | 1.8  |
| 60 and over | 2   | 0.6  | 5   | 0.9  | 7   | 0.8  |
| Unknown     | 21  | 6.3  | 76  | 14.0 | 97  | 11.0 |
| Total       | 333 |      | 546 |      | 879 |      |

Frequency of Suicide Attempts

Of the 879 suicidal callers, 321 had attempted suicide. One attempt had been made by 202 persons; more than two attempts, by 119 (table 1-17). Percentages were approximately the same for males and females.

Methods Used in Suicide Attempts

Information was collected on the methods used in 253 cases of attempted suicide (table 1-18). The most frequently used method was drugs or poison, followed by use of knives and then by gas; the two sexes used drugs and gas proportionately in about the same degree. It is interesting that almost as many women used knives as used drugs or poison. The table also shows percentages for the methods used, by both males and females.

TABLE 1-16
SUICIDE CALLS RECEIVED BY INOCHI NO DENWA,
TOKYO, OCTOBER 1975—SEPTEMBER 1979, BY
OCCUPATION OF CALLERS

| Occupation | Number of male callers | Number of female callers | Total Number | Total Percentage |
|---|---|---|---|---|
| Housewife | — | 130 | 130 | 35.6 |
| Student | 88 | 135 | 223 | 48.0 |
| Jobless | 33 | 20 | 53 | 8.7 |
| Company employee | 32 | 15 | 47 | 10.0 |
| Cab, truck, or other driver | 10 | — | 10 | 2.1 |
| Total | 163 | 300 | 463 | |

TABLE 1-17
FREQUENCY OF SUICIDE ATTEMPTS BY
CALLERS TO INOCHI NO DENWA, TOKYO,
OCTOBER 1978—SEPTEMBER 1979

| Number of attempts | Male Number | Male Percentage | Female Number | Female Percentage | Total Number | Total Percentage |
|---|---|---|---|---|---|---|
| One attempt | 77 | 68.2 | 125 | 60.1 | 202 | 62.9 |
| More than two attempts | 36 | 31.8 | 83 | 39.9 | 119 | 37.1 |
| Total | 113 | 100.0 | 208 | 100.0 | 321 | 100.0 |

TABLE 1-18
METHODS USED IN SUICIDE ATTEMPTS, 1975–1979

| Method | Males | | Females | | Total | |
|---|---|---|---|---|---|---|
| | Number | Percentage | Number | Percentage | Number | Percentage |
| Hanging | 5 | 1.5 | 9 | 1.6 | 14 | 5.5 |
| Self-immolation | 0 | 0 | 1 | | 1 | |
| Electrocution | 4 | 1.2 | 1 | | 5 | 1.9 |
| Drugs or poison | 34 | 10.2 | 65 | 11.9 | 99 | 39.1 |
| Gas | 17 | 5.1 | 25 | 4.6 | 42 | 16.6 |
| Knife or blade | 14 | 4.2 | 53 | 9.7 | 67 | 26.5 |
| Drowning | 3 | 0.9 | 2 | | 5 | 1.9 |
| Jumping from heights | 7 | 2.1 | 5 | 0.9 | 12 | 4.7 |
| Jumping in front of train | 5 | 1.5 | 3 | 0.5 | 8 | 3.2 |
| Total | 89 | | 164 | | 253 | |

SOURCE: Inochi no Denwa, Tokyo.

## Medical Treatment

Medical treatment was given to 243 of the callers, 70 in the hospital and 140 as outpatients; 176 of the patients were female and 67 were male.

## Personality Traits of Callers

Of the personality traits listed (table 1-19), more than half may be described as having to do with depression: lack of motivation or lethargy, 93 persons; depression, 39; inability to concentrate, 4; introversion, 18; insomnia, 62. A small number of people were described as irritable, aggressive, masochistic, or hypochondriacal.

## Mood at Time of Calling

Most of the callers, 278 of the 388 recorded, were either weeping or depressed. A very small number, 43, were in an aggressive mood of excitement or anger.

## Motivations for Suicide Attempts

As some callers gave more than one reason for attempting suicide, there were 1,192 motivations for the 879 clients (table 1-20). They may be grouped under the headings student problems, family problems, love

TABLE 1-19

PERSONALITY TRAITS OF SUICIDAL CALLERS, 1975–1979

| Trait | Male callers | | Female callers | | Total | |
|---|---|---|---|---|---|---|
| | Number | Percentage | Number | Percentage | Number | Percentage |
| Aggressiveness | 14 | 4.2 | 4 | 0.7 | 18 | 4.4 |
| Masochism | 37 | 11.1 | 18 | 3.3 | 55 | 13.5 |
| Hypochondria | 0 | 0 | 25 | 4.6 | 25 | 16.2 |
| Irritability | 10 | 3.0 | 11 | 2.0 | 21 | 5.2 |
| Absenteeism | 2 | 0.6 | 18 | 3.3 | 20 | 4.9 |
| Lack of motivation; lethargy | 62 | 18.6 | 31 | 5.7 | 93 | 23.0 |
| Inability to concentrate | 1 | | 3 | | 4 | .01 |
| Depression | 8 | 2.4 | 31 | 5.7 | 39 | 9.6 |
| Insomnia | 17 | 5.1 | 45 | 8.2 | 62 | 15.3 |
| Introversion | 16 | | 2 | | 18 | 4.4 |
| Other | 30 | 9.0 | 20 | 3.7 | 50 | 12.3 |
| Total | 197 | | 208 | | 405 | |

SOURCE: Inochi no Denwa, Tokyo.

TABLE 1-20

MOTIVATIONS FOR SUICIDAL ATTEMPTS, 1975–1979

| Motivation | Male callers Number | Male callers Percentage | Female callers Number | Female callers Percentage | Total Number | Total Percentage |
|---|---|---|---|---|---|---|
| Entrance exams | 17 | 5.1 | 6 | 1.1 | 23 | 2.6 |
| Studies | 21 | 6.3 | 27 | 4.9 | 48 | 5.5 |
| Child raising or baby care | 0 | 0.0 | 13 | 2.4 | 13 | – |
| Difficulties in relationships | 83 | 25.0 | 41 | 7.5 | 124 | 14.1 |
| Disappointment in love | 54 | 16.2 | 49 | 9.0 | 103 | 11.7 |
| Family troubles | 13 | 3.9 | 33 | 6.0 | 46 | 5.2 |
| Loneliness | 100 | 30.0 | 151 | 27.7 | 251 | 28.6 |
| Illness | 24 | 7.2 | 43 | 7.9 | 67 | 7.6 |
| Physical handicaps | 12 | 3.6 | 10 | 1.8 | 22 | 2.5 |
| Separation | 15 | 4.5 | 8 | 1.5 | 23 | 2.6 |
| Divorce | 15 | 4.5 | 10 | 1.8 | 25 | 2.8 |
| Loss through death | 9 | 2.7 | 15 | 2.7 | 24 | 2.7 |
| Problem pregnancy | 0 | 0.0 | 10 | 1.8 | 10 | – |
| Sexual problems | 4 | 1.2 | 0 | 0.0 | 4 | – |
| Discontent with parents | 32 | 9.6 | 59 | 10.8 | 91 | 10.4 |
| No meaning in life | 82 | 24.6 | 43 | 7.9 | 125 | 14.2 |
| Economic problems | 24 | 7.2 | 11 | 2.0 | 35 | 4.0 |
| Mentally tired of life | 10 | 3.0 | 28 | 5.1 | 38 | 4.3 |
| Marital problems | 2 | 0.6 | 41 | 7.5 | 43 | 4.9 |
| Occupational problems | 3 | – | 12 | – | 15 | – |
| Mental disorders | 2 | – | 60 | – | 62 | – |
| Total | 522 | | 670 | | 1,192 | |

SOURCE: Inochi no Denwa, Tokyo.

problems, difficulties in relationships, attitude toward living, and illness. Difficulties in relationships, together with loneliness in which they usually result, accounted for 375 calls. Love problems, including disappointment in love, separation, divorce, marital problems, problem pregnancy, and loss through death, accounted for 228. Attitude toward living, probably a derivative of other problems, was scored at 125 for meaningless life and 38 for mentally tired of life for a total of 163. Family problems, including the categories of family troubles, discontent with parents, and problems of child care, were motivations for 150 suicide attempts. Illness and physical handicaps were reported as motivations by 89 callers. Student problems with examinations and courses of study ranked quite low, at 71, as a motivation for suicidal attempts. From these responses it is clear that suicidal callers were seriously distressed by interpersonal frictions.

## ADDITIONAL STUDIES

Inochi no Denwa counselors participated in a study published by the Tokyo Children's Education Center on July 1, 1979, under the title *Children's Suicide Attempts and Their Life Histories*. Seventeen counselors from IND, Tokyo, the Tokyo Educational Institute, and the Children's Clinic of Ozuma Women's University studied 38 children who had attempted suicide. The ages of the 26 females and 12 males ranged from 9 to 18, and one young adult aged 22 was included in the survey. The age distribution was as follows:

| Age | Number | Age | Number |
|-----|--------|-----|--------|
| 9   | 1      | 15  | 4      |
| 11  | 1      | 16  | 6      |
| 12  | 2      | 17  | 7      |
| 13  | 4      | 18  | 3      |
| 14  | 6      | 22  | 1      |

Many of the factors in child suicides paralleled those found by Inochi no Denwa in its survey. Personality characteristics were: (1) a strong sense of loneliness; (2) impatience and impetuousness; (3) lack of self-confidence or self-esteem; (4) compulsive perfectionism; (5) inability to face failures; (6) high self-expectations; (7) lack of close friends and confidants.

Parental and family characteristics were: (1) no close relationship to parents in early childhood; (2) domineering parents, causing child's infantile dependence; (3) parents indifferent to child's needs; (4) no mother role model, especially for girls; (5) children not allowed their own identity; (6) negative parental attitudes toward child.

External factors were: (1) child lived in adult setting with no place to play; (2) no friends or confidants among peers; (3) strict and rigid attitude of schools, stressing only cognitive side of child; (4) adverse influence of television.

Other factors were history of depression and psychiatric problems either in child or in family.

## SUMMARY

Inochi no Denwa in Tokyo and elsewhere offers a significant service to distressed, anxious Japanese of all ages and a confidential receptive ear to persons who are trained by their culture to mask weakness or anxiety from others. In 1978 there were 26,372 callers; in 1979, 28,540. For the latter year, 10,479 callers were male and 18,061 were female. As more than half (52.7 percent) of the callers stated clearly that they were concerned about interpersonal frictions, it is probable that most of the remaining callers had similar problems.

For the period 1975–1979, IND surveyed callers who definitely were suicide risks. The peak number of such calls came in from March through July, with another peak in November. Most calls were made from late morning (11 A.M.) to midnight, peaking between 2 and 4 P.M. and 9 P.M. and midnight.

The largest percentages of suicidal callers were in the student and house-wife categories.

A majority of the callers (80.4 percent) were between 10 and 39 years of age, with the largest number between 20 and 29. In general, the percentages for males and females were similar. Female callers covered a wider age span than did male callers.

Of those who had actually attempted suicide—321 out of 879—almost two-thirds had made only one attempt. The most frequent method was drugs or poison, with stabbing second. Primary motivations seemed to be problems in interpersonal relationships.

Since Japan has no network of mental health centers, as some industrially developed countries do, Inochi no Denwa offers immediate responsiveness and concern to suicidal Japanese, particularly to younger persons.

# TAIWAN

**2**

*Editor's Note*

Taiwan has developed substantial manufacturing, especially in light industry, since World War II, although as late as 1973 half the population of this largely agricultural country worked on the land. Industrialization has brought prosperity to Taiwan in the wake of land reforms and with the aid of billions of dollars from the United States, especially in military equipment. The most marked advances have been made in textiles, chemicals, wood processing, machinery, and electronics. The exporting of fish and agricultural products continues on a larger scale than before. The country has good health resources and its population is highly literate.

Taiwan's recent history has centered on its relations with China and the United States. When Chiang Kai-shek was defeated by the Chinese Communists in 1948, he retreated to Taiwan with his army and established his government there. Skirmishes with China, consisting mostly of mutual shelling, have continued since that time. The Korean war of 1950–1953 led to an increase in American support to Taiwan and, in 1954, to the signing of a mutual defense treaty between Taiwan and the United States. As mainland China continued to gain political, economic, and military strength, however, the United States saw the value of recognizing the Communists as the legitimate government of China, despite Taiwan's vigorous protests. Nevertheless, Taiwan's trade with the United States, as with Japan, West Germany, and Hong Kong, continues to flourish, and the political turn of events seems to have caused the island no economic damage.

Hsien Rin earned his M.D. in psychiatry at National Taiwan University and in 1955 went to the United States for further study. He spent a year at Massachusetts General Hospital in Boston as a clinical and research fellow in psychiatry. In 1960 he received a degree in medical science from Hokkaido University, Japan. He did research in psychiatry for a year at McGill University, Toronto, and spent another year, 1965, at the Laboratory of Socio-Environmental Studies, National Institute of Mental Health, Bethesda, Maryland. In the intervals between these periods of foreign study, Dr. Rin was a professor in Taiwan University Hospital Psychiatry Department. He served as chairman of the department from 1966 to 1975, and he is now a professor there. (Taiwan University is the largest university in the country.) Dr. Rin has frequently participated in psychiatric seminars and projects in the South Pacific.

Mrs. Tuan Chen, coauthor of Part I of this chapter, has been working with Dr. Rin as a research assistant for eight years. She is a graduate of Taiwan University in sociology and social work.

The data for Part II of this chapter, dealing with attempted suicides between 1972 and 1980, have been compiled by the Suicide Prevention Center, Mackay Memorial Hospital, in Taipei, through the kind cooperation of Hsien Ming Chen, director of the center. I took the raw statistics from the center's recent survey, presented them in tabular form, and wrote the text, trying to correlate Taiwan's suicide patterns with the patients at the Suicide Prevention Center.

# PART I. HSIEN RIN AND TUAN CHEN[1]

Suicide has occurred at a high rate in Taiwan until very recent years. In this section we describe suicides in Taiwan, which have never been compared cross-culturally, and discuss psychosocial factors that influence Taiwanese suicidal behavior.

Taiwan, formerly known as Formosa, is a 250-mile-long island located 100 miles off the south coast of China. The first migrants to the island were Malayo-Polynesians who came from Southeast Asia some thousand years ago. These people, of whom nine tribes now reside in the mountainous areas of Taiwan, have maintained distinct cultural traditions and primitive skills and methods of cultivation.

The second wave of immigrants were Chinese from southern China, particularly from Fukien; their migration intensified after 1661 when the Dutch were driven out of southern Taiwan by Teng Chen-Kong. The Taiwanese thus consisted of two Chinese subethnic groups, the Fukienese (Holo) and the minority from Canton (Hakka). The third wave of immigration from China occurred in 1949–50, when 2 million mainland Chinese joined the 7 million Taiwanese.

Politically, Taiwan was ceded to Japan at the end of the First Sino-Japanese War, in 1895. After World War II Taiwan called itself the Republic of China, suffering postwar chaos accentuated by the heavy migration after the Communist victory in China. Then, however, Taiwan began to develop industrially, and the economy prospered. With modernization and prosperity came an enormous population growth. Ethnic differences gradually faded, particularly with increasing intermarriage between mainland immigrant Chinese and Taiwanese after 1955. By 1978 Taiwan's population exceeded 17 million.

## ATTITUDES TOWARD SUICIDE

The attitudes toward suicide inherited by the Chinese in Taiwan are rooted in Confucianism, Buddhism, Taoism, and probably in folk hero tales.

[1]We are grateful to Miss Phone-Ming Shieh and Miss Lilias Sung for their diligence and help in preparing data for use in this paper.

Chinese history has many legends about kings or their ministers who suicided after losing a battle for their country. Other tales concern persons who ended their lives to show loyalty to a superior, sometimes in mass suicides. Suicide has also been a means of saving face. The emperor and his court allowed nobles to take their own lives rather than be executed, a practice corresponding to the Japanese institution of hara-kiri. Suicides were honored when they demonstrated loyalty to a family. Many legends tell of women who, in order to remain loyal to their deceased husbands, killed themselves when they were being forced to remarry. This essentially Confucian ethic enjoins the wife to regard her husband as an undisputed leader.

Thus suicides to save face, for family honor and loyalty, and to prove allegiance to a leader-king were respected. Suicides resulting from personal unhappiness or maladjustment or from mental problems are not regarded in the same way. Although such suicides are not condemned, they are met with mixed feelings. Attitudes may range from being pitying or sad and regretful to feeling that the individual has not dealt forcefully with life crises and that either he is weak or he behaved shamefully. Confucian elements in these attitudes are strict; Buddhists are more forgiving. Suicide in Taiwan today is not viewed legally as a crime.

## CULTURAL FACTORS

Adherence to family ties and regard for decorum are still the major emphases in Chinese culture. One should achieve self-fulfillment (in a sense self-expression) and should be obligated to honor his family name. This goal, however, does not necessarily mean continued strict discipline by parents of their children. On the contrary, parents in the Chinese family tend to be permissive with their children, even allowing them considerable freedom from behavioral discipline during preschool years. Marriage arrangement as a means of attaining stability and guaranteeing the safety of family life continues to be a serious concern to parents.

Disregard of the traditional value system by younger people is often an issue in a developing society. While older persons continue to stress family ties in psychological, economic, and cultural aspects, young people are facing difficult decisions in the clash between traditional beliefs and modern values. More than a few of them are frustrated by their elders' disapproval of the free choice of love partners for marriage. As yet there is no agreement about a new model for courting and marriage behavior. Those who follow the new style provided by mass media from Western cultures may have trouble establishing appropriate patterns of behavior. The anger of younger people is also often aroused by the authoritative attitude of parents. A severe strain on youngsters in contemporary society is now being felt in the heavy competition in school entrance examinations and in the search for jobs.

## SOURCES OF INFORMATION

Information on completed suicides provided by the government of Taiwan comes in various forms: Department of Health statistics; vital statistics abstracts; household registration statistics; and the Taiwan Demographic Fact Book. Since there seems to be a positive correlation between the decrease of suicide rates and improved socioeconomic development, four additional governmental reports have been used in compiling this report: (1) annual reports of the Central Bank; (2) the Chinese Maritime Customs Statistical Series; (3) the trade of China (Taiwan); and (4) the Taiwan Trade Directory. The latter reports reflect the annual increase of per capita income and the total amount of trade.

Suicides reported in five large newspapers representing not only Taipei but all of Taiwan were analyzed for the period 1969–1971. Both attempted and completed suicides were investigated as to sex, age, and method. No official reports of attempted suicide in Taiwan are available. Cases handled by the Suicide Prevention Center, Mackay Memorial Hospital, Taipei, were examined for the years 1969 through 1971. A survey was also made of attempted suicides by inpatients at National Taiwan University Hospital for the years 1952–1954 and 1967–1968.

## METHODS OF DATA COLLECTION

Death by suicide is usually reported to a police station by those in the immediate vicinity, especially family members. The on-call public prosecutor accompanies a forensic physician for investigation and certification of the deceased. All the suicide records are filed and kept permanently in the police department; except for the official statistical report, the suicide files are not open to the public. The national vital statistics are based on death certificates presented to the population registration office at each local government level, and these offices are under the direction of the police department. Another source is the data on suicides which are included in the vital statistics reports published by the Health Administration departments of Taipei and of Taiwan provincial governments. We believe that these government statistics, as well as health statistics and household registrations, are well organized and that nonreporting of suicidal deaths is at a minimum. If any family member of the deceased tries to hide the evidence of suicide to protect the name of the family, it is questionable whether the family physician would support the concealment by issuing an

untrue certification, regardless of the social level of the deceased.
Registration of attempted suicides is not required.

## COMPLETED SUICIDES

The annual rate of death by suicide per 100,000 population for the years
1946–1977 is shown graphically in figure 2-1. The average rate is roughly
12 to 13, and the graph shows cycles with three peaks and three declines.
The first peak appeared in 1946, just after the end of World War II.
Although wartime statistics are not available, it is assumed that the suicide
death rates during the war years would be lower than the 1946 rate. The
rate declined sharply toward 1948; however, it then rose steeply until it
reached a peak in 1951. It dropped in 1952 and then gradually rose until it
reached another peak in 1955. An ensuing downward trend continued until
1958 (table 2-1).

The general increase in the suicide rate betwen 1949 and 1958 paralleled
the social disorganization caused by the chaotic mass migration of mainland
Chinese. In the period 1949–1959, 2 million mainland Chinese retreated to
Taiwan along with Chiang Kai-shek's government in exile. The heightened
rates of various mental disorders among migrants observed since that time
have been documented by a series of psychiatric epidemiological studies by
the staff of Taiwan University Psychiatry Department (2, 4, 8). A study of
attempted suicides among psychiatric inpatients (5) revealed that more

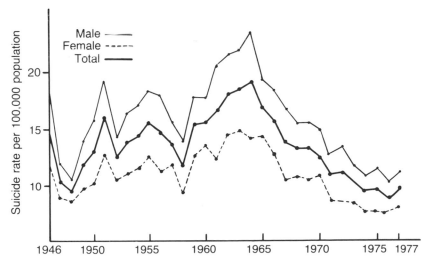

FIG. 2-1.     Suicide rate per 100,000 population in Taiwan, by sex, 1946–1977.
Source of data: Vital statistics abstracts, Ministry of Health, Taiwan.

TABLE 2-1
SUICIDE RATE PER 100,000 POPULATION
IN TAIWAN, 1946–1980

| Date | Rate | Date | Rate |
|------|------|------|------|
| 1946 | 15.4 | 1964 | 19.1 |
| 1947 | 10.4 | 1965 | 16.8 |
| 1948 | 9.5  | 1966 | 15.6 |
| 1949 | 11.9 | 1967 | 13.7 |
| 1950 | 13.0 | 1968 | 13.2 |
| 1951 | 16.0 | 1969 | 13.2 |
| 1952 | 12.4 | 1970 | 12.4 |
| 1953 | 13.8 | 1971 | 10.8 |
| 1954 | 14.3 | 1972 | 11.2 |
| 1955 | 15.5 | 1973 | 10.2 |
| 1956 | 14.7 | 1974 | 9.4  |
| 1957 | 13.7 | 1975 | 9.6  |
| 1958 | 11.6 | 1976 | 8.8  |
| 1959 | 15.3 | 1977 | 9.6  |
| 1960 | 15.6 | 1978 | 9.9  |
| 1961 | 16.6 | 1979 | 9.9  |
| 1962 | 18.0 | 1980 | 10.0 |
| 1963 | 18.4 |      |      |

SOURCE: Vital statistics abstracts, Ministry of Health, Taiwan.

suicidal attempts were made by migrant females, especially middle-aged women, than by migrant males. Migration stresses, which cause social disorganization and alienation of the individual, may elevate the suicidal death rate in the total population.

In 1959 the rate again began to increase, reaching a peak in 1964. A gradual decline beginning in 1965 reduced the suicide rate to 8 to 10 per 100,000 in the years 1974–1977. The increase from 1959 to 1964 and the decline from 1965 to 1974 are attributable to socioeconomic factors. The hectic, unsettled earlier period was a time of modernization, industrialization, and changing value orientations which caused individual disorientation. From 1965 on, sharply increasing per capita income and growing trade improved the economic status of the whole society. In 1978 the per capita annual income was $1,440 and the total trade balance was more than $23 billion.

Because the number of suicides among children under 15 years of age is extremely rare, an increase in the birthrate might be expected to lead to a decrease of the suicide death rate in the total population. To determine the truth of this supposition, the suicide rates in 1957–1977 were recalculated for the population over the age of 15, excluding younger persons. The process, however, revealed no difference in the pattern of the curve between the rising and descending years of suicide rates and no increase in the proportion of young people in the population during these years. As a matter of fact, a family planning project, started in Taiwan in 1965, has just recently begun to show its effect, and once again the evidence denies any correlation between the number of births and the suicide rate.

### Sex Ratio

In general, males suicide more often than females, in a ratio of approximately 1.5:1. The annual suicide death rates of the two sexes paralleled each other in rises and declines in the years 1964—1976 (fig. 2-2). For both sexes the number of suicidal deaths was highest among late adolescents and young adults, with fewer deaths as middle age approached. In their study of suicide in Japan (10), Tatai and Kato point out that the suicide rate among young Taiwan Chinese was extremely high compared with that of other Asian populations. Their observation is based on the World Health Organization report for 1964, when Taiwan's suicide rate was rising to its peak.

Figure 2-2 shows the suicide rates per 100,000 population by age group for males and females in the years 1964, 1968, 1972, and 1976. The rates were highest for the age group 20—24, especially in 1964 when the rate was 50 for males and 39 for females. In the years 1968, 1972, and 1976 the rates for youths were lower, dipping to 13 for males and 11 for females in 1976, when the total annual rate was 9. Another peak in the suicide rate came in the age group 60 and over. The suicide death rate for females is higher than that of males at ages 15—24 and over 70. The highest female rate in the years 1959—1964 was in the 15—24 age group, but from 1965 to 1971 the rate was highest at ages 15—19.

Suicide rates in recent years show less disparity between males and females. In 1978 the rate was 10.9 among males and 8.8 among females; in 1979, 11.3 among males and 8.4 among females; in 1980, 11.0 among males and 8.9 among females.

## ATTEMPTED SUICIDES

No government information on attempted suicides is available. Some material was gathered from records of the early years of the Suicide Prevention Center at Presbyterian Mackay Memorial Hospital in Taipei. The center's lifeline service was established in 1969 with interdisciplinary professionals and trained volunteers from Christian, Buddhist-Taoist, and other backgrounds. As the community responded positively, two numbers were given for the service at the top of the emergency services listing in the telephone book. In 1970 a second lifeline service was established by religious groups in Kaohsung; located in the south, it is the second largest city in Taiwan, with

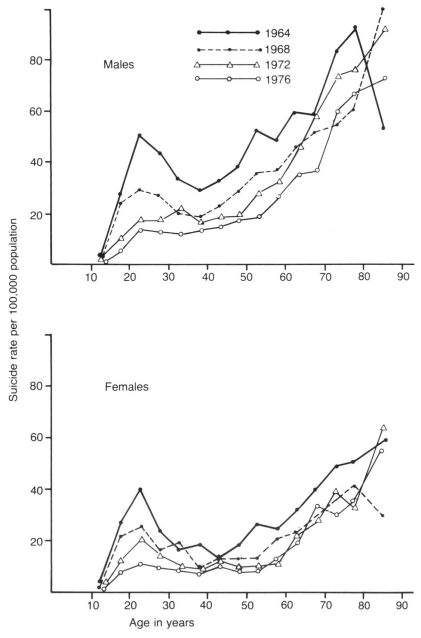

FIG. 2-2.    Suicide rate per 100,000 population in Taiwan, by age, in 1964, 1968, 1972, and 1976. Source of data: Vital statistics abstracts, Ministry of Health, Taiwan.

a population of more than 1 million. Since then more than ten lifeline services have been set up in the major cities of Taiwan.

The Mackay Hospital Suicide Prevention Service found that a high percentage of young suicide attempters, both male and female, came from families of low and lower-middle socioeconomic classes, with high residential mobility. Industrial expansion brought a large number of young workers to the city areas, and social maladjustment among them was evident. Annual rates of suicide attempts seen at Mackay Hospital and at Taiwan University Hospital, which together serve the largest number of emergency cases in Taipei and surrounding communities, increased between 1969 and 1972 and sharply decreased after 1973. These trends suggest that the population mobility accompanying industrial development causes a significant, but transitory, increase in the number of attempted suicides.

## MACKAY HOSPITAL SUICIDE PREVENTION CENTER STATISTICS

The findings during the first three years of operation of the Mackay Hospital Suicide Prevention Center show that 1,286 suicides were attempted in 1969–1971. The sex ratio was about 1:3, males making 318 attempts and females, 968 (table 2-2).

Age and Sex

The highest percentage of cases was in the age group 20–24; the second highest, 15–19; and the third highest, 25–29 (table 2-3). The youngest age was 12 for males and 14 for females; the oldest, 80 for males and 83 for females. Suicide attempts dropped sharply after 45. About 55 percent of the total cases were females aged 15 to 29; the highest percentages for males came in the same age brackets.

Education

The educational level of suicide attempters was slightly higher than that of their counterparts in the general population, with the widest difference in illiteracy; 24 percent of the general population and 8.7 percent of the attempters. The younger attempters were better educated than the older.

Marital Status

More single than married persons were found among suicide attempters because most of the cases were in the younger age groups. In general, the marital status of those who attempted suicide in 1971 does not differ widely from that of the general population (see table 2-4).

## TABLE 2-2
### Number of Suicidal Patents Seen at Suicide Prevention Center, Mackay Memorial Hospital, 1969–1971

| Year | Total number registered | Missing files | Accident, not suicide | Suicide ideas only | | | Suicide ideas and previous suicide attempt | | | Attempted suicides | | |
|---|---|---|---|---|---|---|---|---|---|---|---|---|
| | | | | Male | Female | Total | Male | Female | Total | Male | Female | Total |
| 1969 | 756 | 329 | 40 | 20 | 20 | 40 | 7 | 14 | 21 | 84 | 240 | 324 |
| 1970 | 716 | 53 | 79 | 30 | 33 | 63 | 11 | 16 | 27 | 130 | 366 | 496 |
| 1971 | 633 | 8 | 82 | 22 | 30 | 52 | 11 | 14 | 25 | 104 | 362 | 466 |
| Total | 2,105 | 390 | 201 | 72 | 83 | 155 | 29 | 44 | 73 | 318 | 968 | 1,286 |

Causes of Suicide Attempts

The three main reasons that males attempted suicide in 1969–1971 were conflict with family members, frustrated love affairs, and economic problems with legal complications; for females, marital discord, unhappy love affairs, and conflict with family members were the three major factors precipitating suicide attempts (table 2-5). Older male attempters tended to be more affected by social maladjustment, whereas younger males were more likely to attempt suicide because of frustrated love affairs and family conflicts. For both males and females, therefore, interpersonal problems

TABLE 2-3

AGE AND SEX OF SUICIDE ATTEMPTERS SEEN AT MACKAY HOSPITAL
SUICIDE PREVENTION CENTER, 1969–1971

| Age group | Male | | Female | | Total | |
|---|---|---|---|---|---|---|
| | Number | Percentage | Number | Percentage | Number | Percentage |
| 1–14 | 2 | 1 | 5 | 1 | 7 | 1 |
| 15–19 | 63 | 20 | 185 | 19 | 248 | 19 |
| 20–24 | 82 | 26 | 380 | 39 | 462 | 36 |
| 25–29 | 60 | 19 | 144 | 15 | 204 | 16 |
| 30–34 | 32 | 10 | 95 | 10 | 127 | 10 |
| 35–44 | 36 | 11 | 105 | 11 | 141 | 11 |
| 45–54 | 20 | 6 | 30 | 3 | 50 | 4 |
| 55–64 | 13 | 4 | 12 | 1 | 25 | 2 |
| 65 and over | 8 | 3 | 8 | 1 | 16 | 1 |
| No information | 2 | 1 | 4 | 1 | 6 | 1 |
| Total | 318 | | 968 | | 1,286 | |

TABLE 2-4

MARITAL STATUS OF SUICIDE ATTEMPTERS AND OF
GENERAL TAIWAN POPULATION, 1971
(In percentages)

| Status | General population | | Suicide attempters | |
|---|---|---|---|---|
| | Male | Female | Male | Female |
| Single | 42.00 | 30.80 | 64.10 | 46.30 |
| Married | 54.00 | 60.70 | 28.40 | 42.60 |
| Divorced | 0.08 | 0.07 | 1.60 | 0.08 |
| Widowed | 2.50 | 7.90 | 2.00 | 1.76 |
| Separated | – | – | 2.20 | 0.08 |
| Cohabiting | – | – | 1.60 | 7.70 |

TABLE 2-5
CAUSES OF SUICIDE ATTEMPTS, MACKAY HOSPITAL
SUICIDE PREVENTION CENTER, 1969–1971

| Cause | Male Num-ber | Male Per-centage | Female Num-ber | Female Per-centage | Total Num-ber | Total Per-centage |
|---|---|---|---|---|---|---|
| Frustrated love affairs | 48 | 15 | 233 | 24 | 281 | 22 |
| Marital discord | 38 | 12 | 313 | 32 | 351 | 27 |
| Conflict with family members | 67 | 21 | 147 | 15 | 214 | 17 |
| Conflict with others | 20 | 6 | 47 | 5 | 67 | 5 |
| Economic problems with legal complications | 44 | 14 | 29 | 3 | 73 | 6 |
| Mental illness | 17 | 5 | 29 | 3 | 46 | 4 |
| Nihilism | 15 | 5 | 18 | 2 | 33 | 3 |
| Physical illness | 15 | 5 | 14 | 1 | 29 | 2 |
| Other | 8 | 3 | 15 | 2 | 23 | 2 |
| No information | 46 | 14 | 123 | 13 | 169 | 13 |
| Total | 318 | | 968 | | 1,286 | |

centering on family life and sexual partnerships were the predominating causes of suicide attempts.

Occupations

Among cases of attempted suicide by young females, no particular concentration was found in any occupation, including housewife and student. There were, however, 82 young females who worked in nightclubs, dance halls, wine houses, cabarets, bars, and the like, and they were usually involved in love conflicts with men.

Methods

Roughly 80 percent of both males and females used hypnotics or other drugs or poisons in their suicide attempts (table 2-6). Chemical poisons were largely insecticides and rodenticides. City dwellers tended to use drugs, whereas rural and suburban residents chose chemical poisons. It should be noted that sleeping pills were readily available at dispensaries, although the amounts for single purchase were limited, until 1975, when the law prohibiting public sale of sleeping pills was enacted.

Only a small number of attempters tried cutting or slashing, hanging, drowning, or jumping from high places. In the period covered, 1969–1971, there was no use of violent methods, such as explosions or shooting.

TABLE 2-6
METHODS OF SUICIDE ATTEMPTS, MACKAY HOSPITAL
SUICIDE PREVENTION CENTER, 1969–1971

| Method | Male | | Female | | Total | |
|---|---|---|---|---|---|---|
| | Number | Percentage | Number | Percentage | Number | Percentage |
| Sleeping pills | 205 | 64 | 642 | 66 | 847 | 66 |
| Chemical poisons | 59 | 19 | 109 | 11 | 168 | 13 |
| Cutting or slashing | 11 | 3 | 25 | 3 | 36 | 3 |
| Drowning | 3 | 1 | 7 | 1 | 10 | 1 |
| Hanging | 1 | 1 | 5 | 1 | 6 | 1 |
| Jumping | 0 | 0 | 5 | 1 | 5 | 1 |
| Other | 17 | 5 | 71 | 7 | 88 | 7 |
| Unidentified or no information | 22 | 7 | 104 | 11 | 126 | 10 |
| Total | 318 | | 968 | | 1,286 | |

Severity of Attempts

The severity of a suicide attempt is measured by number of pills taken, maximum degree of consciousness disturbance, and type of treatment necessary. Rankings of degree are severe, moderate, mild, and suicidal gestures. Fifteen percent of the cases surveyed showed no or very slight physical damage, but the individuals were brought in by relatives because of various suicidal gestures. Of the cases surveyed, 31 percent ranked as mild, 22 percent, as moderate, and 28 percent, as severe (table 2-7). A total of 23 attempters (2 percent) died at the hospital. Male attempters tended to show a more severe intensity than female attempters.

## SUICIDES REPORTED IN NEWSPAPERS

Although newspaper reports of suicide do not measure the actual incidence of suicide, they do make it possible to explore suicide patterns. Reports of 435 suicides in 1969–1971 were collected for analysis from *Lien-ho-pao* (United Daily News), one of the most popular newspapers in Taiwan. Of these cases, 364 occurred in the Taipei area and 71 in central and southern Taiwan. By checking several other daily newspapers it was discovered that numerous cases had not been reported in *Lien-ho-pao*. Suicides in 1971 were therefore collected from four other newspapers: *Chung-yang-ju-pao* (Central Daily News), *Chung-kuo-su-pao* (Chinese Times), *Ming-tsu-won-pao* (Racial Evening Post), and *Chung-hwa-ju-pao* (China Daily News). The search of all five papers yielded 568 reports of suicide in 1971.

TABLE 2-7
SEVERITY OF SUICIDE ATTEMPTS, MACKAY HOSPITAL
SUICIDE PREVENTION CENTER, 1969–1971

| Degree of severity | Male | | Female | | Total | |
|---|---|---|---|---|---|---|
| | Number | Percentage | Number | Percentage | Number | Percentage |
| Suicidal gestures | 33 | 10 | 156 | 16 | 189 | 15 |
| Mild degree | 75 | 24 | 320 | 33 | 395 | 31 |
| Moderate degree | 78 | 25 | 202 | 21 | 280 | 22 |
| Severe degree | 118 | 37 | 244 | 25 | 362 | 28 |
| Suicide completed | 8 | 3 | 15 | 2 | 23 | 2 |
| No information | 6 | 2 | 31 | 3 | 37 | 3 |
| Total | 318 | | 968 | | 1,286 | |

Reasons for Suicide

Social maladjustment and criminal and legal matters were the most frequent causes of male suicides (table 2-8). For females, marital conflict, frustrated love affairs, and conflict with family members were the chief causative factors. Both information sources (*Lien-ho-pao* and the four other papers) showed approximately the same distribution by sex and by reason given.

Methods of Suicide

Table 2-9 shows the methods used in the 364 Taipei suicide cases reported in *Lien-ho-pao*, separated into completed and attempted suicides, and the distribution by sex. The use of sleeping pills or chemical poisons was the most common method, accounting for 51 percent of completed suicides and 45 percent of attempted suicides. There was little frequency difference between the sexes. Drowning was a major method for females in both attempted and completed suicides; they used it more often than males did. Hanging was the method in 18 percent of completed suicides but in only 3 percent of attempts, and it was used almost equally by males and females. Cutting or slashing accounted for 13 percent of male attempts but for only 4 percent of male deaths. Violent methods, such as explosives or shooting, were employed more by men than by women.

Degree of Severity

Table 2-10 shows the degree of severity in and the distribution by age and sex of suicide cases reported by newspapers in 1969–1971 and in 1971. Degree of severity is ranked at six levels, the first five relating to attempts:

## TABLE 2-8
### REASONS GIVEN FOR SUICIDES REPORTED IN NEWSPAPERS, 1969–1971 AND 1971

| | Lien-bo-pao (1969–1971) | | | | | | | | Four other newspapers (1971) | | | All cases | | | | | |
| | Taipei area | | | | Central and southern Taiwan | | | | All Taiwan | | | | | | | | |
| | Male | | Female | | Male | | Female | | Male | | Female | | Male | | Female | | Total |
| Reason given | No. | Per-centage | No. | Per-centage | No. | Per-centage | No. | Per-centage | No. | Per-centage | No. | Per-centage | No. | Per-centage | No. | Per-centage | No. | Per-centage |
|---|---|---|---|---|---|---|---|---|---|---|---|---|---|---|---|---|---|---|
| Love affairs | 12 | 6 | 34 | 19 | 2 | 4 | 4 | 17 | 3 | 4 | 10 | 16 | 17 | 6 | 48 | 18 | 56 | 11 |
| Marital conflict | 17 | 9 | 37 | 21 | 4 | 8 | 6 | 26 | 5 | 7 | 13 | 21 | 26 | 9 | 56 | 21 | 82 | 14 |
| Conflict with family members | 15 | 8 | 31 | 17 | 8 | 17 | 4 | 17 | 7 | 10 | 10 | 16 | 30 | 10 | 45 | 17 | 75 | 13 |
| Social maladjustment | 50 | 27 | 18 | 10 | 6 | 13 | 3 | 13 | 19 | 27 | 8 | 13 | 75 | 25 | 29 | 11 | 104 | 18 |
| Physical illness | 14 | 8 | 11 | 6 | 3 | 6 | 0 | 0 | 7 | 10 | 3 | 5 | 24 | 8 | 14 | 5 | 38 | 7 |
| Mental illness | 16 | 9 | 13 | 7 | 4 | 8 | 2 | 9 | 5 | 7 | 6 | 10 | 25 | 8 | 21 | 8 | 46 | 8 |
| Criminal and legal matters | 26 | 14 | 4 | 2 | 14 | 29 | 0 | 0 | 11 | 16 | 1 | 2 | 51 | 17 | 5 | 2 | 56 | 10 |
| Unknown | 36 | 19 | 30 | 17 | 7 | 15 | 4 | 17 | 13 | 19 | 12 | 19 | 56 | 18 | 46 | 17 | 102 | 18 |
| Total | 186 | | 178 | | 48 | | 23 | | 70 | | 63 | | 304 | | 264 | | 568 | |

## TABLE 2-9
### METHODS USED IN COMPLETED AND ATTEMPTED SUICIDES REPORTED IN NEWSPAPERS, 1969–1971 AND 1971

| Method | Completed suicide | | | | | | Attempted suicide | | | | | |
|---|---|---|---|---|---|---|---|---|---|---|---|---|
| | Male | | Female | | Total | | Male | | Female | | Total | |
| | No. | Percentage | No. | Percentage | No. | Percentage | No. | Percentage | No. | Percentage | No. | Percentage |
| Sleeping pills or poisons | 65 | 49 | 61 | 53 | 126 | 51 | 24 | 45 | 28 | 44 | 52 | 45 |
| Drowning | 15 | 11 | 24 | 21 | 39 | 16 | 10 | 19 | 28 | 44 | 38 | 33 |
| Hanging | 23 | 17 | 22 | 19 | 45 | 18 | 1 | 2 | 2 | 3 | 3 | 3 |
| Jumping from a height | 6 | 5 | 4 | 3 | 10 | 4 | 3 | 6 | 3 | 5 | 6 | 5 |
| Cutting or slashing | 5 | 4 | 0 | 0 | 5 | 2 | 7 | 13 | 0 | 0 | 7 | 6 |
| Explosives or shooting | 7 | 5 | 1 | 1 | 8 | 3 | 0 | 0 | 0 | 0 | 0 | 0 |
| Jumping in front of train | 1 | 1 | 1 | 1 | 2 | 1 | 2 | 4 | 1 | 2 | 3 | 3 |
| Burning | 1 | 1 | 1 | 1 | 2 | 1 | 2 | 4 | 0 | 0 | 2 | 2 |
| Banging head | 1 | 1 | 0 | 0 | 1 | 1 | 2 | 4 | 0 | 0 | 2 | 2 |
| Others | 0 | 0 | 1 | 1 | 1 | 1 | 2 | 4 | 0 | 0 | 2 | 2 |
| Unknown | 9 | 7 | 0 | 0 | 9 | 4 | 0 | 0 | 1 | 2 | 1 | 1 |
| Total | 133 | | 115 | | 248 | | 53 | | 63 | | 116 | |

## TABLE 2-10
### SEVERITY OF SUICIDE ATTEMPTS, BY AGE AND SEX, REPORTED IN NEWSPAPERS, 1969–1971 AND 1971

| Severity | Male | | | | | | | | | | Female | | | | | | | | | |
| --- | --- | --- | --- | --- | --- | --- | --- | --- | --- | --- | --- | --- | --- | --- | --- | --- | --- | --- | --- | --- |
| | 29 and under | | 30–49 | | 50 and over | | Unknown | | Total | | 29 and under | | 30–49 | | 50 and over | | Unknown | | Total | |
| | No. | Per-centage | No. | Per-centage | No. | Per-centage | No. | Per-centage | No. | Per-centage | No. | Per-centage | No. | Per-centage | No. | Per-centage | No. | Per-centage | No. | Per-centage |
| Verbal threats | 3 | 2 | 4 | 2 | 0 | 0 | 0 | 0 | 7 | 4 | 6 | 3 | 0 | 0 | 0 | 0 | 1 | 1 | 7 | 4 |
| Suicidal gestures | 1 | 1 | 3 | 2 | 1 | 1 | 0 | 0 | 5 | 3 | 5 | 3 | 1 | 1 | 1 | 1 | 1 | 1 | 8 | 5 |
| Mild degree | 0 | 0 | 0 | 0 | 1 | 1 | 1 | 1 | 2 | 1 | 3 | 2 | 0 | 0 | 1 | 1 | 0 | 0 | 4 | 2 |
| Moderate degree | 3 | 2 | 4 | 2 | 5 | 3 | 1 | 1 | 13 | 7 | 10 | 6 | 4 | 2 | 0 | 0 | 3 | 2 | 17 | 10 |
| Severe degree | 9 | 5 | 10 | 5 | 6 | 3 | 1 | 1 | 26 | 14 | 22 | 12 | 3 | 2 | 1 | 1 | 1 | 1 | 27 | 15 |
| Suicide completed | 37 | 20 | 60 | 32 | 30 | 16 | 6 | 3 | 133 | 72 | 77 | 43 | 21 | 12 | 12 | 7 | 5 | 3 | 115 | 65 |
| Total | 53 | 28 | 81 | 44 | 43 | 23 | 9 | 5 | 186 | 100 | 123 | 69 | 29 | 16 | 15 | 8 | 11 | 6 | 178 | 100 |

verbal threats; suicidal gestures; mild degree (no medical treatment necessary); moderate degree (treatment required but risk not serious); severe degree (life-threatening damage). The rate of completed suicide was higher among males (72 percent) than among females (65 percent), though the difference was slight. The highest degree of severity was shown by males between 30 and 49 and by females of 29 and under. Many attempters who used sleeping pills, with only mild damage resulting, did not come to the attention of reporters, so that cases reported in newspapers were probably either severe in intensity or dramatic in the suicidal action.

Despite the limitations of the information, the figures indicate that suicides among males aged 30 to 39 and females aged 14−29 were most frequently reported in newspapers. According to national suicide statistics, the highest rate for males is in the 20−24 age group, whereas newspapers tend to report more males suiciding at ages 30−39. A possible explanation is that males in the latter group are more likely to be involved in financial and legal difficulties and in interpersonal troubles; homicide-suicide patterns are often found in this group, and newspapers are particularly interested in this type of problem. The number of suicides of females found in the 15−29 age group corresponds to the national suicide death statistics.

## SUICIDES AMONG PSYCHIATRIC INPATIENTS

A study of attempted suicides among psychiatric inpatients at Taiwan University Hospital revealed that 102 persons attempted suicide in the two periods 1952−1954 and 1967−1968. Of this total, 39 attempts or 12 percent of total admissions occurred in the first period, the postmigration era, and 63, or 11 percent of total admissions, in the later period. There was a consistent relationship, in the two periods combined, between attempted suicide and clinical diagnosis, suicide attempts occurring most frequently in patients with reactive depression (48 percent); second, affective disorder (21 percent); third, personality disorder (15 percent). Of schizophrenics, 13 percent make suicide attempts. These figures are similar to those reported from most other countries.

Although the clinical diagnosis was found to be important in attempted suicides, the effect of socioenvironmental factors was also revealed by the survey. A higher rate of attempted suicide by migrant inpatients of both sexes (15−21 percent) than by native Taiwanese (4−9 percent) was found in the first period, but this difference disappeared entirely in the later period. In the first period, migrant housewives aged 30−39 were most affected and showed the highest rate of attempted suicide (27.7 percent). Chaotic mass migration seemingly had affected social, marital, and family solidarity so that migrants were more vulnerable to resulting problems than were native

Taiwanese. If the causes of suicide attempts are divided into two broad categories, socioenvironmental and psychopathological, 51 percent of the patients in the first period were listed under socioenvironmental, whereas only 19 percent were so listed in the later period. As migration pressures gradually wore off, a shift toward psychopathological causes took place.

Drowning and hanging were the most common methods in the first period; use of hypnotics and jumping from a high building, in the second.

In a cross-cultural study of symptomatology and hospitalizations of mental patients (8), the author and his colleagues were able to show differences in symptom patterns between hospitalized Taiwan Chinese and Japanese mental patients. Whereas the Japanese were likely to have disorders of arousal levels (listlessness, sleep disturbances, etc.), to turn against themselves (e.g., depression, the *shinkeishitsu* syndrome), and to find the major source of their problems within themselves, the Taiwan Chinese were much more likely to direct their symptomatology outward, to act out against others with hostility, and to perceive the outside world in unreal ways (paranoid and hypochondriac symptoms).

Another finding of the cross-cultural study was that women in both cultures were more likely than men to show severe symptomatology. Since suicide is one of the most serious deviant behaviors, and since it must obviously be viewed as a psychocultural phenomenon, the following explanation is possible. Japanese suicides turn their aggressions against themselves and are inclined to see the major source of the problems in their intrapsychic areas, whereas Taiwan Chinese suicides tend primarily to direct their aggressions outward and then turn against themselves with a clear intention of protest and communication. Females of both cultures are more likely than men to attempt suicide and to show culturally determined patterns of suicidal behavior.

## CASE HISTORIES

### Case A

A 42-year-old woman, mother of three children, committed suicide by taking thirty sleeping pills. She was a chronic insomniac, taking pills regularly. She was on poor terms with her husband and had frequent quarrels with him. She started a dress shop with another woman but business went badly and they had to close after a year and a half, owing money to creditors. She became more and more irritable with her husband and seemed more unhappy. On the night of her suicide, the couple had a serious quarrel and the wife left home intending to suicide but leaving no note. She took sleeping pills which she had just bought at the dispensary and finally collapsed on the street around 11 P.M. Sent to the emergency clinic, she died two hours later.

## Case B

A 21-year-old college freshman killed himself because of a one-sided love affair. He had been solitary and introverted since childhood. Academically he was doing well, but he was unable to make friends among his schoolmates. He particularly liked his English class taught by a young American woman, and in time he fell in love with her. He invited her to do some photography with him, intending to make a date for the theater, and told her of his love. The teacher told him she was already engaged and would marry in the coming summer. Feeling rejected, he wrote her a letter saying he would die in the classroom if he could not have her love, but the letter did not reach her until after his death. Several days prior to his suicide, he was laughed at by some of his classmates and called antisocial when he refused to attend a fellow student's birthday party. He left a will for his parents, who lived in southern Taiwan, admitting that he was not fulfilling his filial duty and asking that he be buried near the college. He took an overdose of pills and died in the backyard of the school.

## Case C

A 21-year-old girl was brought in a comatose state to the emergency clinic after taking fifty sleeping pills. She was from a small city in southern Taiwan and wanted to come to Taipei to study and work. Her conservative parents did not want her to go but the father compromised and agreed to support her for one year; after that she was to return home. She refused to return, however, and after three years had failed to make a good adjustment. She had met a boyfriend and, although she lived in one room and had borrowed money from relatives (having broken off with her parents), she paid his expenses when they went out. He pressured her to buy him expensive things, which she refused to do, but she became confused and upset. When she discovered that he had another girl friend with whom he was intimate, she was so distressed that she could not take her exams. She then took an overdose.

## Case D

A 35-year-old man, father of five children, attempted suicide by taking a rodenticide. As his parents had divorced soon after his birth, he had been raised by his mother and grandmother, with no contact with the father. In the earlier years he had done well running a factory that made women's handbags, and so he got married. After the marriage the wife found him too demanding sexually, and there were frequent quarrels. He then established a liaison with a divorced woman, which continued for some time. After the wife discovered his infidelity, he wanted to introduce the two women to each other, but the wife refused. Beset by competition and business troubles, he soon had to dismiss employees. About this time a single male friend of his was hospitalized in one of the local hospitals which did not provide food for the patients, and the wife had to take food to the friend and do his laundry. The man soon became jealous, suspecting his wife of intimacy with the friend. Serious quarrels erupted, and the wife often ran away from home.

By this time the man's business had been closed down. On the day of the suicide attempt, one of his friends had come to ask him to repay a large sum of money he had previously borrowed. The husband hinted at suicide to his wife, who did not respond. He then put rat poison on rice noodles and after eating some he forced three of the children to eat the noodles too. Fortunately the dose was not large enough to do serious damage. Regrettably, the couple refused the follow-up service so clearly needed in view of both his immature and hysterical personality and the pressures on the wife.

## CONCLUSION

One is aware of the limitations in basing a discussion of etiological and ecological factors in suicide on information from official documents, newspapers, and clinical records. The same criticism can be leveled at many studies of suicide in varying cultures.

Utilizing four different sources of suicide death statistics—national statistics, clinical case studies of attempts, suicides reported by newspapers, and suicide attempts among inpatient psychiatric cases—one reaches four major conclusions about suicide in Taiwan: (1) social disorganization following the mass migration from China has affected the suicide rate; (2) significantly larger numbers of young persons suicide; (3) the male-female ratio of suicidal deaths is about 1.5:1, whereas the attempt ratio is 1:3; (4) the death rate is higher for younger males. Culturally, Taiwanese patients show angry-aggressive-dependent characteristics, and they attempt to find solutions to problems of frustration and interpersonal relationships through suicidal behavior.

Suicide death rates, with three peaks during the past three decades, are correlated to social changes occurring in the same time period. Suicide rates were high just after wartime; the second peak paralleled the mass migration; the third one accompanied modernization and shifts of population. Stability came with resettlement of the migrant influx, reorganization into a modern economic society based on equality for migrant and host groups, and development of a more stable and cohesive value system. The suicide rate declined to 9 per 100,000 in 1974–1977.

The most characteristic features of young suicides were conflicts with other family members or disappointments in love affairs. These causes stemmed mostly from changes in traditional family life and from identity crises resulting from modernization and changing cultural attitudes. Young suicides were overrepresented by those from rural areas and from the lower and lower-middle classes. Female suicides were most frequently caused (1) by marital friction and the husband's extramarital affairs, and (2) by frustrated love affairs based on incompatibility, abandonment, and unsatisfied dependency needs. Family conflict was often caused by parental disapproval of a prospective marriage partner, for parents continued to believe in traditional values. Conflicts between mother-in-law and wife, however, do not now seem so important a factor, at least in urban areas.

The suicidal death rate of males was higher than that of females, and the difference became larger as the total rate rose. Greater lethality of method seemed to account in part for the higher male rate.

There has been an increase in suicide rates among older persons. They seem to have personal and intrapersonal problems, such as mental and physical illness, loneliness, and hopelessness. Lethality of method is greater among this older group than among younger persons. Loneliness because of separation from children is not common among the causes for suicides of elderly persons for, although population mobility is high, intimate family relationships and filial piety continue to be stressed in the society as deep-rooted values.

## BIBLIOGRAPHY

1. Beall, L. The psychopathology of suicide in Japan. *Internat. J. Social Psychiatry*, 14 (1968):213–225.

2. Chu, H. M. Migration and mental disorder In W. P. Lebra, ed., *Transcultural Research in Mental Health: Mental Health Research in Asia and the Pacific*. Honolulu: East-West Center Press, 1972. II:295–325.

3. Farberow, N. L. Self-destruction and identity. Paper presented at the Institute of Man, Duquesne University, April 1969. Mimeographed. 36 pp.

4. Lin, T., H. Rin, E. K. Yeh, et al. Mental disorders in Taiwan, fifteen years later: A preliminary report. In W. Caudill and T. Lin, eds., *Mental Health Research in Asia and the Pacific*. Honolulu: East-West Center Press, 1969. Pp. 66–91.

5. Rin, H. A study of attempted suicides among psychiatric inpatients. *J. Formosa Med. Assoc.*, 71 (1972):89–96.

6. Rin, H. Suicide in Taiwan. In N. L. Farberow, ed., *Suicide in Different Cultures*. Baltimore: University Park Press, 1975. Pp. 239–254.

7. Rin, H., H. M. Chu, and T. Lin. Psychophysiological reactions of a rural and suburban population in Taiwan. *Acta Psychiatr. Scand.*, 42 (1966):410–473.

8. Rin, H., C. Schooler, and W. A. Caudill. Culture, social structure and psychopathology in Taiwan and Japan. *J. Nerv. Mental Disorders*, 157 (1973):296–312.

9. Rin, H., L. T. Tseng, and T. Chen. Some trends found among suicides reported in a newspaper. *Acta Psychol. Taiwan*, no. 16 (1974):7–24.

10. Tatai, K., and M. Kato, eds. *Nihon no jisatsu o kangaeru* (Thinking of Suicide in Japan). Tokyo: Igaku-Shoin, 1974.

# PART II.  SUICIDE PREVENTION CENTER, MACKAY MEMORIAL HOSPITAL, TAIPEI

The Suicide Prevention Center at Mackay Memorial Hospital, Taipei, in the years 1972 through 1978 saw 2,547 cases of attempted suicide. Some of the attempters were seen for counseling, and some could not be contacted further. Those who were not counseled were usually persons who came to the hospital late at night and left hurriedly after giving a minimum amount of information. In the two years 1979 and 1980, 772 persons came to the emergency center for help, and 328 of them, or almost half (42.5 percent), were seen for counseling. The 1979—1980 cases, which received more intensive treatment, could provide more detailed information, yet the percentages for the two-year period and the seven-year period are approximately the same in the various information categories.

## SEX RATIO

Three and a half times as many women as men came to the emergency center in the period 1972—1978 (77.9 percent female, 22.1 percent male). In 1979—1980, the female-male ratio was 4:1 (80.8 percent females, 19.2 percent males). The male-female percentages were consistent throughout the period 1972—1980. (See table 2-11.)

## AGE

Most attempters were in the 20—24 age group, 35.3 percent in the period 1972—1978. The percentage in that same age group in 1979—1980 was slightly lower, standing at 33.4. The age group 25—29 was second in frequency in both periods. Ages 15—19 and 30—34 had similar percentages of the cases; suicide attempts dropped dramatically after age 54 in both periods. (See table 2-12.)

## METHODS USED

Hypnotics and tranquilizers were the leading methods of attempted suicide, accounting for a little more than 40 percent in both time periods, though the proportion in 1979—1980 would increase to 52.8 percent if

TABLE 2-11
SEX OF ATTEMPTED SUICIDES, SUICIDE PREVENTION
CENTER, MACKAY MEMORIAL HOSPITAL, 1972—1980

|  | Male | | Female | |
|---|---|---|---|---|
| Year | Number | Percentage | Number | Percentage |
| 1972 | 154 | 25.9 | 439 | 74.1 |
| 1973 | 97 | 21.0 | 365 | 79.0 |
| 1974 | 78 | 22.8 | 264 | 77.2 |
| 1975 | 47 | 21.6 | 171 | 78.4 |
| 1976 | 61 | 20.2 | 241 | 79.8 |
| 1977 | 68 | 21.2 | 253 | 78.8 |
| 1978 | 57 | 18.4 | 253 | 81.6 |
| Total | 562 | 22.1 | 1,986 | 77.9 |
| 1979 | 82 | 20.8 | 309 | 79.1 |
| 1980 | 66 | 17.3 | 315 | 82.7 |
| Total | 148 | 19.2 | 624 | 80.8 |

TABLE 2-12
AGE OF SUICIDE ATTEMPTERS, SUICIDE PREVENTION CENTER,
MACKAY MEMORIAL HOSPITAL, 1972—1980

|  | 1972—1978 | | 1979—1980 | |
|---|---|---|---|---|
| Age | Number | Percentage | Number[a] | Percentage |
| 1—14 | 13 | 0.5 | 0 | 0.0 |
| 15—19 | 317 | 12.4 | 32 | 9.9 |
| 20—24 | 900 | 35.3 | 109 | 33.4 |
| 25—29 | 540 | 21.2 | 87 | 26.5 |
| 30—34 | 294 | 11.5 | 36 | 10.9 |
| 35—44 | 267 | 10.9 | 33 | 10.0 |
| 45—54 | 103 | 4.0 | 18 | 5.4 |
| 55—64 | 48 | 1.8 | 6 | 1.8 |
| 65 and over | 28 | 1.0 | 7 | 2.1 |
| Unknown | 37 | 1.0 | — | — |
| Total | 2,547 | | 328 | |

[a]Counseled cases only.

stimulants and hallucinogens and multiple drug ingestions had been included. Chemical poisons—acids, insecticides, rodenticides, household poisons—were used in 17.9 percent of the 1972—1978 cases and in 28.3 percent of the 1979—1980 cases. Cutting or slashing accounted for 5.7 and 7.9 percent in the two periods, respectively, and jumping from a height, for 1.0 and 4.9 percent. (See table 2-13.)

## PRECIPITATING FACTORS

Conflicts with spouse and with other family members were the major precipitating factors leading to attempted suicides: 33.4 percent in 1972—1978 and 32.5 percent in 1979—1980. Boy-girl conflicts caused 18.7 and 22.7 percent, respectively. Financial problems had only a minor impact: 3.9 and 7.6 percent. Academic failure and physical illness were responsible for few suicide attempts. (See table 2-14.)

## TIME OF CALLS

Most calls to the Suicide Prevention Center were received between 6 P.M. and midnight. The period from midnight to 6 A.M. was second busiest; 12 noon to 6 P.M. third; and 6 A.M. to 12 noon, fourth. (See table 2-15.)

TABLE 2-13
METHODS OF ATTEMPTED SUICIDE PREVENTION CENTER,
MACKAY MEMORIAL HOSPITAL, 1972—1980

| Method | 1972—1978 | | 1979—1980 | |
|---|---|---|---|---|
| | Number | Percentage | Number | Percentage |
| Tranquilizers, hypnotics | 1,039 | 40.7 | 132 | 40.4 |
| Stimulants, hallucinogens | — | — | 19 | 5.7 |
| Multiple drugs | — | — | 22 | 6.7 |
| Chemical poisons | 448 | 17.9 | 93 | 28.3 |
| Cutting or slashing | 147 | 5.7 | 26 | 7.9 |
| Jumping from a height | 26 | 1.0 | 16 | 4.9 |
| Drowning | 14 | 0.05 | 0 | 0.0 |
| Hanging | — | — | 3 | 0.9 |
| Other | 241 | 9.4 | 13 | 4.0 |
| Unknown | 632 | 24.8 | — | — |
| Total | 2,547 | | 324 | |

TABLE 2-14
CAUSES OF SUICIDE ATTEMPTS, SUICIDE PREVENTION CENTER,
MACKAY MEMORIAL HOSPITAL, 1972–1980

| | 1972–1978 | | 1979–1980 | |
| Cause | Number | Percentage | Number[a] | Percentage |
|---|---|---|---|---|
| Marital conflict | 477 | 18.7 | 65 | 19.7 |
| Conflict with family | 376 | 14.7 | 42 | 12.8 |
| Boy-girl conflict | 477 | 18.7 | 73 | 22.7 |
| Conflict with others | – | – | 20 | 2.0 |
| Financial problems | 97 | 3.9 | 25 | 7.6 |
| Mental problems | 76 | 2.9 | 29 | 8.5 |
| Physical illness | 55 | 2.1 | 9 | 2.7 |
| Legal problems | 6 | 0.2 | – | – |
| Unemployment | – | – | 1 | 0.6 |
| Academic failure | – | – | 4 | 1.2 |
| Other | 89 | 3.8 | 27 | 8.2 |
| Unknown | 892 | 35.0 | 24 | 7.3 |
| Total | 2,545 | | 319 | |

[a]Counseled cases only.

TABLE 2-15
TIME OF SUICIDE CALLS, SUICIDE PREVENTION CENTER,
MACKAY MEMORIAL HOSPITAL, 1972–1980

| | 1972–1978 | | 1979–1980 | |
| Time | Number | Percentage | Number | Percentage |
|---|---|---|---|---|
| 6 A.M. to 12 noon | 322 | 12.6 | 71 | 21.6 |
| 12 noon to 6 P.M. | 390 | 15.3 | 87 | 26.4 |
| 6 P.M. to midnight | 761 | 29.8 | 101 | 30.8 |
| Midnight to 6 A.M. | 455 | 17.8 | 69 | 21.0 |
| Unknown | 619 | 24.5 | – | – |
| Total | 2,547 | | 328 | |

## CHARACTERISTICS OF SUICIDE ATTEMPTERS

The average suicide attempter at the Suicide Prevention Center was a
primary school graduate, possibly with some junior high school training.
Few were college students or graduate students. (See table 2-16.) Among
the known occupations, housewife, laborer, merchant, and unemployed

TABLE 2-16
EDUCATIONAL LEVEL OF SUICIDE ATTEMPTERS, SUICIDE PREVENTION
CENTER, MACKAY MEMORIAL HOSPITAL, 1972—1980

| Educational Level | 1972—1978 | | 1979—1980 | |
|---|---|---|---|---|
| | Number | Percentage | Number | Percentage |
| Illiterate | 88 | 3.4 | 21 | 6.4 |
| Primary school | 558 | 21.9 | 76 | 23.4 |
| Junior high school | 331 | 12.9 | 70 | 21.3 |
| Senior high school | 371 | 14.5 | 67 | 20.4 |
| College | 112 | 4.3 | 34 | 10.3 |
| Graduate school | 29 | 1.1 | 5 | 1.5 |
| Unknown | 1,058 | 41.9 | 55 | 16.7 |
| Total | 2,547 | | 328 | |

TABLE 2-17
OCCUPATIONS OF SUICIDE ATTEMPTERS, SUICIDE PREVENTION
CENTER, MACKAY MEMORIAL HOSPITAL, 1972—1980

| Occupation | 1972—1978 | | 1979—1980 | |
|---|---|---|---|---|
| | Number | Percentage | Number | Percentage |
| Laborer | 193 | 7.5 | 45 | 13.7 |
| Merchant | 189 | 7.4 | 60 | 18.3 |
| Government employee | 57 | 2.2 | 9 | 2.7 |
| Professional | 161 | 6.3 | 17 | 5.5 |
| Prostitute, dancing girl | 167 | 6.5 | 35 | 10.6 |
| Unemployed | 218 | 8.5 | 47 | 14.4 |
| Housewife | 577 | 22.7 | 71 | 21.6 |
| Student | 135 | 5.5 | 20 | 6.0 |
| Farmer | 13 | 0.05 | 6 | 1.8 |
| Retired | 0 | 0 | 5 | 1.5 |
| Unknown | 837 | 32.9 | 13 | 3.9 |
| Total | 2,547 | | 328 | |

were most common, together accounting for 46.1 percent of the 1972—1978 cases and for 68.0 percent of the 1979—1980 cases (table 2-17). Table 2-18 shows that the largest percentage of attempts were made by single persons, with married persons running a close second. The fact that single people ranked first reflects the youthfulness of many suicide attempters in both time periods.

TABLE 2-18
MARITAL STATUS OF SUICIDE ATTEMPTERS, SUICIDE
PREVENTION CENTER, MACKAY MEMORIAL HOSPITAL, 1972—1980

| Status | 1972—1978 | | 1979—1980 | |
|---|---|---|---|---|
| | Number | Percentage | Number | Percentage |
| Single | 914 | 35.9 | 149 | 45.4 |
| Married | 866 | 34.0 | 129 | 39.3 |
| Divorced or separated | 40 | 1.5 | 11 | 3.5 |
| Cohabiting | 109 | 4.2 | 25 | 7.6 |
| Widowed | 15 | 0.05 | 8 | 2.4 |
| Unknown | 603 | 23.9 | 6 | 1.8 |
| Total | 2,547 | | 328 | |

## SUMMARY

The suicide attempters seen at Mackay Memorial Hospital Suicide Prevention Center in 1972—1978 and in 1979—1980 were most frequently young and female. Three to four times as many females as males attempted suicide. The largest percentage of attempters were in the 20—24 age group, followed by those aged 25—29. Few persons over 55 were seen at the center. The methods most commonly used were drugs of various kinds and household and agricultural poisons. Precipitating causes for the attempts were primarily interpersonal in nature: marital problems were the leading cause; boy-girl difficulties came second; and family conflicts, third. Academic failure accounted for only a very small percentage of attempted suicides. Most calls were received at the hospital between 6 P.M. and midnight; the second-largest number came between midnight and 6 A.M. In general, the largest number of clients were seen in the afternoon and at night. The profile of the suicide attempters was a young, single person with troubled love relationships or a young married person with marital and/or family problems. Housewives were frequently seen, as were merchants, laborers, and prostitutes and dancing girls. The educational level of the clients was most often primary school, with a good possibility of junior and senior high school training.

# HONG KONG 3

*Editor's Note*

I was not able to find a researcher willing to write a chapter on Hong Kong suicides. I obtained raw data from Hong Kong government sources which, though lacking in some respects, would provide some picture of the situation in Hong Kong. I compiled Part I of this chapter from the statistics of these agencies.

The Samaritan Befrienders of Hong Kong supplied valuable information on the problems and stresses experienced by Hong Kong citizens. I wrote the second part of this chapter using their statistics which give a more personalized view of distressed and suicidal individuals. I appreciate the cooperation of Andrew Tu, chairman of the board, and Vanda Scott, director of the Wanchai branch.

## PART I. LEE A. HEADLEY

The following information covers the period 1952–1980, with particular emphasis on the decade 1970–1979. Most of it concerns completed suicides, though the police did provide some information on attempted suicides. A well-known study by Pow Ming Yap[1] dealt with a period of one and a half years (1953–54), and it is possible to compare present information with the conclusions he drew at that time. It is also of interest to relate the findings presented here in Part I to the statistics provided by the Samaritan Befrienders of Hong Kong for Part II.

Hong Kong, like Singapore, may be called a city-state. Essentially a trading center on the south coast of China, this British colony has been awaiting developments after the forthcoming termination of its 99-year lease with China. Within recent months China has indicated that it has no plans to take over Hong Kong, a relief to many in the colony. Chinese banks dominate Hong Kong and the colony is an excellent source of hard currency for China as well as an outlet for Chinese goods.

Although Hong Kong is prosperous and economically expanding, many of its residents are desperately poor. There are refugees from mainland

---

[1] *Suicide in Hong Kong* (Hong Kong: Hong Kong University Press, 1958).

China who have come in enormous numbers every year, swelling the ranks of untrained and uneducated resident Chinese. Many of the immigrants were young farmers lured by tales of wealth and opportunity. Macao was one point of entry for them, but now that the former Portuguese colony is recognized as part of mainland China stricter patrols are curbing the influx.

The immigrants, through supplying cheap labor for Hong Kong enterprises, also created tremendous pressures on all the colony's facilities. For years the government built residential complexes to house the newcomers, but it has recently stopped doing so. Inflation has worsened the housing crisis, and many people cannot afford to pay for shelter. Their plight is increasingly serious as the cost of living keeps pace with wages. Their solution is to resort to the gambling casinos of Macao or humbler gambling spots in Hong Kong or to go to moneylenders. Education becomes vital to enable a person to get a job and to climb out of the slums.

Cultural attitudes are those typical of the Chinese, with Confucian ideals and Buddhist values. Western ideas are incorporated to some extent, and recent immigrants may reflect the egalitarian aims of Revolutionary China. Men remain dominant in the society and women, who have little economic power, find few options open to them.

## SOURCES OF INFORMATION

Information for the following discussion was supplied by the Hong Kong Department of Census and Statistics, the Registry of Births and Deaths, the Royal Hong Kong Police, and the Samaritan Befrienders of Hong Kong. The statistics give the number of registered suicides and the rate per 100,000 population from 1952 to 1979; male and female percentages from 1952 to 1979; and police reports on completed and attempted suicides from 1961 to 1980. The number of suicides, with age and sex, in the period 1970–1979, has been supplied by the Registry of Births and Deaths.

## SUICIDE RATES

Based on data from the Registry of Births and Deaths, the suicide rate per 100,000 population increased from 11.8 in 1952 to 13.5 in 1979. There were, however, fluctuations in that period: the two high points were 14.1 in 1959 and 14.7 in 1976; the two low points, 8.4 in 1965 and 7.2 in 1978. The actual number of suicides was highest in 1979 (661), when Hong Kong's population was just under 5 million. (See table 3-1.)

The number of completed suicides given by the Registry of Births and Deaths was considerably higher for 1961–1980 than the number reported

TABLE 3-1
NUMBER OF SUICIDES AND SUICIDE RATE PER 100,000 POPULATION, 1952–1979

| Year | Male | | Female | | Total | Rate |
| | Number | Percentage | Number | Percentage | | |
|------|--------|------------|--------|------------|-------|------|
| 1952 | 154 | 57.9 | 112 | 42.1 | 266 | 11.8 |
| 1953 | 167 | 62.8 | 99 | 37.2 | 266 | 11.8 |
| 1954 | 183 | 60.6 | 119 | 39.4 | 302 | 13.3 |
| 1955 | 166 | 63.4 | 96 | 36.6 | 262 | 11.2 |
| 1956 | 180 | 60.2 | 119 | 39.8 | 299 | 12.2 |
| 1957 | 177 | 59.8 | 119 | 40.2 | 296 | 11.5 |
| 1958 | 204 | 58.9 | 142 | 41.1 | 346 | 12.6 |
| 1959 | 213 | 52.9 | 190 | 47.1 | 403 | 14.1 |
| 1960 | 210 | 61.6 | 131 | 38.4 | 341 | 11.4 |
| 1961 | 188 | 55.9 | 148 | 44.1 | 336 | 10.6 |
| 1962 | 224 | 61.9 | 138 | 38.1 | 362 | 10.9 |
| 1963 | 216 | 58.4 | 154 | 41.6 | 370 | 10.8 |
| 1964 | 218 | 60.1 | 145 | 39.9 | 363 | 10.4 |
| 1965 | 190 | 63.1 | 111 | 36.9 | 301 | 8.4 |
| 1966 | 191 | 54.4 | 160 | 45.6 | 351 | 9.7 |
| 1967 | 238 | 61.5 | 149 | 38.5 | 387 | 10.4 |
| 1968 | 247 | 54.3 | 208 | 45.7 | 455 | 12.0 |
| 1969 | 180 | 54.5 | 150 | 45.5 | 330 | 8.6 |
| 1970 | 310 | 57.4 | 230 | 42.6 | 540 | 13.6 |
| 1971 | 217 | 55.9 | 171 | 44.1 | 388 | 9.6 |
| 1972 | 276 | 59.6 | 187 | 40.4 | 463 | 11.3 |
| 1973 | 300 | 59.4 | 205 | 40.6 | 505 | 12.1 |
| 1974 | 276 | 57.4 | 205 | 42.6 | 481 | 11.1 |
| 1975 | 326 | 60.9 | 209 | 39.1 | 535 | 12.4 |
| 1976 | 370 | 56.6 | 284 | 43.4 | 654 | 14.7 |
| 1977 | 342 | 54.4 | 287 | 45.6 | 629 | 13.9 |
| 1978 | 204 | 61.8 | 126 | 38.2 | 330 | 7.2 |
| 1979 | 369 | 55.8 | 292 | 44.2 | 661 | 13.5 |

SOURCE: Hong Kong Department of Census and Statistics, Registry of Births and Deaths.

by the Royal Hong Kong Police. In most instances the number of registry deaths was 2 to 3.6 times as large as that shown by police records.

## SEX RATIO

In the 1952–1979 statistics on suicide, males predominated in every year, ranging from a low of 52.9 percent to a high of 63.4 percent (table 3-1). Female percentages during the same period varied from 36.6 to 47.1. Table

3-2 gives the same statistics for a shorter period, 1970–1979, when male percentages varied from 61.8 to 54.4 and female percentages, from 45.6 to 38.2. P. M. Yap found that males predominated in completed suicides but not in attempted suicides.

## AGE

In the decade 1970–1979, the largest number of suicides was in the 60 and over age group; the second largest, 20–29; the third largest, 40–49; and the fourth largest 30–39 (see table 3-3). These data suggest that the most vulnerable ages are 20–49 and 60 and over.

TABLE 3-2
SEX OF SUICIDES, 1970–1979

| Year | Male | | Female | | Total |
| | Number | Percentage | Number | Percentage | |
|---|---|---|---|---|---|
| 1970 | 310 | 57.4 | 230 | 42.6 | 540 |
| 1971 | 217 | 55.9 | 171 | 44.1 | 388 |
| 1972 | 276 | 59.6 | 187 | 40.4 | 463 |
| 1973 | 300 | 59.4 | 205 | 40.6 | 505 |
| 1974 | 276 | 57.4 | 205 | 42.6 | 481 |
| 1975 | 326 | 60.9 | 209 | 39.1 | 535 |
| 1976 | 370 | 56.6 | 284 | 43.4 | 654 |
| 1977 | 342 | 54.4 | 287 | 45.6 | 629 |
| 1978 | 204 | 61.8 | 126 | 38.2 | 330 |
| 1979 | 369 | 55.8 | 292 | 44.2 | 661 |

SOURCE: Hong Kong Department of Census and Statistics, Registry of Births and Deaths.

TABLE 3-3
AVERAGE NUMBER OF SUICIDES PER YEAR, BY AGE AND SEX, 1970–1979

| Age group | Male | | | Female | | | Total number |
| | Number | Average per year | Percentage | Number | Average per year | Percentage | |
|---|---|---|---|---|---|---|---|
| 10–19 | 77 | 7.7 | 41.2 | 110 | 11.0 | 58.8 | 187 |
| 20–29 | 510 | 51.0 | 55.7 | 406 | 40.6 | 44.3 | 916 |
| 30–39 | 469 | 46.9 | 67.0 | 231 | 23.1 | 33.0 | 700 |
| 40–49 | 545 | 54.5 | 66.4 | 276 | 27.6 | 33.6 | 821 |
| 50–59 | 317 | 31.7 | 50.9 | 306 | 30.6 | 49.1 | 623 |
| 60 and over | 693 | 69.3 | 47.7 | 759 | 75.9 | 52.3 | 1,452 |

SOURCE: Hong Kong Department of Census and Statistics, Registry of Births and Deaths.

## AGE AND SEX

The statistics for the 1970—1979 period indicate a widely differing pattern of male-female and age mortalities, the sex patterns showing opposite trends. Of the 10—19 age group 58.8 percent were females. The percentage then declined to 33.0 for the 30—39 group, rose slightly to 33.6 for the 40—49 group, and climbed to 52.3 for those aged 60 and over (table 3-3). The highest percentages of male deaths occurred in the 30—39 and 40—49 groups (67.0 and 66.4, respectively); the percentage declined to 47.7 for the 60 and over age group. Apparently the most difficult years for males are 20—49, whereas these same years are less dangerous for females.

P. M. Yap found a different age-sex profile in his study of 1953-54 cases, based on police statistics and rates per 100,000 rather than on percentages of deaths. According to his data, male deaths were on a plateau between the ages of 30 and 50. The 1970—1979 statistics also show the same plateau, but at a much higher level for males than for females. Yap's observations and the 1970—1979 statistics both show a rapidly rising rate for females after age 60.

## METHODS

The three most common methods of committing suicide are jumping from a height, taking a drug overdose, or shooting oneself.

## ATTEMPTED SUICIDES

Police statistics for 1961—1980 (table 3-4) show that in every year attempted suicides outnumbered completed suicides, often being two to three times as many. As police records for suicide deaths show only 30 to 50 percent of those recorded in the Registry of Births and Deaths, it is likely that attempted suicides also exceeded the number shown in table 3-4. Completed suicides are more often reported to the police than are attempts. Moreover, attempts are more easily concealed, and in any event those making the attempts would usually be taken to medical centers. Consequently, attempts may be as much as 5 to 10 times more numerous than those recorded by the police for these years.

Yap also noted a higher number of attempted than completed suicides, especially among females. He found that most attempts for both sexes occurred in the 20—30 age group and that there were only a few in old age.

Yap concluded that recent immigrants to Hong Kong had higher suicide rates than older inhabitants and that the primary causes of suicide were economic stress and physical illness (half of his cases) and interpersonal difficulties (20 percent). Suicide attempts resulted mainly from interpersonal conflicts and economic stresses. Women, particularly those who were married, were most affected by interpersonal conflict.

TABLE 3-4
COMPLETED AND ATTEMPTED SUICIDES, 1961–1980

| Year | Completed | Attempted | Total |
|------|-----------|-----------|-------|
| 1961 | 174 | 631 | 805 |
| 1962 | 221 | 497 | 718 |
| 1963 | 166 | 382 | 548 |
| 1964 | 127 | 376 | 503 |
| 1965 | 150 | 372 | 522 |
| 1966 | 139 | 409 | 548 |
| 1967 | 129 | 360 | 489 |
| 1968 | 97 | 346 | 443 |
| 1969 | 149 | 390 | 539 |
| 1970 | 130 | 322 | 452 |
| 1971 | 203 | 208 | 411 |
| 1972 | 204 | 234 | 438 |
| 1973 | 210 | 263 | 473 |
| 1974 | 183 | 408 | 591 |
| 1975 | 227 | 458 | 685 |
| 1976 | 195 | 281 | 476 |
| 1977 | 194 | 310 | 504 |
| 1978 | 133 | 384 | 517 |
| 1979 | 194 | 264 | 458 |
| 1980 | 104 | 286 | 390 |

SOURCE: Royal Hong Kong Police.
NOTE: The data did not include sex percentages.

# PART II. SAMARITAN BEFRIENDERS OF HONG KONG

The Samaritan Befrienders of Hong Kong, concerned with helping suicidal persons and those suffering emotional distress, was begun in 1962. The service has an English-speaking branch, Wanchai, with 100 volunteers, and a Chinese-speaking branch, Lok Fu of Lok Fu Estates, which began in 1969; the Homantin branch had to cease operation in February 1980 because of manpower problems. In addition, the organization provides a special service for students in the summer. This program is aimed at assisting students who are depressed and anxious because of difficulties in passing courses or obtaining school placements. The student service also offers practical information and acts as a resource center.

## DATA PRESENTED

The information presented here is derived from overall statistics for the branches for 1978. More detailed information comes from the Wanchai branch for 1977, 1978, and 1979. Suicidal callers to that branch in 1979 are described.

## NUMBER AND SEX OF CLIENTS IN 1978

Table 3-5 reports the work of the three branches and the special summer service for students in 1978. The figures reflect an increase in services since 1977—56 percent in male calls and 70 percent in female calls. For the three branches, the largest number of calls came from the 21−44 age group; the second largest, from those aged 20 and under (table 3-6).

TABLE 3-5
NUMBER AND SEX OF CLIENTS OF SAMARITAN BEFRIENDERS
OF HONG KONG, 1978

| Sex | Branch | | | | |
|---|---|---|---|---|---|
| | Lok Fu | Wanchai | Homantin | Special service | Total |
| Male | 445 | 181 | 260 | 1,157 | 2,043 |
| Female | 601 | 235 | 242 | 1,213 | 2,291 |
| Total | 1,046 | 416 | 502 | 2,370 | 4,334 |

TABLE 3-6
AGE AND SEX OF CLIENTS OF SAMARITAN BEFRIENDERS
OF HONG KONG, 1978

| Age group | Male | | Female | | Total | |
|---|---|---|---|---|---|---|
| | Number | Percentage | Number | Percentage | Number | Percentage |
| 20 and under | 191 | 9.7 | 247 | 12.5 | 438 | 22.2 |
| 21−44 | 532 | 27.1 | 679 | 34.5 | 1,211 | 61.6 |
| 45−60 | 94 | 4.7 | 91 | 4.6 | 185 | 9.3 |
| Over 60 | 38 | 1.9 | 39 | 1.9 | 77 | 3.8 |
| Unknown | 31 | 1.5 | 22 | 1.6 | 53 | 3.1 |

## PRECIPITATING CAUSES

The largest percentages of precipitating causes of calls to the Samaritans were in the field of interpersonal relationships, love problems (13.2 percent) combining with family (12.3 percent) and marital problems (8.2 percent) for a total of 33.7 percent (table 3-7). In these categories a high proportion of callers were female. Money problems were a frequent cause (22 percent). These cases reflect the serious housing and employment problems in Hong Kong, which has been flooded with mainland Chinese emigrants for some time and has lately had Vietnamese refugees add to the overcrowding.

TABLE 3-7
CAUSES OF CLIENTS' CALLS TO SAMARITAN
BEFRIENDERS OF HONG KONG, 1978

| Cause | Male | Female | Total | Percentage of total |
|---|---|---|---|---|
| Marital problems | 50 | 152 | 202 | 8.2 |
| Family problems | | | | 12.3 |
|   With family members | 80 | 170 | 250 | 10.1 |
|   Child abuse | 2 | 1 | 3 | 0.1 |
|   Pregnancy | 2 | 47 | 49 | 2.1 |
| Psychiatric problems | | | | 16.7 |
|   Depression | 79 | 130 | 209 | 8.2 |
|   Other | 101 | 110 | 211 | 8.5 |
| Love problems | 101 | 226 | 327 | 13.2 |
| Drugs or alcohol | 18 | 20 | 38 | 1.6 |
| Sexual problems | 53 | 15 | 68 | 2.8 |
| Rape | 1 | 20 | 21 | 0.7 |
| Education | 80 | 83 | 163 | 6.6 |
| Money troubles | | | | 22.0 |
|   Debts | 41 | 14 | 55 | 2.2 |
|   Poverty | 128 | 66 | 194 | 7.9 |
|   Gambling losses | 7 | 3 | 10 | 0.4 |
|   Unemployment | 89 | 36 | 125 | 5.1 |
|   Housing | 65 | 96 | 161 | 6.4 |
| Legal and criminal problems | – | – | – | 4.5 |
| General inquiry | 34 | 37 | 71 | 2.9 |
| Hoax | 4 | 7 | 11 | 0.4 |
| Other | 59 | 51 | 110 | 4.5 |
|   Total | 994 | 1,284 | 2,278 | |

Housing is so scarce that many families share the same room, people sleep in "hot beds" in shifts, or they rent a cage, a wired-in bunk.

Because of inflation and Hong Kong's limited land space, the price of land has soared. The costs are passed on to tenants and the poor cannot afford to pay the exorbitant rents. Crowded, miserable conditions create tension and aggression; rape and incest result from living in such close proximity. As the government has stopped building apartment blocks for refugees, the resulting price of housing plus inflation has meant that many employed persons do not earn enough to cover necessities. In a desperate last-ditch hope, some residents resort to gambling or borrow from loan sharks, who often ask as much as 60 percent interest. Some wage earners and housewives pledge their identity cards or bank cards to borrow money, lose it in gambling, and borrow again. Loan sharks blackmail debtors for repayment and force housewives into prostitution.

The employment problems are difficult for the Samaritans to alleviate because the unemployed are often over 45 years of age and are unskilled or physically handicapped. The government makes no provision for taking care of such persons. The few callers whose problem was drugs or alcohol were mostly Europeans.

## WANCHAI

This English-speaking branch of the Hong Kong Samaritans received 5,351 hot-line calls in 1979, of which 4,978 were from clients; this number represented an increase of 39 percent over 1978. Eighty percent of the callers telephoned only once, and 53 percent of these calls were from females; 12 percent called two or three times, 63 percent of them females; 6 percent called more than three times, less than half of them females. The percentages were approximately the same in 1978.

The daily average of client calls in 1979 was eleven, an increase of 39 percent over 1978. Almost half of these calls came from known clients. As to sex, 43 percent of the callers were female and 57 percent were male.

### Time of Calls

The sex of the caller varied with the time of day and the day of the week. More males called on Sundays (66.6 percent) and more women on Thursdays (51.6 percent). The high point for male calls was from 7 to 10 A.M., and for women, from 11 P.M. to 1 A.M. Only a small percentage of the calls were received between 1 A.M. and 10 A.M. The busiest day was Saturday and the most active period was from 7 P.M. to 10 P.M., when 20 percent of the calls were received. In the 15-hour period from 10 A.M. to 1 A.M., 88 percent of the calls were received.

Marital Status

Of the 619 new callers in 1979, 54 percent were female and 46 percent were male, and most of them were single. Of the latter, 58 percent were female, and females constituted an even larger proportion of the married persons (71 percent). The same pattern prevailed in 1978, suggesting that single women had less need to call for help than married women.

Ethnicity

Of the Wanchai clients in 1979, 43 percent were Chinese, 37 percent, Caucasian, 9 percent, Indian, and 10 percent, other Asians. All the Asians grouped together accounted for 62 percent of the total. Probably the percentage of Caucasians was high because Wanchai is an English-speaking branch. These figures mean that 1.6 of every 20,000 Asians in Hong Kong called the service, whereas 75 of every 20,000 Caucasian residents called. More Asian clients called in 1979 than in 1978.

Suicidal Clients

In 1979, 49 suicidal clients, or 6.2 percent of the total, called the Wanchai branch; in 1978 the same type of caller accounted for 10 percent of the total. In 1979, 49 percent of the suicidal callers were female; in 1978, 67 percent.

Of the 1979 suicidal callers, 12 percent were under 20 years of age; 72 percent, between 20 and 44; and 8 percent, between 45 and 60. (For age distribution, see table 3-8.)

Problems of Clients

Of the 784 clients in 1979, 81.5 percent described their difficulties as either interpersonal or personal, and 17.5 percent had practical problems (see table 3-9). A case example is a 30-year-old woman, with two children, whose husband has been spending money on other women and using family funds to gamble so that he can keep both family and mistress satisfied. In spite of frequent quarrels, the husband is unwilling to change his ways.

TABLE 3-8

AGE AND SEX OF SUICIDAL CLIENTS, WANCHAI BRANCH,
SAMARITAN BEFRIENDERS OF HONG KONG, 1979

| Age group | Male | | Female | | Total |
| | Number | Percentage | Number | Percentage | |
| --- | --- | --- | --- | --- | --- |
| Under 20 | 2 | 33.4 | 4 | 66.6 | 6 |
| 20–44 | 20 | 57.1 | 15 | 42.9 | 35 |
| 45–60 | 1 | 25.0 | 3 | 75.0 | 4 |
| Over 60 | 1 | 100.0 | 0 | 0.0 | 1 |
| Unknown | 0 | 0.0 | 3 | 100.0 | 3 |

TABLE 3-9
PROBLEMS OF 784 CLIENTS CALLING WANCHAI BRANCH OF
SAMARITAN BEFRIENDERS OF HONG KONG, 1977−1979
(In percentages)

| Problem | All calls | | | Female percentage of calls | | |
|---|---|---|---|---|---|---|
| | 1977 | 1978 | 1979 | 1977 | 1978 | 1979 |
| Interpersonal | | 32.0 | 25.0 | 28.0 | | |
| Marital | 12.0 | 10.0 | 8.5 | 79.0 | 79.0 | 74.0 |
| Family | 5.0 | 6.0 | 8.0 | 59.0 | 69.0 | 75.0 |
| Personal | 12.0 | 5.0 | 7.5 | 28.0 | 43.0 | 48.0 |
| Pregnancy | 3.0 | 4.0 | 4.0 | 100.0 | 91.0 | 80.0 |
| Love (boy-girl) | | 9.0 | 14.0 | 8.5 | 58.0 | 67.0 | 67.0 |
| Sexual | | 7.0 | 6.0 | 8.0 | 15.0 | 13.0 | 18.0 |
| Loneliness | | 11.0 | 7.0 | 14.5 | 37.0 | 60.0 | 35.0 |
| Anxiety | | − | 4.0 | 4.0 | − | 52.0 | 80.0 |
| Depression | | 11.0 | 9.0 | 5.5 | 63.0 | 58.0 | 62.0 |
| Suicidal tendency | | 6.0 | 7.0 | 6.2 | 63.0 | 67.0 | 49.0 |
| Psychiatric | | 1.4 | 1.0 | 1.8 | 75.0 | 37.0 | 50.0 |
| Medical | | 3.0 | 2.0 | 2.3 | 30.0 | 30.0 | 50.0 |
| Alcohol | | 1.5 | 3.0 | 2.0 | 33.0 | 62.0 | 63.0 |
| Drugs | | 0.8 | 1.0 | 0.2 | 40.0 | 50.0 | 100.0 |
| Other addictions | | − | 0.2 | 0.5 | − | 100.0 | 50.0 |
| Education | | 6.0 | 3.0 | 4.0 | 38.0 | 50.0 | 63.0 |
| Money | | 9.4 | 8.0 | 6.5 | | | |
| Housing | 1.4 | 1.0 | 1.5 | 63.0 | 78.0 | 73.0 |
| Unemployment | 5.0 | 5.0 | 3.0 | 32.0 | 22.0 | 44.0 |
| Financial | 3.0 | 2.0 | 2.0 | 35.0 | 38.0 | 29.0 |
| Legal | | 2.7 | 3.0 | 2.0 | | | |
| Civil | 1.5 | 2.0 | 1.0 | 56.0 | 71.0 | 63.0 |
| Criminal | − | 1.0 | 0.5 | − | 20.0 | 25.0 |
| Immigration | 1.2 | − | 0.5 | 43.0 | 0.0 | 33.0 |

## SPECIAL SUMMER STUDENT PROGRAM

Education is a prerequisite for obtaining desirable employment in Hong
Kong. With the large increase in population and a rise in unemployment,
school degrees are increasingly valuable. Many students become anxious,
and some depressed, if they have trouble passing their courses or even

getting into school. Some who wanted to repeat form 5 could not find openings; others hoped to enter form 6 as a preparation for university work but there were insufficient places. In 1978 the Samaritans' special summer service for students had 667 young clients in the first category and 625 in the second.

Teenage suicides increased fourfold from 1978 to 1981. Many blame the fiercely competitive school examinations which began with tests for entry to primary school and continued through secondary school to the university level. A survey of teachers found them nearly unanimous in opposition to the examination system because of the emotional stress on students. Some persons blame parents for pressure on their children to compete successfully, an attitude very similar to that found in Japan. The roots of the examination system lie deep in China's history, when the examination system selected scholars for the ruling bureaucracy. The school system in Hong Kong is now being reevaluated.

Some feel that attitudes have changed to some degree regarding education. It is now recognized that the opportunities to enter a university are limited, as there are only 2,000 openings a year; both parents and students are more realistic about the competition. They are more willing to accept failure in university entrance examinations and to consider alternative schools and types of training. The mass media, as well as education itself, have brought recognition of individual differences in abilities, interests, and potential, so that the university examination does not determine irrevocably the student's future. Students are still keenly aware, however, that they must get as much training as possible, whether as apprentices or in commercial or technical fields. Evening schools are in demand.

The student service offers emotional support and encouragement, career guidance, information, referrals, and practical assistance to these young persons (see table 3-10). A resource handbook put together in 1979 contains data on various types of schools and special training courses which answers some of the questions. In 1978 there were 2,370 calls to the service; in 1979, 4,138 (table 3-11). In 1979 the heaviest work load was in August, when ten hot lines were in service twenty-four hours a day. Nevertheless, the volume of calls was still overwhelming.


## SUMMARY

The clients of the Samaritan Befrienders of Hong Kong are mostly between the ages of 20 and 44, with the second largest group under 20 years of age. Few are over 60 years of age. Females predominate. At the Wanchai branch, females are more common among Caucasian clients than among Asian clients. Most callers are single Asians.

TABLE 3-10
PROBLEMS OF CALLERS, SPECIAL STUDENT SERVICE,
SAMARITAN BEFRIENDERS OF HONG KONG, 1979

| Problem | Calls from males | Calls from females | Total | Percentage of total | Percentage change over 1978 |
|---|---|---|---|---|---|
| Evening schools (form 5) | 107 | 132 | 239 | 5.8 | 115.0 |
| Form 1 to form 4 | 11 | 15 | 26 | 0.6 | − 16.0 |
| Commercial studies | 72 | 239 | 311 | 7.5 | 183.0 |
| Form 5 repeaters | 482 | 519 | 1,001 | 24.2 | 50.0 |
| Nursing | 39 | 72 | 111 | 2.7 | 152.0 |
| Form 6 | 558 | 482 | 1,040 | 25.1 | 66.0 |
| Postsecondary | 136 | 149 | 285 | 6.9 | 148.0 |
| Overseas studies | 44 | 44 | 88 | 2.1 | 105.0 |
| Job placement | 102 | 152 | 254 | 6.2 | 35.0 |
| Referrals | 19 | 40 | 59 | 1.4 | − 3.0 |
| Emotional | | | | | |
| Mild | 13 | 34 | 47 | 1.2 | − 63.0 |
| Serious | 12 | 14 | 26 | 0.6 | 24.0 |
| Other | 331 | 320 | 651 | 15.7 | 188.0 |
| Total | 1,926[a] | 2,212[b] | 4,138 | 100.0 | 74.6 |

[a]46.5 percent of total.
[b]53.5 percent of total.

The most frequent problems leading clients to call the Samaritans are interpersonal difficulties in family, marital, and boy-girl love relationships. Economic problems—housing, unemployment, finances—are also important. Of the 1978 and 1979 clients at the Wanchai branch, 8 to 10 percent were suicidal. During the summer many students, perturbed about obtaining school placements, career information, and technical training, call the special student service for help.

According to government statistics on suicides and attempted suicides, the age group with second-highest vulnerability was 20−49. The Samaritans received their largest number of calls from clients in the 21−44 age bracket, as did also the Wanchai branch. As in other suicide prevention centers, few callers were over 60 years of age, though they are most prone to suicide.

The close percentages of males and females who call the Samaritans reflect the sex proportions of those who actually commit suicide. Whereas females usually predominate in calls to suicide prevention centers and in

TABLE 3-11
VOLUME OF CALLS, SPECIAL STUDENT SERVICE,
SAMARITAN BEFRIENDERS OF HONG KONG, 1977–1979

| Year | Male | Female | Total | Percentage increase |
|------|------|--------|-------|---------------------|
| 1977 | 719 | 749 | 1,468 | |
| 1978 | 1,157 | 1,213 | 2,370 | 61.4 |
| 1979 | 1,926 | 2,212 | 4,138 | 74.6 |

attempted suicides, the proportions here are higher than usual for male calls, which corresponds to the governmental findings. Yap's information was also similar.

The problems experienced by the Samaritan callers are very like those found by Yap in his 1953–54 study; they probably reflect the same difficulties of recent immigrants, employment, and dependency of women. The Samaritan Befrienders are thus serving the high-risk group of Hong Kong residents.

# SINGAPORE 4

*Editor's Note*

After Japan, Singapore is the most prosperous country in Southeast Asia. Its free port is one of the busiest in the world and it is the business and banking center for much of the South Pacific area. Originally merely a transfer point for goods of other nations, Singapore is now exporting raw materials of its own and is manufacturing machinery and textiles, building ships, and making other products requiring technical skills. Of the republic's total wealth, wholesale and retail trade accounts for 28 percent; manufacturing, 25 percent; and transportation and communications, 10 percent. The Chinese are known as traders and businessmen throughout the world, and in Singapore they have reached the ultimate of their skill. Visitors are impressed by the modern and efficient city of Singapore, with its bustle, its luxury goods, and its seeming ability to provide anything that is wanted. Little is seen of the rest of Singapore Island because the city dominates the life of the area; Singapore is essentially a city-state.

Singapore's citizens enjoy a high level of health, long life expectancy (70.8 years), good sanitation and water, and efficient services. The government provides various types of social welfare service and good educational facilities. Literacy is at the 75 percent level, and the number of professional and technologically skilled persons is on the rise. Since recovering from World War II and Japanese occupation, Singapore is politically and economically stable.

The chapter on Singapore is presented in three parts, the first by Hock Boon Chia of the Singapore Medical Center, who had researched suicides and attempted suicides. Parts II and III of this chapter are based on materials from the Samaritans of Singapore. I compiled Part II from statistics provided by that organization, whose director is Mrs. Irene Jacob. Part III, written by Mrs. Kalyani K. Mehta of the Samaritans, analyzes attempted suicides of which the organization was aware between July 1975 and July 1979. Her paper humanizes and puts into focus the stress situations that make people turn to suicide.

## PART I. HOCK BOON CHIA[1]

### INTRODUCTION

The study of suicide is often unsatisfactory as it is beset with many problems, among them the definitions of "suicide" and "attempted sui-

---

[1] I am grateful to the registrar of the University of Singapore for permission to publish data collected during the course of my research for my M.D. thesis in 1978.

cide," the certification of death which varies from country to country, and the reliability of official suicide statistics as reported by the *World Health Statistics Annual* (1977). The problem is simpler, however, in Singapore, which is a small and compact island of 616 square kilometers with a relatively static nonmigratory population, a high standard of medical record keeping, and up-to-date demographic statistics.

The population of Singapore in 1976 was estimated to be 2,278,200, comprising 1,162,000 males and 1,116,200 females. Its plural society is 76 percent Chinese, 15 percent Malay, 7 percent Indian, and 2 percent other ethnic groups. Singapore's population is unique in that it is almost wholly immigrant in origin.

In Southeast Asia, Chinese constitute from 1 to 76 percent of the total population depending on the country concerned (Singapore, Malaysia, Brunei, Thailand, Cambodia, Vietnam, Indonesia, Laos, Burma, Phillipines, and Timor). Scattered in these countries as a minority group among a host population, except in Singapore, the Chinese live, work, and sometimes prosper. They remain a separate community, self-sufficient and independent. Their adaptability, perseverance, and courage are well recognized, and they are known as a pragmatic people.

Of all the Southeast Asian countries, Singapore is the only one that has reliable statistics on population and deaths. The study of suicide in Singapore is therefore mainly a study of suicide among the Chinese. Suicide statistics collected on the other peoples living on the island do, however, provide an opportunity for transcultural study of suicidal behavior among different ethnic groups in one of the most progressive and rapidly advancing cities in Southeast Asia.

## PREVIOUS SUICIDE STUDIES

The first comprehensive study of suicide in Singapore was Murphy's statistical and sociological analysis of data after 1925 (10), concentrating mainly on the periods 1930–1932, 1946–1948, and 1950–1952. Murphy found a steady increase in suicide rates after 1948, especially among females. Among ethnic groups, the Malays had an exceptionally low rate of suicide for both males and females, and the Indian community had the highest incidence. The Chinese rate was fairly high, with different dialectal groups exhibiting rates and patterns that varied closely and indirectly with the size of the group. The Singapore-born population had a much lower rate than immigrants from either Malaya or other overseas areas.

Murphy found that the suicide rate in Singapore did not rise during the world economic depression (1929–1933) which, according to him, affected

Singapore badly. Poverty, overcrowding, poor housing, and the uneven sex ratio (fewer females) seemed not to have a direct effect on the suicide rate. Yet persons who had security of employment were linked with markedly lower rates than were those in economically similar occupations, but with less security.

A. J. Chen (1) used materials collected from coroners' records to determine the trend of deaths from unnatural causes (accidents, suicides, and homicides) in Singapore in the period 1961–1965. She found that suicidal deaths in that period accounted for 1.4 percent of the total number of deaths in Singapore and also that the suicide rate for males was double that for females. Compared with Murphy's figures, her data showed a substantial increase in the Malay suicide rate, from 2.6 to 5.6 per 100,000 for males and from 0.2 to 1.2 for females, whereas for Indians and Pakistanis the rates had fallen. Chen concluded that

> the very low rates of accident, suicide and homicide among the Malays as compared to those of the other ethnic groups are remarkable. This is in contrast to that of the crude death rate and infant mortality rate which are highest among the Malays. One wonders whether this is due to the inherent character of the Malays, or to a stable state of mind in more rural people, or to the fact that immigrant populations are more susceptible to unnatural deaths.

Ting and Tan (17) reviewed briefly the pattern of suicide in Singapore based on postmortem reports during the ten-year period 1955–1964. They observed the effects of economic and social changes on the Indian suicide rate and the inability of certain seasonal and cultural (festive) occasions to influence the Chinese suicide rate.

Hassan and Tan (9), researching suicide files from the coroners' courts in 1968–69, concluded that suicide was related to certain critical life cycles and to areas of residence in Singapore. They also discovered that the highest suicide rates in Singapore were recorded during the Japanese occupation. The highest rates were found in the urban Housing and Development Board (HDB) Estates (high-rise apartment communities), whereas rural areas had the lowest rates. Methods of committing suicide were often related to the area of residence of the suicidal person; for example, high-rise occupants would jump from the buildings. Hassan and Tan also found that certain methods of committing suicide were preferred by certain ethnic groups.

According to the same study, unemployed and retired persons had the highest incidence of suicide, whereas unemployed persons who were looking for work had a very low rate. Among workers in service occupations, industry, and crafts, those engaged in production and processing activities had the highest incidence of suicide. Agricultural, fishery, and forestry workers had the lowest rates. Young and middle-aged persons committed suicide by jumping or taking poison; older persons hanged themselves.

Chia and Tsoi (6), investigating 382 cases of suicide in the period 1969–1971, discovered that, in spite of rapid social, economic, and environmental changes, the rate of suicide in Singapore had not increased; rather, it fluctuated around an annual rate of 9 per 100,000 population. They found that the methods used to commit suicide had changed in frequency. The highest rate was found among those living in the slums of Singapore and not (as they had believed) in the high-rise HDB flats. Mental illness, physical illness, social problems, and troubling interpersonal relationships were the major precipitating factors for suicide in Singapore.

Tsoi and Chia (19) conducted a retrospective study of 112 cases of suicide by persons who had a past record of being admitted to Woodbridge Hospital, the only mental hospital in Singapore. The control in this study consisted of cases admitted just before and just after the first admission to the hospital of persons who had committed suicide. Only 16 percent of all suicides in Singapore in the period 1969–1972 had such a history. Compared with the random control, the cases examined showed a preponderance of female and Chinese; also, the suicide cases were slightly younger and had had more disturbed and aggressive histories.

Tsoi and Chia's (19) other main findings were:

1.  Seventy-eight percent of the suicide cases were diagnosed as suffering from schizophrenia. Of these, 65 percent had been afflicted with the illness for less than five years; 52 percent committed suicide within three months of being discharged from the hospital.
2.  Compared with all suicides in Singapore, there was a notable increase in suicide by drowning and by overdosage of drugs among schizophrenic patients.
3.  The percentage of suicides among Malays who suffered from severe mental illness was found to be the lowest of all ethnic groups. Apparently culture, religious beliefs, and value systems strongly influenced the rate of suicide among mentally ill persons.

I conducted the first and only prospective study of suicide in Singapore (3). Of a total of 1,873 patients registered and treated in my psychiatric practice in 1968–1976, twenty-five were found to have committed suicide. Of these, fourteen suffered from schizophrenia and eleven from depressive illness. The suicide risk of all the patients under different categories was noted and, when possible, was calculated. It was concluded that a schizophrenic patient who has attempted suicide carries the highest suicide risk.

Chia and Tsoi (8) studied 266 suicide letters collected over a period of eight years (1969—1976). Of the writers, 230 were Chinese, 25 were Indians, 4 were Malays, and 7 were from other ethnic groups residing in Singapore. In the study of completed suicides few sources of data are available, and suicide letters are one of them. A critical researcher, however, may question the reliability and the validity of such residual data. In the 1979 study we tried to answer some of the many questions that might be posed. We felt that what had been written in the letters reflected the genuine feelings, reasons, and motives of the suicide victims. A study of suicide letters helps us to understand the mental state of the suicide victims prior to their acts, and therefore it is a prerequisite to the study of suicidal behavior.

There are many reasons for a suicide victim to write a final letter. From our study (8) we noted the following: (1) an obligation to explain, however painfully, to close relatives why he or she had to commit suicide; (2) a desire to alleviate the shock that the suicide might cause to the closest relatives; (3) concern for the victim's body (instructions were given to relatives about disposition of the body after death); (4) deep concern for the loved ones left behind (instructions on how to care for them were included); (5) the desire to punish the person or persons the victim held responsible for his or her death; (6) as a final will; (7) a wish to exculpate others who might be blamed for the suicide; and (8) an appeal for help and a farewell note.

In my study (4) of 137 suicides of persons under 20 years of age in Singapore in the period 1969—1976, I found only one case of suicide of a child below the age of 10 (7 years old). There was also one suicide at age 11 and one at age 12. From the ages of 13 and 14 on, the number of suicides increased very rapidly. In the study I analyzed the pattern of young suicide cases in Singapore as to sex and ethnic group, as well as suicide letters and the methods of committing suicide. When pertinent, I described case histories. The dominant causes for suicide by young people of both sexes were mental illness, physical illness, social problems, and interpersonal problems. For females, interpersonal problems dominated; for males, mental illness. I concluded from this study of youthful suicides that adolescents, feeling alienated from everybody, believed they had no choice and that death was necessary. The tragedy is that parents, who should be closest to their teenage children, often do not understand them and thus cannot help them or prevent suicide.

I also made a study (5) of suicide by the elderly in Singapore, based on data from all coroners' case files for 1969—1976 and on a psychological postmortem of all suicides above 60 in 1974 (39 males and 18 females). Demographic data on suicides among the elderly, the methods used, and the causative factors associated with the suicides were recorded, analyzed, and discussed. The reactions of surviving relatives were also investigated. The unique features of suicides by the aged in Singapore were noted and explained.

Compared with Hong Kong and Japan, Singapore has an extremely high rate of suicide among elderly males. One reason for the disparity may be the migrant population in Singapore. This problem has long been in existence, but only recently has it been recognized. It is noteworthy, however, that the rapid social and environmental changes recently taking place in Singapore have not exacerbated the problem and have not increased the suicide rates.

In Singapore the suicide risk is high for elderly males, single or widowed, who have no close relatives, who live alone in temporary or unsatisfactory abodes, who are retired or unemployed, and who have chronic or incurable physical illnesses and are suffering from clinical depression. For widowed females who are physically or mentally ill, conflicts with their children or their children's spouses or rejection by immediate relatives of the family are important factors in causing suicide. Other factors contributing to or associated with suicides of elderly people in Singapore are poverty, loneliness, bereavement, and opium addiction.

These earlier studies show that in Singapore the suicide rates were highest among the Chinese, followed by the Indian ethnic group; the lowest rate was among the Malays. Murphy (10) indicates that the Indians were most prone to suicide—a tendency perhaps related to their immigrant status—but the rate among Indians has recently declined to a secondary position. Males suicided more than females, and within the Indian group there was a very high rate for young females. High rates for suicide were found in the 20–29 age group, decreasing in middle age and rising again at age 50 and above (table 4-1). Elderly males constituted a high-risk group, particularly if they lacked family connections and were in poor physical or economic circumstances. Under the same conditions elderly females were also suicide risks. The major causes of suicide by the young were physical or psychiatric illness, interpersonal problems, and social difficulties. Females were most affected by family and interpersonal problems.


## PREVIOUS STUDIES ON
## ATTEMPTED SUICIDE

The figures on attempted suicide are so scanty that few countries could ever carry out a survey to estimate the total number of suicidal attempts in any one year. Unlike other countries, however, Singapore is unique in being a small, compact island with a relatively static nonmigratory population, a high standard of medical record keeping, and up-to-date demographic statistics. Moreover, as attempted suicide is still a crime, all patients admitted to government hospitals for treatment after attempting suicide must be reported to the police, who keep records of almost all the cases.

The first survey of attempted suicide conducted in Singapore (7) includes all cases admitted to both government and private hospitals. In 1974 there were 1,133 cases of attempted suicide and 239 cases of completed suicide, or a ratio of approximately 5:1. Females in the 20–29 age group had the highest number, 207, of attempted suicides. Of the different ethnic groups, the Indian group led the rest with 103; the Malay group was lowest, with 18. Poisoning accounted for 94 percent of the cases of attempted suicide, compared with only 14 percent of the suicide cases. The rate of attempted suicide for HDB residents was 41, compared with 63 for the rest of the island population. Within the period covered by the survey, 2.4 percent made more than one attempt to commit suicide. The overall sex ratio was slightly more than 2 females to 1 male.

Tsoi, in a 1974 survey (18), found that suicide and attempted suicide were characteristic of two distinct but overlapping populations. Suicide was associated with males older than 50 who had injured themselves or suffered from ill health (physical or mental), whereas attempted suicide was associated with young adults, mostly females whose interpersonal relationships were disturbing. The method of suicide was poisoning. The main causes for attempted suicide by females were marital difficulties and domestic disharmony; by males, poverty and mental illness.

Thomas, in a 1959 study of thirty-five cases of attempted suicide among Indian women (16), focuses attention on the background of the Indian family, which led to frequent suicide attempts by young Indian women in Singapore. Thomas found that the vulnerable period was five to ten years after marriage, when the woman found herself unable to cope with the

TABLE 4-1

AVERAGE SUICIDE RATE PER 100,000 POPULATION, BY AGE
GROUP, 1968–1971, IN SINGAPORE

| Age group | Male | Female | Total |
|-----------|------|--------|-------|
| 10–19 | 0.8 | 1.9 | 1.3 |
| 20–29 | 13.1 | 12.2 | 12.6 |
| 30–39 | 10.2 | 7.8 | 9.0 |
| 40–49 | 14.3 | 8.6 | 11.6 |
| 50–59 | 33.8 | 13.1 | 24.0 |
| 60–69 | 37.4 | 20.2 | 30.3 |
| 70 and over | 102.8 | 41.7 | 65.5 |

SOURCE: Coroners' records.

increasing responsibilities and demands of married life. Sometimes personality traits of the individuals were responsible for their predisposition to the suicidal act.

Thomas found that 77 percent of the suicidal Indian women belonged to the lowest social class and that few of them had had any formal education. Three of them suffered from mental subnormality. Some of the other pertinent elements in the background of these Indian females were daily quarrels between parents, physical violence, and ill-treatment.

The girls were usually emotionally and physically immature and unprepared for marriage and motherhood. Many of them had been forced to marry middle-aged or elderly men. Because of their unpreparedness for sex life, the husbands' lack of understanding and tolerance, and sexual incompatibility, physical assaults were common. Pregnancies were too frequent and too many children were born.

The same study (16) also revealed alcoholism as a major factor giving rise to unhappiness and thus to quarrels, physical assaults, and economic instability. Poverty was common, and few facilities were available for recreation. Because of the subordinate position of Indian women, Indian wives never retaliated against their husbands; when conflicts arose which could not be solved, the wife often attempted suicide.

Because of the conditions described above, living accommodations were often unsatisfactory; the lack of privacy meant there was no escaping interfering and gossiping neighbors. Physical assaults and abuses by husbands in the presence of neighbors brought shame to the women and precipitated suicidal attempts in 30 percent of the cases surveyed. The Hindu religion, noncondemnatory of and indifferent to suicidal acts, provided no deterrent to suicide.

## AIMS OF THIS STUDY

In this study I propose to determine the reliability of statistics on suicide in Singapore; to discover the demographic factors, particularly concerning the Chinese, associated with suicide; to point out particular aspects of Singapore suicides; and to discuss psychological postmortem studies of suicide cases.

The reported suicide rates in different countries of the world (*World Health Statistics Annual*, 1975) show wide variation. If the differences are real, an explanation may be sought in terms of varying social, cultural, religious, economic, and other factors. If the rates are understated, it is necessary to ascertain how the excess deaths were classified. The personnel responsible for investigating the circumstances surrounding a death and finally deciding that it was a suicidal death, and the procedures employed in reaching that verdict in Singapore, are also described in this study.

## SUICIDE AMONG THE CHINESE

Singapore is the only country in Southeast Asia whose population has a large Chinese majority (76 percent). Little has been written on suicide among the Chinese residents of Singapore. The last comprehensive study of suicide in Hong Kong was done by Yap in 1958 (21). Teoh's 1974 study of completed suicides (15) concerns Kuala Lumpur in Malaysia. It is based on 152 Chinese suicides from coroners' records in the period 1965–1970 and analyzes only nineteen Chinese suicides by psychological postmortem.

In order to provide more information on Chinese suicide, I break down suicide statistics in terms of sex, age groups, ethnic groups, marital status, housing conditions, mental and physical illness, and types of medical treatment received prior to the suicidal act. Whenever possible, sectors of the population particularly vulnerable to suicide are highlighted: lonely, unwanted, and unsuccessful aged emigrant males; those who are medically seriously ill; and alienated and sensitive young females. I also identify stress factors in modern Singapore society which may have precipitated suicide, such as compulsory national service for male youths, competitive school examinations, and cultural customs and values. And I discuss the psychiatric diagnostic classification of mental illness, the main cause of suicide. Included in this study is a psychological postmortem investigation of one year of suicide cases with a view to understanding in greater depth the sociocultural and behavioral patterns among the suicide population.

The aspects of suicide peculiar to Singapore are (1) the methods of leaping from high-rise buildings and taking methyl salicylates (especially by females); (2) the association of suicide and schizophrenia; (3) the effect of massive resettlement programs and rapid rehousing of displaced people in high-rise flats; (4) the effect of religion and the fatalistic attitude toward life on suicide rates (e.g., the influence of Islam); (5) the murder-suicide pattern and suicide pacts in Singapore; (6) the reactions of immediate relatives to suicide.

## CERTIFICATION OF SUICIDE

In Singapore, under the Registration of Births and Death Act, a death must be registered within three days of its occurrence. Observance of the law is ensured by a provision requiring that a death must be reported before a burial permit can be obtained; if there is any doubt that death resulted from other than natural causes, a coroner's inquiry must be held. Two death certificates are required: the one for burial states the cause of death (e.g., hanging) but not the mode (open, misadventure, suicide, homicide, or natural); the second, issued after the coroner's inquest, is for statistical purposes. Case files of all inquests are kept in the same building where the two coroner's courts are located for a period of about three years; they are then transferred to the Supreme Court building for storage. The resulting centralization of record storage facilitates research into suicide in Singapore.

As in most countries, the ascertainment of suicide in Singapore involves legal validation. If the death is thought to have resulted from other than natural causes, an investigation is conducted by the police who collect evidence from relatives, witnesses, doctors, and other persons concerned. The police also visit the site where the death occurred. The comprehensiveness of the investigation varies according to the investigator's skill, motivation, and resourcefulness; it also depends on the cooperation of those who are interviewed.

The coroner may order a postmortem on the body after conferring with the forensic pathologist. The body is then examined by both officials, and the postmortem, when ordered, is performed by a trained forensic pathologist. Blood samples and stomach contents are analyzed in government laboratories to confirm or exclude the presence of drugs, poisons, or alcohol. Suicide letters written in Chinese or Indian are translated into English for the use of the court. The corner's inquest in Singapore is conducted in English. It is open to the public, including newspaper reporters. The coroner, who is a legally trained full-time officer in government service, serves a term that usually varies from two to three years. He is under the jurisdiction of the attorney general and the High Court. Usually two or three coroners serve in each term.

The inquest is normally held in the coroner's court two to three months after a suspected suicide. Police officers, relatives, and occasionally medical doctors and a forensic pathologist give evidence, and they may be questioned by the coroner or by attorneys who are in attendance. Medical reports and suicide letters may be read. Based on all the evidence presented in court, the coroner at the conclusion gives his verdict, which is made public and may be reported by the press. If information collected is insufficient to enable the coroner to arrive at a clear verdict, an open verdict or a finding that the death is due to undetermined cause may be returned.

In Singapore, the coroner has to be satisfied not only that death is self-inflicted but also that the deceased intended to take his own life. A study of eight years of suicide cases revealed that on no occasion did the High Court order that an inquest be repeated. The study showed, however, that the degree of certainty required before a death is considered a suicide varies from coroner to coroner. The decision may depend on various factors: the individual coroner, legal complications, the family's objections to a suicide verdict, the efficiency of the police officer investigating the case, the reports or evidence given by medical personnel, the amount of evidence that had to be evaluated, and the quality and comprehensiveness of the evidence presented in court.

In a study of all suicides occurring in the years 1969–1976, the factors influencing the coroners to reach a suicide verdict were found to be the following:

1. The deceased left a suicide note stating that he or she had committed suicide or that the intent was to commit suicide.

2. Certain modes of death strongly suggested or definitely indicated that the deceased had committed suicide. Examples were burning oneself with kerosene that one had poured over one's body, hanging, and stabbing or slashing. When death resulted from a railroad mishap, the coroner relied on the evidence of witnesses or of the engineer. If it could be proved to the satisfaction of the coroner that the deceased had deliberately placed himself in the way of an oncoming train or astride the railway tracks, a verdict of suicide was returned. Modes of death giving the coroners difficulty in reaching a verdict were poisoning, drowning, or falling or leaping from a high-rise building.

3. There was a history of past suicidal attempt or attempts.

4. There was a history of disturbed mental condition showing that the deceased was depressed because of distressing or shameful circumstances.

5. The deceased was suffering from severe mental illness such as paranoid schizophrenia, agitated depression, or hypochondriasis.

6. The deceased had a painful, incapacitating, or incurable physical illness.

7. Evidence was presented in medical reports by doctors who had treated the deceased prior to the act, in the forensic pathologist's findings, or in laboratory findings.

8. Evidence was given by close relatives as to whether the deceased had communicated an intent to commit suicide or had made burial preparation days, weeks, or months prior to the act. Had the deceased, for example, repeatedly warned a relative that he wanted to die? Had he given all his possessions away, prepared burial clothes, or the like?

9. Witnesses testified to the death act. The deceased may have been seen by a witness near the scene of the act. Often a witness testified that he saw the deceased climbing onto a chair or coming out on a balcony before jumping or falling. A man seen tying a rope attached to a heavy object around his neck before leaping into the sea would be judged to have committed suicide.

10. At the site of death in cases of drowning the watch, clothes, and other personal possessions of the deceased were so neatly placed that police officers investigating an unnatural death would be immediately alerted to the possibility of murder made to look like suicide.

## RELIABILITY OF OFFICIAL SUICIDE RATES

In assessing the reliability of suicide rates in Singapore, the researcher must first discover what percentage of total deaths were certified by nonqualified personnel and, second, must study the procedures adopted by qualified personnel prior to death certification to determine their reliability.

In Singapore, in 1976, 85 percent of all deaths were certified by medical practitioners and coroners and 15 percent by hospital assistants or police officers. In 1967, 80 percent were certified by medical practitioners and coroners and 20 percent by police officers or hospital assistants. The trend, then, is toward more certifications by qualified personnel.

Postmortems were performed on 56 percent of the deaths certified by coroners. Postmortems followed 93 percent of deaths caused by motor vehicle accidents, 55 percent of deaths by other unnatural causes, and 45 percent of deaths by natural causes. Of deaths by the three methods that make it difficult to ascertain suicidal intention—poisoning, jumping, and drowning—66, 58, and 47 percent, respectively, had postmortems performed. In contrast, only 18 percent of the deaths resulting from hanging or strangulation and suffocation, methods in which suicide is more easily established, were followed by postmortems.

Blood alcohol estimations were done in 18 percent of all cases of death certified by coroners. In 5.4 percent of the cases tested, alcohol was found to be present in the blood. Other laboratory investigations included tests for the presence of barbiturates, insecticides, salicylates, and other drugs or poisons in blood samples or stomach contents.

In 1973, Singapore had 69 cases of deaths in which injury, whether accidentally or purposely inflicted, was undetermined. Detailed study of these cases, based on criteria earlier mentioned, revealed that 11 of them could be reclassified as definite suicides and 10 as probable suicides. If the latter are assumed to have been actual suicides, the total of 21 suicides amounts to 30 percent of all deaths attributed to undetermined causes.

Further study of the files showed that of the cases in which coroners returned a verdict of death by natural causes, 11 could be reclassified as definite suicides and 3 as probable. It is noteworthy that all but one of these cases had had medical diagnoses. Two of the victims left suicide notes. Why, then, had coroners ruled that the deaths were owing to natural causes? They had, it turned out, been influenced in some cases by the reports of forensic pathologists. One such report stated that, although "the external injuries are consistent with the fall," death was owing to "the deceased's condition." The death in question was that of a sixteen-year-old Chinese who, suffering from nephrotic syndrome, had leaped from a bathroom window, landing first on a concrete roof and then on the ground. The forensic pathologist reported that "the fracture is a minor one. It would not have contributed to his death. The significant factor is cardiorespiratory failure." A verdict of death by natural cause was therefore recorded. In another questionable case, a sixty-five-year-old Chinese suffering from pulmonary tuberculosis attempted suicide by cutting his throat. He died eight days later from bronchopneumonia. The pathologist's report reads: "The previous neck wound was almost healed before his death. . . . [It] plays a rather insignificant role in his death." Again the verdict was "death by natural cause." Of all the cases in which a misadventure verdict was returned, only one could be reclassified as definite suicide and one as probable suicide.

These data are summarized in table 4-2, which shows that 23 of the deaths attributed by coroners to other causes could be added to the suicide category and that 14 of them could be considered as probable suicides. This reclassification would increase the number of suicides by 37, if probable suicides are included. The total official number of suicides in Singapore for the year 1973 was 240. If these 37 cases had been ruled as suicides, the number for that year would have increased by 15.4 percent. The official annual rate per 100,000 population would have increased from 11.3 to 13.0.

The "undetermined" category of cause of death was first introduced into Singapore official statistics in 1969. It is recorded as "injury undetermined whether accidentally or purposely inflicted." The number of probable suicides within this category is, however, not stated in official statistics. Table 4-3 shows the crude rates of death by accident and violence in the period 1969–1977. The death rates by motor vehicle accident and industrial accident showed a decreasing trend. The homicide death rate in Singapore fluctuated around an annual figure of 1.7 per 100,000 popula-

TABLE 4-2

RECLASSIFICATION OF CAUSE OF DEATH AS DEFINITE OR PROBABLE
SUICIDE IN CASES SEEN BY CORONERS IN SINGAPORE IN 1973

| Cause of death | Number of cases reclassified | |
|---|---|---|
| | Definite suicide | Probable suicide |
| Undetermined | 11 | 10 |
| Natural | 11 | 3 |
| Misadventure | 1 | 1 |
| Total | 23 | 14 |

## Table 4-3
### Rates of Death by Accident and Violence per 100,000 in Singapore, 1969–1977

| Cause of death | 1969 | 1970 | 1971 | 1972 | 1973 | 1974 | 1975 | 1976 | 1977 |
|---|---|---|---|---|---|---|---|---|---|
| Suicide | 9.2 | 8.9 | 10.9 | 10.9 | 11.0 | 10.3 | 11.2 | 11.3 | 9.7 |
| Undetermined | 1.7 | 2.3 | 3.5 | 3.8 | 3.2 | 2.8 | 5.4 | 4.4 | 6.5 |
| Homicide | 1.6 | 1.7 | 2.0 | 2.4 | 1.7 | 2.2 | 1.2 | 1.4 | 1.6 |
| Justifiable homicide | 0.1 | 0.1 | 0.2 | 0.2 | 0.6 | 0.1 | 0.7 | 0.3 | 0.2 |
| Motor vehicle accident | 14.4 | 12.9 | 16.1 | 17.2 | 17.0 | 12.7 | 11.3 | 11.3 | 11.4 |
| Other transport accident | 1.8 | 1.5 | 1.3 | 1.4 | 1.4 | 1.8 | 1.2 | 1.6 | 1.7 |
| Industrial accident | 3.1 | 3.0 | 2.7 | 3.9 | 2.7 | 2.8 | 2.0 | 1.6 | 1.8 |
| All other accidents | 8.5 | 9.9 | 9.3 | 7.5 | 8.6 | 7.7 | 6.5 | 6.5 | 6.9 |

Source: Coroner's office, Singapore.

tion. The suicide rates for 1975 and 1976 were the highest in recent years; in the same years the death rate for undetermined causes was also very high. Thus the increase in the crude suicide rate in recent years is genuine. In 1977, however, the crude suicide rate suddenly dropped, but this sharp decline was accompanied by a marked increase in the undetermined rate. The combined suicide and undetermined rates for the years 1975, 1976, and 1977 were, respectively, 16.6, 15.7, and 16.2, whereas the crude suicide rates were 11.2, 11.3, and 9.7. These figures mean that coroners certified more cases of unnatural death in 1977 in the undetermined category. As noted above, many of the deaths in this group can easily be considered as suicides. Therefore the decrease in the official suicide rate in 1977 is probably not genuine.

## INVESTIGATIVE METHODS

Suicide is an uncommon event. In Singapore there are 200 to 250 suicides a year. For a study of the pattern of those suicides in the period 1969–1976, the major sources of data were (1) files of all inquests on suicide cases kept in the coroner's courts, and (2) psychological postmortems I personally conducted on all cases of suicide in the period of January 1974 to March 1975.

### Coroners' Files

From a pilot study of 100 randomly chosen coroners' records of deaths in the years 1969–1976 on which the verdict of suicide was recorded, a preliminary format giving all the pertinent data from the files was set up. Each file contains all the records and reports presented at the open court inquest held by the coroner. The data include the evidence and reports of the police inspector investigating the case and the evidence of witnesses as recorded by the coroner. The witnesses usually were close relatives of the deceased or persons closely associated with the deceased at the time of the suicide, but occasionally they were colleagues, army officers, hospital nurses, boyfriends or girl friends, and others. At times the files contained the evidence of expert witnesses, such as the doctor or psychiatrist who had attended the suicidal person, a forensic pathologist, and on rare occasions a chemist or an engineer. The files might also include medical or laboratory and postmortem reports, suicide letters and personal diaries, the coroner's summary of the case, and his reasons for handing down a verdict of suicide.

After reading and summarizing all the case files for the years 1969–1976, I recorded the data on a coroner's case files form. Permission had been obtained to use a room in the building where the two coroner's courts were situated and where the case files were stored temporarily. Usually the inquest on a suicide took place about one to three months after the death. To test the reliability of the data I spent many hours collecting data, and to make sure that all cases of suicide in the period 1969–1976 were covered, I studied all coroners' case files for the year 1973, where the verdict recorded was approximate or could be presumed to be suicide: open verdict, misadventure, homicide, natural cause and therefore no inquest. The coroners collaborated very closely with the forensic pathologist before coming to any decision on certification of natural death. From my intensive study I concluded that the number of suicides had been underestimated by 15.4 percent.

The psychiatric diagnostic reliability of the causes of suicide recorded by the coroner was tested by having every tenth case (i.e., 128 cases) independently studied by a psychiatrist colleague. Use of this system placed the reliability of psychiatric diagnostic correlation at nine out of ten cases. Furthermore, all cases of suicide by persons whose psychiatric history had been recorded were thoroughly investigated by correlating that history with clinical notes (whenever possible) at hospitals and medical clinics and by medical attendants.

Psychological Postmortem Investigation

Visits to the homes of all the suicide victims for the year 1974 were made by myself and an assistant within four weeks of the act. We established the approach to be used by making preliminary visits to ten of the homes and asking the respondents unstructured and spontaneous questions. The psychological postmortem form we used contained both structured and unstructured questions. Structured questions were asked first to obtain the personal data essential for the research, such as marital status, economic status, past psychiatric and medical history, and family history. Only after sufficient rapport had been established with the respondent or respondents did we go on to more searching and sensitive inquiries.

The questionnaire was drafted in English, but the questions could be asked in either Chinese, English, or Malay, depending on the language or dialect of the respondent. It is impossible to claim that there was no interview bias, especially when the questions were addressed to relatives on the suicide of a loved one. It was also difficult to adopt a critical, neutral, and scientific attitude in such an interview, for tact and empathy were essential to completion of the interview. Often I had to spend half the time in supportive therapy, trying to ease the grief felt by relatives in their bereavement.

The fieldwork was done between January 1974 and April 1975. I usually made my visits in the evening or on a weekend, when relatives would be home from work. The timing was also planned to accommodate housewives, many of whom were not permitted by their husbands to reveal painful and taboo information about a shameful family crisis. I was invariably accompanied by a lady assistant, as the presence of a female enhanced the chances of an entry and an interview and lessened the strain on the respondent, especially when the latter was a woman. We often took turns interviewing the relatives. One of us would watch the reactions (verbal and nonverbal) of the interviewees and would take notes on what transpired. We correlated our observations immediately after each interview in order to give greater objectivity to the technique of psychological postmortem.

A household that could not be contacted after three attempts was not approached again. On average, the interviews lasted about an hour. Some went on for two hours; a few took only ten minutes. No appointment was made prior to a visit to avoid the risk of rejection. An interview might be refused because an angry and guilty husband had completely withdrawn from society and would not accept visits from anyone; because a protective relative said that the parents of the deceased were very ill and could see no one or that they did not know that the deceased had committed suicide, having been told that the victim had been killed in an accident, for example; or because the members of the family refused to be reminded of the deceased's unnatural death by talking about so painful a subject.

In spite of all our assurances of confidentiality and our emphasis on the academic nature of the study, many respondents were initially suspicious of us and guarded in answering questions. Some were apprehensive that we would report them to the authorities. The majority of the respondents, however, were frank and cooperative, once they became convinced of the legitimacy of our inquiry. We observed that Malays and Indians rather than the Chinese, and that those living in rural rather than nonrural (especially the HDB) areas, were more friendly and easier to inteview.

Among other problems we encountered during the course of the project was the difficulty of finding homes in rural areas. Very often the numbering of residences was not in sequential order, and at times the assistance of mailmen in the various postal districts had to be requested. A car could not be used on some of the roads leading to rural homes, and we had to walk to reach our destination. On a few occasions, especially in the evening, we were chased by dogs. Sometimes, of course, we found that the houses were locked and the occupants were not at home. Four families had moved a few days or months after the suicides. Three of the houses we tried to visit had been demolished.

After all the visits for a day had been concluded, we checked each completed form carefully in order to ensure that all the questions had been properly answered. Some revisits had to be made because certain data had been omitted. When the interview stage was completed, the data were coded and summaries of the cases were recorded on paramount cards.

## SALIENT FINDINGS OF THE STUDY

### Incidence of Suicide in Singapore

In the period 1894–1977, the crude suicide rate in Singapore reached its peak in 1936–1940, just prior to the Japanese occupation of Singapore. Over the years, the annual rate averaged about 10 per 100,000 population. Suicide ranks as the eighth most common cause of death in Singapore. In 1977, 1.9 percent of both male and female deaths were suicides.

### Age and Sex

Suicide rates for different countries must be compared with caution because of the different methods of collecting suicide data. I believe, however, that comparison of the Singapore rates with those of Hong Kong and Japan has some validity. The unusual findings for Singapore were the very high rate of male suicides compared with female suicides in the 65–74 age group and the reverse situation in the 25–34 age group (table 4-4). In Singapore the annual suicide rate for males in the 24–34 group was 10.9 per 100,000 population, whereas it was 13.3 for females.

### Marital Status

A psychological postmortem study of suicide is both essential and rewarding because it not only helps us to understand the psychodynamics of suicide but it gives us a more accurate picture of what suicide statistics really mean. For example, we found that the data on the marital status of

TABLE 4-4
SUICIDE RATES IN 1972 IN SINGAPORE, HONG KONG, AND JAPAN
PER 10,000 POPULATION, BY AGE GROUP AND SEX

| Age group | Singapore | | Hong Kong | | Japan | |
|---|---|---|---|---|---|---|
| | Male | Female | Male | Female | Male | Female |
| 5–14 | — | 0.7 | — | 0.6 | 0.8 | 0.3 |
| 15–24 | 8.0 | 7.9 | 6.8 | 4.8 | 18.5 | 12.4 |
| 25–34 | 10.9 | 13.3 | 25.7 | 13.2 | 22.0 | 14.0 |
| 35–44 | 12.6 | 4.5 | 19.0 | 10.7 | 20.6 | 11.9 |
| 45–54 | 33.7 | 9.5 | 25.7 | 19.0 | 23.5 | 15.0 |
| 55–64 | 58.4 | 7.4 | 32.8 | 17.8 | 33.1 | 23.5 |
| 65–74 | 132.1 | 40.5 | 52.1 | 21.1 | 52.8 | 42.5 |
| 75 and over | 83.2 | 79.9 | 42.0 | 75.1 | 83.4 | 70.0 |

SOURCES: Coroner's Office, Singapore; government offices, Hong Kong and Japan.

suicides as recorded in the coroner's case files were inaccurate, especially for the elderly. The coroner's clerks routinely recorded the marital status of suicide victims as stated on their identity cards. In practice, however, elderly men and women of Singapore, when widowed, seldom bother to have their marital status corrected on the cards. From the psychological postmortem survey, we discovered that many of these elderly suicide cases, especially the women, had to be reclassified in the widowed rather than in the married category. Clearly reports based only on data collected from the coroner's case files may be unreliable.

Table 4-5 presents our findings in the suicide survey. In summary, we found that for females the highest suicide rate, 95 per 100,000 population per year, occurred among divorced women. For both sexes, the rates for the widowed were high: 76.3 for males and 23.4 for females. As to be expected, the suicide rates for single males in all age groups were much higher than those for married men. For females in the 20—24 age group, however, the rate for those who were married was higher than the rate for those who were single. For the young female, presumably, marriage does not bring immunity to suicidal tendencies; it may instead precipitate or contribute to the suicide.

TABLE 4-5

SUICIDE RATES PER 100,000 POPULATION IN SINGAPORE IN 1974
BY MARITAL STATUS, AGE GROUP, AND SEX

| Age group | Single | Married | Widowed | Divorced |
|---|---|---|---|---|
| Male | | | | |
| 10—14 | 0.7 | — | — | — |
| 15—19 | 2.7 | — | — | — |
| 20—24 | 11.7 | — | — | — |
| 25—44 | 44.2 | 8.3 | — | — |
| 45—59 | 117.7 | 12.5 | — | — |
| 60 and over | 514.9 | 34.2 | 124.5 | — |
| All ages | 12.8 | 12.9 | 76.3 | — |
| Female | | | | |
| 10—14 | 1.4 | — | — | — |
| 15—19 | 6.3 | — | — | — |
| 20—24 | 20.5 | 27.2 | — | — |
| 25—44 | 12.6 | 6.6 | 18.1 | 162.5 |
| 45—59 | 60.6 | 18.1 | — | — |
| 60 and over | 23.1 | 9.5 | 34.4 | — |
| All ages | 8.6 | 11.2 | 23.4 | 95.0 |

SOURCE: Psychological postmortem study.

### Causes of Suicide

The main causes of suicide for both sexes were mental illness (29 percent), physical illness (26 percent), interpersonal problems (23 percent), economic and employment problems (13 percent), social problems (6 percent), and chronic alcoholism and opium addiction (2 percent). Interpersonal problems were more important for women than for men in leading to suicide. For the aged male suicide, physical illness was a significant and frequent cause of self-destruction.

### Occupational Status

As to be expected, the highest suicide rates for both sexes were among the unemployed (mainly the chronically unemployed). For unemployed males the rate was 340; for females, 120. Of the economically active, the highest suicide rate for males was 17 among those occupied in sales work; for females, it was 31 among those occupied in various service categories.

### Place of Birth

Through this study we found that 87 percent of male and 100 percent of female suicides above the age of 60 were foreign-born. These figures, however, bear comparison with those for the general population of Singapore: 85 percent of males and 81 percent of females over 60 were foreign born.

### Ethnic Groups

Among ethnic groups, Malays had the lowest suicide rate and Indians had the highest, followed by the Chinese (table 4-6). Besides the markedly different rates, the three main ethnic groups in Singapore also varied in methods adopted, occupational status, major causative factors, frequency of suicide communications, and prevalence of alcoholism and opium addictions among the suicide population.

### Housing

Because of rapid and massive urbanization and resettlement, the housing pattern in Singapore drastically changed in the five-year period 1970–1974. There was a corresponding rise in the suicide rate as it related to living conditions. In 1974, 25 percent of all suicides in Singapore were of persons living in unsatisfactory housing. In Singapore the commonest method of committing suicide is leaping from high-rise flats—51 percent of the total number. Nowhere else in the world is this method so frequently used.

### Suicide Communication

Sixty-one percent of male suicides and 72 percent of female suicides communicated their intent to their immediate relatives by verbal remarks,

TABLE 4-6
SUICIDE RATES PER 100,000 POPULATION IN SINGAPORE IN 1969–1976
BY ETHNIC GROUP, AGE GROUP, AND SEX

| Age group | Chinese | | Indians | | Malays | |
|---|---|---|---|---|---|---|
| | Male | Female | Male | Female | Male | Female |
| 5–9 | 0.1 | – | – | – | – | – |
| 10–14 | 0.5 | 0.6 | – | 1.5 | 0.6 | – |
| 15–19 | 4.9 | 7.2 | 17.7 | 15.6 | 3.4 | – |
| 20–29 | 14.0 | 15.5 | 15.6 | 19.4 | 4.3 | 2.1 |
| 30–39 | 15.1 | 12.3 | 8.6 | 24.3 | 1.7 | 0.8 |
| 40–49 | 14.4 | 9.3 | 19.2 | 13.6 | 0.9 | 3.1 |
| 50–59 | 30.6 | 15.4 | 28.9 | 16.8 | 4.2 | 3.8 |
| 60–69 | 62.4 | 26.1 | 36.4 | 29.0 | – | – |
| 70 and over | 136.1 | 57.8 | 112.9 | – | – | 10.0 |
| All ages | 13.9 | 10.3 | 15.4 | 11.4 | 1.8 | 1.0 |

SOURCE: Coroner's Office, Singapore.

presuicidal acts, suicidal attempts, and suicide letters. The analysis of suicide letters not only reveals the reasons for the suicide but also gives the suicidologist an idea of the presuicide mental state of the victims.

### Physical and Mental Illness

Thirty-four percent of all suicides in Singapore suffered from severe physical illness, and they more frequently used lethal methods to commit suicide. Twenty-two percent of the total male suicides and 25 percent of the total female suicides were suffering from severe mental illness. Schizophrenia, claiming 21 percent of deaths by suicide, was the most common disorder. Of all suicides, 17 percent had in the past been admitted to a mental hospital in Singapore. The survey also revealed that 74 percent of all suicides had received medical or some other kind of care prior to the final act. In spite of treatment received, they still committed suicide.

### Suicide-Murder Pacts

In the series of cases studied, six were infanticide-suicides and four were murder-suicides (three involving lovers). In Singapore, since 1962, there were altogether nine suicide pacts; in 1977 the island experienced its first case of family suicide.

### Reactions of Relatives to Suicide

From three months to a year after a suicide, the reactions of immediate relatives were still intense. In general, Singapore residents see suicide as a shameful, regrettable, pitiful, weak-willed, heartless, or foolish act.

## CONCLUSION

Suicide may be looked upon as the last stage in self-destructive behavior and as a factor that measures social pressure and tension in the community. It may also be considered a useful measure of man's mental distress and physical suffering, as well as of his capacity to tolerate the vicissitudes of life. Suicide is colored by man's attitude toward death and life.

Suicide may be viewed in at least two ways: (1) as a distinct entity in itself, and (2) as a possible manifestation of an underlying disorder. The second view must be adopted if one hopes to be successful in the implementation of any prediction scale or prevention procedure. What this view amounts to is the assumption that suicide in schizophrenia may differ from suicide in other pathologies. Within the given disorder we may perhaps be able to identify the factors that make suicide unique. But to search for the unifying and unique quality in a schizophrenic, a depressive, a psychopathic, an old man dying from an incurable illness, or an unrequited lover—all of whom had committed suicide—may be an impossible task.

Many efforts have been made over the years to develop theoretical approaches to the study of suicide. These are mainly the sociological and the psychological approaches, or a combination of the two. Although both Durkheim's and Freud's theoretical concepts must be regarded as major contributions to the problem of understanding suicide, neither approach is adequate in itself. To understand what motivates suicide one must consider medical, psychological, sociological, and cultural as well as other factors. Values that are important in life, one's attitude to life and death, reasons for dying or for living, and the threshold of suffering (physical and mental) vary not only with individuals but also with different age groups and sexes within a culture and with the culture itself. Thus, in the study of suicide in a particular country, the understanding of cultural, social, economic, and medical backgrounds is most essential. Singapore's unique background of multiracial, multicultural, and multireligious society offers an unusual opportunity to study the influence of such factors on suicide rates and patterns.

As noted earlier, the study of suicide in Singapore is mainly a study of Chinese suicide. The Chinese in Singapore are economically the most prosperous and dominant. For the Chinese, the fear of facing business failure, acquisition of their properties by the government, swindling charges, and failure to gain permission to commence business could all be contributing factors to suicide. Other cultural problems that might lead to suicide among the Chinese are the survival of an eldest son by an aging mother, the inability of Chinese women to bear children to their lovers (married), and the inability of the old and sick to return to China for retirement or treatment. For young people, the difficulty of adapting to life in the army is a growing problem. The Chinese in Singapore have committed suicide for many psychosocial reasons, including marital problems, quarrels, being reprimanded, love problems, and employment and financial difficulties.

Many of the suicide letters written by the Chinese reflect their belief in an afterlife. In such communications they promise to help, or to repay their debts to, their loved ones in the next world. The letters show that filial piety still exists among Chinese youngsters in Singapore. All the opium addicts in Singapore who committed suicide were Chinese, and 94 percent of them were above the age of 44.

Indian females are in general more subordinate to their males than are those of other races. Both as daughters and later as wives they have little freedom to plan their own lives. According to Chia and Tsoi (7), the highest rate of attempted suicide in Singapore is found among young Indian females. In our survey we discovered that they also have the highest rate of taking their young ones with them to their deaths.

Indian men coming to Singapore tend to leave their families at home and to return to India for visits whenever finances permit. Financial difficulties and concern for immediate relatives in India sometimes lead these men to commit suicide. As chronic alcoholism is prevalent among Indians of the lower social classes, it is not surprising that the highest percentage of people so afflicted who committed suicide in Singapore were Indians (8 percent of the total suicides for both sexes).

The Malays in Singapore have the lowest suicide rates. The percentage of Malays who committed suicide because of severe physical illness is found to be the lowest. This rating is understandable because the Malays, as Muslims, look upon suicide as a cardinal sin. To a faithful Muslim life on earth is but a preparation for a better life to come and suicide will deprive him of his passage to Allah. Religion helps the aged Malay to tolerate the pains and hardship of physical illness and prevents him from seeking an easy escape from suffering. In severe mental illness, however, when logical thought has been impaired and severe emotional disturbance exists, this conviction may be overcome. The Malay, in fact, is more fatalistic about life than any of the other races. Their *tida-apa* attitude and the religious teachings they receive combine to produce a less aggressive approach to materialistic pursuits. For example, no Malay committed suicide because of financial difficulties or failure in examinations. Divorce is also more readily accepted by the Malay community. The relative ease of obtaining a divorce, the attitude of Malay women toward marriage, and the strong emotional and economic support they receive from their own kin when divorced explain why no Malay woman commits suicide because of marital problems. Malays do, however, commit suicide because of love problems.

In Singapore the suicide rates for young women are on the rise. Interpersonal problems, especially connected with marriage and love, quarrels, and reprimands, have contributed to the increase. In general, Indian and Chinese women in Singapore are still subordinate to their men; they do not possess complete freedom to organize their lives. Although their role is now changing, an increase in freedom during the transition period may in fact create rather than diminish conflicts for them. Other important factors responsible for the young female suicide are sensitivity, alienation, the generation gap, and the lack of personality traits that would give them strength to solve their emotional conflicts. As Chia (2) has shown, such individuals need to discover a larger number of alternatives in solving problems. In Singapore, marriage for young females is definitely not a protection against suicide; instead, it may precipitate suicide. Females were also found to be most prone to suicide during premenstrual and menstrual periods.

Of the three Asian countries—Singapore, Hong Kong, and Japan—Singapore is the only one where suicide among persons over 65 years of age ranks among the ten leading causes of death. The problem of aged suicides in Singapore is again mainly a Chinese problem. Elderly Chinese with families in Singapore are proud and authoritative. The shame of being old and useless and of becoming a burden on their families, or of seeing their wives working to support their families, was a contributing cause of suicide. Unsuccessful emigrants, alone and without a family, burdened with poverty and ill health, incapacitated with no future in sight, were lost in a harsh world where life had little meaning.

Fortunately, suicide of the very young is rare in Singapore, for of all suicide cases, the most tragic is that of the young. The impact of such a premature death on the parents is severe, and the sorrow is still felt even after many years have passed. Often the parents of young people who commit suicide cannot understand their children's emotional confusion, and so they do not take suicide hints seriously. They do not realize that the young person is mentally ill and needs help and treatment, and they do not support their child during emotional crises. Since they are alienated from their young, they can in no way act to prevent the suicide.

Suicide rates in Singapore have been high and on the rise for the past few years. The possible reasons for the increase are economic recession, rapid and massive resettlement programs, easy availability and increased knowledge of both lethal and passive methods of suicide, and increasing use of insecticides and methyl salicylates.

In Singapore, the most common form of mental illness causing suicide is schizophrenia, the most severe, chronic, and incapacitating mental disorder. Patients unable to tolerate the mental symptoms of schizophrenia or to function adequately even with support from their families, who do not respond satisfactorily to treatment, and who suffer from secondary depression and severe anxiety are likely to commit suicide (19, 20).

Thirty-four percent of the suicides in Singapore were found to suffer from severe physical illness that caused acute or chronic pain and discomfort and led to difficulty in breathing or severe incapacitation. When illness was incurable and worsened in spite of treatment it generated in the victim a feeling of helplessness and hopelessness, leading to suicide.

According to the *Encyclopaedia Britannica* (12), suicide is a complex behavioral problem: "Anyone who states that there are easy answers to these complicated human issues simply does not understand the nature of men. . . . Sometimes especially, the person who does so knows least about his own complicated motives for self-destruction." Suicide—the terminal act—is thus the result of a complicated psychological conflict within the individual. It occurs when the individual (1) is unable to reconcile his own needs and desires with reality; (2) is unable to accept and to adapt to circumstances seen as intolerable in the eyes of the individual; (3) believes in the "purposeless" and feels the weariness of living and the unfairness of society; (4) believes that the life to come in the hereafter is less painful or even that it will be blissful. Suicide is a "last happy escape"; (5) seeks revenge and believes that by dying he will accomplish what he has failed to achieve while alive; (6) refuses to be a burden to his family and feels that it is more honorable to die; (7) suffers conflicts and emotional ambivalence and thinks in an all-or-nothing fashion so that he can no longer, without external help, find a better solution to his difficulties than suicide; (8) feels a driving necessity for relief from tension when his life situation has become too difficult and too stressful to bear; or (9) believes that there is no hope, as in cases of incurable disease.

Finally, it is a well-recognized fact that suicidal attempts are meant to elicit a response from others. Suicidal gestures are attempts to improve relationships with other persons rather than expressions of a wish to die. Suicidal attempts or gestures are often cries for help. If, however, such attempts or repeated attempts to communicate distress to others fail, suicide may ensue. In Singapore 13 percent of male suicides and 17 percent of female suicides had made previous attempts to kill themselves. The study of suicidal behavior should therefore include not only completed suicides but attempted suicides. Although statistically those who commit and those who attempt suicide may be considered as two different population groups, in practice such division is artificial. The concept of a continuum of degree of suicidal behavior is more acceptable.

## SUMMARY

The rates of suicide in Singapore average out to about 10 per 100,000 population. Males rates are higher than female. The most striking feature is the high rate for males aged 65 or over among Chinese and Indians, and the low rate among Malays. Aged females suicide at a rate approximately half that of males. A high suicide rate is found in the 20–29 age group and among females in the 20–24 age group, declining through the forties and rising at 50 years and over. Among young married Indian females there is a significant rate. Methods of suicide are jumping from high places (51 percent), drugs, hanging, and stabbing. Causes appear to be physical and psychological illness, interpersonal problems, and financial difficulties. Females were particularly affected by interpersonal problems.

There are approximately five attempted suicides to one completed suicide; females' attempts were twice those of males. Females in the 20–29 age group had the highest rates. Among ethnic groups, Indians made the most suicide attempts. The most frequent method used for attempted suicide was poisoning.

## BIBLIOGRAPHY

1. Chen, A. J. Recent trend of deaths from unnatural causes (accidents, suicide and homicide) in Singapore, 1961–1965. *Singapore Med. J.*, 10, 2 (1969).
2. Chia, B. H. Suicide in Singapore. M.D. thesis, University of Singapore, 1978.
3. Chia, B. H. Prospective study of suicide in Singapore. *Annals Acad. Medicine* (Singapore). Forthcoming.
4. Chia, B. H. Suicide of the young in Singapore. *Annals Acad. Medicine* (Singapore). Forthcoming.
5. Chia, B. H. Suicide of the elderly in Singapore. *Annals Acad. Medicine* (Singapore), 8, 3 (1979).
6. Chia, B. H., and W. F. Tsoi. Suicide in Singapore. *Singapore Med. J.*, 13, 2 (1972).
7. Chia, B. H., and W. F. Tsoi. A statistical study of attempted suicide in Singapore. *Singapore Med. J.*, 15, 4 (1974).
8. Chia, B. H., and W. F. Tsoi. Suicide letters. *Annals Acad. Medicine* (Singapore). Forthcoming.
9. Hassan, R., and K. Tan. Suicide in Singapore: A sociological analysis. *Southeast Asian J. Sociol.*, 3, 1 (1970).
10. Murphy, H. B. M. Mental health in Singapore: Suicide. *Med. J. Malaya*, 9, 1 (1954).
11. Rin, H. Suicide in Taiwan. In N. L. Farberow, ed., *Suicide in Different Cultures*. Baltimore: University Park Press, 1975.
12. Schneidman, E. S. Suicide. In *Encyclopaedia Britannica*, vol. 21 (1973 ed.).
13. Schneidmann, E. S., and N. L. Farberow. Statistical comparisons between committed and attempted suicides. In E. S. Shneidman and N. L. Farberow, eds., *The Cry for Help*. New York: McGraw-Hill, 1961.

14. Stengel, E. *Suicide and Attempted Suicide*. Harmondsworth: Penguin Books, 1969.
15. Teoh, J. E. An analysis of completed suicide by psychological post-mortem. *Annals Acad. Medicine* (Singapore), 3, 2 (1974).
16. Thomas, A. A study of attempted suicide among young Tamil women in Singapore. Undergraduate dissertation, Department of Social Work, University of Singapore, 1959.
17. Ting, S. K., and K. Tan. Post-mortem survey of suicides in Singapore. *Singapore Med. J.*, 10, 4 (1969).
18. Tsoi, W. F. Suicide and attempted suicide with special reference to Singapore. *Annals Acad. Medicine* (Singapore), 3, 2 (1974).
19. Tsoi, W. F., and B. H. Chia. Suicide and mental illness in Singapore. *Singapore Med. J.*, 15, 3 (1974).
20. Virkkunen, M. Suicide in schizophrenia and paranoid psychoses. *Acta Psychiatr. Scandin. Suppl.*, 250 (1974):1–305.
21. Yap, P. M. *Suicide in Hong Kong*. Hong Kong: Hong Kong University Press, 1958.

# PART II. THE SAMARITANS OF SINGAPORE[2]

On December 1, 1969, the Samaritans of Singapore first offered a confidential listening service, befriending, and emergency services to people needing help. The organization patterned its operations on those of Samaritan services in other countries. The statistical material in this section is mostly for 1979, with comparative information for the years 1971 through 1979. The total number of calls for 1979 was 17,975 from 10,000 individuals; there were 526 interviews and 95 emergency calls (suicide attempts). These figures indicate a remarkable increase from 1971, when the number of interviews was 110 and the number of emergency calls was 20.

## INCIDENCE AND TIME OF CALLS

In the year 1978–79, most calls were received in March, April, May, and June (table 4-7). The daily distribution of calls follows a pattern established over several years, with the largest number of calls coming in on Monday; the number decreased steadily throughout the week, except for a slight rise on Friday (table 4-8). Most calls were received during the afternoon, from 12 noon to 4 P.M., and there were more calls from 4 P.M. to 8 A.M. than in the forenoon. Emergency calls were heaviest between 10 P.M. and 8 A.M. (table 4-9).

[2]I deeply appreciate the cooperation of Mrs. Irene Jacob, director of the Samaritans of Singapore, in providing me with the statistics embodied in this part of this chapter.

TABLE 4-7
MONTHLY INCIDENCE OF CALLS TO THE
SAMARITANS OF SINGAPORE, 1978—79

| Year | Month | Percentage of total calls | Year | Month | Percentage of total calls |
|------|-------|---------------------------|------|-------|---------------------------|
| 1978 | July | 7.3 | 1979 | January | 8.2 |
| | August | 7.7 | | February | 7.6 |
| | September | 7.0 | | March | 9.2 |
| | October | 7.4 | | April | 10.5 |
| | November | 8.2 | | May | 9.4 |
| | December | 8.2 | | June | 9.3 |

TABLE 4-8
DAILY INCIDENCE OF CALLS TO THE SAMARITANS
OF SINGAPORE, 1978—79

| Day | Percentage of total calls |
|-----|---------------------------|
| Monday | 16.5 |
| Tuesday | 15.2 |
| Wednesday | 14.7 |
| Thursday | 14.1 |
| Friday | 15.3 |
| Saturday | 13.1 |
| Sunday | 11.1 |

TABLE 4-9
TIME DISTRIBUTION OF CALLS TO THE
SAMARITANS OF SINGAPORE, 1978—79
(In percentages of total calls)

| Time of day | All calls | Emergency calls |
|-------------|-----------|-----------------|
| 8 A.M. to noon | 17.9 | 19.0 |
| Noon to 4 P.M. | 24.6 | 19.0 |
| 4 P.M. to 7 P.M. | 19.3 | 24.0 |
| 7 P.M. to 10 P.M. | 18.6 | 13.0 |
| 10 P.M. to 8 A.M. | 19.6 | 25.0 |

## PROBLEMS OF CLIENTS

The problems of the people who called the Samaritans of Singapore in 1971–1979 were, in order of importance, (1) interpersonal relationship, (2) psychological, (3) sexual, (4) material, and (5) physical. There were shifts in the rankings of these problems over the years, but the leading issue was consistently interpersonal relationships and the least important problem was always the physical one.

## CALLS RECEIVED

### Frequency

Among those who call the Samaritans of Singapore, 40 percent make one call, 50 percent, two to five calls, and 10 percent, more than five calls.

### Ethnic Distribution

Most of the callers are Chinese, a fact that is in accord with the ethnic distribution of the Singapore population (table 4-10). Eurasians and Caucasians account for only small percentages of the calls to the Samaritans.

### Sources

Emergency calls are made by persons contemplating suicide. Table 4-11 shows that such calls from the client and from the police and fire brigades increased over the period 1976–1979.

## VOLUNTEER STAFF

There are 196 volunteers who assist the Samaritans of Singapore in handling the telephone service and taking care of emergency calls. Of that total, 45 percent are in the 20–29 age group, 34 percent, in the 30–39 group, 13 percent, 40–49, and 8 percent 50 and over. Thus a large majority of the

TABLE 4-10

ETHNIC DISTRIBUTION OF CLIENTS OF SAMARITANS OF
SINGAPORE COMPARED WITH ETHNIC DISTRIBUTION OF SINGAPORE POPULATION
(In percentages)

| Client group | Ethnic group | | | | |
| --- | --- | --- | --- | --- | --- |
| | Chinese | Malay | Indian | Eurasian | Caucasian |
| Interview clients | 83.3 | 7.2 | 5.5 | 2.8 | 1.2 |
| Emergency clients | 70.0 | 6.5 | 13.8 | 1.1 | 8.6 |
| Singapore | 76.1 | 15.1 | 6.9 | a | a |

[a]Eurasians and Caucasians together account for 1.9 percent of the Singapore population.

TABLE 4-11
SOURCE OF CALLS TO SAMARITANS OF SINGAPORE
IN 1976-1979

| Source | Year | | | |
|---|---|---|---|---|
| | 1976 | 1977 | 1978 | 1979 |
| Client himself | 10 | 17 | 18 | 37 |
| Police and fire brigades | 16 | 19 | 32 | 37 |
| Neighbors and friends | 10 | 16 | 8 | 15 |
| Family members | 4 | 5 | 4 | 7 |
| Total | 40 | 57 | 62 | 96 |

telephone force are young adults; apparently the group as a whole is younger than in some other Samaritan services. Length of service is evenly split between those who have volunteered for two to six years and those who have been serving for less than two years. The usual time worked is three to four hours a week. The volunteers, who represent a variety of occupations (table 4-12), attend ongoing in-service training classes and the service offers field training for social work students at the University of Singapore.

# PART III. KALYANI K. MEHTA[3]

## INTRODUCTION

In Singapore, as far as I know, four studies on attempted suicide have been made. The first, in 1959, was conducted by Amini Thomas (9) who interviewed thirty-five South Indian women who had attempted suicide and analyzed the factors that motivated them. The second, by Rosy Yeo (11), was a study of twenty-five Chinese patients who attempted suicide between January 1968 and June 1969. The third was by a psychiatrist, W. F. Tsoi (10), who analyzed 192 patients admitted to Thomson Road Hospital in Singapore. These patients were believed to have attempted suicide in the period 1967-1969. The fourth, entitled "A Statistical Study of Attempted Suicides in Singapore," was by B. H. Chia and W. F. Tsoi (2). After conducting a survey of all the recorded attempted suicides in

[3]I am grateful to Mrs. Irene Jacob, director, and to Mrs. Janice Tan, deputy director, of the Samaritans of Singapore for granting me permission to study the files of the organization. My discussions with them proved to be stimulating as well as helpful.

TABLE 4-12
OCCUPATIONS OF VOLUNTEERS SERVING THE SAMARITANS
OF SINGAPORE

| Occupation | Number |
| --- | --- |
| Administrative and management | 24 |
| Clerical and secretarial | 40 |
| Counseling and social work | 17 |
| Educational work | 32 |
| Housewives | 23 |
| Nursing | 5 |
| Professional (medicine, law, engineering, architecture) | 12 |
| Sales and business | 14 |
| Students | 8 |
| Technical work | 16 |
| Uniformed services | 5 |
| Consultants | |
|   Accounting | 2 |
|   Business and management | 2 |
|   Clergymen | 1 |
|   General practitioners | 6 |
|   Gynecologists | 1 |
|   Lawyers | 7 |
|   Psychiatrists | 4 |
|   Psychologists | 1 |
|   Social work officers | 2 |

Singapore in 1971, they concluded that the ratio of attempted suicides to completed suicides in Singapore was 5:1 and that the ratio of females to males was slightly more than 2:1. This latter finding is in contrast with the completed suicide rate in Singapore, which indicates that more males commit suicide than females.

My intention here is to concentrate less on statistics and more on the personal and situational factors associated with attempted suicides. Bearing in mind Gestalt's theory, I view the individual in the context of his or her cultural and socioeconomic background. In order to emphasize the major cultural influences present in Singapore, I describe two case histories.

## CULTURAL INFLUENCES

Since man is a social being, his life and problems are inevitably linked with the society and cultural milieu in which he dwells. Singapore society may be described briefly as highly urbanized, materialistic, competitive, and cosmopolitan. Although the government is trying to build a distinctively

Singaporean culture, that aim has not yet become a reality. The main cultures existing in Singapore today are Chinese, Malay, Indian, and several minor ones, including Jewish and Japanese. Within each of these cultures there are subcultures: for example, Indian culture consists of North Indian and South Indian cultural patterns. In addition, all these Asiatic cultures are being exposed to Western cultural influences.

Several cultural patterns are common to the three main cultures coexisting in Singapore: Chinese, Malay, Indian. Rather than describe them at length, I merely summarize them here.

1. Dating, especially by one couple alone, is not accepted where marriages are still arranged. In some sectors of the society, however, dating is permitted, but only with strict parental supervision in regard to age, race, and religion.

2. Before and during weddings, certain rituals and expenditures are demanded by the bridegroom's party. These give rise to manifold problems, such as the debts incurred by the bride's family and conflicts between bride and groom and their families. Sometimes a couple cannot get married because of these cultural barriers. Parental approval for marriage is still considered important.

3. On the whole, there is opposition to interethnic and interreligious marriages.

4. Promiscuity by males—keeping a mistress or possessing more than one wife by customary rite—is culturally condoned, although modern women today refuse to accept it.

5. Importance and preferential treatment are still accorded to male children.

6. Superstitious beliefs are held and acted upon. For example, a child who is labeled "unlucky" may be given away or ill-treated by its parents. Temple mediums are resorted to in times of crisis. The belief that a person can be "charmed" or cast under "black magic" when he behaves irrationally continues.

7. The demand for filial piety stresses obedience to and respect for parents. Children are expected to accept parental authority rather than look for affection from and dialogue with their elders. These cultural traits widen the generation gap.

8. The system of "fostering out" children is practiced when the mother needs to go out to work and is unable to look after her young ones. By encouraging women to be economically active, the government increases the extent of fostering. Many times a fostered child feels displaced when he returns to his natural parents, and a stressful situation is thus engendered.

In addition to the above, there is a cultural pattern that relates to each of the three main groups living in Singapore. Among the Chinese today, the customary rites of marriage are still considered very important, perhaps more important than the legal rites. It is common to find a couple who are legally married but do not live together because they have not performed the customary rites. The latter may have been delayed for any one of many reasons, for example, lack of financial ability to give a wedding dinner or the absence of an auspicious date. It is easy to imagine the problems that arise when a person is married and not married at the same time. Among Indians in Singapore, arranged marriages are common, and this practice creates stress among young adults who fall in love and wish to get married. When a marriage is arranged, a subservient attitude is expected of the bride and her family. These cultural expectations are directly opposed to the modern educational system, which strives to mold independent, self-directed, self-supporting, responsible citizens. Among Malays in Singapore, the influence of the Islamic religion is all-important. It is a factor binding all Malays together; any Malay who rejects the religion is considered a non-Malay.

All these cultural influences have both positive and negative effects. They help us to understand the background of the individual who is undergoing particular stresses in life, especially if the stresses are related to any strong cultural practice. A person in a "helping profession" must be familiar with the common cultural patterns of the society he lives in before he can really understand and help the client.

## SOURCE OF DATA

This discussion is based on 255 cases of attempted suicide from the records of the Samaritans of Singapore for the period from July 1975 to July 1979. The Samaritans are a voluntary organization formed mainly to help the distressed and those tempted to commit suicide. Besides maintaining a twenty-four-hour telephone service, the Samaritans provide an emergency squad. When a telephone call comes in reporting that someone is attempting or has attempted suicide and that help is needed, the emergency squad is sent out. The cases here discussed are therefore the emergency clients of the Samaritans of Singapore. After the first contact is made with a client, there is a follow-up in the form of interviews, home visits, and telephone calls until the client is deemed to be stable.

## SEX, AGE, ETHNICITY

In the 255 cases of attempted suicide, the sex ratio was nearly two females to one male (table 4-13). The highest percentage of emergency callers fell within the 20–29 age group (table 4-14). These two findings coincide with

TABLE 4-13
SEX OF SUICIDE ATTEMPTERS WHO CALLED THE SAMARITANS
OF SINGAPORE, JULY 1975—JULY 1979
(In percentages)

|  | Year | | | |
| Sex | 1975—76 | 1976—77 | 1977—78 | 1978—79 |
| --- | --- | --- | --- | --- |
| Male | 22.5 | 35.0 | 35.0 | 36.0 |
| Female | 77.5 | 65.0 | 65.0 | 64.0 |

TABLE 4-14
AGE GROUP OF SUICIDE ATTEMPTERS WHO CALLED THE SAMARITANS
OF SINGAPORE, JULY 1975—JULY 1979
(In percentages)

|  | Year | | | |
| Age group | 1975—76 | 1976—77 | 1977—78 | 1978—79 |
| --- | --- | --- | --- | --- |
| Under 20 | 8.0 | 16.0 | 16.0 | 13.0 |
| 20—29 | 43.0 | 38.0 | 39.0 | 50.0 |
| 30—39 | 24.0 | 33.0 | 25.0 | 20.0 |
| 40—49 | 11.0 | 7.0 | 9.0 | 6.0 |
| 50 and over | 14.0 | 6.0 | 11.0 | 11.0 |

those of Chia and Tsoi (10). Although statistics show that the suicide rate in Singapore is highest for those over 50 years of age, the percentage of emergency calls is comparatively low for this age group. There are two probable reasons for this phenomenon: (1) individuals who are absolutely determined to die will not ring for help and the methods they choose for suicide would be highly lethal; (2) a large proportion of middle-aged and aged persons in Singapore are uneducated and thus probably unaware of the existence of social services, such as the Samaritans of Singapore.

The highest percentage of callers in 1975—1979 were Chinese, followed by Indians, Malays, and others (table 4-15). Although the Malay population in Singapore is larger than the Indian population, the rate of attempted suicide is lower among Malays than among Indians. The surveys by Chia and Tsoi (2) and by Tsoi (10) confirm these findings. The low rate for Malays is probably owing to the influence of the Islamic religion and culture, as well as to close kinship ties and a spirit of *bergotong-royong* (help one another) which has survived the competitive urban climate.

TABLE 4-15
ETHNIC GROUP OF SUICIDE ATTEMPTERS WHO CALLED THE
SAMARITANS OF SINGAPORE, JULY 1975 — JULY 1979
(In percentages)

| Ethnic group | Year | | | | Population of Singapore |
| | 1975 – 76 | 1976 – 77 | 1977 – 78 | 1978 – 79 | |
| --- | --- | --- | --- | --- | --- |
| Chinese | 75.0 | 74.5 | 66.1 | 70.0 | 76.1 |
| Malay | 0.0 | 14.5 | 8.5 | 6.5 | 15.1 |
| Indian | 11.0 | 7.4 | 18.6 | 13.8 | 6.9 |
| Other | 14.0 | 3.6 | 6.8 | 9.7 | 1.9 |

## CAUSATIVE FACTORS

The factors leading an individual to attempt suicide may be classified under five headings: (1) relationship problems; (2) psychological problems; (3) material problems; (4) physical problems; and (5) sexual problems. In each year of the period covered by this survey, 1975 – 1979, these factors were reported in the above order, except that in 1976 – 77 sexual factors ranked fourth and physical factors ranked fifth.

### Relationship Problems

The most frequent problems within this category stem from the boy-girl relationship. When the relationship is broken up because of infidelity or desertion by one party, the other party feels deeply hurt and life becomes meaningless. Parental objection to the relationship may also be a cause of unhappiness. One young adult attempted suicide because his girl friend was pregnant and his parents refused to accept her. In Western societies, where parental approval matters less, the boy-girl relationship seldom suffers if such approval is withheld. The youth of Singapore are in a state of transition; modern and conservative ideas, Western and Oriental values, coexist and sometimes create confusion and lead to dilemmas in the minds of youths and young adults. In a few instances lovers have entered into "suicide pacts" as a result of parental disapproval of their relationship.

Second in importance in this category are marital problems. A high percentage of married women are driven to the brink of despair as a result of marital disharmony and domestic difficulties. A common example is that of a 35-year-old married woman whose children have started to go to school and whose husband, after five to seven years of marriage, finds other women more attractive. This situation is often referred to as the "seven-year itch." In a study entitled "Divorce in Singapore," Tai Ching Ling found that the period from the fifth to the ninth year of marriage was the most dangerous, in terms of proneness to divorce, for Singapore couples. In the past the Chinese culture condoned the practice of keeping a mistress, but the modern Chinese woman in Singapore is not likely to accept such infidelity. Another common cause of stress is marriage of a "liberated" Asian woman to a conservative husband who believes that a woman's place is in the home and that he, as lord and master, is entitled to treat her in whatever way he pleases, even to assaulting her. The wife may have no one to turn to, no one who understands or cares about her. She may have young dependent children; she may also encounter demanding, bossy parents-in-law. Among Asians, who still strongly adhere to the idea of "not washing your dirty linen in public," Indian women especially refrain from discussing their domestic problems with others. When the tension mounts on all sides, and the woman has no outlet for ventilating her problems, she may decide to take her life. On several occasions the husband has been known to taunt his wife by saying "Go and die," little knowing that she will really do it.

Marital relationships are followed by parent-child communication problems, sibling rivalries, and difficulties in working with colleagues. The crux of the problem in parent-child relationships is how much freedom parents should allow their children, especially daughters. One 15-year-old Chinese girl, for example, nearly drove her mother frantic because she had tasted "free love" and was, the mother thought, ruining her life. The parents had lost all control over the girl, and the last resort was the Social Welfare Department. In Singapore, parental consent is not necessary for an abortion to be performed, no matter what the girl's age, a situation that causes parents a great deal of anxiety.

When two persons enter into a relationship, there is a meeting of two unique personalities. Each individual has his own level of maturity, his own ability to relate, his own expectations of the other person as well as of the relationship. A large percentage of the boy-girl relationship problems stem from the immaturity of the parties concerned. Earlier, I referred to the common example of a young adult wanting to attempt suicide following a broken love affair. If this individual had had wider experiences in human relationships, especially of the heterosexual kind, he would probably have been able to handle the situation in a more mature way. Maturity would have helped him to surmount the crisis. Other factors also come into play, but in my opinion the level of maturity of the individual undergoing a crisis is a critical deciding factor. Difficulty in meeting cultural demands, such as parental approval, is another common source of stress. Marital relationship problems arise largely when one party expects too much of the other, or when a conflict arises over the degree of independence each party should have. The friction caused by the "seven-year itch" of the married man and the liberal views of the modern Asian woman can and does lead to misunderstandings, violent scenes, and rash actions, as shown by some of the files on emergency clients.

### Psychological Problems

The common features of urban life-style in other parts of the world—impersonal relationships, competitiveness, high-rise living, and inflation—are also present in Singapore. Stresses in everyday life sometimes prove to be more than an individual can take. Many emergency clients express feelings of depression, anxiety, and tension and, most crucial of all, a sense of hopelessness. Loneliness and a feeling that "life has no meaning" are common. Unless such individuals find understanding persons to confide in so as to get at the root of their problems, they are very likely to take their lives. A particular stressful situation, such as the loss of a loved one, failure in examinations, or rejection by someone close, may cause an individual to sink to the nadir of despair. Reactive depressions, as after a parent or a husband has passed away, afflict a small minority of the total number of clients. An example was the case of a man who experienced a severe trauma at the loss of his homosexual partner. Three common characteristics are found in the majority of the emergency clients in this category: lack of security in childhood, a family background of many siblings, and a history of mental instability.

### Material Problems

This category includes problems pertaining to employment, citizenship, work permits, housing applications, financial situation, and legal matters. A large number of calls dealt with the problem of unemployment, which is also a typical feature of urban environments. As the high standard of living in cities places heavy pressure on the breadwinner of the family, the threat of losing a job or of being unemployed is serious. Many callers were ignorant of the social services and legal advice available in Singapore.

### Physical Problems

Physical causes of concern range from the adolescent's worry over his physical appearance to a person's suffering from an injury; people also became depressed over prolonged illness and the approach of old age and death. A university graduate, for example, confided to the Samaritans of Singapore his worry about a urinary illness for which he had been unable to find a cure, despite several attempts. In addition, he could not obtain employment. These two factors so depressed him that he finally took his own life.

Sexual Problems

Worries about premarital and extramarital sex, unwanted pregnancies, and the risks of abortion make up the bulk of calls in this category. To give a few examples, a girl attempted suicide because she was pregnant and her boyfriend had jilted her. A 15-year-old girl attempted suicide by jumping from a high-rise building because she was too ashamed to face her family after having been raped. A 35-year-old woman twice attempted suicide after the breakup of a lesbian relationship. Remorse over past activities may also lead a person to attempt suicide, as did a 19-year-old girl who had been on drugs and had led the life of a prostitute. When she realized how she had wasted her life she tried to kill herself, but she was saved in time.


## THE ELDERLY

It is noteworthy that, although a high proportion of older residents of Singapore commit suicide, the percentage of those aged 50 or over who are known to attempt suicide is much lower. According to Chia and Tsoi's study (2), people in this age group account for approximately 16 percent of all attempted suicides in Singapore. Records of the Samaritans of Singapore show this age group fluctuating between 6 and 14 percent of the total in any one year in the period 1975–1979 (table 4-14). On the national level, the rate of attempted suicides is five times as high as the rate of suicide deaths, but for older persons (50 and over) the suicide rate is higher than the attempted suicide rate. Several reasons may explain this phenomenon. First, the elderly individual may be so determined in his desire to die that the method he chooses is lethal, and he therefore dies in his first attempt. Second, many unrecorded or unknown suicide attempts by elderly people may have been hushed up by family members for the sake of family honor and reputation.

My data show that during the 1975–1979 period more elderly males than elderly females telephoned the Samaritans for emergency help. The majority of those who phoned were widows or widowers; the second-largest group consisted of people having problems with their wives or family members; third came divorced persons or those separated from their spouses. The last category comprised Caucasians who were either alone or stranded in Singapore; their spouses were traveling or were living in another country, such as the United Kingdom. Unhappy marital relationships, drinking, and depression were common causes of the stresses experienced by the Caucasian group.

The reasons given by clients or deduced by the Samaritans for the suicidal attempts were, in order of importance: (1) family problems, such as the inability to get along with wife, son, or daughter-in-law; (2) physical illness; (3) poverty; (4) mental illness; and (5) loneliness. People facing homelessness were put into the category of poverty. Several clients had overlapping reasons for attempting suicide: for example, an elderly woman who had quarreled with her husband appeared to be mentally ill and had terminal lung cancer. Family friction arises from the confrontation of the eccentric, dogmatic, and extrasensitive disposition of the aged and the intolerant, modern ways of their children. Such friction has been known to culminate in highy tense situations resulting in violent attacks or, alternatively, suicide. Loneliness of the aged stems mainly from the loss of spouse and the ensuing maladjustment of the bereaved to his or her life situation. Two aged persons were known to have been overcome by depression and loneliness at the demise of a favorite pet.

## CASE HISTORIES

To give an insight into the life of the individual who actually attempts suicide, two case histories have been selected. The principle of confidentiality upheld by the Samaritans of Singapore prevents me from relating all the particulars about the cases. The names used are fictional.

### Case A

James has, to date, attempted suicide twice. He rang the Samaritans of Singapore for help after his first attempt. James had had an unhappy childhood and had been forced to struggle for a living from the age of 14. His first marriage ended when his wife deserted him, leaving him with an infant son. He married again, this time to a woman of a different race and religion. As a result of the second marriage, he found himself suspended between two cultures, not accepted by either. James is surrounded by manifold problems—unemployment, care of his son by the first marriage, and cultural dislocation. His only sources of support are his loving wife and the welfare agencies that are trying to help him.

James's personality has been molded by his life experiences. He is basically an insecure person; he has difficulty in relating to people, like his colleagues at work; he feels cheated in life; finally, he is hypersensitive to the reactions of others. He has been diagnosed by a psychiatrist as suffering from reactive depression. When events in his life take a turn for the worse and everything seems hopeless, James gets extremely depressed (sometimes violent) and tries to take his life.

### Case B

Susan had an affair with a man who, as she later found out, was married. She loves him but harbors strong guilt feelings about breaking up his family. These conflicting emotions, together with her boyfriend's inconsistent behavior, drove her to try to kill herself. Before the attempt she dropped hints to her colleagues at work that "they would not see her again" and that she "was going to leave this world." They sought help from the Samaritans of Singapore to prevent Susan from causing harm to herself.

When Susan was 9 years old her parents separated. When she completed her secondary education a family friend financed her through a secretarial course and she later found a job. Her first boyfriend made romantic promises but after borrowing a large sum of money from her he left her and married someone else. Her second affair also disillusioned her when she found out that the man was married. She started to take drugs. The second boyfriend deserted her to return to his wife. On one occasion, his mother cursed Susan for bringing bad luck to her family. As for her own family, Susan feels that she has lost their respect and that they will be ashamed of her and her past misdeeds.

Susan is high-strung and has a tendency to become violent and hysterical. She needs psychiatric help, which she is not willing to accept. The Samaritans of Singapore can give her only limited help, which has to suffice until she accepts the professional help she needs.

## CONCLUSION

Studies focusing on attempted suicide and suicide in a nation are important because they help us to understand how these phenomena occur. Upon further analysis, clues identifying the suicide-prone individual and indicators of the high-risk suicidal population can be deduced. I have discussed these matters with special reference to Singapore in an earlier paper (7). Although one realizes that a social problem like suicide is impossible to eradicate, research can help to direct suicide-prevention programs. Research conducted by organizations such as the Suicide Prevention Center in Los Angeles and the Suicide Prevention Center in Vienna has shown that follow-up procedures and the befriending of persons who have attempted suicide are effective in stabilizing them. Unless they are helped, they will probably try again to take their lives. According to Grollman (4), "twelve percent of those who attempt suicide will make a second try and succeed within 2 years." The Samaritans of Singapore (with its counterparts in many other parts of the world) exists to help persons in despair, as well as to provide a safety valve for those who are undergoing a crisis. Some suicide attempters might be labeled "pseudocides," those whose motive for a suicidal attempt is not to die but to threaten or to frighten close relatives.

In this paper I have tried to convey, by description and by example, the actual emotional conflicts and situational pressures experienced by suicide attempters. These pressures and conflicts have been related to the unique features of Singapore society.

# BIBLIOGRAPHY

1. Chia, B. H. Suicide of the elderly in Singapore. *Annals Acad. Medicine* (Singapore), 8, 3 (1979).
2. Chia, B. H., and W. F. Tsoi. A statistical study of attempted suicide in Singapore. *Singapore Med. J.*, 15, 4 (1974).
3. Ringel, Erwin. Suicide prevention in Vienna. In H. L. P. Resnik, ed., *Suicidal Behaviours: Diagnosis and Management*. London: J. and A. Churchill, 1968.
4. Grollman, E. A. *Suicide: Prevention, Intervention, Post Vention*. Boston: Beacon Press, 1972.
5. Kuo, Eddie C. Y., and Aline K. Wong, eds. *The Contemporary Family in Singapore*. Singapore: University of Singapore Press, 1979.
6. Lennard-Jones, J. E., and R. Asher. Why do they do it? *Lancet*, 1 (1959).
7. Mehta, K. K. Suicide prevention in Singapore: A social worker's viewpoint. Unpublished MS, 1977.
8. Samaritans of Singapore. *Annual Report*. 1975–76, 1976–77, 1977–78, 1978–79.
9. Thomas, A. A study of attempted suicide among young Tamil women in Singapore. Undergraduate dissertation, Department of Social Work, University of Singapore, 1959.
10. Tsoi, W. F. Attempted suicide. *Singapore Med. J.*, 2, 4 (1970).
11. Yeo, R. *Attempted Suicide in Singapore*. Department of Social Work, University of Singapore, 1969.

# 5 THAILAND

*Editor's Note*

Thailand (formerly Siam), with its ample natural resources, plentiful water, extensive forests, and arable land, is one of the most prosperous countries in Southeast Asia. Most Thai people are agricultural workers who own their land. Thailand is unusual in never having been occupied by a European power; its kings have ruled continuously since the thirteenth century. Thailand was a feudal country with powerful nobles until King Mongkut (1851–1868) and his son, King Chulalongkorn (1868–1910), instituted more democratic procedures. This long history is a basis for the respect accorded the Thai royal family.

The literacy rate is high in Thailand because of compulsory education until age 15. Good medical facilities and the elimination of malaria have raised life expectancy to 66 years. It is the tradition for every man to enter the Buddhist priesthood, even if he serves for only a few months. Although Hinyana Buddhism is the state religion and all government employees must be Buddhists, the Chinese mostly adhere to Mahayana Buddhism, with an admixture of Taoism, Confucianism, and ancestor worship. The commingling of ethnic groups is pronounced, and those with more or less pure Thai blood are probably among the mountain dwellers.

Of recent years political unrest, particularly among students, has been considerable, although in comparison with its neighbors Thailand is politically and economically stable.

It was difficult to find a contributor qualified to write the chapter on Thailand for this volume, but the choice of Dr. Somporn Bussaratid proved to be an excellent one. Dr. Bussaratid received his medical training at Siriraj Medical School, Mahidol University, and his psychiatric training at Somdej Choaphya Hospital in Bangkok. He was a fellow in psychiatry at Washington University, St. Louis, Missouri, where he remained for five years. Since 1970 Dr. Bussaratid has been a member of the teaching staff of Siriraj Hospital in Bangkok, presently with the rank of assistant professor. He also gives lectures in psychiatry to medical students at Konkaen University and the Military Medical Academy. He has been an executive member of the Thai Psychiatric Association and an examiner on the Thai Board of Psychiatry. Dr. Bussaratid has numerous publications in the areas of psychosomatic manifestations and the psychiatric aspects of such physical conditions as tuberculosis, amputations, sterility, and insomnia.

Dr. Bussaratid has been active in suicide research since 1974. In the preparation of this paper he tried to obtain statistics from rural areas as well as Bangkok, but the necessary time and assistance were not available. The report therefore concerns only Bangkok, whose large population suggests that the data for the city will give a reasonably accurate perspective on suicide in the whole of Thailand. Dr. Bussaratid's comments on Thai culture point up social and personal reasons for suicide attempts.

Dr. Sompop Ruangtrakool is associate professor in psychiatry and chief of the Psychiatry Department at Mahidol University Faculty of Medicine. Like Dr. Bussaratid, Dr. Ruangtrakool is a graduate of the Siriraj Medical School and was for two years in the Psychiatry Department at Washington University, St. Louis. Presently he is associate professor of psychiatry at Siriraj Hospital Faculty of Medicine. His numerous publications cover the fields of mania, hysteria, filicide, depression, and attempted suicide.

# SOMPORN BUSSARATID AND SOMPOP RUANGTRAKOOL

## THAILAND AND THE THAIS

Thailand borders on the Indian Ocean and Burma in the west, Cambodia and Laos in the east, Laos and Burma in the north, and Malaysia and the Gulf of Thailand in the south. The total area measures approximately 500,000 square kilometers, which is about the size of France. As Thailand is in a tropical zone, the climate is hot and humid; the temperature is about 60 degrees Fahrenheit in the cool season and nearly 100 degrees in the hot season. The northern part of the country is cooler and less humid than the southern part. There are three seasons in Thailand: hot, rainy, and cool. The monsoon climate prevailing across most of the country has a distinct influence on the landscape, its vegetation and animal life, and its human uses. The population is about 40 million. Thai, a language of musical inflection, is the national language. Chinese is the second major language spoken by the Thai, who are Chinese descendants. Thailand is predominantly Buddhist but a small minority of the population are Muslims, Confucians, and Christians of various denominations. Buddhism, professed by more than 90 percent of the inhabitants, is considered the national religion.

The economy of Thailand is based on agriculture, the main crops being rice, sugar, sweet corn, and cassava. Mining and fishing are also important sources of income. Thailand is the world's third-largest producer of tin. The country's gold and foreign exchange reserve increased by 15 percent annually after 1957, and the Thai unit of currency, the baht, is among the world's most stable currencies.

Until 1932 the form of government was an absolute monarchy. Under the constitution established after a revolution in that year the king exercised his legislative power through the National Assembly and his executive power through the courts of law. Since then the constitution has been rewritten several times because of changes in the government, but the provisions are similar. The king is head of state and chief of the armed forces. He is held to be sacred and inviolable. The royal family, regarded as a symbol of national unity, is the protector of national welfare and traditions.

## CULTURE

Family life in Thailand is different from that in Western countries. The extended family unit and close family ties are the basis of the psychological structure of the Thais. Three generations of people live together in the same house or in close contact. After getting married, a couple usually lives with the bride's parents. Traditionally their children are taken care of by the grandparents, freeing the parents to go out to work. In this way children are more secure than if they were left to the care of maids or taken to nurseries. At the same time the grandparents gain the sense of being wanted and can be proud of themselves. The elderly earn respect while the younger generation receives kindness and security in return. It is possible that the extended family pattern may shield some elderly people from loneliness and depression, a service that in turn lowers the incidence of suicide in the old-age group. There are, however, some disadvantages in this system of family life. It intensifies rivalry among children, in-laws, and other younger family members for the love and attention of both parents and grandparents (especially when the grandparents are wealthy). Envy, jealousy, and gossip are common and become part of the life of the people.

A unique characteristic of the Thais is their ability to tolerate unpleasant situations, owing perhaps to the religious belief in the law of karma: hardship is accepted as the payment for a bad deed previously committed. Shyness is also a characteristic of the Thais. Because they are shy they prefer to keep anger, hate, and hostility to themselves, and thus they lack the opportunity to learn to express their feelings properly. On the surface it seems that Thailand is the land of smiles and that the Thais are fun-loving people, but deep down in their hearts there are elements of hostility and aggressiveness. For this reason the number of crimes of violence is very high; the Thais have a tendency to be unpredictably violent. The homicide rate in 1975 was 29.4 per 100,000 population.

The Thais are usually religious. Buddhism as the national religion is the heritage handed down from generation to generation. They believe in the law of karma, that good deeds breed good results and bad deeds breed bad results. A person triumphs over evil by performing noble deeds. These deeply rooted beliefs produce a people who are readily able to forgive and forget. Forgiveness is regarded as highly honorable.

For the past forty years the rapid increase of the population has made life in Thailand more difficult; everyone has to struggle for a living. Many grandparents are not able to support the whole extended family. Housewives have to go out to work and husbands have to work harder. In some families the members rarely see one another. These changes break family ties and split the large extended family into small, lonely, separated units. Many families cannot afford to care for their own young ones. Babies and small children are given into the care of private nurseries or of neighbors whose methods are both psychologically and physically below an acceptable standard.

Another alteration in Thai life has come about because of the changing relationship between the spiritual world of Buddhism and the schools. In the old days the monks were almost everything: moral and ethical sources, social workers, psychiatrists. Today the children are taught in school in Western style, and the school takes over all facets of life from the monks. Religious belief not only is not emphasized, but it is sometimes ridiculed by teachers and intellectuals who have been educated in Western ways. The Thai children of today are confused. These two factors—the breakdown of the extended family pattern and the modernization of the school system—have bred a new generation of people who are not sure of themselves, who have no model they can trust, and who have few leaders they can admire. The situation is certainly not a healthy one. As a result, the Thais may be good prospects for acquiring psychiatric illnesses which in turn will increase the incidence of suicide.

## LEGAL AND SOCIAL ATTITUDES
## TOWARD SUICIDE

Thailand has no law prohibiting suicide. Everyone has the right to control one's own life and everyone is free to commit suicide. It is illegal, however, to encourage or mislead others, especially a minor or a person who cannot control himself, to attempt or to commit suicide.

Kindness is regarded as one of the noblest traits the Buddhist has to learn to practice. A person who commits suicide is disobeying the Buddhist teaching because he has shown that he lacks kindness even to himself. The converse is possible: the suicide victim may really believe that the termination of his own life is the best thing for him to do and thus the act may be seen as a kindness to himself. In such instances it is obvious, of course, that the victim has a distorted view, and that is regarded as a serious sin by Buddhists.

The attitudes of the Thai people toward survivors of suicide attempts vary from sympathy and pity to contempt. Usually an attempt arouses mixed feelings. Nevertheless, most survivors are well treated by their relatives and friends. Quite often the relatives of a suicide victim are blamed for the death. If the victim is blamed, it is usually not done directly. Most people tend to forgive and forget. Members of the family of a suicide victim also suffer from mixed feelings of anxiety, doubt, guilt, shame, and resentment. At times they are anxious to prove their innocence and to be helpful, while suppressing their shame and resentment.

In 1977 Sukatongka and her associate studied the layman's attitude toward suicide, using a group of 170 subjects, 83 males and 87 females (12). Most of the subjects were Buddhists whose educational background was fairly good. Five subjects had a history of suicide attempts and twenty-four had had suicidal thoughts but had never attempted suicide. These subjects had fourteen relatives who had attempted suicide, eight of whom succeeded.

The subjects of the survey thought that most of the suicide victims did not really want to die. The majority (71 percent) believed that suicide was a sinful act because it broke a Buddhist rule and because the victim had not conformed to the teachings of the elderly; they also thought that man has no right to terminate his own life. Others believed that suicide was a shameful act, that killing oneself did not solve problems. A small number of subjects thought that suicide victims had made the attempts in subservience to the law of karma; that sinful acts (sometimes supposedly from a previous life) bring ill luck and trouble to the present life. (These subjects believe in reincarnation.) Only a minority of the laymen surveyed felt that suicide was not a sin; they said that men have the right to do away with their own lives as long as they do not interfere with others. Some of these subjects believed that it is natural to be born and to die, so that it does not matter how one dies; everyone has to die, in one way or another. Another small group saw a suicidal death as an end of misery in this troubled world. The views of these subjects, though gathered from a small number and a limited cross section of people, clearly indicate Thai thinking about suicide.

## SOURCES OF DATA

This report is based upon three sources: statistics from the Ministry of Public Health, Thailand, 1957—1976 (table 5-1); Bussaratid and Vicharn-ratavakan's study (3); and Tosayanonda and Eungprabhanth's survey (13).

Bussaratid and Vicharnratavakan studied 14,000 death certificates randomly drawn from records for 1975 and 1977 available at the Division of Vital Statistics, Ministry of Public Health. Of the 14,000, 208 were identi-

TABLE 5-1
RATE PER 100,000 POPULATION OF DEATHS FROM
ACCIDENTS, HOMICIDE, AND SUICIDE, 1957 – 1976[a]

| Year | Accidents | | | Homicide | | | Suicide | | |
|------|-------|------|--------|-------|------|--------|-------|------|--------|
|      | Total | Male | Female | Total | Male | Female | Total | Male | Female |
| 1957 | 15.4 |      |        | 7.1  |      |        | 2.7 |      |        |
| 1958 | 19.2 |      |        | 12.4 |      |        | 2.8 |      |        |
| 1959 | 18.7 |      |        | 8.7  |      |        | 3.3 |      |        |
| 1960 | 17.5 | 23.8 | 11.2   | 8.7  | 15.1 | 2.3    | 3.5 | 4.3  | 2.7    |
| 1961 | 17.8 | 24.0 | 11.6   | 9.9  | 17.4 | 2.3    | 3.6 | 4.5  | 2.6    |
| 1962 | 19.1 | 26.1 | 12.0   | 11.1 | 19.6 | 2.6    | 3.5 | 4.7  | 2.4    |
| 1963 | 18.4 | 25.2 | 11.7   | 12.0 | 21.2 | 2.7    | 3.4 | 4.4  | 2.4    |
| 1964 | 20.5 | 28.7 | 12.2   | 14.3 | 25.5 | 3.0    | 3.5 | 4.4  | 2.6    |
| 1965 | 23.2 | 31.7 | 14.8   | 15.1 | 26.8 | 3.5    | 3.5 | 4.1  | 2.8    |
| 1966 | 25.0 | 34.1 | 15.8   | 14.6 | 25.7 | 3.6    | 3.7 | 4.3  | 3.2    |
| 1967 | 25.6 | 35.8 | 15.4   | 16.3 | 30.0 | 3.6    | 3.6 | 4.0  | 3.2    |
| 1968 | 24.7 | 35.7 | 13.9   | 16.6 | 29.5 | 3.7    | 3.8 | 4.3  | 3.3    |
| 1969 | 25.5 | 36.4 | 14.6   | 17.1 | 30.7 | 3.7    | 3.7 | 4.1  | 3.3    |
| 1970 | 27.2 | 39.1 | 15.3   | 17.2 | 31.1 | 3.5    | 4.1 | 4.9  | 3.3    |
| 1971 | 27.1 | 40.2 | 14.1   | 16.2 | 28.9 | 3.6    | 3.6 | 3.9  | 3.2    |
| 1972 | 30.3 | 44.3 | 16.5   | 12.6 | 22.4 | 2.9    | 4.5 | 5.0  | 3.9    |
| 1973 | 31.8 | 45.6 | 18.1   | 16.5 | 29.2 | 4.0    | 4.4 | 4.9  | 3.9    |
| 1974 | 32.1 | 45.2 | 19.1   | 19.3 | 34.2 | 4.6    | 4.8 | 5.1  | 4.5    |
| 1975 | 39.2 | 56.2 | 22.4   | 29.4 | 55.0 | 4.2    | 4.9 | 5.0  | 4.8    |
| 1976 | 30.6 | 44.6 | 16.9   | 23.4 | 42.0 | 5.0    | 4.9 | 5.2  | 4.6    |

SOURCE: Division of Vital Statistics, Ministry of Public Health, Thailand.

[a]Figures for 1977 – 1980, updating the suicide rate, have been made available. For 1977, the overall rate, the male rate, and the female rate were, respectively, 5.9, 6.3, and 5.5; for 1978, 5.9, 6.0, and 5.8; for 1979, 6.7, 6.9, and 6.5; for 1980, 7.4, 7.6, and 7.3.

fied as death by suicide. Some of the data compiled in that study are presented in this chapter.

Tosayanonda and Eungprabhanth are forensic physicians who studied the 824 autopsy cases of suicide deaths which were sent to the Department of Forensic Medicine, Siriraj Hospital, between 1953 and 1969. Not all suicide cases are sent to a forensic physician for autopsy; only those in which homicide is suspected or in which death is attributed to undetermined causes are referred. As most of these autopsy cases were sent by the police, the samples used for the study did not represent suicide cases in general. According to this study, the highest incidence occurred between the ages of 20 and 39 (table 5-2). For all ages, almost twice as many men as women committed suicide, suggesting that men have a tendency to kill themselves by violent means. The differences between the findings of

Tosayanonda and Eungprabhanth and other statistics, given in table 5-2, show that hospital or police cases do not accurately reflect the overall suicide picture in the general population. The government statistics for table 5-2 were gathered from all suicide deaths reported to registrars in 1975.

## METHOD OF COLLECTING
## VITAL STATISTICS

At the end of each month, birth, death, and stillbirth certificates are sent from provincial medical offices to the Division of Vital Statistics to be compiled. The process follows a set pattern established by law. The vital event—birth, death, or stillbirth—is reported by the head of the household or a relative to the municipal registrar in urban areas or to the commune registrar in nonmunicipal areas. A birth must be reported within fifteen days; a death, within twenty-four hours. Registrars are responsible for collecting vital records and sending them to the Division of Vital Statistics, Ministry of Public Health, where they are compiled and kept.

Although registration of births and deaths is compulsory throughout the country, the process is not always complete. A sample survey conducted in 1964 by the National Statistical Office showed that only 65.2 percent of male deaths and 60.0 percent of female deaths were registered. The major reasons for failure to register were the informant's lack of interest, particularly in rural areas, and the registrar's underestimation of the necessity of recording all events within the specified periods. Although the funeral or cremation ceremony cannot be performed without permission, especially in the municipal area, evidence from the 1964 study shows that in remote villages, where close personal relationships exist between villagers and the communal registrar, the practice is not always followed. Sometimes cremations take place outside the crematorium, so that official documents are unnecessary.

Since 85 percent of the population lives outside the municipal area, it is inevitable that the registration of deaths will remain incomplete to a high degree. Most of those who live outside the municipal area die at their own residences without receiving modern medical treatment from qualified physicians. Instead, they depend upon indigenous doctors or unqualified medical personnel, or they treat themselves. Consequently the details of a death, particularly its cause, given by informants to the communal registrar are inaccurate, unreliable, or ill-defined, or the death is attributed to unknown causes. Only 16.2 percent of all deaths occurred in hospitals, which are accurate and reliable in reporting deaths. About a third of the fatalities outside hospitals are regarded as death by known causes; approximately 37—42 percent, as death by ill-defined or unknown causes. Other

## TABLE 5-2
### SUICIDE RATE PER 100,000 POPULATION IN THAILAND, BY AGE AND SEX, BASED ON STATISTICS FROM THREE SOURCES, FOR VARYING DATES

1975: DIVISION OF VITAL STATISTICS, MINISTRY OF PUBLIC HEALTH

| Sex | Under 15 | 15–24 | 25–34 | 35–44 | 45–54 | 55–64 | 65 and over | Unknown | Total |
|---|---|---|---|---|---|---|---|---|---|
| Male | 3 | 405 | 190 | 168 | 91 | 55 | 52 | 25 | 989 |
| Female | 3 | 543 | 154 | 81 | 52 | 37 | 25 | 23 | 918 |
| Total | 6 | 948 | 344 | 249 | 143 | 82 | 77 | 48 | 1,907 |

1975, 1977: BUSSARATID AND VICHARNRATAVAKAN (3)

| Sex | Under 15 | 15–24 | 25–34 | 35–44 | 45–54 | 55–64 | 65 and over | Unknown | Total |
|---|---|---|---|---|---|---|---|---|---|
| Male | 1 | 46 | 17 | 11 | 7 | 13 | 7 | – | 102 |
| Female | 7 | 58 | 17 | 5 | 5 | 4 | 9 | 1 | 106 |
| Total | 8 | 104 | 34 | 16 | 12 | 17 | 16 | 1 | 208 |

1953–1969: TOSAYANONDA AND EUNGPRABHANTH (13)

| Sex | 19 and under | 20–39 | 40–59 | 60 and over | Unknown | Total |
|---|---|---|---|---|---|---|
| Male | 54 | 195 | 139 | 49 | 66 | 503 |
| Female | 109 | 146 | 39 | 10 | 17 | 321 |
| Total | 163 | 341 | 178 | 59 | 83 | 824 |

reasons for underregistration are the inadequate system of compiling and keeping records and the inability to maintain orderly records because registrars, who are assigned various other duties, are often overworked.

## COMPLETED SUICIDES

Suicide rates in Thailand are available from 1957, the year when the rate was 2.7 per 100,000 population, the lowest ever recorded. Since then the suicide rate has steadily increased, reaching 4.9 in 1976 and 7.4 in 1980 (table 5-1). The apparent increase may be owing to errors in collecting and compiling the data or to underestimation of the size of the population. If, however, these figures are accepted as accurate, what are the possible causes of changes in the rates? Nobody really knows the answer, but we do know that there were many changes in the country between 1957 and 1976. One of them was the rapid growth of the population, from 26 million in 1960 to 34 million in 1970 and 39 million in 1976. Undoubtedly the rapidity of this increase created considerable stress in the Thai people. Many a housewife was forced to leave her young children in the care of others in order to go out to work because her husband did not earn enough to support the family. Family ties and extended family patterns were not so strong as they needed to be. Some families were disrupted because of economic problems. The elderly were not as well treated as in the old days. Many youngsters, left alone without being properly disciplined, turned to drugs, and some became antisocial. People of working age suffered from guilt over not treating their parents and senior relatives properly, or from the stress of not earning enough money for the family. Sometimes problem children drove parents to distraction. These problems may have hit some people so hard that they felt their lives were no longer bearable.

In view of the way in which the suicide death rate is estimated by the Division of Vital Statistics, it is possible that the stated rate is lower than the real one. The 1964 survey of population by the National Statistical Office revealed that only 60 percent of the total deaths in the country were reported to registrars' offices. Bussaratid and Vicharnratavakan (3) estimated from their study of 14,000 death certificates that the 1976 suicide rate was 15 per 100,000 population, whereas the official figure released by the Division of Vital Statistics was only 4.9. It is likely, therefore, that suicide deaths in Thailand are higher than officially stated.

### Age

In 1975 the 20−24 age group had the highest rate of suicide, 14.8 per 100,000 (table 5-3). The rate dropped sharply to 5.8 at the 30−34 age group and stayed in that area until the 50−54 age group, when it again began to rise. The total rate, however, did not exceed the high rate for the 20−24 age

TABLE 5-3

SUICIDE RATE PER 100,000 POPULATION, BY AGE AND SEX, 1960–1976

| Age | 1960 | | | 1961 | | | 1962 | | | 1963 | | | 1964 | | | 1965 | | |
|---|---|---|---|---|---|---|---|---|---|---|---|---|---|---|---|---|---|---|
| | T | M | F | T | M | F | T | M | F | T | M | F | T | M | F | T | M | F |
| Total | 3.5 | 4.3 | 2.7 | 3.6 | 4.5 | 2.7 | 3.5 | 4.7 | 2.4 | 3.4 | 4.4 | 2.4 | 3.5 | 4.4 | 2.6 | 3.5 | 4.1 | 2.8 |
| 0–4 | | | | | | 0.1 | | | | | | | | | — | 0.1 | .. | 0.1 |
| 5–9 | | | | | | | | | | | | | | | | .. | 0.1 | — |
| 10–14 | 0.5 | 0.6 | 0.3 | 0.5 | 1.0 | 0.3 | 0.5 | 0.6 | 0.4 | 0.4 | 0.4 | 0.4 | 0.7 | 0.7 | 0.8 | 0.8 | 0.6 | 1.0 |
| 15–19 | 5.5 | 3.4 | 7.6 | 5.2 | 4.8 | 5.5 | 4.8 | 3.8 | 5.7 | 5.5 | 4.8 | 6.1 | 5.9 | 4.9 | 6.8 | 6.2 | 4.8 | 7.6 |
| 20–24 | 7.8 | 8.3 | 7.4 | 8.0 | 8.5 | 7.4 | 7.7 | 9.2 | 6.2 | 7.2 | 8.4 | 6.0 | 6.9 | 7.8 | 6.1 | 7.0 | 7.5 | 6.5 |
| 25–29 | 5.0 | 6.2 | 3.8 | 5.1 | 6.3 | 4.0 | 6.3 | 7.9 | 4.8 | 6.1 | 7.9 | 4.3 | 5.8 | 6.9 | 4.8 | 6.2 | 6.7 | 5.7 |
| 30–34 | 3.9 | 4.2 | 3.5 | 4.6 | 6.2 | 2.9 | 5.1 | 7.4 | 2.9 | 4.6 | 5.5 | 3.6 | 5.6 | 7.4 | 3.9 | 5.0 | 6.8 | 3.2 |
| 35–39 | 4.3 | 5.9 | 2.9 | 5.8 | 8.2 | 3.4 | 5.5 | 8.1 | 2.9 | 4.5 | 7.3 | 1.6 | 5.0 | 7.6 | 2.4 | 4.9 | 6.5 | 3.3 |
| 40–44 | 4.9 | 7.3 | 2.5 | 5.3 | 7.3 | 3.2 | 5.2 | 7.7 | 2.7 | 5.4 | 8.0 | 2.7 | 4.1 | 6.6 | 1.6 | 4.1 | 6.1 | 2.1 |
| 45–49 | 6.3 | 10.3 | 2.3 | 6.6 | 10.1 | 3.0 | 4.9 | 7.8 | 2.0 | 5.2 | 7.6 | 2.7 | 3.7 | 3.2 | 1.7 | 4.9 | 7.1 | 2.6 |
| 50–54 | 5.6 | 8.9 | 2.4 | 5.6 | 9.3 | 1.9 | 7.0 | 12.3 | 1.9 | 4.1 | 5.9 | 2.3 | 6.9 | 10.5 | 3.4 | 4.3 | 6.4 | 2.2 |
| 55–59 | 4.7 | 8.7 | 0.9 | 5.7 | 9.7 | 1.8 | 5.0 | 8.1 | 2.0 | 5.3 | 8.8 | 2.0 | 5.4 | 7.8 | 3.1 | 5.0 | 7.0 | 3.0 |
| 60–64 | 8.6 | 15.7 | 2.0 | 7.1 | 11.0 | 3.6 | 5.4 | 10.7 | 0.4 | 6.0 | 11.2 | 1.1 | 5.6 | 9.0 | 2.5 | 5.8 | 11.0 | 1.1 |
| 65–69 | 6.0 | 10.0 | 2.4 | 4.3 | 7.1 | 1.8 | 6.2 | 9.3 | 3.4 | 6.5 | 10.8 | 2.7 | 4.7 | 5.8 | 3.6 | 5.5 | 10.6 | 1.0 |
| 70–74 | 6.5 | 10.2 | 3.6 | 4.4 | 5.4 | 3.5 | 6.0 | 10.5 | 2.5 | 9.8 | 20.1 | 1.6 | 8.1 | 17.4 | 0.8 | 5.7 | 10.2 | 2.2 |
| 75–79 | 8.5 | 14.1 | 4.4 | 8.1 | 11.7 | 5.6 | 7.1 | 16.9 | 1.8 | 5.3 | 9.1 | 2.6 | 5.9 | 8.7 | 3.8 | 8.5 | 15.2 | 3.6 |
| 80–84 | 14.5 | 28.7 | 5.3 | 9.4 | 12.0 | 7.7 | 6.1 | 11.8 | 3.6 | 9.0 | 19.1 | 2.5 | 7.3 | 3.7 | 9.6 | 5.7 | 14.6 | — |
| 85 and over | 11.0 | 30.9 | — | 10.7 | 24.1 | — | 8.3 | 17.5 | 3.2 | 4.0 | 5.7 | 3.1 | 3.9 | 5.5 | 3.1 | 5.7 | 5.9 | 4.7 |
| Unknown | 112.6 | 132.6 | 87.8 | 111.2 | 123.0 | 96.8 | 120.6 | 137.3 | 100.9 | 112.6 | 147.9 | 71.5 | 179.9 | 263.4 | 85.3 | 134.1 | 178.7 | 84.8 |

TABLE 5-3—Continued

| Age | 1966 T | 1966 M | 1966 F | 1967 T | 1967 M | 1967 F | 1968 T | 1968 M | 1968 F | 1969 T | 1969 M | 1969 F | 1970 T | 1970 M | 1970 F | 1971 T | 1971 M | 1971 F |
|---|---|---|---|---|---|---|---|---|---|---|---|---|---|---|---|---|---|---|
| Total | 3.7 | 4.3 | 3.2 | 3.6 | 4.0 | 3.2 | 3.8 | 4.3 | 3.3 | 3.7 | 4.1 | 3.3 | 4.1 | 4.9 | 3.3 | 3.6 | 3.9 | 3.2 |
| 0–4 | | | | | | | | | | | | | | | | | | |
| 5–9 | | | | | | | | | | | | | | | | | | |
| 10–14 | 1.1 | 0.9 | 1.3 | 0.8 | 1.0 | 0.5 | 0.7 | 0.6 | 0.9 | 0.8 | 0.8 | 0.8 | 0.6 | 0.6 | 0.6 | 0.8 | 0.7 | 0.8 |
| 15–19 | 6.4 | 5.3 | 7.5 | 6.1 | 3.9 | 8.2 | 7.7 | 5.5 | 9.9 | 7.8 | 5.4 | 10.2 | 7.5 | 5.7 | 8.6 | 7.0 | 3.9 | 10.0 |
| 20–24 | 8.1 | 7.7 | 8.5 | 7.5 | 6.0 | 7.3 | 8.6 | 8.1 | 9.0 | 8.2 | 7.7 | 8.7 | 9.6 | 9.1 | 10.1 | 8.8 | 9.4 | 8.2 |
| 25–29 | 6.6 | 7.2 | 6.0 | 6.8 | 6.5 | 7.2 | 4.9 | 6.5 | 3.3 | 5.1 | 5.6 | 4.7 | 6.0 | 7.3 | 4.8 | 5.5 | 6.3 | 4.7 |
| 30–34 | 4.4 | 5.5 | 3.3 | 5.4 | 5.9 | 4.9 | 3.7 | 3.8 | 3.6 | 4.6 | 5.7 | 3.5 | 4.4 | 6.1 | 2.8 | 4.4 | 5.7 | 3.2 |
| 35–39 | 5.7 | 7.3 | 4.0 | 5.4 | 8.1 | 2.8 | 5.3 | 6.9 | 3.7 | 4.4 | 5.8 | 3.0 | 5.8 | 8.4 | 3.2 | 5.6 | 6.5 | 4.7 |
| 40–44 | 4.9 | 8.0 | 1.8 | 4.7 | 6.2 | 3.1 | 5.4 | 7.9 | 2.9 | 5.2 | 7.8 | 2.7 | 5.7 | 7.7 | 3.6 | 5.4 | 8.4 | 2.3 |
| 45–49 | 5.2 | 6.8 | 3.6 | 4.9 | 7.7 | 2.0 | 6.5 | 9.5 | 3.5 | 5.1 | 6.6 | 3.6 | 5.7 | 8.6 | 2.8 | 4.5 | 7.3 | 1.6 |
| 50–54 | 5.2 | 7.7 | 2.8 | 5.8 | 9.1 | 2.6 | 5.1 | 7.8 | 2.5 | 6.8 | 10.7 | 3.1 | 6.6 | 9.7 | 3.7 | 5.6 | 8.1 | 3.2 |
| 55–59 | 4.5 | 7.5 | 1.6 | 6.8 | 10.0 | 3.7 | 4.7 | 7.5 | 2.1 | 6.3 | 10.2 | 2.5 | 8.6 | 14.3 | 3.0 | 3.6 | 6.0 | 1.2 |
| 60–64 | 6.2 | 10.3 | 2.4 | 5.9 | 10.0 | 2.0 | 5.2 | 8.0 | 2.6 | 6.5 | 11.2 | 2.2 | 6.2 | 9.6 | 3.1 | 3.4 | 6.7 | 0.3 |
| 65–69 | 6.9 | 11.3 | 2.9 | 3.4 | 6.7 | 0.5 | 5.9 | 11.5 | 0.9 | 8.4 | 15.9 | 1.7 | 5.7 | 8.8 | 2.9 | 4.2 | 8.1 | 0.8 |
| 70–74 | 5.1 | 8.1 | 2.8 | 4.1 | 8.6 | 0.7 | 7.2 | 13.2 | 2.6 | 2.1 | 1.6 | 2.5 | 3.7 | 7.7 | 0.6 | 6.1 | 10.3 | 2.8 |
| 75–79 | 5.4 | 13.0 | — | 2.6 | 4.7 | 1.1 | 7.0 | 12.1 | 3.3 | 3.0 | 4.4 | 2.1 | 4.7 | 9.8 | 1.0 | 1.7 | 2.7 | 1.0 |
| 80–84 | — | — | — | 2.7 | 7.0 | — | 5.3 | 6.8 | 4.4 | 1.3 | 3.3 | — | 5.0 | 113.0 | — | 7.4 | 12.7 | 4.1 |
| 85 and over | 3.7 | — | 5.7 | 5.4 | 10.1 | 2.8 | 1.7 | — | 2.7 | 6.8 | 9.6 | 5.3 | 4.9 | 9.3 | 2.6 | 3.2 | 9.0 | — |
| Un-known | 184.4 | 212.1 | 154.5 | 192.3 | 202.6 | 181.5 | 245.9 | 313.7 | 175.9 | 174.1 | 191.5 | 156.6 | 350.4 | 473.3 | 229.1 | 206.4 | 217.2 | 196.0 |

## TABLE 5-3—Continued

| Age | 1972 T | 1972 M | 1972 F | 1973 T | 1973 M | 1973 F | 1974 T | 1974 M | 1974 F | 1975 T | 1975 M | 1975 F | 1976 T | 1976 M | 1976 F |
|---|---|---|---|---|---|---|---|---|---|---|---|---|---|---|---|
| Total | 4.5 | 5.0 | 3.9 | 4.4 | 4.9 | 3.9 | 4.8 | 5.1 | 4.5 | 4.9 | 5.0 | 4.8 | 4.9 | 5.2 | 4.6 |
| 0–4 | | | | | | | | | | | | | | | |
| 5–9 | | | | | | | | | | | | | | | |
| 10–14 | 0.6 | 0.5 | 0.8 | 1.1 | 0.8 | 1.4 | 1.2 | 1.0 | 1.4 | 0.1 | 0.1 | 0.1 | 1.2 | 1.0 | 1.3 |
| 15–19 | 8.5 | 6.1 | 10.8 | 9.3 | 7.2 | 11.2 | 9.2 | 7.0 | 11.4 | 11.5 | 8.5 | 14.3 | 10.1 | 7.2 | 12.9 |
| 20–24 | 11.1 | 11.6 | 10.6 | 12.5 | 13.1 | 11.8 | 14.5 | 14.2 | 14.8 | 14.8 | 15.5 | 14.1 | 14.6 | 14.4 | 14.7 |
| 25–29 | 7.9 | 10.3 | 5.7 | 7.2 | 7.7 | 6.7 | 8.9 | 10.4 | 7.5 | 8.8 | 9.2 | 8.5 | 9.1 | 9.8 | 8.4 |
| 30–34 | 5.6 | 6.7 | 4.7 | 5.3 | 7.6 | 3.2 | 5.8 | 7.0 | 4.7 | 5.8 | 7.4 | 4.3 | 6.7 | 8.3 | 5.2 |
| 35–39 | 5.8 | 6.7 | 0.5 | 5.9 | 7.6 | 4.2 | 6.5 | 6.9 | 6.0 | 6.1 | 8.3 | 3.9 | 5.6 | 7.6 | 3.6 |
| 40–44 | 5.6 | 7.3 | 3.9 | 5.3 | 7.2 | 3.4 | 5.9 | 7.6 | 4.2 | 6.1 | 8.1 | 4.0 | 6.6 | 8.9 | 4.2 |
| 45–49 | 5.4 | 7.3 | 3.5 | 5.5 | 7.8 | 3.1 | 7.2 | 9.1 | 5.3 | 5.5 | 6.9 | 4.0 | 6.6 | 8.4 | 4.8 |
| 50–54 | 5.8 | 9.6 | 2.2 | 5.7 | 9.4 | 2.1 | 6.4 | 9.3 | 3.6 | 6.6 | 8.7 | 4.6 | 6.6 | 9.9 | 3.5 |
| 55–59 | 6.5 | 9.9 | 3.3 | 5.3 | 7.7 | 3.0 | 6.6 | 7.8 | 5.5 | 6.5 | 8.6 | 4.5 | 6.3 | 9.1 | 3.5 |
| 60–64 | 5.7 | 9.7 | 2.0 | 4.8 | 7.9 | 2.0 | 5.4 | 7.4 | 3.6 | 4.8 | 5.2 | 4.5 | 7.5 | 8.1 | 3.9 |
| 65–69 | 5.1 | 8.2 | 2.3 | 4.3 | 6.7 | 2.2 | 5.3 | 9.3 | 1.8 | 6.4 | 10.1 | 3.1 | 5.4 | 9.4 | 2.0 |
| 70–74 | 2.1 | 3.5 | 1.1 | 6.8 | 9.5 | 4.7 | 5.4 | 11.8 | 0.5 | 5.4 | 9.5 | 2.4 | 5.0 | 8.5 | 2.3 |
| 75–79 | 3.8 | 7.8 | 0.9 | 2.6 | 5.0 | 0.9 | 7.6 | 14.6 | 2.6 | 5.4 | 7.0 | 4.2 | 6.6 | 11.3 | 3.2 |
| 80–84 | 12.1 | 18.5 | 7.9 | 4.7 | 9.1 | 1.9 | 8.1 | 17.7 | 1.9 | 7.9 | 11.5 | 5.5 | 0.5 | 11.3 | 1.8 |
| 85 and over | 3.1 | 4.4 | 2.4 | 19.6 | 42.7 | 7.0 | 2.9 | 4.2 | 2.3 | 5.7 | 4.0 | 6.6 | 4.1 | 11.8 | — |
| Un-known | 380.4 | 480.4 | 285.9 | 197.2 | 239.5 | 158.1 | 179.5 | 233.7 | 130.4 | 114.0 | 126.5 | 103.0 | 123.6 | 170.6 | 92.9 |

SOURCE: Division of Vital Statistics, Ministry of Public Health, Thailand.

group. The incidence of suicide by age groups in Thailand is different from that for Americans, Europeans, Japanese, or Ceylonese, possibly because Thai youths are subject to more stressful situations than are youths of other countries. Thai children usually are raised in a protective atmosphere, pampered by parents, grandparents, and other senior relatives who live together in an extended family unit. Thai children are therefore not well prepared to cope with life situations faced by young adults. When competing with others they are on their own, as their parents are unable to fight for them. Those who fail the tests of adulthood may be desperate enough to do away with themselves.

Elderly people in Thailand are treated with respect and gratitude. Those who are negligent in taking good care of their parents are blamed and looked down upon and regarded as outcasts. Elderly people usually live their lives with dignity and efforts to preserve their self-esteem. Most of them are religious and follow the Buddhist way of life, which is quiet and peaceful, until the end of their lives. These characteristics probably account for the low suicide rate among the elderly. Now things are changing, especially in the big cities where people have to work so hard that they may not have time to give proper attention to their parents. The elderly then experience a sense of rejection, desperation, and loneliness while their children feel guilty for not fulfilling their obligations. If this trend of social changes continues it is likely that the suicide rate among the elderly will increase. It is noteworthy that the suicide rate is rather low at ages 30−59, the most active years of adult life. In this period men find that their physical and mental capacities are at the maximal level. The ability to cope with the stresses of life is at its best.

Sex

In 1960 the rate of male suicides per 100,000 population, 4.3, was roughly 50 percent higher than the female rate of 2.7 (table 5-3). Over the years since then the gap has narrowed, as the female rate steadily increased while the male rate remained fairly constant. Between 1960 and 1976 the latter stayed within the narrow 4−5 range except for three years (3.9 in 1971, 5.1 in 1974, 5.2 in 1976), while the female rate almost doubled in the same time span (table 5-3). The rate according to age group also differs, being highest for females aged 15−24 and highest for males of 60 and over. The female rate in the 15−24 age group has increased gradually since 1960, strongly suggesting that Thai females encounter most difficulties in that period. After 25 they lead happier lives; even in the climacteric period the suicide rate does not exceed the expected level. In Thai culture girls are expected to help their mothers do housework, a responsibility from which boys are usually exempt. Sometimes the eldest girl has to assume the role of mother in the absence of her mother. But the social structure is now changing, as women are trying to compete with men and are rejecting their customary role. Yet in doing so they suffer from guilt feelings for not being good daughters to their parents. This conflict is a possible reason for the high suicide rate among adolescent and young adult females.

## Marital Status

Data on the relationship between marital status and suicide are not complete because the marital status of the victims was frequently not known or recorded. The figures in table 5-4 are composites derived from the studies by Bussaratid and Vicharnratavakan (3) and by Tosayanonda and Eungprabhanth (13). Of the 208 suicidal deaths reported in the former, only 75 had marital status recorded; in the latter, such data were recorded for 581 deaths. From the tabulation, more single than married persons committed suicide, but no statistics on marital status in the general population are available for comparative purposes. In fact, a good number of young adults kill themselves before they reach the age of marriage. There is no reason to assume that those who remain single (beyond the usual age of getting married) are likely to kill themselves more frequently than those who are married. Divorced and widowed persons were also suicide victims, but it is not known whether the risk of suicide among them is higher than among other groups.

## Education

The data in table 5-5 are derived from Bussaratid and Vicharnratavakan's study (3), though it does not supply a complete record of educational background. Since the figures given do not differ markedly from census data on the educational level of the general population, it may be assumed that people of different educational levels and perhaps of different classes and occupation are at the same risk of suicide.

### TABLE 5-4
### MARITAL STATUS OF 656 SUICIDE VICTIMS IN THAILAND, 1975
### AND 1977 AND IN THE PERIOD 1953–1969

| Status | Male | Female | Total |
|--------|------|--------|-------|
| Single | 130 | 137 | 267 |
| Married | 138 | 106 | 244 |
| Widowed | 10 | 6 | 16 |
| Divorced | 3 | 2 | 5 |
| Unknown | 102 | 22 | 124 |
| Total | 383 | 273 | 656 |

SOURCES: Bussaratid and Vicharnratavakan, 1978 (3); Tosayanonda and Eungprabhanth, 1969 (13).

TABLE 5-5
EDUCATIONAL LEVEL OF 208 SUICIDE VICTIMS IN THAILAND,
1975 AND 1977

| Level | Male | Female | Total |
|---|---|---|---|
| Illiterate | 0 | 1 | 1 |
| Primary school | 38 | 42 | 80 |
| Secondary school | 5 | 5 | 10 |
| University or college | 1 | 2 | 3 |
| Unknown | 61 | 53 | 114 |

SOURCE: Bussaratid and Vicharnratavakan, 1978 (3).

## Methods

Of the 1,032 deaths by suicide from the studies by Bussaratid and Vicharnratavakan (3) and by Tosayanonda and Eungprabhanth (13), 579 were caused by poison, the means most frequently used to commit suicide (see table 5-6). The insecticide parathion was the most common poison chosen. Other pesticides, including organic phosphates, DDT, zinc phosphates, and arsenic, were also used. Drugs, such as tranquilizers and hypnotics, were the third most commonly used drugs. Other poisons occasionally employed were strychnine, cyanide, corrosives such as Lysol, acetic acid, and methyl salicylates. Women tended to use poisons more than men. The second most frequent means of suicide was hanging, which accounted for 291 cases of the 1,032. Men hanged themselves more frequently than women. Firearms, the third most common means of committing suicide, were also used by more men than women. Other infrequently used methods were drowning, stabbing, jumping from high places, and jumping in front of a train.

## Seasonal Variations

The seasonal variations of suicide presented in table 5-7 are derived from Bussaratid and Vicharnratavakan's study of 208 suicidal deaths (3). During the first four months of the year death by suicide occurred much less frequently than in the rest of the year. Suicidal deaths occurred most frequently in May, July, and December. It would, however, be incorrect to draw any conclusions from these data, and there is no possible explanation for the seasonal variations reported.

## Psychiatric Illness

It would be interesting to know what those who committed suicide thought and felt prior to the act. Robins tried to study this question retrospectively by interviewing and collecting all available information

TABLE 5-6
METHODS OF COMMITTING SUICIDE IN THAILAND, BASED ON
STATISTICS FROM TWO SOURCES, FOR VARYING DATES

| Method | Male | Female | Total |
|---|---|---|---|
| 1975, 1977: BUSSARATID AND VICHARNRATAVAKAN (3) | | | |
| Poison | 48 | 71 | 119 |
| Hanging | 37 | 24 | 61 |
| Firearms | 17 | 6 | 23 |
| Other | 3 | 2 | 5 |
| Total | 105 | 103 | 208 |
| 1953−1969: TOSAYANONDA AND EUNGPRABHANTH (13) | | | |
| Poison | 232 | 228 | 460 |
| Hanging | 164 | 66 | 230 |
| Firearms | 63 | 12 | 75 |
| Other | 55 | 4 | 59 |
| Total | 514 | 310 | 824 |

TABLE 5-7
SEASONAL VARIATIONS IN 208 SUICIDES IN THAILAND, 1975 AND 1977

| Month | Male | Female | Total |
|---|---|---|---|
| January | 7 | 4 | 11 |
| February | 3 | 7 | 10 |
| March | − | − | − |
| April | 9 | 2 | 11 |
| May | 10 | 17 | 27 |
| June | 8 | 5 | 13 |
| July | 14 | 11 | 25 |
| August | 8 | 13 | 21 |
| September | 8 | 10 | 18 |
| October | 9 | 9 | 18 |
| November | 7 | 14 | 21 |
| December | 13 | 13 | 26 |

SOURCE: Bussaratid and Vicharnratavakan, 1978 (3).

from the relatives, friends, and fellow employees of victims (7). He found
that the victims of suicidal deaths were psychiatrically ill. But in Thailand
no study has been undertaken to establish a diagnosis for those who have
already killed themselves. Among twenty-nine victims of suicide reported
by Tosayanonda and Eungprabhanth (13) whose histories were available,
four were known to have been psychotic. Ruangtrakool et al. (10) studied

psychiatric patients at Siriraj Hospital who succeeded in killing themselves.
They found that the majority of Ruangtrakool's patients who ended in
suicide were depressed (63 percent) and that 20 percent were schizophrenic,
10 percent were alcoholics, and 7 percent were neurotics. These data show
that some suicide victims were psychiatrically ill and that depression,
schizophrenia, alcoholism, and neuroses were the disorders often found
among the victims of suicide.

## ATTEMPTED SUICIDE

Suicide is not a crime in Thailand. An individual who attempts but fails to
commit suicide is usually treated with tender, loving care; as a result, some
people make the attempt in order to gain attention from relatives and
friends. It is at times a useful device for a person to get what he wants.
There are, then, two groups of people who attempt suicide: those who
really want to die and those who do not. Attempters in the second category
usually do not harm themselves seriously and need no hospitalization. Most
of those who really want to die but fail in suicide attempts inflict serious
injuries on themselves and need hospitalization.

### Age and Sex

In 1973 Bussaratid and his associates conducted a survey of attempted
suicides in Bangkok. The subjects were suicide attempters who came or
were brought to Siriraj Hospital in 1973, separated into three groups: 33
nonhospitalized failed attempters; 130 hospitalized failed attempters; and
33 successful attempters who were dead on arrival. The results of the
survey are shown in table 5-8.

TABLE 5-8
ATTEMPTED AND COMPLETED SUICIDES IN BANGKOK, 1973

| Age group | Attempted suicides | | | | | | Completed suicides | | |
|---|---|---|---|---|---|---|---|---|---|
| | Nonhospitalized | | | Hospitalized | | | | | |
| | Male | Female | Total | Male | Female | Total | Male | Female | Total |
| Under 21 | 1 | 13 | 14 | 14 | 32 | 46 | 7 | 4 | 11 |
| 21−30 | 7 | 9 | 16 | 21 | 23 | 44 | 3 | 6 | 9 |
| 31−40 | 1 | 1 | 2 | 8 | 12 | 20 | 3 | 4 | 7 |
| 41−50 | – | – | – | 7 | 3 | 10 | 2 | 1 | 3 |
| 51−60 | 1 | – | 1 | 5 | 2 | 7 | 2 | 1 | 3 |
| Over 60 | – | – | – | 3 | – | 3 | – | – | – |
| Total | 10 | 23 | 33 | 58 | 72 | 130 | 17 | 16 | 33 |

SOURCE: Bussaratid et al., 1975 (2).

The ratio of men to women was approximately 1:2 among the nonhospitalized attempters, almost 6:7 among hospitalized attempters, and about 1:1 among completed suicides. Most of the nonserious attempters were 30 or under, and very few of them were over 30. Those who really wanted to die and failed to do so (hospitalized group) were found in all age groups, with the heaviest concentration being under 40. The same generalization is true of the successful attempters. The logical conclusion is that people over 30 who attempt suicide are likely to be serious in wanting to die, whereas those under 30 may or may not intend to kill themselves. This conclusion is contrary to the national statistics on suicide, which suggest that the 20–24 age group has the highest rate of suicidal death. A possible explanation is that younger people attempt suicide much more frequently than older persons even though the rate of success is much less than among the elderly. Bussaratid et al. (2) estimated that there were roughly fifty failed attempts to one successful attempt.

Marital Status

The number of cases surveyed by Bussaratid and his associates (2) is far too small to be definitive (table 5-9); moreover, no census of marital status in the general population exists, so comparison is impossible. As noted earlier, younger people attempt suicide more frequently than older people, and many of the former are under the age for marriage. It is not surprising, then, that more single than married people kill themselves. No study concerning suicide among divorcees, widows, and widowers has been made. It is noteworthy that more boys than girls attempt suicide because of disappointment in love affairs. More females than males try to take their own lives because of marital disharmony.

Occupation

Maids and housekeepers and those who own small businesses run by the family accounted for more than half the suicide attempts in Bangkok in 1973 (table 5-10), according to the sample survey conducted by Bussaratid and

TABLE 5-9
MARITAL STATUS OF NONHOSPITALIZED FAILED SUICIDES
IN BANGKOK, 1973

| Marital status | Male | Female |
|---|---|---|
| Single | 5 | 10 |
| Married | 4 | 13 |
| Buddhist monk | 1 | 0 |

SOURCE: Bussaratid et al., 1975 (2).

TABLE 5-10
OCCUPATION OF NONHOSPITALIZED FAILED SUICIDES
IN BANGKOK, 1973

| Occupation | Number | Percentage |
|---|---|---|
| Family business | 8 | 24 |
| Maid, housekeeper | 10 | 30 |
| Factory worker | 3 | 9 |
| Skilled manual laborer | 4 | 12 |
| Civil officer | 1 | 3 |
| Student | 2 | 6 |
| Farmer | 2 | 6 |
| Buddhist monk | 1 | 5 |
| Unemployed | 2 | 6 |

SOURCE: Bussaratid et al., 1975 (2).

associates (2). Other victims were factory workers, skilled manual laborers, civil officers, students, farmers, unemployed persons, and one Buddhist monk. Again the number of cases surveyed is too small for us to draw conclusions; besides, the figures reported in table 5-10 were obtained from the emergency room at Siriraj Hospital, where upper-class people seldom go for treatment. From our own clinical experience we believe that people in all social classes and in every type of occupation, ranging from illiterates to physicians and from criminals to Buddhist monks, attempt or commit suicide.

Educational Level

Of the sample of 33 persons who attempted suicide in Bangkok in 1973, surveyed by Bussaratid and associates (2), 23, or 70 percent, had completed primary school; those with a secondary school education accounted for 27 percent of all the attempters (table 5-11). Only 3 percent had had a college education. There were no illiterates among the victims in the sample. Even without a valid study from which conclusions can be drawn, we believe that people at all educational levels attempt suicide. The acts of those who have a higher education are, however, not always reported.

Psychiatric Illness

Table 5-12, derived from the survey by Bussaratid and associates (2) of nonhospitalized suicide attempters, shows that more than a third were clinically depressed and that almost a fifth suffered from personality disorders. The remaining attempters were schizophrenic, anxiety neurotic, mentally retarded, or undiagnosed. No studies on psychiatric disorders of serious attempters have been prepared, but some differences would be

TABLE 5-11
EDUCATION OF NONHOSPITALIZED FAILED SUICIDES
IN BANGKOK, 1973

| Educational level | Number | Percentage |
|---|---|---|
| Primary school | 23 | 70 |
| Secondary school | 9 | 27 |
| University or college | 1 | 3 |
| Illiterate | 0 | 0 |

SOURCE: Bussaratid et al., 1975 (2).

TABLE 5-12
PSYCHIATRIC DIAGNOSIS OF NONHOSPITALIZED FAILED
SUICIDES IN BANGKOK, 1973

| Diagnosis | Number | Percentage |
|---|---|---|
| Depression | 12 | 36 |
| Personality disorder | | 18 |
| Sociopathic | 2 | 6 |
| Nonsociopathic | 4 | 12 |
| Schizophrenia | 2 | 6 |
| Anxiety neurosis | 1 | 3 |
| Mental retardation | 1 | 3 |
| Undiagnosed | 1 | 3 |

SOURCE: Bussaratid et al., 1975 (2).

revealed. Our clinical impression is that serious attempters would suffer from depression, schizophrenia, organic brain syndrome, alcoholism, or personality disorders. Most of both the successful suicide attempters and the failed attempters were depressed. In some instances there was no evidence of psychiatric illness, but that situation was less common and was usually found among nonserious attempters.

Methods

Ruangtrakool and his associates (9) found that three-fourths of 105 attempters at Siriraj Hospital took poison as a means of attempting suicide. One-tenth stabbed themselves, and another tenth tried hanging. Other methods employed were jumping from a height, biting one's tongue, and jumping into the river (the victim did not swim).

Table 5-13 compares the methods employed by would-be suicides, both nonserious and serious, and actual suicides. Again the data came from the study by Bussaratid and associates (2). Nonserious attempters tended to use

## TABLE 5-13
### METHODS USED IN ATTEMPTED AND COMPLETED SUICIDES IN BANGKOK, 1973

| Method | Attempted suicides | | | | | | Completed suicides | | | Total |
| --- | --- | --- | --- | --- | --- | --- | --- | --- | --- | --- |
| | Nonhospitalized | | | Hospitalized | | | | | | |
| | Male | Female | Total | Male | Female | Total | Male | Female | Total | |
| Poisons, drugs | | | 31 | | | 97 | | | 20 | 148 |
| Rodenticides | 2 | 6 | 8 | 2 | 4 | 6 | – | – | – | |
| Insecticides | 3 | 2 | 5 | 19 | 30 | 49 | 9 | 7 | 16 | |
| Drugs | 4 | 11 | 15 | 7 | 18 | 25 | – | – | – | |
| Other poisons | 1 | 2 | 3 | 7 | 10 | 17 | – | 4 | 4 | |
| Knives | – | 1 | 1 | 14 | 3 | 17 | – | – | – | 18 |
| Firearms | – | – | – | 5 | 1 | 6 | 7 | 1 | 8 | 14 |
| Hanging | – | – | – | 4 | – | 4 | 1 | 4 | 5 | 9 |
| Drowning | – | – | – | – | 4 | 4 | – | – | – | 4 |
| Jumping from height | – | 1 | 1 | 2 | 2 | 4 | – | – | – | 5 |

SOURCE: Bussaratid et al., 1975 (2).

drugs, such as tranquilizers or hypnotics, in small dosages. Dangerous poisons, insecticide and rodenticides, for example, were less frequently used. Some nonserious attempters might try dangerous methods, like stabbing or jumping from a height, but they would apply them lightly: for instance, a young lady jumped from a window only 10 feet high and her only injury was a sprained ankle. Poisons and drug overdosages were also frequently taken by serious attempters as well, but they chose the more dangerous poisons and took lethal amounts of the drugs. Successful attempters used poisoning more than other methods, but they also tried the more dangerous methods of firearms and hanging.

## CASE HISTORIES

### Case A

A 25-year-old married Thai housewife from a provincial town was admitted to Siriraj Hospital in January 1973 after attempting suicide by ingesting an insecticide. In her family she is the youngest of three children. Her parents got a divorce and both of them remarried when she was very young. She and her siblings were raised by their father and stepmother and had little contact with their mother. The father, a taxi driver, paid more attention to the patient's half siblings than to his children by his first marriage. The patient described the environment in which she grew up as insecure and miserable. She kept looking forward to leaving the family, dreaming of getting married to a good man. At fifteen she met a man with whom she finally fell in love and ran away with him when she was sixteen. Her husband took her to live with his sister. The in-laws did not like her but she had to live with them because she had no other place to go.

Two years later the patient had her first child. Two months after that she began to suffer from rheumatoid arthritis, which prevented her from carrying on her usual housework. She became a burden to her sister-in-law, who increasingly expressed hostility toward her. Ensuing friction with her husband created a sense of desperation and depression, but she went with him when he moved to another town a year later. He began to gamble and they continued to quarrel.

The young woman, finally deciding to leave her husband, went to live with her father. She helped her stepmother run the small family business and took care of her retarded half brother. The life imposed a heavy burden on her. Her husband lost his job and went to live with her, staying four months. He then got a job in another city but soon quit it and went back to live with his wife. She became pregnant for the second time. The husband again left for a new job in Bangkok and sent her some money, but he did not come to see his second child when it was born.

When the patient learned that her husband was living with another woman, her world fell apart. She became depressed and could not sleep; she lost her appetite and lost weight. She blamed herself for not being a good housewife. She wanted to die and frequently expressed her death wishes to her sister. When the second child was eighteen months old her husband came to take the child to live with him in Bangkok, and he promised to send his wife money every month. He kept his promise for about a year, but then he quit sending the money. After the patient had received nothing for three months, she went to see her husband in Bangkok. He told her to go back home because he no longer cared for her. She decided to go and took her children with her.

On her way home she suddenly developed a strong desire to kill herself. She bought two bottles of insecticide and rented a room in a hotel. She mixed the poison with milk and drank a cup of the mixture. Then, realizing that her children would be left with their father and stepmother, she decided to take them along with her. She mixed another cup of poison and milk and gave it to the children to drink. The elder child got sick and left the room, the bellboy found him, and all of them were sent to the hospital. The younger child died a few days after hospitalization, but the elder one survived.

During the first two weeks in the hospital the patient was somnolent and confused; she began to regain consciousness in the third week, when she learned that her small child had died. In her imagination she saw and heard her dead son. Her mood was labile; she did not eat or sleep. When treatment with antipsychotic and antidepressant drugs was started she stopped hallucinating, but she continued to be depressed. She began to get better, but when she learned that a charge had been brought against her for attempting murder she again became depressed. After the charge was lifted on the ground of insanity, she recovered. A year after leaving the hospital she was in good health, having obtained a divorce and gone to live with her sister.

## Case B

A single Thai 18-year-old male was hospitalized after hanging himself. He was the oldest of six children. He had quit school while he was in eighth grade because his father committed suicide. His father had been suffering from high blood pressure for five years and was worried about his illness. Approximately five days before his death he began to have trouble sleeping and developed a severe headache. The day before his death he disappeared, and on the following day his body was found floating in the river. He had drowned after jumping off a bridge. The son quit school to help his mother run the small family business, which yielded a profit barely large enough to support the family.

In his early years the boy had been quite happy because he was his father's and grandparents' favorite. He was described by his mother as a quick-tempered child. He threw things and broke glasses when he could not get his way. When his mother tried to reprimand him, he looked upon her scolding as maternal rejection, but he did go through his early developmental period without getting into serious problems.

About a year before the youth's hospitalization his mother started an affair with an old friend of his father's, a man with a wife and three children. In spite of the son's strong objection, the mother and her lover lived together openly as man and wife. The patient, disgusted and humiliated, felt that his stepfather was taking away his mother's love. Hostility and frequent friction arose between the patient and his stepfather.

Three months prior to hospitalization the boy fell in love with a girl but the girl's mother did not like him. He began to worry about the future and could not sleep well at night. He was irritable, argued with his mother, had headaches, and got tired of working. He became depressed and lost interest in everything, feeling that his life was empty and not worth living. He could see no way of solving his problem. He expressed his death wish to his siblings and mother, as he thought suicide was the only way out of his difficulties.

On the day of hospitalization his mother became angry at him because he had quarreled with a customer. The patient looked deeply disappointed and desperate. He went home early and did not help his mother as usual. A few hours later his mother found him hanging in his room. He was taken to the hospital but he died two days later.

## SUMMARY

The suicide rate in Thailand in 1957, according to government statistics, was 2.7 per 100,000 population, rising to 4.9 in 1976. In comparison, a study of 14,000 death certificates by Bussaratid and Vicharnratavakan indicated a suicide rate of 15 per 100,000 in 1976. The highest incidence was found in the 20–24 age group, both males and females. The number of suicides fell dramatically in the age group 30–60, and then made a significant but variable rise after age 60. The ratio of male to female rates was 4.3:2.7 in 1960 and 5.0:4.8 in 1975, indicating both a rise in the overall suicide rate and a larger number of female suicides.

The main means of suicide were, in order of frequency of use, poisons, hanging, and firearms. The poisons used were usually those intended for agricultural or household use.

Most attempted suicides were found among persons under 21 years of age and between the ages of 20 and 30. The survey by Bussaratid et al. showed a ratio of 1:2 (male to female) attempts among nonserious cases and 6:7 in serious attempts. As those who fail in suicide attempts are usually treated with kindness and concern, an attempt becomes a useful method of gaining attention. The major methods employed were poisons and pills, followed by stabbing and hanging. There is evidence that untrained workers and small businessmen were more prone to attempt suicide than people in other occupations. Many female attempts are made in response to family problems.

## BIBLIOGRAPHY

1. Brooke, M. *Suicide and Attempted Suicide.* Public Health Paper no. 58. Geneva: World Health Organization, 1974.
2. Bussaratid, S., K., Kaewpanukrungsee, K. Puranasamriddhi, and S. Ruang-trakool. Attempted suicide in Bangkok. *J. Med. Assoc. Thailand,* 58 (1975): 138–142.
3. Bussaratid, S., and T. Vicharnratavakan. Suicide rate in Thailand. *J. Psychiatr. Assoc. Thailand,* 2 (1978):158–167.
4. Eungprabhanth, V. Combined suicide by cut throat and caustic soda ingestion. *Forensic Science,* 2 (1973):471–474.
5. Eungprabhanth, V. Suicide in Thailand. *Forensic Science,* 5 (1975):43–51.
6. Ministry of Public Health. Division of Vital Statistics. Thailand. *Statistics, 1973–1974.*
7. Robins, E., G. Murphy, R. Wilkinson, S. Gassner, and J. Kayes. Some clinical considerations in the prevention of suicide based on a study of 134 successful suicides. *Amer. J. Public Health,* 49 (1959):888.
8. Ruangtrakool, S., O. Thongtang, and K. Kaewpanukrungsee. A study of successful suicide in eight patients. *Siriraj Hospital Gazette,* 11 (1974): 2077–2093.
9. Ruangtrakool, S., O. Thongtang, K. Kaewpanukrungsee, and K. Sukhatunga. A study of 105 cases of attempted suicide. *Siriraj Hospital Gazette,* 3 (1975): 317–335.
10. Ruangtrakool, S., O. Thongtang, K. Kaewpanukrungsee, and K. Sukhatunga. Characteristics of successful suicide: A clinical study of 27 cases. *Siriraj Hospital Gazette,* 6 (1975):771–785.
11. Ruangtrakool, S., O. Thongtang, K. Kaewpanukrungsee, K. Amatayakul, V. Eungprabhanth, and S. Srivannaboon. Filicide cases report with medico-legal comment. *J. Psychiatr. Assoc. Thailand,* 21 (1976):9–25.
12. Sukatonga, K., and Kowit Buranasamrit. The layman attitude toward suicide. *J. Clinical Psychol.* (Thailand), 8 (1977):36–43.
13. Tosayanonda, S., and V. Eungprabhanth. Suicide. *Siriraj Hospital Gazette,* 11 (1969): 393–409.

# SRI LANKA 6

*Editor's Note*

Sri Lanka is one of the many Asian countries that gained independence from foreign colonial rule after World War II. The republic has general suffrage, compulsory education, and therefore a high literacy rate. The governmental system is comparatively well organized, thanks to British colonialism. Major products are tea, rubber, cotton, rice, spices, graphite, and precious stones.

This beautiful, fertile land is plagued by serious problems which thus far have defied solution. Although Sri Lanka is a large rice producer, it has to import rice to meet the needs of its people. Free rice rations have been provided for some time (now only to the poor), but when the government occasionally attempts to drop the program, vigorous protests follow. The high literacy rate has created an oversupply of educated youth who cannot find jobs; the resulting resentment leads to periodic rioting against the government for not stimulating more employment. Twenty percent of the population lives in cities, which look much the same as they did in colonial times. The Tamil Hindu population in the north agitates for self-rule—a not surprising manifestation in view of the country's historical roots. Conquerors from north India founded the Sinhalese dynasty in the sixth century b.c.; later there were invasions by southern Indian Tamils. The country had two separate kingdoms of these Indian invaders until European conquests began in the sixteenth century. The Tamils want their own language and governing bodies, and they have succeeded to some extent in obtaining these objectives. They are the most vocal of the groups living in Sri Lanka: Sinhalese, Tamils, Moors (of Arab blood), European–Sri Lanka mixtures, Malays, and the few remaining Veddas, the original inhabitants. Socialist groups dissatisfied with the economy are a political force.

S. A. Wijaya Dissanayake, FRC Psych., FRCP(E), DPM (UK), has been chairman of the Department of Psychiatry, Faculty of Medicine, University of Colombo, since 1970 and also served as consultant-psychiatrist at General Hospital in Colombo. A graduate of the University of Sri Lanka, he took postgraduate work in the United Kingdom, receiving a degree in psychological medicine. While there he was on the staff of several National Health Service hospitals. He is a member of the Royal College of Physicians, Edinburgh (1965), and of the Royal College of Psychiatrists. His special interests are epidemiological and transcultural psychiatry. The rapid increase in suicides in Sri Lanka prompted him to begin his studies in that field in 1960.

Padmal De Silva is also a graduate of the University of Sri Lanka. He obtained his M.A. in psychology at the University of Edinburgh. After working with Dr. Dissanayake in Colombo and lecturing in clinical psychology, he received his M. Phil. (Clinical Psychology) in England and is now a lecturer at the Institute of Psychiatry, Mandsley Hospital, London.

# S. A. W. DISSANAYAKE and PADMAL DE SILVA[1]

## INTRODUCTION

Sri Lanka is situated in the Indian Ocean, separated from the southern extremity of India by a narrow strip of sea about twenty miles across. This tropical island is 270 miles long and at its broadest point about 170 miles wide, covering an area of 25,332 square miles (65,630 square kilometers). It is comparable in size to the state of West Virginia or the Republic of Eire. In the center of the island is a mass of mountains, the highest of which is over 8,000 feet, surrounded by coastal plains. The northern end of the island tapers into a peninsula called Jaffna.

As Sri Lanka is close to the equator—its southern shore is about 6° north latitude—temperatures are high, around 27°C (80°F). The climate is equable, however, because of the sea all around the island and the mountains in the interior. In the hill country the temperature is much cooler, ranging from 12° to 22° (55°−70°F). Rainfall varies widely in the different parts of the island. The southwestern part of the island and the mountains have heavy monsoonal rains, whereas the northern and eastern parts are comparatively dry.

The population of the island in 1978, estimated from a census taken in 1971, was 14,184,000. A large proportion of the inhabitants live in the southwestern part of the island, which is dominated by the capital city of Colombo, Sri Lanka's main commercial center. It is a seaport with a population of 652,000.

In spite of its relatively small size, the country has many linguistic or ethnic groups, living in specific areas. The largest group, the Sinhalese, who number more than 10 million, are mostly descendants of migrants

[1]We are grateful to Mr. R. I. Abeysekera, chief statistician, Registrar General's Department, Colombo; to Mr. E. Gunawardene, superintendent, Planning and Research, Police Headquarters, Colombo; and to Mr. D. P. Gunaratne of the Department of Census and Statistics, all of whom supplied statistical data on suicide. A special debt is owed to Mr. V. Navaratnam, assistant director, Department of Census and Statistics, for valuable comments and advice, and to the chief magistrate, Colombo, for permission to consult coroner's records in Colombo.

from north India who settled in the island about 500 B.C. The low-country Sinhalese, numbering 6,097,000, live in the southwestern and southern coastal plains. As they have experienced the impact of European administration, commerce, and missionary enterprise since the beginning of the sixteenth century, their traditional way of life and their outlook have been affected to a higher degree than those of other ethnic groups. Somewhat more than 4 million Sinhalese live in the valleys and the plateaus of the hill country and on the north central plains, around the city of Kandy, the seat of government of the Kandyan Kingdom up to 1815. Referred to as the Kandyan Sinhalese in census reports, they form a subcultural group of inhabitants who are more rural, traditional, and conservative in their way of life than others.

The main minority community, the Tamils, also comprises two subgroups. The Ceylon Tamils have been living on the island, mainly in the northern part, from the earliest centuries of its history. They number 1,578,000. The second group, the Indian Tamils numbering about 1 million, have lived in the central hill country since the middle of the nineteenth century, when the British brought them from south India to the island as indentured laborers to work on the tea plantations. Some of them are presently being repatriated to India under an Indo–Sri Lanka agreement.

The other communities in the island are the Moors (952,000), descendants of the North African and Arabian seafaring merchants of the Middle Ages, and the Burghers (49,000) or the Eurasians, who are of mixed Portuguese and Dutch ancestry.

Almost two-thirds of the population follow the Theravada or the orthodox Southern School of Buddhism, found also in Burma, Thailand, and Cambodia. This form of Buddhism was introduced to the island in the third century B.C., when Asoka was the Indian emperor. The Tamils are mainly Hindus; the Moors form the bulk of the Muslim population of the island. By and large, except for Christianity, religious faith closely parallels ethnic groups: more than 92 percent of the Sinhalese are Buddhists, and a similar percentage of Tamils are Hindus. Nearly a million (987,660) Christians, including a minority of Sinhalese and Tamils and the entire Burgher community, live in Sri Lanka. A large majority of the Christians profess to the Roman Catholic faith.

In addition to language, religious and cultural differences separate the various communities in Sri Lanka, with very little intermarriage among them. Ethnically these communities can hardly be called "races," though they are so classified. The population of Sri Lanka is of mixed origin, predominantly Caucasian from northern India, with some admixture of Mediterranean from western Asia and the prehistoric Australoid race.

Politically Sri Lanka was an independent kingdom from the time of its earliest recorded history. Various dynasties of Sinhalese kings ruled the country until the advent of the European powers. The Portuguese, arriving in 1505, occupied the maritime regions of Sri Lanka until they were displaced by the Dutch in 1658. The British, who took over these areas from the Dutch in 1796, were able to annex the hitherto independent Kandyan Kingdom in 1815, and the whole of Sri Lanka became a crown colony of the British Empire. In 1948 the island became independent and in May 1972 it was declared a republic within the British Commonwealth.

Sri Lanka is one of the few countries in Asia with a ruling parliament, chosen by Western-style free elections. On three occasions since independence the governing party has been ousted from power through the ballot. In 1978 the newly elected government of the conservative United National Party promulgated a new constitution giving wider powers to the president.

Some years ago the government introduced a free rice ration for everybody, a largess a developing country could ill afford. The practice has recently been discontinued, except for the very lowest income groups.

Under British colonial administration a predominantly self-sufficient agricultural economy was transformed into one that devoted a vast acreage to cash crops like tea and rubber, after the evergreen tropical forests of the southwestern and mountainous regions had been felled. The importance of tea to the national economy is shown by the fact that it accounts for more than half the value of all exports from the island. Of late a determined effort has been made to supplant the traditional plantation economy with crop diversification and expansion of light industry, so as to make the country self-sufficient in cereals and other essential foodstuffs.

In spite of the changes brought about by British rule, about 62 percent of the people of Sri Lanka still live by agriculture, a majority of them practicing age-old methods of paddy cultivation and growing other subsidiary foodstuffs on small holdings. Only 20 percent of the Sri Lankans live in urban or developed areas. Sri Lanka's population is increasing rapidly, about 2 percent a year, as the birthrate remains high (27.9 per thousand) and the mortality rate is relatively low (7.4 per thousand). It is also noteworthy that more than 8 million inhabitants are young people under 24 years of age (60 percent of the population). Sri Lanka is thus a south Asian country with a distinctive Buddhist culture which has remained intact, by and large, despite several centuries of European domination and influence. It is also a developing country that is predominantly agricultural and has a literacy rate of 80 percent and a life expectancy of 65.9 years. These figures are high by Asian standards.

## METHODS OF DATA COLLECTION

The two main sources of statistical information about suicide in Sri Lanka are annual reports of (1) the registrar general and (2) the inspector general of police. Some researchers have used data from the former (e.g., Strauss and Strauss, 1953 [16] and others have relied on the latter (e.g., Jayawardane and Ranasinghe, 1966 [10]. The registrar general's reports are somewhat more reliable than those of the police; the latter consistently reports lower suicide figures than the former (table 6–1). The differences occur because the two agencies have different ways of collecting suicide data from their respective sources and of recording them. The methods of both reflect the thoroughness and the relative efficiency with which data were collected by a British colonial administration in an Asian country where circumstances were favorable. Such data are available from the year 1880 onward.

The investigation and recording of suicides in Sri Lanka follow a set pattern. By law, in the event of a sudden or an accidental death, or if death occurs within twenty-four hours of admission to a hospital, an inquest must be held by a coroner or an inquirer into sudden deaths (2). A postmortem examination or an autopsy is peformed by an authorized medical officer. After ascertaining the cause of death and obtaining all the relevant evidence from key witnesses, the coroner reaches a verdict. A total of 617 coroners cover all areas of the island. Although they all work part-time, they are expected to hold inquests into sudden deaths without delay. The only full-time coroner in the island is the one who serves Colombo. Many of them, especially those in provincial and urban centers and towns, are practicing lawyers or attorneys; those in rural areas are community leaders or important government officials who have been nominated to perform the duties of a coroner.

Upon reaching his verdict, the coroner issues a letter to the party of the deceased. All documents concerning the inquest proceedings are kept in the local magistrate's courts. When the coroner's letter is forwarded to the registrar of births and deaths in the area, the death is registered and a death certificate issued. These particulars are then sent to the registrar general's department through the district registrars. Altogether there are 764 registrars of births and deaths and 25 district registrars on the island. The police data come to police headquarters from the district stations where deaths are reported. It is likely that many cases of which the police have not been informed, or for which police assistance has not been sought, are recorded only in the registrar general's office. The police may lack knowledge of many cases of attempted suicide whose victims later die in the hospital.

Thus it is evident that police data in Sri Lanka underestimate the total number of suicides, but it is also probable that the registrar general's data do not reflect the actual number of suicides. The underestimation is unavoidable and understandable. Relatives would, if possible, attempt to conceal suicides, for obvious social reasons. Coroners' verdicts are occasionally inconclusive, even though the evidence is adequate for a suicide verdict. The criteria of proof for a coroner's verdict of suicide in Sri Lanka are rigid and are bound by legal codes and conventions. Many cases are therefore

TABLE 6-1
NUMBER OF SUICIDES EACH YEAR IN SRI LANKA, 1958–1960

| Source of data | 1958 | | | 1959 | | | 1960 | | |
|---|---|---|---|---|---|---|---|---|---|
| | Male | Female | Total | Male | Female | Total | Male | Female | Total |
| Registrar general | 580 | 197 | 777 | 549 | 243 | 792 | 693 | 284 | 977 |
| Police | 483 | 188 | 671 | 559 | 216 | 775 | 640 | 203 | 843 |

recorded with an "open verdict" or as "accidental death." Such anomalies are also common in countries with a tradition of more efficient data collection, such as the United States or the United Kingdom. In America, for example, the number of suicides is probably higher by one-fourth to one-third than the number recorded (5).

Sainsbury's study of suicide in 1968 [14] demonstrates, however, that differences between national suicide rates are valid and should not be attributed to differences in reporting methods, especially in Euro-American cultures. In particular, Sainsbury has shown the reliability with which coroners in England and Wales report suicide, and that the differential rates for suicide in certain districts of England and Wales cannot be attributed to differences in procedure or criteria of suicide. He concludes that "Suicide, like any other cause of death, is certainly under-reported, but this type of error must operate randomly, otherwise correlations such as we have been describing would not be found. For suicide statistics to be useful the absolute rate is not required; some constant proportion of it is enough, and as the procedures used to record suicides apparently achieve this, we may now go on to compare the incidence of suicide at different times, in different places, and in various kinds of people" (14:5).

It may be said that the recording system in Sri Lanka is relatively satisfactory. A good communication network covering all parts of the island facilitates proper recording of deaths. Further, it is statutory that all deaths be registered and that in the case of sudden death an inquest be held. There are few religious beliefs and practices or social traditions in the country which hinder the smooth functioning of this process. In fact, as Strauss and Strauss note, the "registration system of Ceylon (Sri Lanka) is unusually good in comparison with those of other Asian countries and it is likely that the figures are directly comparable to similar statistics for western nations, which of course, includes all the usual deficiencies to which such figures are subject" (16:461).

Since the 1950s Sri Lanka's suicide rate has sharply increased, but there have been no corresponding changes in the criteria coroners use in reaching suicide verdicts or in the methods of data collection and recording. Therefore it may be concluded that the rates reflect a real increase.

The suicide data used in this chapter, unless otherwise stated, are based on figures published in the annual reports of the Registrar General's Department.

## SOCIAL AND FAMILY STRUCTURE

The traditional social structure in Sri Lanka, with its characteristic caste stratifications and the extended family system, is pertinent to the analysis of suicide in the country.

The caste system, which in earlier centuries was based on occupations of people, is still a factor of some importance in the social structure. Stratification was possible because there was almost no intermarriage between different castes; people practiced their distinctive age-old crafts and occupations and passed their skills on to succeeding generations. The largest caste group among the Sinhalese is the Cultivator or Goigama caste, which has a relatively high status. Among the others are the Fishermen caste and the Artisan caste, while the Scavenger caste is at the lower end of the hierarchy. The caste system among the Sinhalese is a relic of centuries of Hindu influence from India. It has survived into modern times even though Buddhism is strongly opposed to it. It is less rigid in its application, however, than that of the Hindu Tamils. Among the latter the caste system is more institutionalized, and it includes the lowly Untouchables.

Family life in Sri Lanka is based on the extended family system. Grandparents are often considered an integral component of the family unit. Strong bonds commonly exist among relatives, who have a bigger say in the management of family affairs than in the West. The caste barriers and bonds, and the extended family organization, are generally stronger among the Hindu Tamils and the Kandyan Sinhalese than among other ethnic groups in Sri Lanka.

These two traditional social institutions, with their associated codes and values, have felt the impact of the Western way of life and Western education. The caste system is visibly crumbling, especially among the low-country Sinhalese of the urban areas. But the extended family unit, including grandparents, is still quite popular, though how long the system will remain in its traditional form is unpredictable. The decline of the caste system and of family social organization is an aspect of the social disintegration that is evident today.

## ATTITUDES TO SUICIDE

Many factors, such as religious beliefs and cultural norms and values, influence the attitude of the people toward suicide.

The Christian and Islamic views on suicide professed by about 15 percent of the people are well known. With regard to Buddhism, the faith of the majority of the population, there seems to be a misconception in the Western mind that it encourages suicide (5:96). The tragic immolation of Buddhist monks in South Vietnam has also been cited in support of this claim (15:67). Traditional ancient suttee, which was practiced in some parts of India, has colored and dominated the Westerner's view of the Hindu attitude toward suicide.

Buddhism of the orthodox Southern School has influenced the beliefs and the way of life of the Sinhalese from the beginning of their history.

Likewise, Hindu philosophy and culture are dominant among the Tamils in the northern part of Sri Lanka. In contrast with the Judeo-Christian religions, one theme dominates the world view of both Buddhism and Hinduism: the doctrine of rebirth. According to this doctrine, an individual is subject to repeated cycles of birth and death before he achieves the ultimate salvation of Nirvana.

Buddhism extols the value of human life, for birth as a human being is the culmination of the individual's efforts through many previous cycles of births. Suicide is thus considered either as an empty, fruitless act from the point of view of man's salvation or as a behavior that will delay his ultimate enlightenment. Neither Buddhism nor Hinduism condemns man to an eternity of suffering for whatever misdeeds he has done in this short span of life, and suicide in comparison with many other acts is considered more as an error or a mistake than as a grave offense.

Self-sacrifice at the cost of one's life is also commended as meritorious in both Buddhism and Hinduism, but not suicide. Nowhere in orthodox Buddhist texts is there any reference that can be interpreted as supportive of suicide. In the Vinaya Pitaka (Book of Disciplines)—one of the three principal texts of the Southern School—which is said to contain the authentic word of the Buddha, there is a reference to suicide. When a monk who attempted suicide by throwing himself down onto a rock survived, he was brought before the Buddha, who admonished him for the act, stating that while it was a wrongful deed, it was not serious enough to oblige him to leave the monastic order (9:I, 142).

Suttee as practiced in various parts of India was never a custom among the Hindus of Sri Lanka in ancient times, showing that factors other than religious ones help to perpetuate a custom. Orthodox Hinduism does not encourage suicide in any way, yet the religious restraints against suicide in a Buddhist or Hindu culture are not as condemnatory as in Judeo-Christian or Islamic cultures. The belief in rebirth, the vision of a future existence free of suffering, may in fact—at least for some individuals—serve as a catalyst in precipitating suicide. One can visualize cults and sects emerging in such cultures which sanction or condone suicide in some form or other.

A Historical Perspective

In ancient Sri Lanka suicide was looked upon as a tragedy. This attitude is reflected in ancient chronicles which refer to kings who committed suicide after losing a battle, or to queens who chose death after some misfortune.

Two eminent Englishmen who lived in Sri Lanka during the early part of the nineteenth century have written on suicide in that country and the social attitudes toward it. Both men had intimate knowledge of the people and their customs. Dr. John Davy, brother of the renowned scien-

tist Sir Humphrey Davy, was stationed in Sri Lanka as medical officer to
the British army from 1816 to 1820. His book, *An Account of the Interior of
Ceylon and of Its Inhabitants with Travels in That Island* (3), refers to the
procedure adopted in the case of suicide. The investigation was the responsibility of Sake Ballande, a body functioning as a coroner's court. In fact the
term means investigation of evidence. If the suicide had been preventable,
the inhabitants of the village were subjected to a fine equal to about
29 shillings for their negligence. Davy notes, however, that "from all
I could learn, neither suicide nor murder was common amongst the
Sinhalese" (3:180—181).

Sir John D'Oyly, British commissioner in Sri Lanka at the time of the
capture of the Kandyan Kingdom by the British in 1815, throws further
light on the same subject in his book, *A Sketch of the Constitution of the
Kandyan Kingdom*. Unlike Davy, D'Oyly claims that suicide was not infrequent (4:32, 34). In general, he writes, suicide was owing to contempt for
life and a desire for revenge. It was, in many instances, a way of gaining
publicity for a grievance, such as an injury, a slander, or a debt. The person
would climb a tree and then proclaim his grievance. If he in fact jumped off
the tree and died, the provincial chief who conducted the death inquiry
would inflict a fine on the person responsible for the grievance. Interest-
ingly, D'Oyly points out that some people attempted suicide merely as a
threat, in order to draw attention to their grievances.

The contemporary attitudes toward suicide in Sri Lanka have also been
influenced by Western laws and ethics, first introduced to the island by the
Dutch and then by the British. These views are crystallized in the present-
day legal position of suicide in Sri Lanka, which is, in effect, a legacy of the
laws of the United Kingdom of an earlier period. According to the penal
code of Sri Lanka, aiding and abetting suicide is still an offense punishable
by death (2: chap. 32, sec. 362). Section 102 of the same chapter specifies
that a person found guilty of attempting suicide may be punished by a
one-year prison sentence, with or without hard labor, or by a fine, or by
both. In practice, however, judicial officers have been lenient toward such
offenders; rarely, if at all, is the maximum penalty ordered. Often the guilty
party is discharged or bound over for a short period.

Today, apart from legal prohibitions, suicide is usually considered a
disgrace and a social stigma by family members and other relatives. It is
neither condoned nor encouraged by any section of the population. A
family invariably reacts promptly to an attempted suicide, immediately
offering help and sympathy to the survivor and ignoring the undercurrents
of hostility and resentment which may have precipitated the attempt. Often
the appeal element in attempted suicide is recognized and the survivor may
win concessions from those concerned, thus realizing his objective. The

rejection of a survivor by his family and the community is almost unheard of.

## COMPLETED SUICIDES

### Suicide Rates

As noted earlier, suicide figures are available from the year 1880, yielding rates for each successive year. The trend, since 1880, has been steadily on the increase. The rates for a few representative years are given in table 6-2, which shows a slow and steady upward trend in the early years, followed by a more rapid increase in the past twenty-five years or so. Between 1900 and 1950 the rate increased by only 87 percent, whereas in the much shorter period 1950–1974 (table 6-3) it increased by about 450 percent. This remarkable growth overshadows the fluctuations in the rate over the decades. It may be explained as reflecting the rapid socioeconomic changes during the period after political independence was achieved in 1948. The breaking down of the older social structure, together with the shift from a sedate, basically agricultural socioeconomic pattern to a definitely competitive one, may have effected this change.

It is noteworthy that in this period of stress and tension the homicide rate increased far more slowly than the suicide rate. Table 6-4 gives the homicide rate from 1951 through 1969.

The suicide rates for 1975, 1976, and 1977 (19.5, 20.4, and 20.1, respectively, from table 6-3), however, show a slight decline from the all-time high of 22.1 recorded for 1974. Whether the trend indicates a slight reduc-

TABLE 6-2
SUICIDE RATE PER 100,000 POPULATION,
EVERY TENTH YEAR, 1880–1970

| Year | Rate |
|------|------|
| 1880 | 2.3 |
| 1890 | 2.9 |
| 1900 | 3.7 |
| 1910 | 5.2 |
| 1920 | 5.6 |
| 1930 | 5.2 |
| 1940 | 6.3 |
| 1950 | 6.9 |
| 1960 | 9.9 |
| 1970 | 19.2 |

SOURCE: Annual reports, Registrar General's Department, Sri Lanka.

TABLE 6-3
SUICIDE RATE PER 100,000 POPULATION
IN SRI LANKA, 1930–1977

| Year | Rate | Year | Rate |
|------|------|------|------|
| 1930 | 5.2  | 1954 | 8.0  |
| 1931 | 5.8  | 1955 | 7.0  |
| 1932 | 6.6  | 1956 | 7.8  |
| 1933 | 6.5  | 1957 | 8.0  |
| 1934 | 5.6  | 1958 | 8.3  |
| 1935 | 7.4  | 1959 | 8.2  |
| 1936 | 6.7  | 1960 | 9.9  |
| 1937 | 6.9  | 1961 | 9.7  |
| 1938 | 7.2  | 1962 | 11.6 |
| 1939 | 5.2  | 1963 | 12.1 |
| 1940 | 6.3  | 1964 | 14.7 |
| 1941 | 6.9  | 1965 | 13.7 |
| 1942 | 6.2  | 1966 | 13.7 |
| 1943 | 6.6  | 1967 | 16.9 |
| 1944 | 6.3  | 1968 | 17.2 |
| 1945 | 5.8  | 1969 | 19.7 |
| 1946 | 5.9  | 1970 | 19.2 |
| 1947 | 5.8  | 1971 | 18.2 |
| 1948 | 6.3  | 1972 | 21.0 |
| 1949 | 6.7  | 1973 | 22.0 |
| 1950 | 6.9  | 1974 | 22.1 |
| 1951 | 7.4  | 1975 | 19.5 |
| 1952 | 6.9  | 1976 | 20.4 |
| 1953 | 7.0  | 1977 | 20.1 |

tion in the rate of increase so as to form a plateau, or merely a transient interruption in the steady rise, is uncertain at this stage. The increase of 4.7 percent in the suicide rate over the eight-year period 1970–1977 is significantly lower than the 70.0 percent in the preceding eight years (1962–1969), suggesting that the sociopsychological stresses that may have led to a steep rise in the suicide rate in the 1960s are gradually becoming less intense, or that compensatory stabilizing responses of the community are making themselves felt. Similarly, the high birthrate of Sri Lanka maintained over several decades (29.4 per 1,000 in 1971) has shown a slight decline in recent years. In view of the social transformations that are taking place in the island, the drop in the suicide rate between 1974 and 1977 cannot be taken as the beginning of a substantial or a rapid decline.

Table 6-3 also shows a drop in Sri Lanka's suicide rate in relationship to World War II. Data for the country have also been viewed by Sainsbury as

TABLE 6-4
HOMICIDE RATE PER 100,000 POPULATION
IN SRI LANKA, 1951–1969

| Year | Rate |
| --- | --- |
| 1951 | 4.7 |
| 1952 | 5.1 |
| 1953 | 5.2 |
| 1954 | 5.7 |
| 1955 | 5.4 |
| 1956 | 5.5 |
| 1957 | 5.7 |
| 1958 | 7.5 |
| 1959 | 6.8 |
| 1960 | 5.4 |
| 1961 | 5.3 |
| 1962 | 5.8 |
| 1963 | 5.4 |
| 1964 | 5.7 |
| 1965 | 6.0 |
| 1966 | 5.6 |
| 1967 | 6.6 |
| 1968 | 6.0 |
| 1969 | 6.7 |

reflecting a decline in the suicide rate during wartime (14:5). The decline between 1938 and 1944 shown in table 6-3 is 12.5 percent. The mean suicide rate for the war years 1939–1945 is below the rate for 1938 and below the mean for the four immediate prewar years, with significance at the 5 percent level. There seems to be no corresponding decline in the rate during World War I, but that war had little impact on Sri Lanka even though the country was officially at war. On the other hand, the country was very much more involved and affected by World War II; the Japanese bombed many cities and there was a real invasion scare. Even during this time, however, the drop was not all that remarkable compared with that in many European countries. This result is perhaps only to be expected in a country that entered the war as a territory of the British Empire and would not have been psychologically motivated in a struggle that was, in a sense, imposed upon it.

As table 6-5 clearly shows, the suicide rate was at a high level for the 15–24 age group in the years 1951–1977, followed by decline in the middle years, with the lowest rate for the 35–44 age group. The upward trend then continued toward old age. This pattern held for most of the years for which age-specific suicide rates are available (see table 6-5). The peak in the rate for the younger age group puts Sri Lanka in contrast with the pattern found in most Western countries for which data are available. Usually the curve rises

TABLE 6-5

SUICIDE RATE PER 100,000 POPULATION BY AGE GROUP,
IN SELECTED YEARS BETWEEN 1951 AND 1977

| Year | | | | | Age group | | | | |
| | 5–14 | 15–24 | 25–34 | 35–44 | 45–54 | 55–64 | 65–74 | 75 and over | All age groups |
|---|---|---|---|---|---|---|---|---|---|
| 1951 | 0.9 | 11.6 | 9.3 | 9.8 | 10.1 | 10.2 | 17.8 | 23.1 | 7.4 |
| 1961 | 0.8 | 16.1 | 15.1 | 12.1 | 15.1 | 19.0 | 24.1 | 42.4 | 9.7 |
| 1966 | 1.6 | 25.9 | 20.9 | 16.4 | 20.3 | 21.9 | 34.9 | 52.9 | 13.7 |
| 1969 | 2.4 | 42.8 | 29.6 | 21.4 | 22.4 | 28.4 | 53.0 | 58.7 | 19.7 |
| 1971 | 1.3 | 39.1 | 26.8 | 21.5 | 22.2 | 26.2 | 41.3 | 57.8 | 18.2 |
| 1974 | 3.0 | 44.7 | 33.5 | 20.7 | 25.9 | 29.2 | 39.9 | 72.1 | 22.1 |
| 1977 | 2.6 | 42.3 | 32.4 | 18.8 | 20.0 | 23.9 | 31.8 | 57.5 | 20.1 |

SOURCE: Annual reports, Registrar General's Department, Sri Lanka.

with age, in a steady increase. On the other hand, the picture found in Japan is similar to that in Sri Lanka (11:Pt. I, chap. 1, p. 65) and unlike that in Hong Kong, which was found by P. M. Yap to be like that in many Western countries (19:274).

In 1973, 44.3 percent of all suicides were in the 15–24 age group; in 1977, the latest year for which such data are available, the corresponding figure was 43.7. If the 1977 suicides for the 15–24 age group are added to those for the 25–34 group, together they account for 65 percent of all suicides in the country. Despite the high proportion of young people in Sri Lanka's population (60 percent below 24), this percentage is unusually high. The corresponding percentage for the 15–24 age group in 1951 was 35 and for the 15–34 group, 54. Thus the proportion of young people committing suicide is increasing. In Sri Lanka, it seems, young people are generally the most vulnerable to suicide. The figures also show that in the 1971–1977 period thirty children between the ages of 5 and 9 were recorded as having committed suicide. It is evident from table 6-3 that in Sri Lanka, as in many other countries, the suicide rate for the older age groups—65 and over—is high, that it has risen sharply over the past few years.

In Sri Lanka, as in most countries, suicide is more common among males than among females. The figures for the decade 1961–1971 illustrate this fact (see table 6-6). In 1960 the male-female ratio of suicide was 2.51:1 and in 1969 it was 2.60:1. These figures are comparable to the ratios in many European countries: West Germany (1959), 1.81:1; France (1959), 2.65:1; England and Wales (1959), 1.49:1. The corresponding United States figures varied from 3:1 to 4:1 for the younger age group; the ratio was 10:1 for those over the age of 85 (5:23–25).

TABLE 6-6
ANNUAL SUICIDE RATE PER 100,000 POPULATION BY SEX, 1961–1971

| Year | Male | Female | Both sexes |
|------|------|--------|------------|
| 1961 | 12.7 | 6.3   | 9.9  |
| 1962 | 16.2 | 6.5   | 11.6 |
| 1963 | 16.9 | 6.7   | 12.0 |
| 1964 | 19.9 | 9.0   | 14.7 |
| 1965 | 18.7 | 8.2   | 13.7 |
| 1966 | 18.6 | 8.5   | 13.7 |
| 1967 | 23.3 | 10.0  | 16.9 |
| 1968 | 24.0 | 9.8   | 17.2 |
| 1969 | 25.0 | 11.4  | 19.7 |
| 1970 | 26.3 | 11.45 | 19.2 |
| 1971 | 25.5 | 10.42 | 18.2 |

SOURCE: Annual reports, Registrar General's Department, Sri Lanka.

As shown in table 6-7, in 1969 the female rate tended to rise steadily after a decline in middle age, except for a drop at age 75. The rate for males rose sharply in later years, reaching the highest point for any age group, with no evidence of a drop in any of the years after 1951. P. M. Yap has drawn attention to the high suicide rates for elderly females in Sri Lanka, Hong Kong, and Japan (19:274–275), whereas in many European countries the rate for this age group showed a decline. The male-female ratio for the old-age group (those 75 and over) was 6:1 in 1969.

Methods

Data are available on the methods of committing suicide in Sri Lanka, both in the registrar general's reports and police records. These figures, however, cover only completed suicide.

The registrar general's reports, which are, as noted earlier, more reliable than police records, show that taking poison is the most common method of committing suicide in Sri Lanka. In 1969, 72 percent of all suicides died by poisoning. Beginning in 1960, poison replaced hanging as the preferred method. Table 6-8 illustrates this change and shows that the taking of poison has become progressively more popular over the past decade or so.

From 1900 to 1949 hanging was the most popular method of suicide in Sri Lanka, with drowning the second choice. In the period 1940–1949, 53 percent of suicides hanged themselves and 15 percent chose drowning (8:140). Most of the latter jumped into the deep wells used in rural areas for drawing fresh water for household purposes. By 1969, however, drowning accounted for only 1.6 percent of male and 4.1 percent of female suicides. In general, more violent methods, such as the use of firearms, are rare in Sri Lanka, in contrast with countries like the United States.

TABLE 6-7
ANNUAL SUICIDE RATE PER 100,000 POPULATION
BY AGE GROUP AND SEX, 1969

| Age group | Male | Female | Both sexes |
|---|---|---|---|
| 5–14 | 2.8 | 1.9 | 2.4 |
| 15–24 | 52.2 | 33.1 | 42.8 |
| 25–34 | 45.4 | 14.7 | 29.6 |
| 35–44 | 31.0 | 10.2 | 21.4 |
| 45–54 | 34.0 | 7.9 | 22.4 |
| 55–64 | 41.0 | 11.5 | 28.4 |
| 65–74 | 77.0 | 22.9 | 53.0 |
| 75 and over | 96.3 | 15.7 | 58.7 |
| All groups | 25.0 | 11.4 | 19.7 |

SOURCE: Annual report, Registrar General's Department, Sri Lanka.

TABLE 6-8
FREQUENCY OF SUICIDE BY POISONING
AND HANGING, IN SELECTED YEARS, 1959–1969
(In percentages)

| Year | Poisoning | Hanging |
|------|-----------|---------|
| 1959 | 37 | 40 |
| 1960 | 41 | 37 |
| 1961 | 47 | 33 |
| 1962 | 53 | 29 |
| 1966 | 66 | 19 |
| 1969 | 72 | 15 |

SOURCE: Annual reports, Registrar General's Department, Sri Lanka.

The reason for the increasing use of poison as a means of suicide is quite obvious. Acetic acid, as it is needed for rubber processing, is freely available, and in 1960 it accounted for 75 percent of all suicides by poisoning (10:31–40). If more detailed data are examined, in recent police records, for example, it becomes apparent that a large number of suicides are caused by the intake of organophosphorous insecticides.

Poisoning is more popular among females than among males. In fact, even before 1960, in certain years women preferred poison to any other single method of taking their lives. Hanging is more frequent among males, as also is the occasional use of cutting and piercing instruments and of firearms. Only a very few women in Sri Lanka have resorted to firearms as a means of suicide (e.g., none at all in 1951, 1953, and 1966). On the other hand, drowning has always been more popular among female suicide victims than among male victims. (See table 6-9.)

The records of the Colombo city coroner of 122 cases of suicide in 1971 give a more detailed picture of the methods employed in the city and its

TABLE 6-9
SEXUAL PREFERENCES IN METHOD OF
COMMITTING SUICIDE, 1969
(In percentages)

| Method | Male | Female |
|--------|------|--------|
| Poison | 71.0 | 77.0 |
| Hanging | 17.0 | 9.0 |
| Drowning | 1.6 | 4.1 |
| Firearms | 0.8 | 0.3 |

SOURCE: Annual report, Registrar General's Department, Sri Lanka.

suburbs (table (6-10). Poisoning accounted for 50.2 percent of these suicides. Of deaths by poison, 50.8 percent followed the ingestion of insecticides. Hanging and firearms were used only by males. A fairly common
method was jumping in front of a moving train, chosen by more than 16
percent, perhaps because there are many more rail lines in Colombo and its
suburbs than in outlying areas. Seventeen of the victims covered by this
study set themselves on fire after dousing themselves with kerosene or
gasoline; of these twelve, or 11 percent, were women. This method, which
is rare in other countries, is not uncommon in Sri Lanka, especially among
women. Kerosene is easily available, as it is used in almost every household
in the island for lighting or cooking purposes. It is also ingested by many
suicide attempters, but this method is often nonlethal.

Taking poison as a common method of suicide in Sri Lanka is related to
the free availability of insecticides and acetic acids, as noted above. In
contrast, the most frequently used method in the United States is firearms,
and in the United Kingdom, hypnotic drugs and coal gas. If availability
were the only criterion, however, many more suicides in Sri Lanka would

TABLE 6-10
METHODS OF SUICIDE IN 122 CASES IN COLOMBO AND
SUBURBS, 1971

| Method | Male | Female | Total |
|---|---|---|---|
| Burning | 5 | 12 (9.8%) | 17 (14%) |
| Poisoning | | | |
|     Insecticide | 25 | 7 | 32 |
|     Corrosive | 6 | 4 | 10 |
|     Rat poison | 1 | 2 | 3 |
|     Arsenic | 2 | 2 | 4 |
|     Cyanide | 1 | 1 | 2 |
|     Barbiturate | 1 | 0 | 1 |
|     Other | 1 | 0 | 1 |
|     Unknown | 6 | 4 | 10 |
| | 43 | 20 | 63 (50.2%) |
| Jumping in front of train | 16 | 5 | 20 (16.4%) |
| Hanging | 9 | 0 | 9 (7.4%) |
| Jumping from height | 4 | 0 | 4 |
| Cutting injury | 4 | 0 | 4 |
| Firearms | 1 | 0 | 1 |
| Jumping opposite bus | 1 | 0 | 1 |
| Drowning | 2 | 0 | 2 |
| | 85 | 37 | 122 |

SOURCE: Records of Colombo city coroner.

use cutting instruments. Knives are in fact freely used in the island, and the most common method of murder is stabbing. But the use of such implements for suicide is extremely rare: in 1969 only six of 2,407 victims used knives. It would seem that in Sri Lanka choice of method depends upon availability coupled with the victim's desire for a less violent method of ending his life. A third possible factor in choice of method is "fashion"; that is, a person contemplating suicide may be inclined to imitate others in the method used. As suicides are freely reported in Sri Lankan newspapers, it is probable that an important factor in determining the method to be used is a desire to imitate.

Use of the unusually violent method of suicides setting themselves on fire (burning) may be regarded as reflecting an inner psychological need to die in suffering and pain. Such an explanation would be more plausible, however, if people who chose this method displayed an exceedingly high sense of guilt and a desire for self-punishment. In the absence of corroborating data, it is hardly warranted to draw such a conclusion. Even here, the availability of kerosene in almost every kitchen in Sri Lanka, and the fashion of imitation, may be more relevant. It is noteworthy that cremation on a public funeral pyre of logs and firewood is a much practiced method of disposal of the dead, sanctioned by both Buddhism and Hinduism. The idea of death and extinction is thus often associated in such a culture with fire.

### Urban-Rural Differences

A large majority of the people of Sri Lanka are still rural, although the proportion of urban population has been increasing slowly over the years. City dwellers increased from 15.4 percent in 1946 to 21.5 percent in 1969.

Data are available in the registrar general's reports on the number of suicides in rural and urban areas separately. From the statistics for the years 1963 to 1969 (table 6-11), it is at once noticeable that the urban rate was

TABLE 6-11
URBAN AND RURAL SUICIDE RATES PER 100,000 POPULATION, 1963–1969

| Year | Rural rate | Urban rate |
|------|------------|------------|
| 1963 | 10.5 | 19.2 |
| 1964 | 12.9 | 22.5 |
| 1965 | 11.5 | 22.7 |
| 1966 | 12.1 | 20.8 |
| 1967 | 13.6 | 28.5 |
| 1968 | 15.8 | 23.3 |
| 1969 | 18.2 | 29.0 |

SOURCE: Registrar General's Department, Sri Lanka.

higher than the rural rate. The mean rate for these years for urban areas was 23.7, while for rural areas it was only 13.5.

These data are in general agreement with the findings in many other countries. While rural-urban differences are not so wide in the United States, they are marked in Europe (5:50−51). In Hong Kong, too, as Yap has found (19:283), there is a substantial difference between rural and urban rates. Asuni, on the other hand, working with limited data in western Nigeria, reports a higher incidence of suicide among rural peoples (1:1094).

The interpretation of urban-rural differences must be undertaken with some caution. Of the many issues involved, the criteria used to define urbanity are particularly important. Figures on urban-rural distinction arrived at by one criterion cannot be compared with figures based on a different criterion. In Sri Lanka, local government administrative areas of certain types—municipal, urban, and town councils—are considered urban for recording purposes, while all other areas are considered rural. The type of local administration in a given area is determined not only by the density of population but also by the amenities and the extent of development.

Marital Status

Neither the registrar general's reports nor police records include data on the marital status of suicide victims. The information used here is derived from Dissanayake's study of the Colombo coroner's records. No data whatever are available on the marital status of suicide attempters. The coroner's records for 1971 show that 38 percent of the 122 persons who committed suicide in Colombo were single and that 43 percent were married; the status of the remaining 19 percent was unknown. The group included seven unidentified cases (table 6-12). Case notes of 17 other suicides recorded by coroners of suburban areas were found in the Colombo magistrate's courts. Although the data are inadequate, this sample shows a preponderance of single persons over married persons in suicide cases (table 6-12). Thus considerable differences exist among coroners' areas regarding the proportions of married and single persons.

Superficially, the figures indicate that marital status is not correlated either positively or negatively with suicide in Sri Lanka. This finding is in contrast with the general trend observed elsewhere in the world, that single marital status is associated with a high rate of suicide whereas marriage is considered an insurance against suicidal tendencies, as illustrated by data for the United States, England, and Sweden (5:26−29). Yap's data show that Hong Kong's experience is consistent with this trend (19:283). Nevertheless, the trend is by no means universal according to figures for London (13:65−67, 79−81) and for western Nigeria (1:1094).

The samples for Sri Lanka are obviously too small to allow extrapolations

TABLE 6-12
SUICIDE AND MARITAL STATUS IN COLOMBO
AND SUBURBS, 1971

| Sex | Marital status | | | Total |
| | Single | Married | Unknown | |
|---|---|---|---|---|
| | CITY OF COLOMBO | | | |
| Male | 27 | 36 | 22 | 85 |
| Female | 19 | 17 | 1 | 37 |
| Total | 46 (38%) | 53 (43%) | 23 (19%) | 122 |
| | SUBURBS OF COLOMBO | | | |
| Male | 10 | 3 | 3 | 16 |
| Female | 1 | 0 | 0 | 1 |
| Total | 11 (64%) | 3 (18%) | 3 (18%) | 17 |
| Grand total | 57 (41%) | 56 (40%) | 26 (19%) | 139 |

SOURCES: Colombo city coroner; Colombo magistrates' courts (for suburban areas).

for the country as a whole. Furthermore, the high proportion of suicides whose status was unknown (18.7 percent) render the data unreliable. It is likely that a majority of persons in this group are unmarried. Third, the classification here does not include the significant categories of "divorced" and "widowed." In view of these limitations, it seems wisest not to interpret these data as indicating anything conclusive. It is likely that a larger sample with a smaller number of cases in the "unknown" category would in fact show a higher incidence of suicide among single persons in a country where a large proportion of those who commit suicide are in a younger age group.

Employment and Social Status

No data are available in the registrar general's reports on the social and employment conditions of suicides. The discussion here is therefore confined to data derived from Dissanayake's study of the Colombo city coroner's records.

Figures on the occupations of suicide victims in 1971 are given in table 6-13. These data, however, are merely suggestive because of the smallness of the sample and the unavailability of corresponding occupational category figures for the parent populations. The latter information would have permitted the calculation of rates of suicide by occupation.

No data on the relationship between suicide and social status are available. As one's occupation does not necessarily reflect one's social status in

Sri Lanka, even an indirect assessment of occupational differences in relation to the suicide rate is not possible.

On the whole, then, it may be said that no firm conclusions can be drawn on suicide in relation to employment or to social class in Sri Lanka until further research is done. It seems that in the group reported in table 6-13 the unemployed, retired persons, and petty traders are overrepresented, compared with their numbers in the general population. Petty traders like small shopkeepers, vendors, and hawkers seem to be the most affected in this sample of an urban and semiurban population.

TABLE 6-13
OCCUPATIONS OF SUICIDE VICTIMS IN COLOMBO, 1971

| Occupation | Male | Occupation | Female |
|---|---|---|---|
| Professional, managerial | 2 | Domestic service | 1 |
| Clerical | 3 | Laboratory technician | 1 |
| Skilled worker | 6 | Student | 1 |
| Semiskilled worker | 5 | Estate worker | 1 |
| Petty tradesman | 10 | Housewife and unknown | 33 |
| Cultivator | 5 | | |
| Laborer | 11 | | |
| Other (student, prisoner) | 2 | | |
| Retired (over 60) | 9 | | |
| Unemployed | 10 | | |
| Unknown | 15 | | |
| Unidentified | 7 | | |
| Total | 85 | | 37 |

SOURCE: Colombo city coroner.

Seasonal Variations

Many studies of suicide in Europe and North America have revealed different rates in different seasons of the year. The peak has been found to occur in early summer, and Yap (19:297) has found similar results for Hong Kong despite its tropical location. Asuni (1:1096) tried to correlate variations in suicide rates in western Nigeria with the pattern of rainfall.

In Sri Lanka, where seasonal changes are not marked, one might expect the suicide rate to be uniform throughout the year. There is no marked difference in rainfall even between monsoonal and intermonsoonal months, and the temperature is relatively stable throughout the year. As no monthly data on suicide are published in the registrar general's reports, statistics had to be obtained from the Colombo city coroner's records. The averages given in table 6-14 are for the periods 1963—1966 and 1970—1972. The averages, standardized for a 30-day month, are also presented. Statistical evaluation of these monthly data, using the chi-square distribution for individual months or for three 4-month periods, failed to show any significance. It becomes clear from these data that, as expected, there are no seasonal variations in the suicide rate in tropical Sri Lanka, in contrast with countries that have a temperate climate.

TABLE 6-14
SEASONAL VARIATIONS IN SUICIDE IN COLOMBO,
1963—1966 AND 1970—1972

| Month | Average number of suicides | Number of suicides standardized for a 30-day month |
|---|---|---|
| January | 63 | 61 |
| February | 56 | 60 |
| March | 64 | 62 |
| April | 54 | 54 |
| May | 56 | 54 |
| June | 57 | 57 |
| July | 55 | 53 |
| August | 61 | 59 |
| September | 58 | 58 |
| October | 61 | 59 |
| November | 56 | 56 |
| December | 68 | 66 |

SOURCE: Colombo city coroner's records.

### Precipitating and Predisposing Factors

Suicide is the culmination of a series of causative factors or the result of a combination of predisposing circumstances. The evidence in a coroner's court, however, is the interpretation or explanation of suicide by a key witness. Hence, one or two factors taken in isolation from the background and highlighted by witnesses as causative of suicide may be an oversimplification and give an incomplete picture. Nevertheless, such data are useful in identifying some of the motives for and the causes of suicide in Sri Lanka.

As many researchers have pointed out, it is impossible to be certain of the specific precipitating factor in a given case of suicide. Since the investigation is essentially retrospective, much reliance has to be placed on the evidence of relatives and friends and on past records. Second, what is usually taken as the precipitating cause is the one that is, according to the evidence, dominant. Third, a factor that precipitates suicidal behavior in one person does not necessarily have the same effect on another person, the difference being determined by individual, psychological, and constitutional factors. These difficulties in interpreting data must be borne in mind in any analysis of precipitating factors.

For our discussion of such factors operating in Sri Lanka, as no relevant information was available in the registrar general's reports, data were drawn from the study of the records of the Colombo city coroner. Of the 122 cases studied for 1971, acute interpersonal disputes accounted for 16.4 percent and thwarted love, for 9.0 percent (table 6-15). Taken together, these interpersonal problems were responsible for 25.4 percent of the cases. It is noteworthy that the corresponding figure for Hong Kong was about 38 percent (19:291). These conclusions, of course, reflect the layman's attitude to the causation of suicide, for relatives and friends giving evidence after a suicide often attribute the act to interpersonal problems. In fact, in some cases other causes, whose significance the layman does not see, may be operating. Even if one makes allowance for this kind of distortion, the number of suicides owing to interpersonal conflicts is high in Sri Lanka. The number of suicides attributable to such conflicts also partly explains the high peak found in the younger age group. It is notable that, as in Hong Kong, females (9.8 percent) tend to outnumber males (6.6 percent) in this group.

These data from the Colombo city coroner may be analyzed further (see table 6-15). Thwarted love is generally considered by the public as a more frequent cause of suicide than the 9 percent found in this study would indicate. Perhaps this erroneous impression is created by the wide newspaper publicity given such suicides. Of the six males in this category, two committed suicide because their partners left them and the other four because of objections by elders. Three of the five females were jilted by their lovers.

The traditional concept of matrimony in Sri Lanka is a marriage arranged by the elders in a family with the consent of the young couple. The Western idea of marriage for love often conflicts with caste and ethnic barriers and the status of the family. Though more and more young people are marrying for love, especially in urban areas, the social restraints imposed on them, particularly by tradition-bound conservatives, may impel some of them to commit suicide. That the traditional family life pattern is still preserved to some extent, even in the Colombo area, is emphasized by some of these suicides.

It may be, however, that some of those committing suicide because of interpersonal problems also have a personality disorder of some kind. In fact, a detailed assessment of witnesses' statements revealed that in four cases out of twenty in which family dispute was the main cause some personality abnormality of the victim was evident. "He was stubborn"; "He did not help in the field"; "He did not try to get a job"; "He was a very hot-tempered person"—these were some of the descriptions given by relatives who were witnesses. The reference usually was to an abnormal trait in the person rather than to a mental derangement. One such person was described by his father as a lawbreaker who had a court case pending. Another was called a "bad character" who was wanted by the police and the village headman for violent behavior. He had also quarreled with his parents. A few of them could have been chronic schizophrenics. What is significant, however, is that both the relatives and the coroner interpreted the suicide as a consequence of an interpersonal dispute.

In sixteen cases of suicide (13.1 percent) alcoholism was the primary cause. Of these, eleven were "dependent," three showed acute intoxication with no clear history of addiction, and two drank heavily after a particularly stressful event. In fourteen of the sixteen suicides there were other contributing factors. Some had had family disputes; three had financial problems; three were unemployed; and one showed evidence of personality disorder. In this study they are all categorized as alcoholics because drinking was the main precipitating factor. Thus only eleven of the sixteen were chronic alcoholics in the usual sense. Even this figure is high, though it is not surprising in view of the large amount of alcohol consumed in Sri Lanka today. As Stengel says (15:64), "There is a positive connection between the alcohol consumed in a country and its suicide rate." On the other hand, drug addiction is relatively rare in the island, and only one opium addict was found among the suicides studied.

Organic disease also accounted for a fair proportion of suicides in the study—13 out of 122, or 10.7 percent. All except one of them were male (table 6-16). All had a history of physical illness, as mentioned by witnesses, and this testimony was usually confirmed by the postmortem. These suicides, whose mean age was 47.9, suffered from chronic ailments with little prospect of cure within the foreseeable future, cancer accounting for four of them (table 6-16). The percentage of suicides suffering from physical illness in our study (10.7) is less than the 27.9 percent Yap found in Hong Kong (19:290, table 12). Between our figure and Yap's is Sainsbury's 18 percent for London (13:60–61, 81–92). In Asuni's study of suicide in western Nigeria the corresponding figure was 20 out of 221, or 9 percent (1:1096).

A large proportion of the Colombo 1971 suicides, 20 out of 122, or 17.3 percent (table 6-15), gave evidence of serious psychiatric illness, here called probable psychosis. In most cases this diagnosis had been arrived at by the victims' relatives, who used expressions like "mentally deranged," "mentally ill," and "severely depressed" in describing the victims. Figures on mental disturbances found in other societies vary from 7.8 percent in Hong Kong (19) to 37 percent in London (13). Metropolitan Life Insurance

TABLE 6-15
PRECIPITATING FACTORS IN 122 SUICIDES IN
COLOMBO, 1971

| Factor | Male | | Female | | Total | |
|---|---|---|---|---|---|---|
| | Number | Percentage | Number | Percentage | Number | Percentage |
| Probable psychosis | | | | | | |
| Affective | 4 | | 4 | | | |
| Schizophrenia | 5 | | 3 | | | |
| Unclassified | 2 | | 2 | | | |
| | 11 | 9.0 | 9 | 7.4 | 20 | 17.3 |
| Alcoholism | 16 | | 0 | | | |
| Interpersonal disputes | | | | | | |
| With spouse | 0 | | 7 | | | |
| With parent | 5 | | 3 | | | |
| With brother | 1 | | 2 | | | |
| With son or daughter | 2 | | 0 | | | |
| | 8 | 6.6 | 12 | 9.8 | 20 | 16.4 |
| Thwarted love | | | | | | |
| Involving partner | 2 | | 3 | | | |
| Involving parent | 2 | | 1 | | | |
| Involving brother | 2 | | 1 | | | |
| | 6 | 4.9 | 5 | 4.1 | 11 | 9.0 |
| | 6 | 4.9 | 5 | 4.1 | 31 | 25.4 |

| Economic | | | | | |
|---|---|---|---|---|---|
| Unemployment | 3 | | 0 | 3 | |
| Stress on job | 3 | | 1 | 4 | |
| Financial problems | 8 | | 0 | 8 | |
| | 14 | 11.5 | 1 | 15 | 12.3 |
| Organic disease | 12 | 9.8 | 1 | 13 | 10.7 |
| Grief reaction | 1 | | 2 | 3 | |
| Marital unhappiness | 1 | | 1 | 2 | |
| Other | 5 | | 3 | 8 | |
| Unknown | 4 | | 3 | 7 | |
| Unidentified persons | 7 | | 0 | 7 | 5.7 |
| Total | 85 | | 37 | 122 | |

SOURCE: Colombo city coroner's records.

TABLE 6-16
ORGANIC ILLNESSES LEADING TO SUICIDE
IN COLOMBO, 1971

| Illness | Number | Illness | Number |
|---------|--------|---------|--------|
| Cancer | 4 | Leprosy | 1 |
| Tuberculosis | 1 | Bronchial asthma | 1 |
| Heart disease | 2 | Skin disease | 1 |
| Epilepsy | 2 | Other | 1 |

SOURCE: Colombo city coroner's records.

Company data show 20 percent for the United States (5:170). Jayawardane and Ranasinghe, in their study of suicide in Sri Lanka (10), obtained a figure of 20 percent for the mentally ill group.

Of the twenty in our study, eight suffered from a significant depressive illness, eight were schizophrenics, and the other four could not be placed in any specific category of psychosis on the evidence available. Even for the sixteen definitely classified, the diagnosis was by no means certain. Four of the eight cases of schizophrenia had received treatment at a psychiatric hospital, one at the General Hospital, Colombo, and one at a private hospital. They had probably suffered from these illnesses for some time, as relatives had said all of them were of "deranged mind."

Probable affective psychosis was diagnosed on the description of the patient by relatives as "severely depressed" for several months. Of these eight, two had attempted suicide earlier. Three had had treatment from a general practitioner, one had been treated at a psychiatric hospital, one by a private psychiatrist, and another by a native practitioner in psychiatry. One was a patient at the Eye Hospital, Colombo, at the time of suicide. Three of the eight had expressed suicidal intentions, according to the evidence, some time before the actual event.

The four unclassified suicide victims were also described as "deranged." One of them had had treatment at a psychiatric hospital and one at a provincial hospital. In another case a nineteen-year old girl was described by relatives as having suffered from a state of hysteria.

Thus a large proportion of the probable psychosis group—about 75 percent—had earlier had either psychiatric therapy or medical treatment. In fact, a history of previous treatment was taken into consideration in classifying some of the suicides in this group.

According to the available evidence, 15 of the 122 victims, or 12.3 percent, committed suicide because of economic troubles (table 6-15). Economic factors, however, may have played a role in some of the other suicides, as, for example, in those attributed mainly to alcoholism or family disputes. Specific financial problems leading to suicide were debts, unem-

ployment, or loss of employment. The proportion of females committing
suicide for economic reasons was very low.

Eight of the cases studied were classified as having committed suicide for
"other" reasons (table 6-15). They included two males with court cases
pending, one prison inmate, one opium addict, one suffering from impotence, and a girl who had failed an examination. Seven of the 122 committed
suicide for unknown reasons (table 6-15). Relatives of three of them were
ignorant of a precipitating cause. Three others had shown some evidence of
an affective disorder, but the evidence was not conclusive enough to list
them in the probable psychosis group. According to relatives, two of these
seven persons were apparently suffering from aches and pains and had been
treated at local hospitals. There were, however, no clues as to organic
disorders, and the postmortems were negative. Many patients suffering
from endogenous depression in Sri Lanka present themselves with somatic
symptoms, and it is probable that these two belonged to this category.
Seven other persons in the study who had obviously committed suicide
were unidentified, and their motives for suicide were unknown to the
coroner.

### Precipitating Factors in Old Age

In the same sample of Colombo suicides, fifteen were persons over the
age of 60. As shown in table 6-17, the probable psychosis group with four
persons—three of them classified as affective—and the three who had
organic diseases together account for almost half the total. In the two cases
of grief reaction, suicide was in response to the recent death of the spouse.
Economic problems and alcoholism also claimed some victims. An old man
who started to drink after his daughter's elopement committed suicide six

TABLE 6-17
PRECIPITATING FACTORS IN FIFTEEN SUICIDES OF
PERSONS OVER 60 IN COLOMBO, 1971

| Factor | Male | Female | Total |
|---|---|---|---|
| Probable psychosis | 3 | 1 | 4 |
| Organic disease | 3 | 0 | 3 |
| Alcoholism | 2 | 0 | 2 |
| Interpersonal disputes | 1 | 0 | 1 |
| Economic problems | 2 | 0 | 2 |
| Grief reaction | 1 | 1 | 2 |
| Other | 1 | 0 | 1 |
| Total | 13 | 2 | 15 |

SOURCE: Colombo city coroner's records.

months later. Of particular interest is the fact that interpersonal disputes were of little importance in causing suicide in old people.

Why the suicide rates for old people are high in a culture that accords them an honored place, with many privileges in the extended family, is not clear. Factors that are often causative elsewhere—organic disease and affective disorder—are found in Sri Lanka as well. The existence of an extended family seems to provide no insurance against an old person's committing suicide, perhaps out of altruistic motives. It may also be true that the extended family, in a society where traditional social norms are breaking down, may, though existing superficially, be responding to undercurrents of stress.

### Psychology of Suicide: An Illustrative Case

The case presented here illustrates some of the individual psychological factors affecting suicidal behavior in Sri Lanka. This case, an attempted suicide referred to Dissanayake for psychiatric investigation and help, has been chosen because it highlights some of the culturally determined psychological factors in the individual which are characteristic of the average suicide.

A. S. D., 18 years old, an unmarried male Sinhalese, comes from a rural area. He has been unemployed for a year, although he had been a casual rubber tapper and had also worked on a farm. He was brought to the hospital with acetic acid poisoning. He has three brothers—a rubber estate worker, a waiter, and an unemployed man—and a sister who is in school. His father died when he was eight years old, and he had to give up school. There is no personal or family history of mental illness and no history of a previous suicidal attempt.

On the day of the incident, the elder brother (23) gave him money for marketing. He went to town with the money in his shirt pocket, but he lost the shirt and so also the money. When he returned home the brother abused him for his carelessness in losing what was, for them, a large sum. The patient then got very angry at his brother, but he did not retaliate, although he wanted to. ("It's a sin to abuse elders," he said.) For three hours he lay in bed with depressive preoccupations. He thought about his losses and about his brother's harsh words. (When asked whether, at that time, he did not think of earning the money and paying it back to the brother, he said, "How could I do that, being unemployed?") He then bought a quarter-bottle of acetic acid, commonly available in rubber-growing areas, and drank some of it, but he could not bring himself to drink the whole lot. The desire to remain alive came back almost immediately. When he was brought to the hospital he was filled with regret for his act.

Upon interviewing the patient later, Dr. Dissanayake discovered that, although the brother's abuse had triggered the suicide attempt—especially because he had, on moral and religious grounds, no way of retaliating and therefore had to suppress his own aggression—the act had really been determined by a multiplicity of causes. First and foremost, he was unemployed. The family's poverty meant that they often had to do without a meal. Yet what upset the patient most was that he had no way of earning money so that he could repay his brother. The brother's abuse certainly was the immediate cause of the suicide attempt, but it was obviously not the main reason. Later, when the brother who abused him came to see him in the hospital with tears in his eyes, the patient became quite remorseful. In a way, the act had had the desired effect of arousing feelings of guilt and sympathy in the person who had abused him, but the patient was still very regretful. He had no intention of repeating the attempt.

This case shows both the multiplicity of causes in suicide and the cultural factors that play a part in determining a person's behavior in stressful situations.

Suicide Rates and Ethnic Groups

As the population of Sri Lanka is multiracial, it is of particular interest to compare the suicide figures for the various ethnic groups.

Suicide in Sri Lanka seems to have aroused the interest of many American social anthropologists and sociologists. Among the earliest were Strauss and Strauss, who analyzed the data on suicides and homicides in Sri Lanka up to 1950 (16). While making general comments on the figures for the island in comparison with other countries, they were mainly concerned with the differential rates for suicide and homicide of the Sinhalese and the Tamils. The rates they found for all the main ethnic groups in 1946 are given in table 6-18. Strauss and Strauss explain the very high rate for Europeans by pointing out that, as aliens whose roots were in Europe, they were socially isolated. In fact, Europeans constituted only 0.08 percent of

TABLE 6-18
SUICIDE RATE PER 100,000 POPULATION BY ETHNIC GROUP IN SRI LANKA, 1946

| Ethnic group | Rate |
| --- | --- |
| Sinhalese | 4.9 |
| Ceylon Tamils | 10.6 |
| Indian Tamils | 7.9 |
| Muslims | 2.1 |
| Burghers (Eurasians) | 4.8 |
| Europeans | 80.0 |
| Other | 19.5 |
| All groups | 5.9 |

SOURCE: Strauss and Strauss, 1953 (16).

the total population. Today the European population in Sri Lanka is negligible, as most expatriates returned to the United Kingdom after Sri Lanka became independent.

The other remarkable feature commented on by Strauss and Strauss is the wide difference between the suicide rates of the Sinhalese and the Tamils, the two major communities on the island. In adducing a theoretical explanation for the variance, they observe Tamil society as cohesive and more closely structured than the Sinhalese, with rigid observances of caste and familistic behavioral norms. In such a society where the identity of the individual merges with that of the group, Strauss and Strauss argue, suicide occurs for seemingly trivial causes. The high suicide rate among Tamils, by this analysis, is explained in terms of a large number of altruistic suicides in Durkheim's terminology. Sinhalese society, on the other hand, is more loosely structured and is tolerant of deviance (16:467−469).

Gibbs and Martin (7), in reexamining some of the data of Strauss and Strauss, have sought to explain these differential rates according to status integration, which they measure in terms of an index of marital integration. They endeavor to show that the Tamils are less integrated socially and that their higher suicide rate is owing to this circumstance. Gibbs and Martin also show that the suicides in Sri Lanka conform more to Durkheim's egoistic model than to the altruistic model.

It is our view, however, that the differential suicide rates for ethnic groups are more profitably analyzed within the context of regional differences. In fact, the only reliable data available yield regional variations rather than ethnic variations. In the following paragraphs, therefore, we examine data for the districts of Colombo, Galle, Kurunegala, and Jaffna.

Although Sri Lanka is a small country, the different ethnic groups live in more or less exclusive regional areas, except for Colombo and its suburbs. The population of the Jaffna district, the northernmost part of the island, is almost exclusively Ceylon Tamil (92 percent). On the other hand, the Galle district in the Southern Province is exclusively Sinhalese (93 percent), and Kurunegala district in the northwestern part of the island is predominantly Kandyan Sinhalese (75 percent). The population of the Colombo district is mixed, but even there the majority are Sinhalese (80 percent).

A comparison of district figures thus yields a reasonable basis for conclusions on ethnic group differences in relation to suicide. The suicide rates for these districts for the years 1963−1971 are given in table 6-19. The figures show that the mean suicide rate is the highest in the Jaffna district and therefore among the Ceylon Tamils. The high rate in the Tamil community, noted by Strauss and Strauss for 1946, was still maintained some years later. It is worth observing, however, that the mean figure for the Kurunegala district, with its almost exclusively Sinhalese population, is very close to that for the Jaffna district. In some years the Kurunegala rate in fact

TABLE 6-19
SUICIDE RATE PER 100,000 POPULATION IN FOUR DISTRICTS
OF SRI LANKA, 1963–1971

| | District | | | |
|---|---|---|---|---|
| Year | Colombo | Galle | Kurunegala | Jaffna |
| 1963 | 6.6 | 6.6 | 21.1 | 17.9 |
| 1964 | 8.6 | 12.8 | 20.3 | 21.4 |
| 1965 | 6.7 | 11.6 | 18.1 | 19.0 |
| 1966 | 8.4 | 10.0 | 16.5 | 20.5 |
| 1967 | 8.2 | 13.3 | 23.9 | 24.1 |
| 1968 | 8.7 | 14.7 | 23.8 | 20.4 |
| 1969 | – | – | – | – |
| 1970 | 9.1 | 17.2 | 25.0 | 28.3 |
| 1971 | 8.2 | 12.7 | 19.9 | 28.2 |
| Mean | 8.1 | 12.4 | 21.1 | 22.5 |

SOURCE: Registrar general's annual reports.

exceeded the Jaffna rate. The differential suicide rates for districts seem to be related less to ethnic divisions than to cultural and socioeconomic factors. Thus no firm conclusions can be drawn from the apparent ethnic differences in suicide rates. What is particularly significant is that the rate in the most populous, least cohesive, westernized Colombo district was relatively low, with the Jaffna and Kurunegala rates running almost three times as high, and that these rates were consistent over a period of years. Galle district occupied an intermediate position in this respect.

The Kandyan Sinhalese inhabiting the Kurunegala district, who are largely rural and tradition-bound, strictly observe the caste system and maintain the conservative familistic social organization. Among the Ceylon Tamils of the Jaffna district these values are even more rigidly cherished and observed.

At a superficial glance, the explanation of differential suicide rates for the districts based on Durkheimian principles is by no means an easy one. If one applies these principles, one would expect the rate in Colombo district to be the highest in the island. The same could to some extent be said about the Galle district. As the Jaffna and Kurunegala districts are still very traditional and socially cohesive, one would expect a low rate in those areas. The data, however, do not conform to these predictions (table 6-19), and one is compelled to look for other explanations.

It may be argued that three main factors must be taken into account. First, as social bonds and traditions are still quite strong in Kurunegala and Jaffna, deviance is less tolerated there than in more westernized areas, and that should lead to a higher suicide rate. Second, owing to rapid socioeconomic changes, especially after independence, the social and economic pressures on the people are strong. Social changes have introduced new hierarchies into the traditional caste-ridden social organization. Such strains, which are felt most deeply in the Cultivator community (Goigama caste), have been observed by A. L. Wood, who has proposed the well-known frustration-aggression hypothesis. On the basis of Wood's theory suicides in Sri Lanka could be looked upon as acts of aggression on the part of those who are victims of the social change from a traditional ascribed status system to a modern, urban-oriented, achieved-status system (18:107).

The Jaffna and Kurunegala districts have less rainfall, fewer natural resources, and higher unemployment than other areas. The younger generation there is thus under heavier pressure to compete for an achieved status, with all the attendant tensions and frustrations. This situation could easily lead to a higher suicide rate, especially among young people. The third point, in a sense a combination of the two noted above, is that the peoples of the Colombo and Galle districts often resort to outward-directed crime in response to stress. As the traditional values and norms have given way, over the past few decades, to a self-centered competitive philosophy of life, outward-directed crime has become a common phenomenon in those areas. In the more traditional and conservative rural areas, however, where the old values and norms are still very much a living force, a person under stress is more likely to react to his frustrations by self-destruction rather than by aggression toward others. In fact, evidence in support of this notion is seen in the high rate of murder and other crimes in the Colombo district, whereas the lowest murder rate is observed in the Jaffna district.

In summary, the higher suicide rates among some tradition-bound communities of Sri Lanka seem to be a result of the varied and serious strains imposed upon them, plus their predilection to react to social tensions in a mode that is characteristic of suicidal behavior.

### Suicide and Youth

One of the most striking features of suicide in Sri Lanka is that it occurs predominantly in youth. In the seven years from 1971 to 1977, 42.4 percent of those who committed suicide were between the ages of 15 and 24, with a mean rate of 42.3 per 100,000 population. A further breakdown reveals that the peak suicide rate occurred consistently between the ages of 20 and 24 (table 6-20); the second-highest rate was found in the adolescent 15–19 group. The mean rates for the two age groups were 50.2 and 36.2 per 100,000, respectively, in the five-year period ending in 1977. The age-specific rates show a regular predictable pattern. The high rates among young people should also be seen in the context of rapid growth of the youthful population and the island's relatively stagnant economy. The

TABLE 6-20
SUICIDE RATE PER 100,000 POPULATION BY AGE
GROUP, SRI LANKA, 1973—1977

| Year | Age group | | | | | | | | |
|------|-----|-------|-------|-------|-------|-------|-------|-------|-----------|
|      | 5—9 | 10—14 | 15—19 | 20—24 | 25—29 | 30—34 | 35—39 | 40—44 | All groups |
| 1973 | 0.2 | 3.8 | 40.1 | 52.2 | 35.4 | 28.0 | 25.3 | 21.3 | 22.0 |
| 1974 | 0.4 | 5.0 | 35.2 | 54.8 | 37.5 | 28.3 | 23.1 | 17.8 | 22.1 |
| 1975 | 0.5 | 4.3 | 29.5 | 48.1 | 32.9 | 22.6 | 24.9 | 15.7 | 19.5 |
| 1976 | 0.2 | 4.0 | 40.2 | 47.3 | 35.3 | 24.1 | 20.2 | 18.9 | 20.4 |
| 1977 | 0.3 | 4.9 | 36.3 | 48.8 | 38.4 | 24.7 | 20.6 | 16.6 | 20.1 |

SOURCE: Registrar general's annual reports.

population in the 15—24 age group has doubled since 1946, reaching 2,940,000 with a growth rate of 3.8 percent.

Although the rate of suicide in relation to unemployment and economic status in Sri Lanka could not be established owing to inadequate statistical evidence, it is our impression that the unemployed and the poverty-stricken are more vulnerable to suicidal acts than are the more affluent members of the community.

Social stresses among young people have also found expression through channels other than suicide. In addition to many instances of student lack of discipline and strikes, which of course may be considered a worldwide phenomenon, in 1971 Sri Lanka experienced the horrors and convulsions of a well-planned but abortive ultraradical youth uprising aimed at overthrowing the moderately socialist government elected in 1970. The uprising resulted, according to official estimates, in about 1,300 deaths and 15,000 arrests.[2] The young people responsible belonged exclusively to the Sinhalese community, with the majority drawn from the less privileged castes.

Over the past few years some Tamil youth have been indulging in acts of terrorism, especially in the Northern Province, demanding a separate Tamil-speaking state. As a result the government has declared a state of emergency in those areas. The most important cause of this unrest has been identified as unemployment, particularly among educated young people.

The figures of the Department of Census and Statistics show that the island's unemployment rate in 1971 was 7.3 percent (table 6-21), which was higher than the corresponding rates in Europe and the United States. When classified by age, 82.7 percent of the unemployed were in the 15—24 bracket. To understand the full significance of this high unemployment

[2]All those arrested were subsequently released unconditionally from prison.

TABLE 6-21
OCCUPATIONS OF SRI LANKA POPULATION, AGE 15 AND OVER,
BY SEX, 1971

| Occupation | Male | | Female | | Total | |
|---|---|---|---|---|---|---|
| | Number (× 1,000) | Percentage | Number (× 1,000) | Percentage | Number (× 1,000) | Percentage |
| Employed | 2,730.6 | 73.1 | 804.8 | 21.6 | 3,535.4 | 47.4 |
| Unemployed | 332.8 | 8.9 | 213.0 | 5.7 | 545.8 | 7.3 |
| Own housework | 31.6 | 0.8 | 2,174.3 | 58.3 | 2,205.9 | 29.5 |
| Student | 355.5 | 9.5 | 298.4 | 8.0 | 653.9 | 8.8 |
| Retired, old, disabled | 261.9 | 7.0 | 224.7 | 6.0 | 486.6 | 6.5 |
| Other | 24.0 | 0.7 | 14.7 | 0.4 | 38.7 | 0.5 |
| Total | 3,736.4 | 100.0 | 3,729.9 | 100.0 | 7,466.3 | 100.0 |

SOURCE: Department of Census and Statistics.

rate, it is necessary to consider the youth problem in a historical perspective. The traditional precolonial culture, with its authoritarian hierarchical caste system, was marked by inbuilt apprenticeship and full employment associated with complete integration. The traditional center of learning in the village was the Buddhist temple, where the vernacular was taught and Buddhist ethics were explained.

Under the British administration (1815 – 1948) the stability of the old system was shaken to its foundations, and a new caste—the English-educated upper and middle class—emerged with high status. The quest for white-collar jobs began as mass education was introduced in schools controlled by the government or by Christian missionaries. The introduction of free and compulsory education in 1947 without a corresponding change in educational policy further accentuated the problem. As one observer wrote in 1969, "The rationale of this system was that the young men who got a smattering of English shunned manual occupations and became misfits in a society" (17:32). These youths had rejected the way of life, the values, and the manner of dress of their fathers along with the traditional occupations that were still available. Their job aspirations, work experience, and training were not compatible with an agricultural economy in which the number of white-collar jobs and occupations in industry was severely limited.

In spite of the postindependence educational "explosion," about 92 percent of the students were compelled to return to hereditary occupations. Unemployment rates correlate positively with rising levels of education. In 1970, 55 percent of university graduates in Sri Lanka, or 12,000, were without jobs. Most of them were graduates in liberal arts. Many of them had come from the poorer, rural sections of the community, where the schools were ill-equipped to prepare young people for science and professional courses with better prospects for employment. Unemployment and alienation among the educated youth within a rapidly changing socioeconomic system, coupled with the disintegration of a traditional caste-bound social organization, may be turning them toward suicidal behavior, while their more assertive peers express their disenchantment through rebellion. At least these are some of the identifiable strands within a complexity of etiological factors.

Suicide Notes

It is not uncommon for a suicidal victim to leave behind a suicide note. The average number of those who do so, in relation to the total number of suicides, is estimated at 15 percent (15:43 – 44). Although no figures are available regarding suicide notes for the whole of Sri Lanka, press reports suggest that quite a number of suicides do leave notes. The study of the Colombo city coroner's records revealed that 25 of a total of 122, or 18.2 percent, left suicide notes in 1971. (Of these, 16 are in Sinhalese, 4 in Tamil, and 5 in English.) The number of suicide notes may be a reflection, at least in part, of the high rate of literacy in the island.

In content, suicide notes in Sri Lanka are similar to those in other countries. Revenge, remorse, guilt, and forgiveness are the feelings often expressed. What is different, perhaps, is a reference to a future life which reflects the concept of rebirth found in Buddhism and Hinduism. The following translation of a suicide note of a 22-year-old girl who committed suicide by jumping under the wheels of a moving train underlines this point. According to the evidence of relatives, she had been jilted by her lover.

> I am writing to my dear [elder] sister with love. Did you ever imagine that such a fate as this would befall me? Yet, what we expect and wish for does not always happen. Death is inevitable, however long a person may live. Therefore Aunt and you should not grieve. It is only Aunt and yourself who might feel sorrow about me. Death is better for me than this life. My love is for the little daughter [niece]. I do not wish to continue living this miserable life any longer. *Although I have led an unhappy life in this existence, I hope to lead a life free of misery in my future births at least* [italics added]. May the Triple Gem[3] protect you all.

## ATTEMPTED SUICIDES

In Sri Lanka, as in many other countries, every case of suicide is the subject of a coroner's inquest and subsequent registration. The same rules do not apply, however, to attempted suicides. It is possible that many cases of attempted suicide never reach the hospital. According to the Sheffield study, attempted suicides in the United Kingdom amount to about 20 percent of completed suicides (2:135–136). In Sri Lanka, many suicide attempters who do obtain treatment at a hospital do not divulge the truth because of the risk of prosecution in accordance with existing laws. An accurate estimate of the extent of this problem is therefore difficult, or even impossible. Whatever data are available are unreliable and underestimated.

Law enforcement officers—policemen and magistrates—in Sri Lanka often take a lenient view of attempted suicide. The police tend to overlook many of the cases reported, and inquiries are not vigorously pursued. The few cases that do reach the courts are dealt with leniently by magistrates. Incomplete data on attempted suicides are thus available at police stations and at police posts in the larger hospitals. The police post in Colombo's General Hospital maintains records of all patients treated in or admitted to the hospital after any injury, self-inflicted or otherwise, and after poisoning.

[3]The Trinity in Buddhism (Buddha, his doctrine, and the order of monks).

A study was made of police records on cases admitted to General Hospital in the period 1970–1972 for poisoning, as about 72 percent of all suicides in the island are a result of self-poisoning (table 6-22). The data on police interviews with 270 of the 857 such patients admitted in 1972 were reviewed. The survey revealed that 131 persons—about 49 percent of those interviewed—admitted taking poison or an overdose of drugs in order to commit suicide. The remaining 139 claimed that the poisoning was accidental. This information on attempted suicide had been given to police interviewers in spite of the interviewees' awareness of the risk of legal prosecution. Although the actual percentage of attempted suicide could be much higher, the available data suggest that about half of those admitted to General Hospital with a history of poisoning took poison with intent to commit suicide or as a suicidal gesture.

With these insufficient data it is impossible to make an accurate assessment of the prevalence of attempted suicide and of its relationship to completed suicide in Sri Lanka. Still, the figures may be profitably compared with the number of persons brought to the hospital as emergencies after suicide attempts who died either before or after admission. There were 42 such deaths by poisoning and another 21 were pronounced dead at the outpatients' department in 1971, and a verdict of suicide was returned by the coroner for these 63 cases. If this number, 63, is compared with 332, the number of persons who could have taken poison in 1971 in order to commit suicide (49 percent of 679, using the percentage arrived at for 1972 because the geographical area is the same), the ratio of successful to attempted suicide is approximately 1:5. It is apparent that this ratio and the data underestimate the true incidence of attempted suicide. Many surveys conducted in the United States and the United Kingdom have in fact shown that the incidence of attempted suicide is six to ten times that of completed suicide (15:89), at least in urban communities.

It has also been found that those who attempt suicide and those who are successful belong to two distinct "populations," with a certain amount of overlap. A higher proportion of females and of those in younger age groups have been found among attempted suicides (12:136–137). Similar conclu-

TABLE 6-22
ADMISSIONS TO GENERAL HOSPITAL, COLOMBO,
FOR POISONING, 1970–1972

| Year | Male | Female | Total |
|------|------|--------|-------|
| 1970 | 398 | 268 | 666 |
| 1971 | 429 | 250 | 679 |
| 1972 | 541 | 316 | 857 |

sions have been reached for Hong Kong (19:276—279). If the poisoning cases at General Hospital in Colombo are any guide to attempted suicide in Sri Lanka, the male preponderance in completed suicides is maintained in the attempted suicide group by a ratio varying from 1.5:1 to 1.7:1 (see table 6-15). The 131 persons of the 1972 group who admitted to attempted suicide reflected this trend by a male-female ratio of 1.9:1.

A study of a sample of 104 hospital case notes of patients admitted to General Hospital with a history of poisoning also showed that the male-female ratio was 1.9:1, with a mean age of 24.3 compared with the mean age of 35.6 for the 122 suicide cases recorded by the Colombo coroner in 1971. In contrast with police records, the hospital records gave no further information on this sample. In 75 percent of the cases, the medical officers did not record whether the poisoning was accidental or was attempted suicide. Of the 26 cases for which such information had been recorded, nearly 40 percent admitted to attempted suicide. Apparently the medical officers did not think it necessary to find out and record whether the poisoning was an accident or a suicide attempt. This task seems to have been relegated to the police in view of the medicolegal aspects of the problem.

In this sample of 104 cases, the poisons and drugs used covered a wide spectrum, with kerosene and copper sulphate—which is relatively non-lethal—constituting about 35 percent. Kerosene is often ingested by many of those who are merely making suicidal gestures or ambivalent attempts, whereas those who are determined to kill themselves pour kerosene on their bodies and set themselves on fire.


## SUICIDE PREVENTION

Programs for suicide prevention in a developing country like Sri Lanka encounter special problems.

Most known cases of attempted suicide in Sri Lanka, if hospitalized, are referred to a psychiatric unit or clinic and the patient is seen by a psychiatrist. In this way, for those who have attempted suicide, some medical or psychiatric service is available. Apart from general practitioner service and the small number of private hospitals, the state runs a free comprehensive health service at 328 general, district, and rural hospitals distributed throughout the island. Not all areas of the island, however, have enough psychiatrists attached to large provincial hospitals. Further, the legal position of attempted suicide prevents many persons from admitting to such attempts. It seems likely, therefore, that only a minority of individuals who attempt suicide obtain social or psychiatric help.

Apart from treating potential victims in state-run hospitals and clinics, suicide prevention activities sponsored by other organizations are still in a rudimentary stage. The main voluntary organization was inaugurated under the patronage of the president of the Republic in May 1974 to help the depressed and the suicidal. The Sri Lanka Sumitrayo (Samaritans), which is affiliated with the London-based Samaritans International, has offices in the two main urban centers of the island, Colombo and Kandy. Its seventy-five volunteers have helped 2,686 clients during the past five years. Another voluntary organization is the Family Services Institute, which has associations with the Catholic church. It has started a skeleton counseling service for those in distress, helping many individuals who have suicidal intentions. The activities of this organization are confined for the present to Colombo.

Methods of suicide prevention used with some success by voluntary organizations in the West may be unsuitable or unrewarding when applied in other cultures with divergent traditions and ways of life. Multifarious socioeconomic and educational systems and levels may call forth distinctive methods to deal with the problem. That a suitable preventive organization in Sri Lanka cannot be based on telephone service is shown by the fact that the island has only 40,000 telephone subscribers. This service caters mainly to a small minority of town dwellers who belong to the upper middle class. Most public telephones are located in post offices, and even this service is nonexistent in the villages where the vast majority of the population lives. The Sri Lanka Sumitrayo, aware of the scarcity of telephones, advertises its services regularly through the medium of newspapers, encouraging correspondence or personal interviews. By and large, the services provided by these organizations are urban-oriented, with hardly any appreciable impact on village communities.

The question arises as to whether a suicide prevention service run on the same lines as those in Europe or America is feasible or practicable in a predominantly agricultural Asian country. Even in the West, "despite years of experimentation, there is still a question as to exactly what kind of organisation is needed and feasible" (6:Pt. III, p. 205).

It may seem that the contribution of suicide prevention organizations is marginal. The central issue—especially in reducing suicides among the youth—is the alleviation of unemployment. The government of Sri Lanka has moved to overcome this problem by enhancing the status of agriculture as a profession and by reorganizing the educational system to slant it toward vocational training and agriculture, in conformity with the country's economy and employment opportunities. The stress is on agriculture rather than industrialization. What spurred the government to implement these changes, however, was not the high suicide rate among young people but their armed uprising in 1971.

What is the best form of suicide prevention service suitable for a country like Sri Lanka? What should be its role? How should it be organized? These problems need clarification by further research and experimental work in suicide prevention agencies.

## CONCLUSION

Sri Lanka, a small, developing Asian country with a rich tradition and culture nourished by a Buddhist civilization, has remained substantially intact despite foreign influences. Its statistics on suicide and other demographic data could well be compared with those of developed countries, in view of a relatively efficient system of data collection, the manageable size of the country and its population, and the high literacy rate. In general, in earlier years, Sri Lanka's suicide rate was lower than that of most countries where such data were available and has remained relatively stable over the decades.

Factors of considerable sociological and psychological interest, however, are (1) the steep rise in the suicide rate, a trend that emerged in the decades following independence from the United Kingdom, and (2) the high rate of suicide among young people, especially in the age group 15–24. The subsequent political changes, economic transformations, and social upheavals seem to have affected the suicide rate of the country.

The popularity of insecticides and other poisons, which account for a large majority of cases, as a method of committing suicide is perhaps an aspect of the "green revolution" and the easy availability of such poisons.

It is perhaps in the past few years that Sri Lanka has begun to feel the full impact of the postwar rise in population and unemployment. The post-independence social and economic changes are apparently causing a breakdown of the traditional social norms and values; increasing demands and expectations are not being met in a society that is trying to cope with these problems within a liberal and democratic tradition.

Leaving aside those who commit suicide because of a major psychiatric disorder or psychosis, the main causative factors seem to be hypereridism, alcoholism, and unemployment or financial problems. Perhaps they too are characteristic of a traditional society in a state of transition. This trend may continue till such time as a new equilibrium or stability is achieved.

## BIBLIOGRAPHY

1. Asuni, T. Suicide in western Nigeria. *Brit. Med. J.* (1962).
2. Ceylon. *Criminal Procedure Code.* Part VIII.
3. Davy, John. *An Account of the Interior of Ceylon and of Its Inhabitants with Travels in That Island.* London: Longman, Hurst, Rees, Orme, and Brown, 1821.
4. D'Oyly, John. *A Sketch of the Constitution of the Kandyan Kingdom.* Colombo: Ceylon Government Press, 1928. Reprint.
5. Dublin, L. I. *Suicide: A Sociological and Statistical Study.* New York: Ronald Press, 1963.
6. Gibbs, J. P. *Suicide.* New York: Harper and Row, 1968.
7. Gibbs, J. P., and W. T. Martin. Status integration and suicide in Ceylon. *Amer. J. Sociol.*, 64, 6 (1959):585–591.

8. Gunasekera, N. D. Some observations on suicide in Ceylon. *J. Ceylon Branch Brit. Med. Assoc.*, 46, 11 (1951).
9. Horner, I. B., trans. *Vinaya Pitaka* (Book of Disciplines). London.
10. Jayawardane, C. H. S., and H. Ranasinghe. Suicide in the Southern Provinces. *Ceylon J. Med. Science*, 15, 1 (1966):31−40.
11. Labovitz, Sanford. Article in *Suicide*, ed. J. P. Gibbs. New York: Harper and Row, 1968.
12. Parkin, D., and E. Stengel. Incidence of suicidal attempts in an urban community. *Brit. Med. J.* (1965).
13. Sainsbury, P. *Suicide in London*. London: Chapman and Hill, 1955.
14. Sainsbury, P. *Suicide and Depression*. London: R.K.P.A., 1968.
15. Stengel, E. *Suicide and Attempted Suicide*. Harmondsworth: Penguin Books, 1969.
16. Strauss, J. H., and M. A. Strauss. Suicide, homicide and social structure in Ceylon. *Amer. J. Sociol.*, 58 (1953):461−469.
17. Wijesinghe, C. P. Youth in Ceylon. In *Youth: A Transcultural Psychiatric Approach*, ed. J. M. Massermann. New York: Grune and Stratton, 1969.
18. Wood, A. L. Crime and aggression in changing Ceylon. *Trans. Amer. Phil. Soc.*, 51 (1961).
19. Yap, P. M. Suicide in Hong Kong. *J. Mental Science*, 104 (1958).

# 7 INDIA

*Editor's Note*

Tamil Nadu, where Madurai Medical College and Erskine Hospital are located, is one of the states with the highest reported incidence of suicide in India. The neighboring state of Kerala, in south India, also has a high suicide rate, though it is lower than the rates prevailing in some of the union territories. South India is poor compared with areas where some industrialization has taken place. In general, wealth and prosperity are found in India's cities rather than in the countryside, although a visit to Calcutta makes it abundantly clear that severe poverty also exists in the cities.

Overpopulation continues to be a major problem in India despite government attempts to educate the people on birth control. Religious leaders, fearing that Muslims would outnumber Hindus and thereby gain more power, oppose such plans. Many of the progressive actions of the government have not really altered ways of thinking in India. Caste is still a potent force. Education has been improved but not enough to touch the life of the peasant. India has developed the atomic bomb but it has not been able to solve the problem of poverty of the masses. Marriages arranged on an economic basis, still in vogue, cause explosive frictions leading to suicidal acts.

Dr. Venkoba Rao is professor of psychiatry at Madurai Medical College and chief psychiatrist at Erskine Hospital. He received his training in England. Dr. Rao has been active in bringing the suicide problem to the attention of government and community bodies, and he has published numerous articles on the subject. The establishment of the Suicide Prevention Center at Erskine Hospital was a significant accomplishment, in view of the difficulties.

## A. VENKOBA RAO[1]

Suicide and attempted suicide, as universal phenomena, naturally have not spared the Indian subcontinent. Of late, there has been a growing interest in the field of suicidology in India, and a number of publications on different aspects of the subject have appeared. Madurai, Bangalore, Luck-

[1]I am grateful to Dr. M. Narayanan, director of medical education, Tamil Nadu, for permission to publish this paper.

now, Bombay, and Delhi and the state of Gujarat are some of the centers where work on various aspects of suicidal behavior has been in progress. The government of India has published annual statistical reports on suicide.

## RELIGIOUS AND HISTORICAL CONSIDERATIONS

Suicide was commented on by the ancient Indians in the Vedas, or sacred literature of the early inhabitants. In the early Vedic period (4000–2000 B.C.), killing oneself was allowed, but in the later Upanishadic period (approximately 800 B.C.) the sacred writings strongly opposed such an action.

The early inhabitants of India, as nature worshipers, made sacrifices for good harvests, protection from dangers, and the like. The best sacrifice that could be offered in early Vedic times was human life, and various verses or sutras can be so interpreted: "These great beings attained to heaven where the gods and the ancient Sadhyas reside." Scholarly interpreters, however, have differed as to whether the Vedas permitted suicide as sacrifice.

In the period of the Upanishads the attitude was entirely different. The Upanishads were mystic presentations and interpretations of the Vedic literature regarding the soul. (Hindu sacred writings are deeply concerned with the relationship of the individual, primarily his soul, to the whole cosmos.) The seers of this period condemned suicide in strong terms. A verse from Isavaya Upanishad declares: "He who takes his self [life] reaches after death, sunless regions covered with darkness." Later concessions were made for the sanyasin, one who has achieved full insight into himself and the cosmos: "The sanyasin may enter upon the great journey, or choose death by voluntary starvation, by fire, by a hero's fate, or by drowning."

In the dharmasastras there is considerable discussion as to whether man has a right to kill himself. Religious suicides were permitted in some circumstances: by ascetics; drowning at the junction of the sacred rivers—the Ganges and the Jamuna—as a sacrifice; wandering and self-starvation in the last years of one's life; suttee, in which a woman was immolated on her husband's funeral pyre, thus following him into the next world. Persons who suffered from incurable diseases, or who were so old and enfeebled as to wish to end their lives, were also permitted to commit suicide.

Although religious suicides were condoned, ordinary suicides were not. Kautilya, the ancient lawgiver, prescribed severe penalties for the body of the suicide. Hindu philosophy, however, holds that death does not end existence, for it is the body that dies; the soul remains immortal. With its theory of reincarnation, the Vedanta (the whole of Indian religious thought on the relationship of the individual, the soul, worldly manifestations, and the universal principle) views death as a door to the next life. The individual's rebirth will depend upon his actions in this life. Death can thus be an opportunity for a new life in accordance with the individual's views on and acceptance of Hindu philosophy.

Suttee, or the immolation of a widow, is well known and has had a long history in India. Other peoples, such as the Scythians and the Thracians, have followed similar practices. Originally the practice was voluntary on the part of the widow, but later it became obligatory. Many women were forced against their will to end their lives in this way, either through social pressure or through physical force. Raja Ram Mohan Roy attacked the custom in 1818, arousing public opinion by agitation and pamphlet writing. Among his other important moves against suttee, he examined all the legal texts from the most ancient times, showing that not all the authorities in Hindu law were agreed on approving the practice and that many of the later jurists who did permit it stated that it should be a voluntary act free of pressure. Suttee, declared illegal in 1829, has died out, and only rarely is a case reported from remote areas.

Two other forms of suicide are known or recorded in history. Mass suicide (*jauhar*) took place in Rajput when women killed themselves to avoid humiliation and molestation by invading armies. Similar mass suicides occurred during other invasions. The Jain religion, an Indian sect, allows suicide by self-starvation, but only by ascetics.

Hunger strikes in India are a form of satyagraha or "soul force." Mahatma Gandhi originally used this method to combat British rule in India, with considerable success. The type of satyagraha in which one deprives himself of food and water, even though politically motivated, has a religious aura akin to that of ascetics. It is not uncommon in India today for a person or a group to begin a fast of indefinite length as a means of gaining attention and achieving redress for real or fancied wrongs. There may also be token fasts to protest government or other agency actions and measures. Potti Sriramuda of Madras, by fasting for 51 days, succeeded in triggering the reorganization of India into linguistic divisions. In a recent instance of death from fasting, Pheruman suffered the ordeal in vain; he had hoped for the inclusion of the city of Chandigarh into the Punjab.

## LEGAL AND SOCIAL ATTITUDES

The Indian penal code regards attempted suicide as a legal offense. Consequently, families fail to report suicidal attempts both for fear of legal consequences and to avoid social disadvantage. Survivors of suicide attempts and family members are looked upon with suspicion, and such a family "taint" can damage marriage prospects. Society's attitude toward the suicide and his family is compounded of fear, censure, shame, and condescension, all of which may injure a family's economic and social status.

## CULTURAL FACTORS

In discussing the causes of suicide and suicidal attempts, one cannot remain unconcerned about the sociocultural context. Marriages in India today, notwithstanding modernization, are still conservative in nature. Usually they are arranged and approved by the elders in the family; usually they take place within the caste and between parties of social and economic parity. Hence marriages disapproved of by the parents, in the event of self-selection of the mate or selection from outside the caste, are not favored and are held to be against tradition. In such instances it is not uncommon for either or both of the lovers to attempt suicide. Similarly, suicides are known to result as a tragic consequence of unwanted forced marriages.

Marriage negotiations can be stressful for families, and particularly so for the prospective bride. The parents approach the boy's family and describe her age, appearance, education, accomplishments, and disposition. They outline their own economic standing, family lineage, and caste and mention family members of prominence and any other factors that might seem positive. The girl's family is questioned about possible dowry and wedding gifts.* If these matters proceed well and the horoscopes of both parties are found to be auspicious, the next step is a meeting of the boy and the girl. Demanding or sometimes critical remarks may be addressed to the girl, and she may be asked to display her accomplishments. If she is accepted, protracted negotiations for wedding arrangements, gifts, and money follow. This process may be time consuming and expensive and thus work a hardship on the parents. For the girl the experience may be embarrassing and depressing. If it happens more than once, it can be a traumatic ordeal for her. Girls have attempted suicide when no husbands can be found for them, both from depression and from feelings that they have failed their parents.

Intrafamily conflicts often lead to self-destructive behavior. Mother-in-law and daughter-in-law confrontations not uncommonly lead to suicide of the latter. Since a barren woman is often held to be unlucky, and her state is inauspicious in Indian culture, she may turn to suicide. Parenthood is

---

*Editor's note: Although demanding a dowry is illegal and punishable by law, such demands continue. "Bride burning" for insufficient dowries has allegedly increased. Women's groups, leading the protest against these murders, have presented petitions against the practice to Prime Minister Indira Gandhi.

cherished and usually a son is preferred because he is required to carry out the obsequies and observe the death anniversaries of the parents. The ancient sacred texts of India state that a son prevents the entry of the parents, after their death, into a specific type of hell called *puth*. Hence a high premium is placed on a son in the Indian family. A woman's chastity is highly valued in the Indian cultural system. This quality has been enshrined in the Indian epic, Ramayana. Rama, the hero of the epic, submits his wife Sita to a trial by fire when she returns to him after her captivity in the abode of Ravana, a demon, to test her purity. Sita emerges unscathed, thereby proving her innocence of marital transgression. I have come across cases of women attempting or consummating suicide when they are baselessly accused of marital infidelity. Such a solution is likely to occur to the wives of paranoids who harbor delusions or suspicions about their wives' conduct.

Sexual adequacy is seen as the mark of manliness or, more precisely, as an expression of a healthy and sturdy youthfulness. Marital disharmony is all too common a consequence of sexual dysfunction. Impotence in men, with a few exceptions, is certainly psychogenic; without being a component of any psychiatric syndrome, it may be an isolated handicap resulting from several psychological traumas, especially masturbation. It is a popular notion in India that impotence and other disorders follow masturbation. Although one may recognize that whatever harm there is in masturbation comes from the idea rather than its practice, the public and the professions alike still believe that the act carries the germs of sexual failure. Impotence is but one example of several situations in medicine where there is a time lag between folklore and science. I know of many instances of suicides and suicide attempts stemming from this psychological disability.

## SOURCES OF DATA

This report includes all India government statistics on completed suicides for 1965–1977 and police statistics for Bangalore in the period 1958–1967. Suicide studies in Madurai, state of Tamil Nadu, include Department of Forensic Medicine autopsy reports for 1956–1972. Other data come from my study of attempted suicides at Erskine Hospital, Madurai, in 1964 and a follow-up study in 1972 on attempted suicides by students in 1971. Further data come from the Suicide Prevention Clinic in Erskine Hospital for the period 1974–1978.

Government statistics on completed suicides are collected in the following way. Section 40 (i)(d) of the Criminal Procedure code assigns the legal responsibility for reporting unnatural deaths and deaths under suspicious circumstances to officials such as village headman, accountant, watchman, police officers in villages, landowner or occupant of land or his agent, and officers in charge of revenue collection. Reports are made to the nearest magistrate or to the police station. The magistrate, should he receive the information first, forwards the report to the police station. Reports of unnatural deaths and deaths under suspicious circumstances are also available to the police from hospitals. Autopsies are conducted invariably in all such cases and the findings are forwarded to the concerned police department and to the magistrate. Several factors affect the reliability of statistics on suicidal deaths: efficiency and willingness of the reporting persons, efficiency of the police in conducting investigations, and the ability of the police surgeon to determine that the death is a suicide. Many cases of attempted suicide which are treated in private hospitals or nursing homes or which end fatally in the patients' homes are likely to go unreported.

The government statistics presently available offer data on the following: (1) suicides in different geographical areas of the country; (2) suicides in different age groups; (3) causes of suicides; (4) sex distribution; and (5) means of committing suicide. The deficiencies in government data are that they do not offer details about religions, rural-urban distribution, prevalence of suicide at different socioeconomic levels, marital status, seasonal variations, and the literacy level of suicides. The list of causes for suicide is inadequate; in fact, 52 percent of the cases are listed under the heading "other causes."

The statistics on suicide, together with accidental deaths, have been compiled by the Central Bureau of Investigation, government of India, from 1964. Prior to that year the government was not collecting data for the whole country. Although India today is the second most populous nation in the world, it stands sixteenth in number of suicides when compared with other countries where government statistics are available. It has been estimated that 110 of the 1,000 individuals who commit suicide every day in the world are Indians.

## COMPLETED SUICIDES

That there has been an upward trend in the occurrence of suicide in India during recent years has been borne out by the data collected by the government of India. The number of suicides per 100,000 population in the country increased from 6.3 in 1965 to 8.1 in 1969. Furthermore, the increase in the suicide rate is approximately four times the increase in India's population during the same period. Whereas the number of suicides rose by 43.3 percent, the population increased by only 10.2 percent. Table 7-1 indicates the rising rate of suicide for the country for the period 1965–1969. In 1972 the number of suicides had declined slightly, to 43,601 from the 43,633 in 1969. Table 7-2 shows suicide data for smaller geographical units.

TABLE 7-1
ESTIMATED POPULATION, NUMBER OF SUICIDES,
AND SUICIDE RATE PER 100,000
POPULATION IN INDIA, 1965–1969 AND 1972

| Year | Estimated midyear population (× 1,000) | Number of suicides | Suicide rate |
|------|------|------|------|
| 1965 | 4,869 | 30,669 | 6.3 |
| 1966 | 4,937 | 37,848 | 7.6 |
| 1967 | 5,113 | 38,386 | 7.5 |
| 1968 | 5,235 | 40,688 | 7.3 |
| 1969 | 5,366 | 43,633 | 8.1 |
| 1972 | – | 43,601 | 7.8 |

SOURCE: Central Bureau of Investigation.

EDITOR'S NOTE: Dr. K. Sathyavathi of the National Institute of Mental Health and Neurosciences in Bangalore has kindly provided data on the all-India suicide rate for later years: 1973, 7.1; 1974, 7.8; 1975, 7.1; 1976, 6.8; 1977 (the last year for which data are available), 6.3.

In addition to government documents, there are reports based on police statistics indicating the frequency of suicide in different parts of the Indian subcontinent. In 1960 the rate in Sourashtra State (now part of Gujarat) was estimated at 14.1 per 100,000 (11) and in Bangalore city, at 8.8 (9). In discussing the mean annual rate of suicide in south India, Aiyappan and Jayadev (1) commented: "Suicide in Coimbatore is as common as it is in Scotland and higher than in Italy and Holland." In 1954 suicide in Madurai, according to the same authors, was comparable to that in Spain.

Autopsy Studies in Madurai

The autopsies conducted by the Department of Forensic Medicine in the five-year period, 1958–1962, in Madurai have been investigated by Ganpathi and Rao (4). Of the total of 1,500 autopsies, 912 or 60.8 percent, were suicides. The average number of suicides a year was 182.4. Based on the Madurai census of 1961, the suicide rate was 43 per 100,000 population. In a later study, Rao and Paul (23) found that 42.1 percent of the 3,313 autopsies in 1963–1972 were suicides. The increase in the occurrence of suicide has been out of proportion to the increase in the population of Madurai. In Madurai, it seems that an autopsy is performed every other day for a death judged to be a suicide.

Table 7-3 gives the autopsy and suicide data from the records of Erskine Hospital, Madurai, for the seventeen years from 1956 through 1972. When the annual number of suicides in 1958–1962 is compared with the annual

TABLE 7-2

SUICIDE RATE PER 100,000 POPULATION AND PERCENTAGE DISTRIBUTION
OF SUICIDES IN STATES AND UNION TERRITORIES OF INDIA, 1972

| State or union territory | Estimated midyear population (× 1,000) | Number of suicides | Suicide rate | Percentage of total suicides |
|---|---|---|---|---|
| *States* | | | | |
| Andhra Pradesh | 44,571 | 3,286 | 7.37 | 7.5 |
| Assam | 15,192 | 1,215 | 8.00 | 2.8 |
| Bihar | 57,649 | 920 | 1.60 | 2.1 |
| Gujarat | 27,544 | 1,324 | 4.81 | 3.0 |
| Haryana | 10,317 | 445 | 4.31 | 1.0 |
| Himachal Pradesh | 3,506 | 49 | 1.40 | 0.1 |
| Jammu and Kashmir | 4,735 | 33 | 0.70 | 0.1 |
| Karnataka | 30,042 | 3,539 | 11.78 | 8.1 |
| Kerala | 21,971 | 4,500 | 20.48 | 10.3 |
| Madhya Pradesh | 42,959 | 3,362 | 7.83 | 7.7 |
| Maharashtra | 51,815 | 4,278 | 8.26 | 9.8 |
| Manipur | 1,102 | 20 | 1.81 | 0.1 |
| Meghalaya | 1,038 | 127 | 12.23 | 0.3 |
| Nagaland | 526 | 8 | 1.52 | 0.0 |
| Orissa | 22,522 | 2,461 | 10.93 | 5.7 |
| Punjab | 13,874 | 649 | 4.68 | 1.5 |
| Rajasthan | 26,533 | 513 | 1.93 | 1.2 |
| Tamil Nadu | 42,216 | 4,769 | 11.30 | 10.9 |

TABLE 7-2 (Continued)

| State or union territory | Estimated midyear population (× 1,000) | Number of suicides | Suicide rate | Percentage of total suicides |
|---|---|---|---|---|
| Tripura | 1,598 | 258 | 16.15 | 0.6 |
| Uttar Pradesh | 90,216 | 4,049 | 4.49 | 9.3 |
| West Bengal | 45,560 | 7,271 | 15.96 | 16.7 |
| Total | 555,486 | 43,076 | 7.75 | 98.8 |
| *Union territories*[a] | | | | |
| Andaman and Nicobar Islands[b] | 118 | 62 | 52.54 | 0.2 |
| Chandigarh | 263 | 23 | 8.75 | 0.1 |
| Dadra and Nagar Haveli[c] | 76 | 38 | 50.00 | 0.1 |
| Delhi | 4,313 | 149 | 3.45 | 0.3 |
| Goa, Daman, and Diu[d] | 830 | 57 | 6.48 | 0.1 |
| Lakshadweep | 33 | 0 | 0.00 | 0.0 |
| Mizoram | 334 | 9 | 2.69 | 0.0 |
| Pondicherry | 484 | 187 | 38.64 | 0.4 |
| Total | 6,501 | 525 | 8.08 | 1.2 |
| Grand total | 561,987 | 43,601 | 7.76 | 100.0 |

SOURCE: Central Bureau of Investigation.
[a]Union territories are administered directly by the government of India.
[b]Andaman and Nicobar Islands are southeast of Madras. Many of their inhabitants are migrants from the mainland, although there are local tribes. During British rule Andaman Island was used to confine criminals sentenced to life imprisonment. The island is covered by malaria-infested forests.
[c]Nagar Haveli was originally a Portuguese settlement.
[d]Goa, Daman, and Diu were originally Portuguese settlements.

TABLE 7-3
AUTOPSIES AND SUICIDES IN ERSKINE HOSPITAL, MADURAI, 1956–1972

| Year | Number of autopsies | Number of suicide autopsies |
|------|---------------------|-----------------------------|
| 1956 | 154 | 36 |
| 1957 | 157 | 68 |
| 1958 | 180 | 58 |
| 1959 | 330 | 205 |
| 1960 | 260 | 164 |
| 1961 | 370 | 247 |
| 1962 | 360 | 238 |
| 1963 | 358 | 194 |
| 1964 | 353 | 187 |
| 1965 | 328 | 180 |
| 1966 | 329 | 191 |
| 1967 | 303 | 163 |
| 1968 | 332 | 125 |
| 1969 | 326 | 95 |
| 1970 | 306 | 90 |
| 1971 | 345 | 81 |
| 1972 | 333 | 121 |

number in 1963–1972, a decline is obvious. Table 7-3 reveals a sharper drop from 1969 onward, with a rise again in 1972. The steep decline may be attributed to various factors: a larger number of bodies from suicidal deaths being handed over to relatives without autopsy; improved facilities at Erskine Hospital, especially a central resuscitation section to handle cases previously cared for in medical and surgical wards; and the activities of the Suicide Prevention Center. Also, the cases treated by private clinics are not recorded. Furthermore, the counseling offered to suicide attempters in the hospital may have helped to prevent repetition of the act.

Table 7-3 also discloses that autopsies for suicide were fewer in the years 1956–1958. Does the smallness of these numbers reflect a periodic fall in suicide frequency with an intervening decade of upward trend? It is difficult to answer this query at present. The admission of suicide attempters into Erskine Hospital has been increasing, however; in 1971 there were 981 cases; in 1972, 1,062 cases. The completed suicides for these years were 182 and 201, respectively, figures far higher than those shown in table 7-3. Thus there is evidence that suicides have been on an upward trend in Madurai.

Using police records for the ten years 1958–1967, Sathyavathi (8) has clearly demonstrated an increase in the rate of completed suicides for the

TABLE 7-4
SUICIDE RATE PER 100,000 POPULATION
IN BANGALORE, 1958–1967

| Year | Rate |
|------|------|
| 1958 | 8.5 |
| 1959 | 7.5 |
| 1960 | 11.5 |
| 1961 | 11.9 |
| 1962 | 14.6 |
| 1963 | 14.6 |
| 1964 | 17.8 |
| 1965 | 17.9 |
| 1966 | 18.7 |
| 1967 | 18.7 |

SOURCE: Dr. K. Sathyavathi, National Institute of Mental Health and Neuroscience, Bangalore, India.

city of Bangalore. From 8.7 per 100,000 in 1958, it rose to 18.7 per 100,000 in 1967 (table 7-4).

Sex Distribution

The vulnerability of the female sex to suicide has been reported by several Indian researchers. Aiyappan and Jayadev (1) reported in 1956 that the male-female ratio in south India was 47.3:52.7, and Sathyavathi and Rao (9) found a ratio of 1:1.06 in Bangalore in 1961. In 1970, however, Sathyavathi (8) reported a male rate varying from 16.3 to 24.4 per 100,000 and a female rate varying from 17.6 to 18.7 for the five-year period 1963–1967 in Bangalore. In the state of Saurashtra, Shah (11) found in 1960 that women outnumbered men in reported suicides. In 1971 Singh and associates (12) reported a female-male ratio of 3.50:2.76 in Delhi State. In Madurai, however, male suicides exceeded female suicides by a ratio of 3:2 in 1966, and males consistently predominated over a period of almost fifteen years (23). This observation is in keeping with the Western world's sex distribution of suicides, which is three males to one female. According to an all-India survey conducted by the government males constituted 59.5 percent of all suicides in 1968 and 60.1 percent in 1969. The percentage was 61.7 in 1972. Table 7-5 shows the complete geographical distribution of suicides, by sex, in India in 1972. Table 7-6 shows the incidence of suicide in states with the highest rates and in those with the lowest rates in 1968–1972.

A significant increase in the incidence of suicide per 100,000 population took place in the century between 1872 and 1972 in some states in India

TABLE 7-5

SEX DISTRIBUTION OF SUICIDES IN STATES, UNION TERRITORIES,
AND CITIES OF INDIA, 1972

| State, union territory, or city | Male | | Female | | Total |
|---|---|---|---|---|---|
| | Number | Percentage | Number | Percentage | |
| *States* | | | | | |
| Andhra Pradesh | 1,936 | 58.9 | 1,350 | 41.1 | 3,286 |
| Assam | 848 | 69.8 | 367 | 30.2 | 1,215 |
| Bihar | 544 | 59.1 | 376 | 40.9 | 920 |
| Gujarat | 726 | 54.8 | 598 | 45.2 | 1,324 |
| Haryana | 284 | 63.8 | 161 | 36.2 | 445 |
| Himachal Pradesh | 25 | 51.0 | 24 | 49.0 | 49 |
| Jammu and Kashmir | 27 | 81.8 | 6 | 18.2 | 33 |
| Karnataka | 2,342 | 66.2 | 1,197 | 33.8 | 3,539 |
| Kerala | 3,107 | 69.0 | 1,193 | 31.0 | 4,500 |
| Madhya Pradesh | 2,099 | 62.4 | 1,263 | 37.6 | 3,362 |
| Maharashtra | 2,638 | 61.7 | 1,640 | 38.3 | 4,278 |
| Manipur | 14 | 70.0 | 6 | 30.0 | 20 |
| Meghalaya | 111 | 87.4 | 16 | 12.6 | 127 |
| Nagaland | 8 | 100.0 | 0 | 00.0 | 8 |
| Orissa | 1,514 | 61.5 | 947 | 38.5 | 2,461 |
| Punjab | 527 | 81.2 | 122 | 18.8 | 649 |
| Rajasthan | 288 | 56.1 | 225 | 43.9 | 513 |
| Tamil Nadu | 3,189 | 66.9 | 1,580 | 33.1 | 4,769 |

TABLE 7-5 (Continued)

| State, union territory, or city | Male | | Female | | Total |
|---|---|---|---|---|---|
| | Number | Percentage | Number | Percentage | |
| Tripura | 130 | 50.4 | 128 | 49.6 | 258 |
| Uttar Pradesh | 2,460 | 60.8 | 1,589 | 39.2 | 4,049 |
| West Bengal | 3,759 | 51.7 | 3,512 | 48.3 | 7,271 |
| Total | 26,576 | 61.7 | 16,500 | 38.3 | 43,076 |
| *Union territories* | | | | | |
| Andaman and Nicobar Islands | 48 | 77.4 | 14 | 22.6 | 62 |
| Chandigarh | 16 | 69.6 | 7 | 30.4 | 23 |
| Dadra and Nagar Haveli | 24 | 63.2 | 14 | 36.8 | 38 |
| Delhi | 90 | 60.4 | 59 | 39.6 | 149 |
| Goa, Daman, and Diu | 41 | 71.9 | 16 | 28.1 | 57 |
| Lakshadweep | 0 | 00.0 | 0 | 00.0 | 0 |
| Mizoram | 8 | 88.9 | 1 | 11.1 | 9 |
| Pondicherry | 120 | 64.2 | 67 | 35.8 | 187 |
| Total | 347 | 66.1 | 178 | 33.9 | 525 |
| Grand Total | 26,923 | 61.7 | 16,678 | 38.3 | 43,601 |

| Cities | | | | | |
|---|---|---|---|---|---|
| Ahmedabad | 75 | 46.9 | 85 | 53.1 | 160 |
| Bangalore | 290 | 79.2 | 76 | 20.8 | 366 |
| Bombay | 107 | 61.1 | 68 | 38.9 | 175 |
| Calcutta | 19 | 57.6 | 14 | 42.4 | 33 |
| Delhi | 82 | 62.6 | 49 | 37.4 | 131 |
| Hyderabad | 92 | 59.7 | 62 | 40.3 | 154 |
| Kanpur | 32 | 61.5 | 20 | 38.5 | 52 |
| Madras | 130 | 58.8 | 91 | 41.2 | 221 |
| Total | 827 | 64.0 | 465 | 36.0 | 1,292 |

Source: Central Bureau of Investigation.

## TABLE 7-6
### SUICIDE RATE PER 100,000 POPULATION AND PERCENTAGE OF TOTAL SUICIDES IN STATES WITH HIGHEST RATES AND STATES WITH LOWEST RATES IN INDIA, 1968–1972

| State | 1968 Rate | 1968 Percentage of total suicides | 1969 Rate | 1969 Percentage of total suicides | 1970 Rate | 1970 Percentage of total suicides | 1971 Rate | 1971 Percentage of total suicides | 1972 Rate | 1972 Percentage of total suicides |
|---|---|---|---|---|---|---|---|---|---|---|
| *Highest rates* | | | | | | | | | | |
| Tamil Nadu | 14.71 | 13.80 | 12.78 | 11.38 | 13.14 | 10.74 | 12.40 | 11.73 | – | – |
| Kerala | 14.38 | 7.20 | 14.38 | 7.20 | 14.75 | 6.50 | 15.55 | 7.62 | 20.48 | 10.30 |
| West Bengal | 13.49 | 14.10 | 12.82 | 12.86 | 15.42 | 14.32 | 17.81 | 18.20 | 15.96 | 16.70 |
| Orissa | 11.36 | 5.80 | 11.86 | 5.75 | 11.64 | 5.20 | – | – | – | – |
| Karnataka | 11.02 | 7.60 | 11.12 | 7.31 | – | – | – | – | 11.78 | 8.10 |
| Maharashtra | – | – | – | – | 11.43 | 11.83 | – | – | – | – |
| Tripura | – | – | – | – | – | – | 12.78 | 0.46 | 16.15 | 0.60 |
| Haryana | – | – | – | – | – | – | 11.89 | 2.73 | – | – |
| Meghalaya | – | – | – | – | – | – | – | – | 12.23 | 0.30 |
| *Lowest rates* | | | | | | | | | | |
| Jammu and Kashmir | 1.09 | 0.10 | 0.35 | 0.03 | 0.12 | 0.01 | 0.00 | 0.00 | 0.70 | 0.10 |
| Punjab | 2.16 | 0.70 | 4.61 | 1.52 | – | – | – | – | – | – |

| | | | | | | | | | | |
|---|---|---|---|---|---|---|---|---|---|---|
| Rajasthan | 2.88 | 1.80 | 1.29 | 0.75 | 1.00 | 0.55 | 1.24 | 0.74 | – | – |
| Nagaland | 3.83 | 0.04 | 4.93 | 0.05 | 0.92 | 0.01 | 0.39 | – | 1.52 | – |
| Bihar | 4.06 | 5.50 | 3.19 | 4.12 | 3.92 | 4.68 | 1.41 | 1.83 | 1.60 | 2.10 |
| Himachal Pradesh | – | – | – | – | 2.98 | 0.22 | 1.69 | 0.13 | 1.40 | 0.10 |
| Manipur | – | – | – | – | – | – | – | – | 1.81 | 0.10 |

SOURCE: Central Bureau of Investigation.

(table 7-7). The comparative figures for England and Wales are 6.56 (1872) and 11.30 (1972). Also, the suicide rate was higher among females than among males in 1872, a trend reversed in the course of a hundred years (tables 7-8, 7-9). In England and Wales, in contrast, the male rate in 1872 (9.75) was substantially higher than the female rate (3.54).

## Age Distribution

Suicide and attempted suicide seem to be associated with comparatively younger people in India, in contrast with more advanced countries. The number of suicides and attempted suicides in Madurai has been highest for the age group 10−29, with the peak coming in the 20−29 range. Singh and associates, surveying 108 cases in one year in Delhi State, found the peak numbers in the 20−29 and 45−59 age groups for males and in the 20−29 group for females (12). In Gujarat, the highest number of suicides occurred in the age group 21−24, with the range of 25−29 a close second (6). In persons over the age of 50, the incidence of completed and attempted suicides has recently shown a rising trend, although adolescents still contribute most heavily to the toll. Suicides in the age group 18−29 years constituted 43.7 percent of all suicides in India in 1968 and 44.7 percent in 1969 (5). The comparable figure in 1972 was 45.4 percent (table 7-10).

## Methods

In India, completed and attempted suicides have been primarily attributable to the ingestion of an organophosphorus compound, a common insecticide, according to surveys by Ganapathi and Rao (4), Bagadia et al. (3), and Rao and Paul (23). Insecticide accounted for 45.5 percent of the suicides studied by Ganapathi and Rao (4). It is likely that organophosphorus compounds are preferred by potential suicides because they are cheap and easily accessible.

Other researchers have come to different conclusions. For example, Singh and his associates found that the "most common methods are hanging

TABLE 7-7
INCREASE IN SUICIDE RATE PER 100,000 POPULATION IN
SELECTED STATES IN INDIA BETWEEN 1872 AND 1972

| State | Rate in 1872 | Rate in 1972 |
|---|---|---|
| Bengal (West Bengal) | 2.36 | 15.96 |
| Bombay Presidency (Maharashtra) | 4.73 | 8.26 |
| Madras Presidency (Tamil Nadu) | 7.85 | 11.30 |
| Central Provinces (Madhya Pradesh) | 6.10 | 7.83 |

SOURCE: D. N. Nandi, G. Banerjee, and G. C. Boral, "Suicide in West Bengal," *Indian Journal of Psychiatry* (April 1978).

TABLE 7-8

MALE AND FEMALE SUICIDE RATES PER 100,000 POPULATION
IN SELECTED STATES IN INDIA IN 1872

| State | Male | | Female | |
|---|---|---|---|---|
| | Number | Rate | Number | Rate |
| Bengal (West Bengal) | 532 | 1.78 | 883 | 2.93 |
| Bombay Presidency (Maharashtra) | 337 | 3.99 | 429 | 5.56 |
| Central Provinces (Madhya Pradesh) | 202 | 5.41 | 241 | 6.85 |

SOURCE: D. N. Nandi, G. Banerjee, and G. C. Boral, "Suicide in West Bengal," *Indian Journal of Psychiatry* (April 1978).

and throwing oneself in front of the train" (12). A Gujarat suicide inquiry found drowning to be the most common method of committing suicide (2,164 cases out of a total of 4,537). There were 831 instances of burning, 682 hangings, and 506 poisonings, and 239 persons threw themselves in front of a train (6).

The government of India report (5) shows that the important methods were poisoning (20.22 percent in 1968 and 21.30 percent in 1969) and drowning (23.71 percent in 1968 and 21.30 percent in 1969). Self-destruction by firearms and other weapons, setting oneself on fire, and jumping from a height were observed less frequently.

TABLE 7-9

SEX DISTRIBUTION OF SUICIDES IN
SELECTED STATES IN INDIA IN 1972

| State | Male | | Female | |
|---|---|---|---|---|
| | Number | Percentage | Number | Percentage |
| Assam | 848 | 69.8 | 367 | 30.2 |
| Bihar | 544 | 59.1 | 376 | 40.9 |
| Gujarat | 726 | 54.8 | 598 | 45.2 |
| Kerala | 3,107 | 69.0 | 1,393 | 31.0 |
| Uttar Pradesh | 2,460 | 60.8 | 1,589 | 39.2 |
| West Bengal | 3,759 | 51.7 | 5,512 | 48.3 |
| Bombay | 107 | 61.1 | 68 | 38.9 |
| Calcutta | 19 | 57.6 | 14 | 42.4 |
| Delhi | 82 | 62.6 | 49 | 37.4 |
| Madras | 130 | 58.8 | 91 | 41.2 |

SOURCE: D. N. Nandi, G. Banerjee, and G. C. Boral, "Suicide in West Bengal," *Indian Journal of Psychiatry* (April 1978).

TABLE 7-10

## SUICIDE BY AGE GROUP IN THE STATES OF INDIA, 1972

| State | Age group | | | | | | | | |
| --- | --- | --- | --- | --- | --- | --- | --- | --- | --- |
| | Below 18 | | 18–29 | | 30–49 | | 50 and over | | Total |
| | Number | Percentage of total | Number | Percentage of total | Number | Percentage of total | Number | Percentage of total | |
| Andhra Pradesh | 344 | 10.4 | 1,619 | 49.3 | 988 | 30.1 | 335 | 10.2 | 3,286 |
| Assam | 139 | 11.5 | 501 | 41.2 | 424 | 34.9 | 151 | 12.4 | 1,215 |
| Bihar | 149 | 16.2 | 372 | 40.4 | 329 | 35.8 | 70 | 7.6 | 920 |
| Gujarat | 198 | 15.0 | 621 | 46.9 | 441 | 33.3 | 64 | 4.8 | 1,324 |
| Haryana | 126 | 28.3 | 179 | 40.2 | 108 | 24.3 | 32 | 7.2 | 445 |
| Himachal Pradesh | 5 | 10.2 | 28 | 57.1 | 11 | 22.5 | 5 | 10.2 | 49 |
| Jammu and Kashmir | 1 | 3.0 | 32 | 97.0 | – | – | – | – | 33 |
| Karnataka | 335 | 9.5 | 1,598 | 45.1 | 1,285 | 36.3 | 321 | 9.1 | 3,539 |
| Kerala | 823 | 18.3 | 1,970 | 43.8 | 1,357 | 30.1 | 350 | 7.8 | 4,500 |
| Madhya Pradesh | 608 | 18.1 | 1,245 | 37.0 | 1,055 | 31.4 | 454 | 13.5 | 3,362 |
| Maharashtra | 766 | 17.9 | 1,876 | 43.9 | 1,353 | 31.6 | 283 | 6.6 | 4,278 |
| Manipur | 3 | 15.0 | 5 | 25.0 | 12 | 60.0 | – | – | 20 |
| Meghalaya | 16 | 12.6 | 34 | 26.8 | 23 | 18.1 | 54 | 42.5 | 127 |
| Nagaland | – | – | 55 | 62.5 | 3 | 37.5 | – | – | 8 |
| Orissa | 313 | 12.7 | 803 | 32.6 | 913 | 37.1 | 432 | 17.6 | 2,461 |
| Punjab | 51 | 7.9 | 274 | 42.2 | 247 | 38.1 | 77 | 11.9 | 649 |
| Rajasthan | 53 | 10.3 | 249 | 48.5 | 183 | 35.7 | 28 | 5.5 | 513 |
| Tamil Nadu | 699 | 14.6 | 2,260 | 47.4 | 1,510 | 31.7 | 300 | 6.3 | 4,769 |

| | | | | | | | | | |
|---|---|---|---|---|---|---|---|---|---|
| Tripura | 76 | 29.5 | 112 | 43.4 | 45 | 17.4 | 25 | 9.7 | 258 |
| Uttar Pradesh | 610 | 15.1 | 1,798 | 44.4 | 1,426 | 35.2 | 215 | 5.3 | 4,049 |
| West Bengal | 1,268 | 15.3 | 3,962 | 54.5 | 1,898 | 26.1 | 143 | 2.0 | 7,271 |
| Total | 6,583 | 15.3 | 19,543 | 45.4 | 13,611 | 31.6 | 3,339 | 7.7 | 43,076 |

SOURCE: Central Bureau of Investigation.

Causes of Suicide

The causes of suicide and attempted suicide in India are usually not psychiatric illnesses, although the importance of mental diseases in leading to suicide should not be overlooked. Their contribution to the incidence of suicide is, however, significantly less than that of disturbed interpersonal relationships, socioeconomic factors like poverty, unemployment, and indebtedness, marital unhappiness and discord, disappointment in love affairs, childlessness or excessive fecundity, failure in examinations, and a fear of, or actual, loss of prestige. Thus nonpsychiatric factors are more significant in causing suicide than psychiatric disorders.

The causes of suicide in India in 1968 and 1969 as revealed by a survey are shown in table 7-11. Allowances should be made for the inherent difficulties in the accurate collection of data by governmental machinery and the reporting of suicidal deaths. The table confirms the fact that mental illnesses (listed here as insanity) do not occupy a prominent place. Apart from the other causes, despair over serious physical illness and quarrels with parents-in-law or spouses show up as important causes.

Although mental illnesses are not a prominent cause of attempted suicide and suicide in India, among psychiatric conditions that do lead to suicide are schizophrenia, depression, hysterical reaction, immature personality, alcoholism, and drug dependency. The linear relationship that exists between depressive illness and suicide in Western countries is not characteristic of India. Fewer depressives commit suicide in India than elsewhere. Ideas of guilt and sin possess a low suicide potential in the Indian culture. Besides, many patients who contemplate suicide do not proceed to its

TABLE 7-11
CAUSES OF SUICIDE IN INDIA, 1968–1969
(In percentages)

| Cause | 1968 | 1969 |
|-------|------|------|
| Failure in examinations | 3.86 | 3.90 |
| Quarrel with parents-in-law | 8.24 | 7.50 |
| Quarrel with spouse | 6.20 | 7.70 |
| Poverty | 4.38 | 4.30 |
| Love affair | 3.30 | 3.30 |
| Insanity | 3.04 | 2.30 |
| Dispute over property | 1.49 | 2.20 |
| Despair over serious illness | 17.37 | 14.40 |
| Other | 52.12 | 52.40 |
| Total | 100.00 | 100.00 |

SOURCE: Central Bureau of Investigation.

completion because of overwhelming economic, religious, moral, ethical, or social considerations. The care of children and of marital partners, a fear of the stigma that would descend upon the family, and a fear of damnation in hell after suicide are given serious attention by potential suicides. Indian philosophy does not permit *moksha* (salvation) for the suicidally dead. All these factors indicate the functioning of conscience. It may be argued that the high toll of suicide among Western depressives is owing to the functioning of conscience. How is it, then, that the same feature acts as a counter-force in Indian culture? The answer seems to lie in the type of family living, which stresses personal responsibility in the West but a collective or family responsibility in the East. The latter makes the patient look toward other family members and to realize his obligations to them. In the West, the individual blames himself and acknowledges his responsibility. The ultimate answer may be found in the Indian philosophical outlook: the Indian patient, in contrast with his Western counterpart, is more conscious of his obligations than of his rights, more aware of his duties than of his privileges. Not all Indian researchers, however, agree that ideas of sin and guilt play a lesser role among Indian depressives (2, 13).

Suicides among schizophrenics are owing to commanding voices or delusions or impulsiveness. Immature personality and hysterical reactions are diagnosed in youthful attempters. I have come across typical cases of Cotard syndrome[2] terminating in suicide, although admittedly they are rare. Overt mental illness was observed in 24.14 percent of the suicides studied by Singh and his associates (12). A psychiatric diagnosis was made in 15 of the 114 suicide attempts reported by Rao (15). Mental etiology was found in only 944 of the 4,537 suicides studied by the second Gujarat Suicide Inquiry Commission (1966).

Chronic sickness and physically debilitating illnesses contribute heavily to the suicide toll. The relation between abdominal pain and suicidal behavior has been investigated at length in a study I conducted in 1971. In the 1961 survey by Sathyavathi and M. Rao (9), the heaviest toll was taken by stomachache. Physical illnesses and handicaps came second among the causes found by the Gujarat Suicide Inquiry Commission, the first place being occupied by sociocultural factors like domestic unhappiness, ill-treatment, discord, and the like. This section is not intended to underestimate the importance of psychiatry in suicide and suicide attempts, but to emphasize that there are more reasons for suicide than mental illness.

Multiple Suicide Pacts

Sathyavati reported in 1976 (8) that 25 percent of the total suicides in Bangalore in the ten-year period beginning in 1967 were owing to suicide

[2]The Cotard syndrome is presence of nihilistic ideas concerning the content of the body.

pacts. Of the twenty-three double suicides, fourteen were of husband and wife; four, of love partners; four, of friends; and one, of sisters. Most of the individuals were between the ages of 26 and 38, with males in the older brackets. Almost all the victims were Hindu, and they were either housewives, students, workers in unskilled trades, or unemployed. The married couples all had children, and the single individuals lived with their families. Forty of the individuals—thirteen pairs of husband and wife, three pairs of lovers, and four pairs of friends—poisoned themselves with insecticides. One husband and wife hanged themselves; the two sisters died by drowning.

The suicides of eight couples were owing to poverty, debts, and financial disasters; two couples suicided because of friction in the extended family. Three pairs of girls killed themselves because of tensions brought about by marriage negotiations, primarily because they did not wish to marry the persons chosen for them by the parents. Four of these girls had had the wedding dates set and had protested unsuccessfully against the marriages. The other two girls had become depressed over the complex and often humiliating process of meeting families of prospective husbands and being critically surveyed: they killed themselves to avoid further experiences of that kind.

## ATTEMPTED SUICIDES

Table 7-12 gives the number of attempted suicides seen at Erskine Hospital, Madurai, in each year from 1974 through 1978. The figures show that an average of approximately one patient a day was admitted for attempted suicide in Madurai in 1974, 1975, and 1976, and that two or more a day were the average in 1977 and 1978. In Bangalore, hospital records show an average of seven suicide attempters admitted each day. If the figures in

TABLE 7-12
REGISTRATIONS AT SUICIDE PREVENTION CENTER,
ERSKINE HOSPITAL, MADURAI, 1974–1978

| Year | Number of registrations |
|---|---|
| 1974 | 350 |
| 1975 | 450 |
| 1976 | 434 |
| 1977 | 782 |
| 1978 | 1,440 |
| Total | 3,456 |

table 7-12 are compared with completed suicides in Madurai, the ratio of completed to attempted suicide ranges from 1:12 to 1:9.

Sex Distribution

No definite figures for the male-female distribution of suicide attempters are available from centers other than Madurai. Of the 114 suicide attempts I surveyed in 1965 (15), 65 were by males and 49 by females. The male dominance persisted when projected against the sex distribution of the population of Madurai (1:0.93). A 1967 study of 198 suicide attempters at Erskine Hospital, Madurai, also showed more males than females—108 as against 90.

Age Distribution

The 1967 study also revealed that the largest proportion of attempters (88 percent) were between the ages of 10 and 29; slightly more were in the 10−19 group than in the 20−29 group (table 7-13). Only three patients were over 50 years of age. Interviews with teenagers showed that attempts by them were often impulsive and that the precipitating causes were trivial in nature.

Causes and Methods

The dominant feelings of attempters were depression, anger, spite, jealousy, and a desire to get attention. My 1965 study of 114 suicide attempts revealed that 63 percent of those who tried to commit suicide had consumed bug poison (15).

## STUDENTS AND SUICIDE

Research on attempted suicide and suicide among students in India has been very meager. In association with R. Chinnian, I made a modest

TABLE 7-13
AGE DISTRIBUTION OF PATIENTS AT ERSKINE HOSPITAL,
MADURAI, WHO ATTEMPTED SUICIDE, 1967

| Age group | Male | Female | Total |
| --- | --- | --- | --- |
| Below 10 | 0 | 0 | 0 |
| 10−19 | 53 | 38 | 91 |
| 20−29 | 42 | 42 | 84 |
| 30−39 | 10 | 7 | 17 |
| 40−49 | 2 | 1 | 3 |
| 50 and over | 1 | 2 | 3 |
| Total | 108 | 90 | 198 |

beginning in this direction in 1972 (24). We found that in the ten-month period beginning April 1, 1971, the thirty-five suicide attempts by students in Madurai amounted to 31 percent of all attempts registered. We used the term "student" in its broadest sense to include school and college students and student nurses. Twenty-two of the thirty-five were in college, in the following fields: medicine, six; arts and sciences, fourteen; agriculture, two. Three were student nurses. Ten were in lower schools, five each in S.S.L.C. and elementary and middle grades. Of all the students, nineteen were male and sixteen were female. Table 7-14 shows the age distribution of these thirty-five students who attempted suicide. Twenty-seven of the students made one attempt each; five attempted twice and three attempted four times. Clinical diagnosis showed that twenty students were hysterical, with inadequate and immature personalities; eight had schizophrenia; three were dependent on drugs; two stammered; one was an epileptic; and one suffered from toxic psychosis. Insecticides were employed in seventeen instances and sleeping pills, in eleven. The absence of depression is striking. The report, while highlighting such factors as intellectuality, marriage, and family history, makes a strong plea for the institution of suicide prophylaxis measures in schools and on college and university campuses.

## SUICIDE PREVENTION ACTIVITY

There is very little activity on programs for suicide prevention in India. During the past five years, however, suicide prevention clinics have begun to function in some cities, notably in Madurai, Bangalore, Bombay, and Delhi. The centers in Madurai and Delhi are located in the Department of Psychiatry of the teaching medical college hospital in the two cities, which are run by the state. The others are operated by social agencies like the Medico-Pastoral Association in Bangalore. Training programs for volun-

TABLE 7-14
AGE DISTRIBUTION OF STUDENTS WHO ATTEMPTED SUICIDE
IN MADURAI, APRIL 1971 – JANUARY 1972

| Age group | Number |
|---|---|
| 10 and below | 3 |
| 11–15 | 6 |
| 16–20 | 18 |
| 20 and over | 8 |
| Total | 35 |

SOURCE: Suicide Prevention Center, Erskine Hospital, Madurai.

teers, who are mostly members of the lay public, are conducted regularly at these centers. In some centers psychiatric social workers and educationists play an active role in the program. A society for mental health, named Sanjivini, was started by a band of volunteer social workers in New Delhi three years ago. It offers services for the suicide-prone individual as well as crisis intervention facilities.

## CONCLUSION

That half a million people commit suicide annually in India and nine to twelve times as many attempt suicide should alarm anyone who is concerned with the country's public health problems. Yet these figures reflect modest research data and do not include cases that go unreported and unrecorded. Suicide continues to be shrouded by stigma, and efforts are made to hide the fact or to attribute deaths to accidents or to "heart attacks." In India today, since attempted suicide is legally punishable, attempters avoid hospitalization to escape entanglement with the police. The bodies of suspected suicides are subjected to autopsy, which in Indian culture is not viewed with approval. In these respects, suitable modification of the existing law is called for. Illegitimate pregnancy, as well as unwanted pregnancy in wedlock, accounts for quite a few attempted and completed suicides. The liberalization of abortion laws by the Indian Parliament on April 1, 1972, should help to some extent to mitigate the agony of these potential self-killers.

The magnitude of the suicide problem in India should be brought to the notice of the public by the media of mass communication. Adequate efforts must be expended to spread the dictum that thoughts of suicide arise only in a distressed mind and measures must be employed to screen and "catch" such suicide-prone individuals in the community. Psychological and emotional examinations in schools, colleges, and industries should be instituted. The attitude of the family and of the community in general toward a survivor must be drastically changed if the latter is to be usefully and healthily rehabilitated. There is clearly a need to alter the teaching program of psychiatry at the undergraduate level and to give adequate importance to suicidology in the curriculum. Future doctors should be trained to identify the potential suicides in their clienteles. At present the few suicide prevention centers in India do not touch even the fringe of this enormous problem. As many suicide prevention clinics as possible should be opened in such places as general hospital psychiatry departments, mental hospitals, seminaries, and mental health centers. Even though the question as to whether these clinics really diminish the death rate from suicide has not been conclusively answered, their institution is urgently called for as a means of improving the quality of mental health in the community.

## SUMMARY

The Indian government reports that between 1965 and 1972 the highest incidence of completed suicides was 8.1 per 100,000 population and the lowest was 6.3. The incidence based on autopsy records of suicides at Madurai, however, was estimated to be an average of 43 per 100,000 a year in the period 1958–1962.

Slightly more males than females attempted suicide. Eighty-eight percent of the attempters were between 10 and 29 years of age. The numbers of those aged 10–19 and 20–29 were almost equal. Attempted suicides are increasing in Madurai. The ratio of completed to attempted suicides ranges from 1:12 to 1:9.

Suicides are concealed because of legal consequences from felony statutes and because of the need to protect family honor and status. Attempted and completed suicides are concealed as accidents, heart attacks, and the like.

Madurai had more male suicides, but Bangalore and Saurashtra State had more female victims; government figures say that men commit 60 percent of the suicides. In Madurai the predominance of men over women is 3:2. India's overall rate shows that in 1972 15.3 percent of suicides were below the age of 18; 45 percent were between 18 and 29; and 31 percent were between 30 and 50. Few suicides are over 50. In Madurai the highest incidence was between the ages of 10 and 29, with the peak at 20–29. In Gujurat the peak was in the 21–24 age group, followed by 25–29.

Government statistics list poisoning as the method of suicide in about 21 percent of the cases and drowning, in 21–24 percent. Gujurat State reported that approximately half the suicides drowned themselves. Madurai investigations showed ingestion of insecticide poisons to be 45 percent of the autopsy cases and 63 percent of attempted suicides.

Causes for suicide are largely family friction, failure in examinations, unsuccessful love affairs, poverty, and chronic illness. In Madurai, in a ten-month period in 1971, students accounted for 31 percent of the attempts.

## BIBLIOGRAPHY

1. Aiyappan, A., and C. J. Jayadev. Suicide in south India. In *Society in India*. Madras: Social Science Publications, 1956.
2. Ansari, S. A. Symptomatology of Indian depressives. *Trans. All-India Inst. Mental Health*, 9 (1969):1.
3. Bagadia et al. A prospective psycho-social study of 52 consecutive cases during one year. *VITA*, 5 (1969):15.
4. Ganapathi, M. N., and A. Venkoba Rao. A study of suicide in Madurai. *J. Indian Med. Assoc.*, 46 (1966):18.
5. India. *Accidental Deaths and Suicides in India, 1968, 1969*. New Delhi: Bureau of Police Research and Development, Ministry of Home Affairs, 1971.

6. Motives and modes of suicide. *The Hindu* (English-language daily newspaper in Madras), Dec. 2, 1966.

7. Sarma, D. S. Article in *Bhavan's J.* (Bombay bimonthly), Oct. 15, 1972.

8. Sathyavathi, K. Male and female suicide in Bangalore: A longitudinal study over a ten-year period. *Trans. All-India Inst. Mental Health*, 10 (1976):105.

9. Sathyavathi, K., and D. L. N. Murti Rao. A study of suicide in Bangalore. *Trans. All-India Inst. Mental Health*, 2 (1961):1.

10. Sethi, B. B., S. S. Nathawat, and S. C. Gupta. Depression in India. *J. Social Psychol.* 91 (1973):3.

11. Shah, J. H. Article in *Indian J. Social Work*, 21 (1960):167.

12. Singh, K., N. R. Jain, and B. M. P. Khullar. A study of suicide in Delhi State. *J. Indian Med. Assoc.*, 57 (1970:412.

13. Teja, J. S., R. L. Narang, and A. K. Agarwal. Depression across cultures. *Brit. J. Psychiatry*, 119 (1971):253.

14. Thakur, U. *The History of Suicide in India.* Delhi: Munshiram Manoharlal, 1963.

15. Venkoba Rao, A. Attempted suicide: An analysis of 114 medical admissions. *Indian J. Psychiatry*, 7 (1965):253.

16. Venkoba Rao, A. Depression in southern India. Proceedings of the 5th World Congress on Psychiatry, Madrid. Excerpta Medica series, 150, 3 (1882). 1968.

17. Venkoba Rao, A. Impotence: Some psychiatric aspects of etiology and treatment. *J. Indian Med. Assoc.*, 51 (1968):177.

18. Venkoba Rao, A. History of depression: Some aspects. *Indian J. Hist. Medicine*, 14 (1969):46.

19. Venkoba Rao, A. A study of depression as prevalent in south India. *Transcultural Psychiatr. Research Rev.*, 7 (1970):166.

20. Venkoba Rao, A. The history and philosophy of suicide. *Indian J. Hist. Medicine*, 17 (1972):37.

21. Venkoba Rao, A. Depressive illness and guilt in Indian culture. *Indian J. Psychiatry*, 15 (1973):231.

22. Venkoba Rao, A. Marriage, parenthood, sex, and suicidal behaviour. *Indian J. Psychiatry*, 16 (1974):92.

23. Venkoba Rao, A., and P. G. Paul. Suicide in Madurai: A comparative study of its pattern in two different periods. *VITA*, 10 (1974):14.

24. Venkoba Rao, A., and R. Rawlin Chinnian. Attempted suicide and suicide in "students" in Madurai. *Indian J. Psychiatry*, 14 (1972):389.

# 8                  IRAN

*Editor's Note*

As seen by the brevity of the bibliography to this chapter, little interest has been evinced in the subject of suicide in Iran. Earlier, there were discussions at the University of Tehran about conducting a survey of suicidal persons, but the problems proved overwhelming. Now, under the present regime, and for some time in the future any such project is out of the question. Conversations with Europeans, Americans, and natives of Iran suggest that the suicide rate may be high in rural areas, but documenting that supposition would be impossible because Iranian cultural attitudes lead to concealment of suicidal acts.

My observations on several visits to Iran suggest that a wide gap existed between seemingly westernized city officials and businessmen and the mass of the poverty-stricken population. Although civil liberties and more freedom and prosperity were promised, little seemed to have changed for the average Iranian. The power of the religious hierarchy remained, and the traditional lines of power within the family and in the community seemed to be the same as in past centuries. Young people were under the strict control of their elders until mid life, and women were dominated by men and by the religious law, which does not operate in their favor. The better life promised by Western technology accrued mainly to the higher social classes. Knowledge of and skill in the new technologies were not widespread because of Iran's high illiteracy rate and the system of rote learning, which does not encourage flexibility of mind. The shah's increasingly autocratic and repressive government added to the pressures on the mass population. These worsening conditions put immense stress on young people, stress that is reflected in the data gathered for this chapter.

Dr. Hassan Farzam is an internal medicine specialist who headed the Poison Center at Massmoomin Hospital in Tehran for fifteen years. He has had seventeen years of experience in toxicology. His interest in research is evidenced by the fact that he began collecting data about attempted suicides at a time when there was no concern at all about the problem in Iran. I was impressed by Dr. Farzam's willingness to investigate suicide attempts in spite of work overloads and the negative attitudes to any such inquiry.

The task was gargantuan. Dr. Farzam had no statistical assistants or computer technologists to help him gather the data. The statistics derived from the replies of willing respondents had to be tabulated by hand. A significant number of people who had attempted suicide were ready to answer questions and thus gave Dr. Farzam the opportunity to see the dimensions of the problem in the largest and most important city in Iran.

His humanitarian concern for these patients was shown in his attempts to establish a suicide prevention center, but the conditions now prevailing in Iran make it impossible to set up such a service. Dr. Farzam retired from government service after gathering these data and is now on the staff of Mehr Hospital. In the deteriorating conditions that led to the overthrow of the shah, no updating of information was possible, and in the present chaotic conditions prevailing in Iran there is little likelihood that any work will be done on suicide and suicide attempts in the foreseeable future.

# HASSAN FARZAM[1]

Iran, formerly Persia, is a country with 2,500 years of recorded history. In the early history of the Persian Empire, of Cyrus the Great, Darius, and Xerxes, the empire's power spread from India to southeastern Europe. The caliphs of Baghdad, during the Muslim conquests, ruled Iran and made its centers of learning, poetry, architecture, and wealth paramount in the world. Thereafter, from approximately the thirteenth century until 1900, when oil was discovered, Iran declined into a backward, poverty-stricken nation of negligible importance.

Iran is a large country (more than 600,000 square miles) surrounded by mountain chains on the west, north, and east, with 12,000 miles of coastline on the Persian Gulf and the Gulf of Oman on the south. Russia borders the north, Iraq and Turkey the west, Afghanistan and Pakistan the east. The Caspian Sea on the north has commercial importance for the fishing industry, especially for caviar sturgeon, and the Persian Gulf for the shipping industry, particularly petroleum. Iran is a high plateau with widely differing regions: lofty mountains, the fertile Caspian Sea coast, two very large barren deserts, one of which is covered with salt, and the Khuzistan plain which contains the country's most lucrative petroleum fields. Much of the land is too poor for productive agriculture. Owing to the mountains encircling Iran, the climate tends to extremes of hot and cold with intense heat in the summer and bitter cold in the winter. Since almost no rain falls in Iran, rivers are few and water is scarce. Streams originating in the mountains are used for irrigation and reclamation of land. Much of Iran's agricultural wealth comes from these irrigated areas.

Most of the population (56 percent) is rural and consists of peasants and nomadic tribes. The best-known tribes are Kurdish, Bakhtiari, Baluchi, Lurs, and Quashqai. The tribes are fiercely independent and have resisted attempts to settle them on the land. Their produce comes from cattle,

[1]I wish to express my appreciation for the encouragement and assistance of Shahnaz Shahnavaz, director of the John F. Kennedy Training Center for Retarded Children in Tehran.

camels, and other livestock. The more settled small farmers may be tenant farmers, may rent their land, or own their own land. Some attempts were made in 1950−1960 to redistribute the large landowner blocks of farmland, but more land reform is still needed. Sixty-five percent of the Iranians earn their livelihood from farming or livestock raising, and methods are often primitive. Traditional life continues in the nomadic tribes and the small villages of the farmers. Few schools, stores, or other supply centers are found in these villages. Modern city life exists only in the very large centers such as Tehran, Isfahan, and the industrial cities focusing on oil production. Although public education under the shah's government was theoretically free and universal, children from farm areas often had no schools to attend. The illiteracy rate is 70 percent. Most of the country's newspapers are published in Tehran, and radio stations operate only in large cities. Few people are trained in modern skills, a circumstance that adversely affects the potential for industrialization.

Iran produces cereals, fruits and nuts, tea, tobacco, and fish. Opium was formerly a large crop but it was outlawed by the shah. Iran's exports and its wealth are primarily in petroleum; the country stands third in the Middle East and sixth in the world in production of oil. Fifty percent of the oil goes to western Europe, 22 percent to Japan, 8 percent to Africa, and about 8 percent to North America. Chief exports are petroleum, cotton, carpets and fruits.

## GOVERNMENT

Before the overthrow of Mohammed Reza Pahlavi's government in 1979, Iran was a constitutional monarchy. Literate men and women were entitled to the vote. Reza Shah, father of the shah, began the Pahlavi dynasty in 1925 by overthrowing the then ruling shah. Among his reforms were expropriation of lands belonging to the Muslim clergy and institution of civil law rather than ecclesiastical law, abolition of the veil for women, universal education as a goal, and an attempt at industrializing the country. Wealth tended to remain in the cities among business groups and professionals. More women than before were going into higher education and were employed professionally and in offices. Now, under the regime of Ayatollah Ruhollah Khomeini, all government and secular functions are under the control of conservative mullahs.

## RELIGION

Iran is 98 percent Muslim. Most Muslims belong to the Shiah sect, a minority branch of Islam more conservative than the majority branch of

Sunnites. The minority religious groups are 20,000 Zoroastrians (a remnant of Iran's past), a small number of Orthodox and Catholic Christians, a few Protestants, and approximately 40,000 Jews. All these groups enjoyed religious freedom under the constitutional monarchy. Many uneducated people follow the Quran for guidance in their daily lives; some settle their various problems by opening the "Divan" of the poet Hafiz at random and taking whatever action or direction the text indicates. Polygamy is authorized by Muslim law with the provision that the husband must be able to support another wife. As many Iranians cannot do so, the practice is declining. In 1972, when traditional Muslim divorces became illegal, divorces were handled by civil courts. Either husband or wife could request a divorce. Muslim law specifies the grounds for divorce, the primary one being infertility, which is presumed to be on the wife's side.

## LEGAL ATTITUDES TOWARD SUICIDE

The Quran strictly prohibits suicide, stating that suicides will not be permitted to enter Heaven and that they will be punished in Hell. Although suicide and attempted suicide are felonies, in practice the perpetrators are not prosecuted. It is important for rural and traditional families to conceal attempted and completed suicides, preferably by listing them as accidents, because such actions are embarrassing and bring shame to the family, causing lack of status and threatening the marriageability of children. Within the family, however, suicide attempts are often met with concern and sympathy.

## FAMILY LIFE AND CULTURAL ATTITUDES

In spite of a veneer of Westernization in the cities, traditional life continues in Iran, especially among the peasants and nomadic tribes. Since 56 percent of the population is rural, modern influences are not very strong and most people follow their traditional beliefs and occupations. Highest in the power structure of the family are males and elders. The extended family system remains in force in rural areas and to a certain extent in cities, where relatives can find apartments within the same building or nearby. Marriages are usually arranged, although the tendency for young men and women to choose their own partners is gaining strength. Parents of both young people must agree to the marriage, and families take the time to become acquainted. The parents of the groom pay the wedding expenses; the bride's parents must provide her with a dowry. After the marriage the couple lives with the husband's parents; the bride must fit into her husband's home, showing respect for and giving obedience to the elders. The bride's responsibility is to bear children, preferably sons, and to teach children the traditional values.

Families stress respect for the authority of the father and elders, virginity and modesty for women, submissiveness of women, good behavior and conformity to family standards for children. Girls are restricted in movement in the community; they are closely guarded and their friendships, especially with boys, are carefully supervised. Marriage is considered essential. Parents believe that children who are unhappy or who suffer from psychiatric difficulties will be cured by getting married, and such marriages are often arranged despite the problems that may ensue. Approved attitudes are entrenched early in the child's life by encircling maternal care. During the first four or five years the child is in very close affectionate contact with its mother, who is permissive and giving. The father is a more distant, authoritative figure and the child is encouraged to respect his authority as a man and an elder. When a son is approximately six years old the father becomes more closely associated with him; the eldest son is particularly favored as the father's deputy and successor. Girls are trained to stay at home, help their mothers, and in general become dependent on her. Sexual matters are discussed before children so that they are usually aware of the physical facts of life.

Stress in this traditional life arises from modern conditions. Marriage may be delayed among the middle and upper classes to allow for education. Students who attend coeducational classes may form romantic alliances that are not approved of by parents. Young people move to the cities for jobs in industry, leaving behind their parents who had expected to be cared for by their children in their old age. The latter feel guilty about not observing this obligation; parents become depressed and hurt. Traditional life also has its frictions. Parents continue to direct their adult children's lives; brides do not get along with their in-laws; mothers-in-law are demanding and domineering.

According to H. Davidian (2), the Iranian reactions to stress situations are anxiety attacks and depression. For his research, Davidian chose an area comprising a small city and many traditional villages of less than 500 population each. Physicians interviewed a sample of 488 persons over 15 years of age to determine whether any psychiatric conditions existed. The sample was selected from half of the population, as 52 percent of those living in the area were under 15. The interviews showed that 43.03 percent of the sample had some kind of psychiatric condition. Of this group, 56 percent were diagnosed as having varying degrees of depression, 40 percent of these as needing psychiatric care. More women than men suffered from depression (66 percent). It was speculated that the higher incidence for women might be owing to their more burdensome responsibilities and their heavier workload, as they cared for the house and children and also worked in the fields. In contrast, men had more time for themselves and were able to gather together for relaxation and recreation.

In another study (1), Davidian found that of 3,461 clinical cases of neuroses he had seen in the period 1959–1967, 50.6 percent were depressives and 18.43 percent showed anxiety reactions. Hysterical reactions among women were seven times more frequent than among men, and conversion hysteria and disassociation reactions were four times more frequent. The most common (90 percent) reactions to anxiety were bodily complaints, apprehension, and restlessness. The reasons given for these anxiety-depression states were primarily interpersonal problems: marital conflict, family conflict, heavy responsibilities, pressure of work, divorce, loss of loved ones, and failure in love affairs. Thus it seems that, in Iran, interpersonal difficulties are frequently expressed through somatic complaints. These data fit with the life situations of those who attempt suicide, as discussed later.

## METHODS OF DATA COLLECTION

Because of the lack of interest in suicide and suicide attempts in Iran, information about the problem is sparse. Tehran's official statistics for completed suicide are based on cases sent for autopsy to the Department of Legal Medicine of the Ministry of Justice. The question to be decided in these cases is the cause of death and its classification as accident, homicide, or suicide. There is no overall compilation of suicide figures for Iran as the various districts and cities do not send data to a central office. Obtaining the material would be almost impossible and, in addition, evaluation of the varying methods of reporting would be difficult. Figures for completed suicides in Tehran were obtained from the Ministry of Justice only for the period 1964–1974. Data on attempted suicides are not collected by the Ministry of Justice.

## SOURCE OF INFORMATION

As director of Massmoomin Hospital's Poison Center in Tehran, I became interested in the number of attempted suicides that came to the unit; I was especially concerned about the number of young people attempting suicide. Massmoomin Hospital, a government institution, has the largest number of admissions in the city. Two other hospitals to which poisoning cases are sent may have 1,000 cases yearly between them, whereas Massmoomin Hospital receives 20,000 to 28,000 such cases a year[2] out of the city's population of 3 million or more.

[2]In 1965–1973, 11,000 to 16,000 cases each year were food poisoning.

The first inquiry was made at Massmoomin for the 1967, 1968, and 1969 poisoning cases. The factors considered were time of arrival at the hospital, time between attempt and time of arrival at the hospital, time between attempt and beginning of treatment, marital status, living in a family or alone, presence of a stepmother or a stepfather in the home, financial situation, time of year, number of repeat suicide attempts, and suicides in family history. It was not possible to get data in all cases, and the highest number of replies on any one item was 5,494.

A questionnaire concerning age, education, marital status, number of previous attempts, reasons for attempt, family history of suicide, and living arrangements (alone or not) was used to obtain data for 1970, 1971, and 1972. Although again it was not possible to obtain all the information in all cases, the replies were sufficient to indicate a certain pattern. Another difficulty in obtaining questionnaire data was the shortage of personnel and time. The total number of cases surveyed was 8,928.

These data may be compared in some instances with those published in the only other study of suicide in Iran, a psychiatric survey of 100 suicide attempts in Shiraz in southern Iran, over a ten-month period in 1971—72 (3).

It is important to note that this report from Massmoomin Hospital deals only with suicide and attempted suicide by poisoning and that other means are not reported or are unknown.

## COMPLETED SUICIDES

Data from the Ministry of Justice, Tehran, for the eleven years from 1964 through 1974 (table 8-1) show little yearly variation in reported suicides, which may simply mean that the number of cases referred for autopsy is fairly constant. The total number of completed suicides for the period is 379. Age and sex were not obtainable. Means of suicide were predominantly hanging (50.1 percent) and shooting (25.5 percent), followed by cutting and stabbing (10 percent). Self-immolation was reported in nineteen cases and poisoning in only nine. Forty-two cases, the highest annual number, were reported in 1967; in 1974, when the population was much larger, the number was only twenty-three.

In the Shiraz study (3) seventeen cases were reported from the two major hospitals and the Department of Forensic Medicine. Since the total population of Shiraz was 300,000, the completed suicide rate was 5.6 per 100,000 population. Poisoning deaths at Massmoomin Hospital are reported for 1965—1973.

The actual rate of completed suicides in Iran remains unclear because comprehensive statistics are unavailable. In this study, therefore, I can merely indicate that the incidence is higher than governmental statistics suggest.

## TABLE 8-1
### METHODS OF COMMITTING SUICIDE IN TEHRAN, 1964–1974

| Year | Hanging | Shooting | Cutting and stabbing | Burning | Jumping | Poison | Self-electrocution | Drinking petrol | Total |
|------|---------|----------|----------------------|---------|---------|--------|---------------------|------------------|-------|
| 1974 | 12 | 8 | 1 | – | 1 | – | – | 1 | 23 |
| 1973 | 18 | 3 | 2 | 5 | – | – | – | – | 28 |
| 1972 | 20 | 8 | 6 | 1 | – | 1 | – | – | 36 |
| 1971 | 22 | 8 | 2 | 3 | – | 3 | – | – | 38 |
| 1970 | 16 | 14 | – | 2 | – | – | – | – | 32 |
| 1969 | 17 | 13 | 5 | 2 | – | 3 | – | – | 40 |
| 1968 | 12 | 10 | 5 | – | 3 | – | 1 | – | 31 |
| 1967 | 20 | 9 | 6 | 4 | 1 | – | 2 | – | 42 |
| 1966 | 21 | 12 | 2 | 2 | 3 | 1 | – | – | 41 |
| 1965 | 19 | 8 | 9 | – | 1 | 1 | – | – | 38 |
| 1964 | 13 | 15 | 1 | – | 1 | – | – | – | 30 |
| Total | 190 | 108 | 39 | 19 | 10 | 9 | 3 | 1 | 379 |

SOURCE: Department of Legal Medicine, Ministry of Justice, Tehran.

## ATTEMPTED SUICIDES

### Sex Distribution

In the period 1970–1972, 5,388 females and 3,540 males attempted suicide in Tehran, according to Massmoomin Hospital records (table 8-2). The ratio of males to females was 1:1.5. The predominance of females was particularly marked in the 10–14 age group but less so in the 15–19 age group, except in 1970. Thereafter female attempts exceeded male attempts, except for some leveling off at age 65.

### Age Distribution

Thirty percent of the 1970–1972 cases were found in the 10–19 age group. The largest number of suicide attempts took place between 15 and 24 years of age: 57.8 percent in 1970, 46 percent in 1971, and 51 percent in 1972. If the 25–34 age group is added to the 15–24 group, the percentages rise to 79.6, 70.4, and 74.7 for the three years, respectively. The incidence drops sharply at age 45 and continues to decline through the 65 and over group. (See table 8-3.) Government estimates put the Tehran population at 2.5 million in 1970 and at 3 million in 1972. The rates of attempted suicide per 100,000 population was therefore 146.2 in 1970, 87 in 1971, and 96.4 in 1972. The total population of Iran in 1972 was estimated to be approximately 30 million.

In comparison, the ten-month study of 100 suicide attempts in Shiraz (3) found a total of 340 cases of attempted suicide recorded at the two major general hospitals in the city and the Department of Forensic Medicine. The population of Shiraz was estimated at 300,000 and the attempted suicide rate per 100,000 was 113.3. Shiraz is much less westernized than Tehran, and its surrounding territory is rural and traditional. These facts perhaps account for the lower rate of attempted suicide in Shiraz.

A comparison of the age and sex distribution of attempted suicides in Tehran and Shiraz in 1970–1972 is interesting. In Tehran, the age group 10–19 accounted for 30 percent of the three-year total; in Shiraz, the age

TABLE 8-2
SUICIDE ATTEMPTS IN TEHRAN, BY SEX, 1970–1972

| Year | Female | Male |
|------|--------|------|
| 1970 | 2,236 | 1,435 |
| 1971 | 1,348 | 1,016 |
| 1972 | 1,804 | 1,089 |
| Total | 5,388 | 3,540 |

SOURCE: Poison Center, Massmoomin Hospital, Tehran.

## Table 8-3
### Age and Sex of Attempted Suicides by Poisoning, Tehran, 1970–1972

| Age group | 1970 | | | 1971 | | | 1972 | | | Total |
|---|---|---|---|---|---|---|---|---|---|---|
| | Male | Female | Total | Male | Female | Total | Male | Female | Total | |
| 10–14 | 29 | 76 | 105 | 30 | 50 | 80 | 11 | 61 | 72 | 257 |
| 15–19 | 363 | 824 | 1,187 | 243 | 283 | 526 | 237 | 462 | 699 | 2,412 |
| 20–24 | 423 | 512 | 935 | 223 | 350 | 573 | 372 | 416 | 788 | 2,296 |
| 25–34 | 338 | 462 | 800 | 260 | 305 | 565 | 251 | 423 | 674 | 2,039 |
| 35–44 | 136 | 232 | 368 | 120 | 150 | 270 | 125 | 371 | 496 | 1,134 |
| 45–54 | 36 | 55 | 91 | 56 | 83 | 139 | 47 | 35 | 82 | 312 |
| 55–64 | 22 | 31 | 53 | 34 | 44 | 78 | 18 | 7 | 25 | 156 |
| 65 and over | 40 | 22 | 62 | 20 | 38 | 58 | 5 | 3 | 8 | 128 |
| Unknown | 48 | 22 | 70 | 30 | 45 | 75 | 23 | 26 | 49 | 194 |
| Total | 1,435 | 2,236 | 3,671 | 1,016 | 1,348 | 2,364 | 1,089 | 1,804 | 2,893 | 8,928 |

Source: Poison Center, Massmoomin Hospital, Tehran.

group 12−19 accounted for 34 percent. The succeeding age groupings are not divided in the same way: in Shiraz the age group 20−39 had 59 percent of the attempts; in Tehran, the age group 20−34 had 48 percent. Therefore the distribution curve for age is approximately the same: 30−34 percent of the attempted suicides in both cities were under age 19; 48−59 percent were in the 20−39 group in Shiraz and in the 20−34 group in Tehran. (See table 8-3 for Tehran data.) These figures, when rounded, show that about a third of the attempted suicides were under 19 and that almost two-thirds were in the 20−39 age range. The number of attempts dropped rapidly after age group 40−45 and continued to decrease thereafter. Among the 100 Shiraz cases almost twice as many males as females attempted suicide (3), in contrast with Tehran data. The educational level in Shiraz also differed from that in Tehran; more than half the cases in the former city had had high school and university training, indicating a higher socioeconomic rank.

The number of females attempting suicide in Tehran seems to have been related to severe family problems and limited means to alleviate the distress thus caused. These women seemed to have exhausted all possibilities for getting assistance and, receiving neither sympathy nor understanding, sought to end their lives.

Marital Status

The distribution of suicide attempts by marital status is shown in table 8-4. As expected, single persons predominated from 10 through 24 years of age because most individuals in those groups are of premarital age.

TABLE 8-4
MARITAL STATUS OF SUICIDE ATTEMPTERS, BY
AGE GROUP, TEHRAN, 1970−1972

| Age group | Single | Married | Total |
|---|---|---|---|
| 10−14 | 199 | 0 | 199 |
| 15−19 | 1,612 | 265 | 1,877 |
| 20−24 | 1,122 | 950 | 2,072 |
| 25−34 | 404 | 1,062 | 1,466 |
| 35−44 | 92 | 693 | 785 |
| 45−54 | 25 | 230 | 255 |
| 55−64 | 13 | 111 | 124 |
| 65 and over | 14 | 73 | 87 |
| Unknown | 72 | 126 | 198 |
| Total | 3,553 | 3,510 | 7,063 |

SOURCE: Poison Center, Massmoomin Hospital, Tehran.

TABLE 8-5
CAUSES OF SUICIDE ATTEMPTS IN 7,553
CASES IN TEHRAN, 1970—1972

| Age group | Love affairs | Family problems | Social problems | Financial problems |
|-----------|--------------|-----------------|-----------------|--------------------|
| 10—14 | 67 | 86 | 4 | 1 |
| 15—19 | 632 | 1,268 | 134 | 108 |
| 20—24 | 669 | 1,121 | 272 | 155 |
| 25—34 | 377 | 944 | 139 | 75 |
| 35—44 | 269 | 423 | 116 | 67 |
| 45—54 | 36 | 161 | 44 | 10 |
| 55—64 | 24 | 78 | 11 | 5 |
| 65 and over | 9 | 87 | 26 | 6 |
| Unknown | 35 | 61 | 17 | 15 |
| Total | 2,118 | 4,229 | 763 | 443 |

SOURCE: Poison Center, Massmoomin Hospital, Tehran.

A reversal appears at age 25, and thereafter married individuals outnumber single ones. The earlier data, for 1967—1969, indicate that many more single than married individuals attempted suicide, but few cases of age 25 or more were recorded, and that would affect the results.

Precipitating Causes

The 1970—1972 questionnaire divided the causes of suicide attempts into four large categories: love affairs, family problems, social problems, and financial problems. Family problems included marital disharmony, in-law frictions, grandparent difficulties, child-parent friction, and relationships within the extended family. Social problems included problems of housing and employment and status problems among ethnic and social groups. The same category was used for failure in school examinations, inability to get into the school of one's choice, and general social adjustments.

Family problems, or difficulties in relationships with relatives or in-laws, were reported in an overwhelming 56 percent of attempted suicides. The largest number of individuals reporting family problems as the cause were in the 15—19 age group; the second-largest, in the 20—24 group (table 8-5). These two age groups together accounted for 56 percent of those who reported family problems; another 22 percent were in the 25—34 group. Respondents between the ages of 10 and 34 accounted for almost 81 percent of those who reported they attempted suicide because of family problems. Of those aged 10—14 who attempted suicide, 33 percent cited family problems as a causative factor.

Love affairs were a second most frequent cause of suicide attempts, reported by 28 percent of the total (table 8-5). Understandably, most of these—61 percent—were in the 15−24 age group.

Social problems came third as a cause, with the largest number falling in the 20−24 age group. The 15−19 and 25−34 groups were almost equal in this category, and together they accounted for almost exactly the same number as the 20−24 age group alone. Few of the 10−14 age group reported social problems as the cause of their suicide attempts; their major precipitating causes were family problems and love affairs. (See table 8-5.)

Financial problems were listed by only about 6 percent of the total cases. Most of those so reporting were in the 15−24 age group (table 8-5), which accounted for approximately 37 percent of the total in this category.

The Shiraz study reported that 50 percent of the suicide attempters surveyed specifically named personal relationship difficulties, mostly with family members, as the cause (3).

Methods

The drug most commonly used in attempted suicides is opium, closely followed by barbiturates. Although the government of Shah Pahlavi had legally prohibited the production and sale of opium, it was still easily available. Sleeping pills of various kinds could be obtained by prescription and saved for a suicide attempt with little difficulty. The time and personnel at my disposal were not sufficient to permit a systematic survey of all the drugs used. Among others, however, are mercury chloride, cyanide, aspirin, plant toxins, household poisons, and insecticides.

The Shiraz study (3) showed that poisons were used in 95 percent of the cases surveyed. Opium headed the list, accounting for almost half the attempts, and was followed by tranquilizers. Other frequent agents were phenobarbital, arsenic, and farm and home poisons. Most of the respondents in the Shiraz study were middle- and upper-class persons.

Table 8-6 shows the number of deaths at the Poison Center, Massmoomin Hospital, Tehran, in the period 1965−1973 which were attributable to substances most frequently used in suicide attempts. Although relatives were eager to assert that the substance was taken by mistake in order to deny the possibility of suicide in the family, most of the deaths here listed were probably suicides. Besides opium, sleeping pills, and other barbiturates, substances ranking high in this survey were not likely to have been taken by mistake: rat poison, cyanide, insecticides, kerosene, and Zarnich. Zarnich, a depilatory, is a gray doughy paste whose unpleasant and distinctive odor makes it unlikely to be ingested accidentally. As no antidote for Zarnich is known, a substantial dose is surely lethal. Aspirin, in order to be lethal, would have to be taken in massive doses and often in combination with other pills. Other substances unlikely to be taken by

## TABLE 8-6
### DEATHS ATTRIBUTABLE TO POISONS MOST FREQUENTLY USED BY SUICIDE ATTEMPTERS, TEHRAN, 1965–1973

| Year | Opium | Barbiturates | Rat poison | Cyanide | Aspirin and analgesics | Insecticides | Kerosene | Zarnich[a] | Carbon monoxide | Total | Total suicides |
|---|---|---|---|---|---|---|---|---|---|---|---|
| | | | | | | Poison | | | | | |
| 1965–66 | 3 | 5 | 4 | 0 | 2 | 9 | 5 | 0 | 2 | 30 | 53 |
| 1966–67 | 12 | 8 | 2 | 0 | 0 | 10 | 8 | 4 | 1 | 45 | 76 |
| 1967–68 | 14 | 4 | 0 | 0 | 0 | 6 | 7 | 3 | 4 | 38 | 58 |
| 1968–69 | 6 | 6 | 0 | 0 | 0 | 11 | 6 | 5 | 0 | 34 | 69 |
| 1969–70 | 15 | 6 | 3 | 0 | 1 | 12 | 5 | 4 | 1 | 47 | 80 |
| 1970–71 | 18 | 2 | 3 | 0 | 0 | 1 | 8 | 3 | 3 | 38 | 64 |
| 1971–72 | 13 | 4 | 0 | 1 | 0 | 6 | 1 | 6 | 2 | 33 | 62 |
| 1972–73 | 10 | 6 | 2 | 2 | 1 | 15 | 3 | 4 | 2 | 45 | 82 |
| Total | 91 | 41 | 14 | 3 | 4 | 70 | 43 | 29 | 15 | 310 | 544 |

SOURCE: Poison Center, Massmoomin Hospital, Tehran.
[a]Zarnich is a depilatory.

mistake were amenable to treatment and caused no deaths: nail polish remover (82), Mercurochrome (88), mothballs (902), ammonia (22); possibly double that number if peroxide had been included, and liquid glue (44).

Financial Condition and Work Satisfaction

An investigation of these two items supported the earlier finding that financial problems were not a major precipitating cause in most suicide attempts in Tehran in 1970—1972. Dissatisfaction with jobs was reported by 767 respondents to the questionnaire; satisfaction, by 3,194. In answer to the question whether the financial situation was good to very good, fairly good, or poor, the large majority (6,147) replied "fairly good"; 432, "good to very good"; and 581, "poor" (table 8-7). As the differences among age groups were not large, one could not conclude that the very young or the very old were either particularly disadvantaged or particularly fortunate. It thus appears that the major predisposing factor in these suicide attempts was distressing personal relationships, either with family members or with a love partner. The most striking finding in this survey was the preponderance of family frictions as a cause for attempting self-destruction.

Living Conditions

The 1970—1972 survey brought 5,588 replies to the question of whether the individual was living alone or with a family. Those who lived alone varied from 10 to 22 percent in the three-year period. The higher percentage

TABLE 8-7
FINANCIAL CONDITION OF SUICIDE ATTEMPTERS IN 7,160
CASES IN TEHRAN, 1970—1972

|  | Condition | | |
|---|---|---|---|
| Age group | Good to very good | Fairly good | Poor |
| 10—14 | 23 | 171 | 16 |
| 15—19 | 95 | 1,904 | 112 |
| 20—24 | 130 | 1,707 | 159 |
| 25—34 | 62 | 1,219 | 133 |
| 35—44 | 106 | 625 | 71 |
| 45—54 | 6 | 239 | 11 |
| 55—64 | 3 | 106 | 7 |
| 65 and over | 3 | 79 | 6 |
| Unknown | 4 | 97 | 66 |
| Total | 432 | 6,147 | 581 |

SOURCE: Poison Center, Massmoomin Hospital, Tehran.

TABLE 8-8
YOUNG PEOPLE LIVING WITHOUT A PARENT OR WITH
A STEPMOTHER IN TEHRAN, 1970—1972
(In percentages)

| Age group | Without a mother | | | Without a father | | | With a stepmother | | |
|---|---|---|---|---|---|---|---|---|---|
| | 1970 | 1971 | 1972 | 1970 | 1971 | 1972 | 1970 | 1971 | 1972 |
| 10—14 | 4.2 | — | — | 8.9 | — | 10.6 | 14.7 | — | 1.4 |
| 15—19 | 14.8 | 3.8 | 17.0 | 1.8 | 1.1 | 8.0 | 17.0 | 3.8 | 7.2 |
| 20—24 | 27.7 | 4.4 | 34.0 | 25.0 | 26.0 | 30.3 | 19.0 | 4.6 | 6.5 |

SOURCE: Poison Center, Massmoomin Hospital, Tehran.

was for 1970, when an unusually large number of 15- to 19-year-olds reported that they were living alone. This way of living at so early an age does not fit into the culture, and it may be that those who attempted suicide did not want relatives to know about their actions. The percentage for 1971 was 10 and for 1972, 14. The 1967—1969 figures also showed a small number of individuals living alone.

Living without a parent or with a stepmother may also affect the rate of attempted suicides. I was therefore particularly concerned to gather as many data as possible about suicide attempters in the 10—14 age group to determine whether their difficulties lay in family problems. If they did not live alone, it would be of interest to note the absence of a parent or the presence of a stepmother. The inquiry showed (table 8-8) that the largest percentages of those living with a stepmother were in the 15—24 age group. Parental absence was a significant factor, especially in the 20—24 bracket. The percentages of those affected by parental absence in the 10—14 group were low, even though the impact of parental loss would be strongest on children in this age group.

Another facet of living conditions which might have an effect on suicidal attempts is the presence in a household of family members who had attempted suicide. Both surveys (1967—1969 and 1970—1972) revealed that only a small number of respondents had had similar suicidal acts in their family history: 183 out of 4,647, or 4 percent, with no history and 283 out of 5,273, or 5 percent with such a family history.

Educational Level

Of a total of 6,812 suicide attempters in the 1970—1972 surveys 1,641, or 24 percent, were illiterate. This percentage is lower than that of the general population. Primary school education was reported by 72.9 percent, and 3 percent had attended secondary schools or higher institutions of learning. Those with primary school education and illiterates were concentrated in the 15−34 age groups. After age 45 there were few replies that indicated any schooling. Almost no respondents had had higher education.

### Number of Attempts

Very few second and third attempts were recorded in the 1970−1972 questionnaire (table 8-9), although about 16−17 percent of those in the 10−14 age group did try a second time to commit suicide. Asked whether they would attempt suicide again in the future, 170 respondents answered affirmatively; 6,084 said they would not. The largest number of those who would make another attempt were in the 15−34 age range.

### Seasonal Fluctuation

December, January, and February were the months in which most suicide attempts took place in Tehran; June and July came second; and May was the lowest point in the year. Many attempts were made by adolescents between 14 and 18 years of age in the late summer, after failing their school examinations. The winter months in Iran may be very cold and miserable. Also, the winter months follow Ramadan, the ninth month of the Muhammadan year, which is observed with daily fasting. It is therefore a time of less social interaction.

### Time of Day

Suicide attempts tended to peak in the 8−9 A.M. period and at 5, 8 and 9 P.M. At these hours some family member was usually at home. Another peak occurred at 1−2 P.M., again a family gathering time. (Seee table 8-10.) These data are verified by two measures used in the 1967−1969 report: time of arrival at the hospital and time interval before treatment began. The majority of the attempters were seen at the hospital by the first or second hour after taking poison. Seventy-three percent had arrived by the fourth

TABLE 8-9
NUMBER OF SUICIDE ATTEMPTS MADE IN 5,826 CASES
IN TEHRAN, 1970−1972

| Age group | Number of attempts | | |
|---|---|---|---|
| | One | Two | Three |
| 10−14 | 225 | 37 | 0 |
| 15−19 | 2,040 | 67 | 9 |
| 20−24 | 1,770 | 84 | 15 |
| 25−34 | 1,443 | 130 | 6 |
| Total | 5,478 | 318 | 30 |

SOURCE: Poison Center, Massmoomin Hospital, Tehran.

TABLE 8-10
TIME OF DAY OF 5,707 SUICIDE ATTEMPTS IN
TEHRAN, 1970−1972

| Hour | Number of attempts | Hour | Number of attempts |
|---|---|---|---|
| 1 A.M. | 32 | 1 P.M. | 345 |
| 2 A.M. | 38 | 2 P.M. | 302 |
| 3 A.M. | 31 | 3 P.M. | 217 |
| 4 A.M. | 72 | 4 P.M. | 216 |
| 5 A.M. | 56 | 5 P.M. | 380 |
| 6 A.M. | 93 | 6 P.M. | 312 |
| 7 A.M. | 285 | 7 P.M. | 312 |
| 8 A.M. | 384 | 8 P.M. | 382 |
| 9 A.M. | 472 | 9 P.M. | 624 |
| 10 A.M. | 286 | 10 P.M. | 309 |
| 11 A.M. | 215 | 11 P.M. | 72 |
| 12 noon | 248 | 12 P.M. | 24 |
| Total | 2,212 | | 3,495 |

SOURCE: Poison Center, Massmoomin Hospital, Tehran.

hour after ingestion. From reports of the exact time of arrival at the hospital it seems that the largest number of arrivals coincided with the largest number of attempts at the hours stated, with a lag of one to two hours. Hospital arrivals rose sharply from 94 cases at 8 A.M. to 274 cases at 9 A.M. The number of attempts (ingestions) rose sharply at 7 A.M., indicating that two hours had elapsed before arrival at the hospital. Hospital arrivals then increased at 1 P.M. and 2 P.M., decreased in the afternoon, and rose sharply at 7 P.M. Arrivals were high until midnight and then dropped sharply at 1 A.M.

From these data it may be concluded that suicide attempts take place at hours when family and friends are nearby. Thus someone is at hand to receive the attempter's message, whatever it may be: help, threat, accusation, retaliation, or the like.

## CASE HISTORIES

### Case A

Hassan, a 21-year-old teacher, had had a traumatic childhood. His father had married several wives, rapidly divorcing one to marry another. When Hassan was a child his father had divorced his mother, throwing both of them out into the street. Through help from family members the mother and son survived in passable condition, and the boy eventually got teacher's training. He then fell in love with a girl whose parents would not permit him to marry her because his parental background lowered his status in their eyes. He was depressed and frustrated by this disappointment, for the stated reasons for refusal were not only beyond his control, but they were also demeaning. Furthermore, the refusal aggravated the hurt he had suffered in childhood. He took poison and died because he was not taken to the hospital in time.

### Case B

A 15-year-old girl, a high school student, was a talented and intelligent youngster. Her paintings, poems, and writings seemed to reflect sensitivity and depression in spite of her family's excellent financial situation and congenial relationships with the daughter. The girl's performance in school had always been superior, and she was considered a top student. One day she came home very upset and crying. Her mother was quite alarmed, went to the girl's room, and urged her to say what was the matter. The girl finally told her mother that her mathematics teacher had done her a very great injustice. She had completed her exams but her teacher had not given her full credit, although all her answers were correct. When she asked the teacher why he had not given her full credit, he said before the whole class, "I gave you a low mark because I don't like your face." The girl was crushed; burning with the insult and the injustice, she subsequently took poison.

## SUMMARY

A complete picture of suicides and attempted suicides in Iran is not available owing to difficulties in obtaining overall statistics. Data obtained from cases of poisoning taken to Massmoomin Hospital indicate that the rate of attempted suicide in Tehran is rather high; this may or may not be true of the rest of the country. Available data suggest that the largest number of attempted suicides take place between 15 and 24 years of age and that the rate declines with increasing age. Females make more attempts than males, but the ratio, 1 male to 1.5 females, is not so disproportionate as it is in Western countries. Most attempters beyond the normal age for marriage are married individuals, so that the preponderance of single individuals who attempt suicide below the age of 25 is not significant. The primary reason for attempting suicide is disturbed personal relationships, especially family problems. Troubled love affairs come second and social problems third. Financial difficulties and employment problems were of minor importance. Most suicidal individuals lived with a family and had primary school education or were illiterate. There is evidence that lack of a parent or presence of a stepmother was a contributing factor in attempts by younger persons, especially in the 15–24 age group. Most attempts took place in the late morning, evening, and before midnight, increasing at times of family gathering such as mealtimes. A higher rate for females apparently is related to their disadvantaged position in society.

The rate for attempted suicide varied from 146 per 100,000 to 87 per 100,000 in the surveys I conducted.

## BIBLIOGRAPHY

1. Davidian, H. Aspects of anxiety in Iran. *Austral. New Zealand J. Psychiatry*, 3 (Nov. 1969):254–258.
2. Davidian, H. Study of mental disease in the Caspian Sea area. *Iranian J. Public Health*, 3 (Winter 1975):145–159.
3. Gharagozulu-Hamadani, H. Psychiatric evaluation of 100 cases of suicide attempts in Shiraz, Iran. *Internat. J. Social Psychiatry*, 18 (Summer 1972): 140–144.

# 9 PAKISTAN

*Editor's Note*

Pakistan is among the twenty poorest nations in the world. The economy is still largely agricultural, with exports of cotton and cloth. Forty-one percent of the national income is derived from agriculture, forestry, and fishing; landownership and business are concentrated in the hands of a few. Life expectancy is 54 years for men and 49 for women. The literacy rate for persons over 5 years of age was estimated in 1975 to be 25 percent, of which women represented 7 percent. Concern over population increase is reflected in the national budget which places family planning third, after military needs and railroads.

Rapid urban expansion has caused living conditions to deteriorate for city dwellers, especially those in the lower income groups. The government estimated in 1967 that 72 percent of the urban population lived in makeshift shacks with little water and few sewer facilities. The tribal areas in the northwestern provinces live very much in the traditional past. The population there is fluid, as tribes move freely back and forth between Pakistan and Afghanistan.

Pakistan's present situation is difficult. The country needs to develop a wider economic base than its present largely agricultural products. The proposed projects require large amounts of borrowed capital, and in addition a trained technical force is lacking. The main rallying cry is Islam, but the problems to be solved are mostly outside the scope of religion. Pakistan and Iran, both having declared themselves Islamic states, face the serious problem of large, illiterate, untrained populations attempting to cope with unmet basic economic needs. Both countries have resorted to religious slogans which may unify their people but supply no practical answers to pressing problems.

Dr. Syed Haroon Ahmed, trained in psychiatry in England, has been at Jinnah Postgraduate Hospital since returning to Pakistan. He became interested in depression and suicide, but it has been difficult for him to obtain material on these subjects because of lack of time and of modern research facilities. He has also been hampered by resistant attitudes to the seriousness of the problem in Pakistan. The nonmedical professionals with whom I talked asserted that there was no suicide in Pakistan. The opinion of psychiatrists with whom I discussed this matter was that suicide was as frequent in Pakistan as it is in England, but that legal attitudes made it unlikely that proof could be obtained.

So far as I know, the material presented in this chapter is the only complete body of information on Pakistani suicides and the only material to be published outside the country. The chapter is particularly important because it is not based on government statistics, which are not reliable in Pakistan. It took nine years to accumulate these data, which may therefore be somewhat dated. Under present circumstances it is impossible to update the material.

# SYED HAROON AHMED

Pakistan was formed in the last days of British colonial rule of the Indian subcontinent on the basis of the Muslim religion. Hindu-Muslim tensions in India, both economic and political, were the precursors of the partition that took place in 1947, presumably gathering together a people of common culture and religious belief but ignoring historical, geographical, and economic divergences. The two parts of the country, East Pakistan and West Pakistan, had differing ethnic, historical, and linguistic backgrounds and were separated by 1,000 miles. Karachi is in the province of Sind which contains many excavated remains of the Moenjodero and Harrapa cultures, highly developed civilizations dating back to 2500 B.C. These cultures were thriving for 1,000 years before Aryans from central Asia invaded the area, bringing with them their own culture and customs. Owing to invasions by Greeks, Persians, Moguls, and Arabs, the culture of West Pakistan has been shaped by Aryan, Arab, and Hindu influences. Muslim influences came late in Pakistan's history, with conquerors from Afghanistan.

The partition resulted in mass migrations on an enormous scale, with Muslims leaving India and Hindus leaving Pakistan. The migrations were unusual in that two sets of populations were forced to uproot and move to new areas, causing more disruption than usual in movements of people. The population of West Pakistan now consists of Aryans, Persians, Greeks, Pathans, Moguls, Arabs, and Indians. The language is 66 percent Punjabi and 13 percent Sindhi. English, the official language, is spoken by only 2 percent of the population.

Hostilities between East Pakistan and West Pakistan erupted in armed conflict in 1965 and 1971. Economic disparity and differences in languages and culture divided the two sections, despite uniformity in religion, and led eventually, in December 1971, to the establishment of Bangladesh. It replaced East Pakistan, and West Pakistan is now known as Pakistan.

According to a government census, the population of Pakistan in 1972 was 64,892,000, in an area of 307,374 square miles. In addition to the four provinces—Punjab, Sind, North-West Frontier, and Baluchistan, there is a tribal area in the northwest (FATA). There is considerable disparity in economic wealth among the four provinces, and the tribal area is the most traditional and primitive part of the country. These factors created friction, and the events of 1971 in East Pakistan helped to build severe tensions in the country. Attempts have been made to alleviate these insecurities and hostilities through religious emphasis and slogans, and leaders of the various Muslim sects are active in national politics. At present there is a strong emphasis on being a Muslim state with traditional laws and customs, some of which date to much earlier times.

Rapid growth in urban populations has come with industrialization efforts and as a result of villagers seeking better jobs. In 1972 the urban sector contained a fourth of the total population; Karachi, the former capital (the present capital is Islamabad), alone accounted for 20 percent. Karachi, in Sind, is a cosmopolitan city and the most important industrial and commercial center of the country. Its growth as the principal seaport of Pakistan has been phenomenal. In the wake of the massive dislocations caused by partition, Karachi attracted migrants from both India and the Pakistani provinces with the hope of better prospects, and it continues to do so. The city's population is about 4 million. From 136,000 in the 1941 census, it swelled to 1.126 million in 1951, to 2.048 million in 1961, and to 3.56 million in 1972 (1.97 million males; 1.59 million females). The languages spoken in Karachi are Urdu, Sindhi, Punjabi, Gujarati, and English. The city is a melting pot of various ethnic groups and religious sects, as these languages suggest.

## SOCIAL AND CULTURAL FACTORS

In spite of such diversity, economic factors have kept the family bound together around a common kitchen. Low incomes, underemployment, shortage of accommodations, and traditional respect for elders have perpetuated the extended family, though it is undergoing some change. The earning member of a family has to take care not only of his dependents but of deserving relatives as well. A study of disturbed schizophrenics and their acceptance by relatives, which I conducted in 1971, shows that more than 18 percent of the patients, together with their family members (0–7 individuals), were economically dependent on someone other than husband, wife, or immediate blood relations (i.e., parents or siblings).

In our culture the elderly enjoy a particularly privileged role and are given care and respect. The elder remains the wise old man whose idiosyncrasies are tolerated and whose needs, however childish, are catered to. He is not isolated; he is not poorer than his relatives nor is he discarded from society. Because of innumerable preventable diseases, few people in Pakistan survive to a ripe old age. Many who do survive have found a purpose in life by running the lives of their grown-up children and their great-grandchildren.

As in traditional Muslim life, cousin marriages are preferred. Males and elders are dominant; women are submissive. The woman, whose position in the family is low, is expected to attend to her duties as wife and mother.

She gains a small share of prestige and power if she is an urban woman who must work to help provide for the family or if she is a member of a trade union.

Industrialization and urbanization are having an effect on traditional views and values. Mobility and competition lead to a more materialistic approach to life, especially in the poorer sections of the city whose residents have minimal comforts. The clash of these new conditions with old values and traditions has brought stresses and strains perhaps as yet unrecognized.

## RELIGION

Pakistan is 97 percent Muslim, mostly Sunni and of the orthodox Hanafi view. There are a few Shiah Muslims. Members of another small yet influential sect, called Ahmadis or Qadianis, do not regard Muhammad as the final prophet. The Hindu population is very small, only 0.5 percent of the total, and Christians account for 1.4 percent. Islamic thought and traditions are extolled as the central force in the country, to the neglect of other ancient cultural roots.

## ATTITUDES TOWARD SUICIDE

The attitude toward suicide in Pakistan is determined by religion and law. Suicide is primarily a sin and subsequently a crime. Islam condemns suicide (Koran IV:29, 30); the Hadith gives explanations and unequivocally forbids suicide. The law governing the fate of those attempting suicide is the same as it was in England and Wales until 1961. Section 309 of the criminal code reads: "Whoever attempts to commit suicide and does any act towards the commission of such offense shall be punished with simple imprisonment for a term which may extend from one year to a maximum of five."

Cases in which suicide or attempted suicide is suspected are not treated by any doctor or in private and public hospitals except those authorized to handle medicolegal cases. In Karachi only two centers were so authorized until 1974, when a third was added. When the patient is brought to the emergency center, the medical officer first takes the history of the case and makes an examination; he then determines the nature of the case and, if he suspects a suicide attempt, informs the police station in the area of the patient's residence. A police inquiry follows, whether the individual lives or dies.

If the patient dies a postmortem is carried out by the police surgeon; if he lives, the articles he used are impounded and the gastric wash—if ingestion of poisonous material is suspected—is sent for chemical analysis. In the investigation the individual and the family members, sometimes even neighbors, are interrogated. After completion of the inquiry the case is brought before a magistrate who then passes judgment. He may discharge the case, levy a fine, or, rarely, hand down a prison sentence.

## SOURCES OF DATA

The circumstances outlined above greatly magnify the problem of collecting data on suicide. Because of a variety of penal, religious, and moral factors, a suicidal act is kept secret, sometimes even to the extent that proper medical aid is denied. The cases reported at recognized emergency medical centers are only those to which no other resource is available, in which a life is in danger, or in which the participants are ignorant of the legal implications. In spite of the law, medical aid is privately sought by those who can afford it. Resourceful people thus manage to evade medicolegal registration by reporting attempted suicides either as accidents or as the result of psychiatric illness. Medical men, who are sympathetic, extend treatment as in an accidental or psychiatric case.

Apparently only a fraction of patients are registered at the medicolegal centers. It was planned to procure the data for the period 1976–1978 from all the medicolegal center in order to obtain an idea of the pattern of suicide and attempted suicide in Karachi. Because of faulty record-keeping procedures, complete data are not yet available. Information is available, however, about all the cases reported at the emergency department of a federal hospital, Jinnah Postgraduate Medical Centre (JPMC), Karachi, in the three years (1976, 1977, 1978) and about those admitted to the intensive care unit (ICU) of this center in the same period.

Data are presented separately for consummated suicides and attempted suicides from the emergency department and the ICU. At the emergency department, for purposes of tabulation, attempted suicides (medicolegal) and "accidental" cases (nonmedicolegal) have been added together. This means that pleas of accident have been ignored. The medicolegal register consists of printed forms on which all cases reporting at the emergency department—accidents, suspected homicides, suicides, or instances of foul play—are recorded. Nonmedicolegal cases are entered in a separate register. Using ICU records, Hamida Jamil and her associates (2) have surveyed the cases of poisoning admitted in 1976. With her permission, further data were collected from her records for 1977 and 1978 so that figures for the three-year period could be presented here.

In addition to the information gleaned from the emergency department and the ICU, a third source was the patients admitted to the ICU as suspected attempted suicides in the first quarter of 1979. Of the total of twenty-six, only one died. The twenty-five survivors and their relatives were interviewed on the basis of a structured questionnaire, and the results are presented here. In these interviews much useful information was withheld by the relatives and even by the patients. To allay fears of prosecution and also to avoid the possibility that a male doctor could be mistaken for a police officer, female psychologists were employed for the interviews.

## COMPLETED SUICIDES

A survey of suicidal deaths in Karachi in the five-year period 1959–1963, conducted by Muhammad Ashraf (1), showed a range of 9 to 24 deaths a year with an average of 18. The data for the study were all obtained from the Karachi Police Department.

My own study of 44 deaths at the Jinnah Postgraduate Medical Centre's emergency ward and the ICU in 1976–1978 (which includes Jamil's 1976 ICU cases) showed an average of 14.6 suicides a year. Since JMPC is only one of the three centers in Karachi which receive such cases, and since the number of patients seen by private physicians is unknown, this statistic does not tell the whole story.*

### Sex Ratio

Ashraf's study (1) showed that male deaths were 2.5 times as numerous as female deaths. The JMPC emergency ward suicide deaths were 60 percent female (table 9-1); the ICU deaths, 52.9 percent female.

TABLE 9-1
SUICIDES AT JINNAH POSTGRADUATE MEDICAL CENTRE,
KARACHI, BY AGE AND SEX, 1976–1978

| Age group | Emergency ward | | | | ICU | |
|---|---|---|---|---|---|---|
| | Male | Female | Total | Percentage | Number | Percentage |
| 5–14 | 1 | — | 1 | 10 | 1 | 2.94 |
| 15–24 | 2 | 5 | 7 | 70 | 20 | 58.80 |
| 25–34 | — | 1 | 1 | 10 | 8 | 23.50 |
| 35–44 | 1 | — | 1 | 10 | 1 | 2.90 |
| 45–54 | | | | | 4 | 11.80 |
| 55–64 | | | | | | |
| 65–74 | | | | | | |
| 75 and over | | | | | | |
| Total | 4 | 6 | 10 | | 34 | |

*Editor's note: According to a recent unpublished study by S. Haroon Ahmed, Humra Zuberi, and Shezad Qamar, based on information from three medicolegal centers (JPMC, Civil Hospital, and Abbasi Shaheed Hospital), the average suicide rate for the years 1974–1978 was 1.24 per 100,000 population.

## Age

The earlier study (1) showed that 67.4 percent of the suicides surveyed were under 30 years of age, 15.7 percent were in the age range 16−20, and 51.7 percent were in the 21−30 age group. The group 31−40 accounted for 25.8 percent of the cases; the number of deaths above age 40 was insignificant.

The JMPC reports show roughly the same percentages: 61.7 percent were under 25 years of age (ICU) and 80 percent were under 25 (emergency ward). The age group 15−24 was the most common, with 58.8 percent for ICU and 70.0 percent for the emergency ward. Although the older age groups showed very few cases, there was a slight rise (11.8 percent) in the 45−54 age group for ICU cases, and emergency cases showed 10.0 percent of the deaths at ages 35−44. (See table 9-1.)

## Method

An overwhelming percentage of the suicides at JPMC in 1976−1978 used insecticides (50 percent at ICU; 55.9 percent at the emergency ward), tablets, and other poisons (table 9-2). Of the emergency cases, 17.6 percent swallowed tablets and 14.7 percent used acids; 20 percent used poison and 10 percent hanged themselves. Ashraf's study (1) showed that 39.3 percent used drugs, tablets, and other poisons. Hanging and burning had equal percentages, 17.9 each. Males were inclined to use drugs and hanging. Female methods were (1) burning, with twice as many females as males using this method, and (2) drugs and poisons.

## Reasons for Suicide

Family problems were given by relatives as the reason for 38.2 percent of the suicides at the ICU in 1976−1978; financial problems, for 17.7 percent; and unhappy love affairs, for 14.7 percent (table 9-3). These three cate-

TABLE 9-2

METHODS OF SUICIDE AT JINNAH POSTGRADUATE MEDICAL CENTRE,
KARACHI, 1976−1978

| Method | Emergency ward | | ICU | |
|---|---|---|---|---|
| | Number | Percentage | Number | Percentage |
| Insecticides | 5 | 50 | 19 | 55.9 |
| Tablets | − | − | 6 | 17.6 |
| Poisons [a] | | 20 | 8 | 23.5 |
| Hanging | 1 | 10 | − | − |
| Other | 2 | 20 | 1 | 8.3 |

[a]Kerosene, acid, copper sulphate.

TABLE 9-3
REASONS FOR SUICIDES AT INTENSIVE CARE UNIT, JINNAH
POSTGRADUATE MEDICAL CENTRE, 1976–1978,
AS STATED BY RELATIVES
(In percentages)

| Reason | | Percentage |
|---|---|---|
| Family problems | | 38.2 |
| With parents | 20.6 | |
| With spouse | 8.8 | |
| With in-laws | 8.8 | |
| Financial problems | | 17.7 |
| Lack of money | 11.8 | |
| Unemployment | 5.9 | |
| Failure in love | | 14.7 |
| Chronic illness | | 5.9 |
| Other | | 23.5 |

gories together accounted for 70.6 percent of the cases. Of the family problems, conflict with parents caused 20.6 percent, conflict with spouse, 8.8 percent, and in-law troubles, 8.8 percent.

Occupational Status

Data about occupations of the persons who committed suicide were available only from ICU records. Most females were housewives or students. Among males, 68.8 percent were skilled and semiskilled workers, 18.8 percent, students, and 14.3 percent, unemployed. Most of the victims were in the lowest and middle income groups (52.9 and 35.3 percent, respectively). Only 11.8 percent were in the upper income group.

Marital Status

Twice as many suicides were married as single.

Monthly Incidence

February had three times as many suicides as any other month. No cases were reported in July, August, November, and December. In each of the remaining seven months the number of suicides was the same. A survey covering a longer period would be necessary to show a more accurate monthly trend.

ATTEMPTED SUICIDES

The attempted suicides in the JPMC emergency ward and ICU in 1976–1978 totaled 825. Of these, 272 cases occurred in 1976, 215, in 1977; and

338, in 1978. These figures include both the medicolegal cases and the accidental or nonmedicolegal cases that were clearly suicidal attempts. Using the figure of 4 million for Karachi's population in 1978, the rate of attempted suicides in that year was 8.45 per 100,000. Ashraf (1) found from police records 102 attempts in five years for an annual average of 21.

## Age

The age range for suicide attempters was somewhat broader than for completed suicides. Of the ICU cases, 46.3 percent were under 24 years of age; 79.1 percent in the range 10–34. Of emergency ward cases, 42.1 percent were in the 5–24 age groups; 60.7 percent, in the 5–34 age group. As in completed suicides, the number of cases after age 40 was infinitesimal. (See table 9-4.) Ashraf's survey (1) showed roughly similar figures: 71.5 percent were in the 16–30 range.

## Sex Ratio

Females accounted for 54 percent of the ICU attempted suicides and for 59 percent of the emergency ward cases. In contrast, Ashraf (1) found that the ratio of males to females was almost 7:1.

## Method

Both the earlier study (1) and the JPMC study show approximately the same results. Tablets and pills, insecticides, and poisons were the major methods used in suicide attempts. Tablets were taken in 39.4 percent of the

TABLE 9-4
ATTEMPTED SUICIDES AT JINNAH POSTGRADUATE MEDICAL CENTRE,
KARACHI, BY AGE AND SEX, 1976–1978

| Age group | Emergency ward | | | | ICU | |
|-----------|------|--------|-------|------------|--------|------------|
|           | Male | Female | Total | Percentage | Number | Percentage |
| 5–14        | 4   | 9   | 13  | 3.60  | 14  | 3.01  |
| 15–24       | 67  | 72  | 139 | 38.50 | 201 | 43.30 |
| 25–34       | 39  | 28  | 67  | 18.60 | 152 | 32.80 |
| 35–44       | 18  | 8   | 26  | 7.20  | 57  | 12.30 |
| 45–54       | 6   | 6   | 12  | 3.30  | 30  | 6.46  |
| 55–64       | 6   | 1   | 7   | 1.90  | 4   | 0.88  |
| 65–74       | 2   | 1   | 3   | 0.83  | 5   | 1.07  |
| 75 and over | 2   | 2   | 4   | 1.11  | 1   | 0.21  |
| Unknown     | 33  | 57  | 90  | 24.90 |     |       |
| Total       | 177 | 184 | 361 |       | 464 |       |

ICU cases; insecticides, in 35.8 percent; poisons, plus kerosene and acid, in 14.26 percent. In emergency ward cases, 26.9 percent used insecticides; 31.9 percent, tablets; and 32.2 percent, poisons. (See table 9-5.) Ashraf, in his survey (1), found that pills and insecticides were used by 42 percent of attempters.

The sexual differences in method were not striking in the JPMC study. Females used tablets, insecticides, and poisons in that order in emergency cases, and male usage was approximately the same (table 9-5). Females in Ashraf's study (1) showed no pattern; males used drugs and poisons, stabbing and drowning, in that order.

Reasons for Attempted Suicide

The study by Jamil and associates (2), covering the year 1976, showed that family problems—conflict with parents, in-laws, or spouse—precipitated 40.62 percent of suicide attempts. Unhappy love affairs accounted for 45.8 percent; financial problems and unemployment, for 7.30 percent.

The distribution was different among the ICU cases in 1976–1978. Family problems (including difficulties with parents, in-laws, or spouse) led to 29.7 percent of the attempts; failure in love affairs, to 24.6 percent; financial and employment difficulties, to 7.3 percent; and illness, to 4.5 percent.

Ashraf's study (1) showed 44 percent of attempts were caused by family problems; 8 percent, by unhappy love affairs; and 18.6 percent, by financial difficulties.

TABLE 9-5
METHODS OF ATTEMPTED SUICIDE AT JINNAH
POSTGRADUATE MEDICAL CENTRE,
KARACHI, 1976–1978

| Method | Emergency ward | | | | ICU | |
|---|---|---|---|---|---|---|
| | Male | Female | Total | Percentage | Number | Percentage |
| Tablets | 55 | 60 | 115 | 31.9 | 163 | 39.40 |
| Insecticides | 42 | 54 | 96 | 26.6 | 166 | 35.80 |
| Poisons[a] | 42 | 28 | 70 | 19.4 | 26 | 7.35 |
| Kerosene | 11 | 21 | 32 | 8.9 | 32 | 6.89 |
| Acid | 5 | 9 | 14 | 3.9 | 8 | 1.72 |
| Gas | | | | | 1 | 0.22 |
| Other | 22 | 12 | 34 | 9.4 | 48 | 10.34 |
| Total | 177 | 184 | 361 | | 444 | |

[a]Including copper sulphate, Dhatura, Engro-Urea.

### Occupational Status

Among female attempters at JPMC in 1976–1978, housewives formed the largest category, 61.9 percent. Students were 17.1 percent of the total; professional women, 5.2 percent; skilled and semiskilled workers, 2.8 percent. Among male attempters, 52.9 percent were skilled and semiskilled workers; 22.8 percent, students; 8.5 percent, professional men; 3.7 percent, businessmen; 6.6 percent, unemployed.

Jamil's yearlong study (1) showed that 78.75 percent of female attempters were housewives and 15.00 percent were students. Among males, 36.4 percent were laborers; 23.4 percent, students; 15.6 percent, clerks.

### Marital Status

In his 1964 study (1), Ashraf found that more suicide attempters were married (56.8 percent) than single. Contrarily, most of the emergency ward cases at JPMC in 1976–1978 were single. Of the ICU attempts by males, twice as many were made by married men as by single men; among females, there were 50 percent more single women than married women. In the total ICU group of attempters, very slightly more persons were married than single. A significant proportion of attempters in both groups were below the average marriage age.

### Income Status

Only the ICU had collected data about the income status of attempters in 1976–1978. They were almost equally divided among low, middle, and high income groups.

### Monthly Incidence

Suicide attempts at the JPMC emergency ward in 1976–1978 reached a peak in April, followed by March and February. There was little variation for the rest of the year, except for a slight rise in December. (See table 9-6.)

## CASE STUDY

A case study of twenty-five attempted suicides registered at ICU was made in the first quarter of 1979. The findings were very similar to the previous reports as to age, sex, marital status, methods, and reasons.

The average age was 24, with ages ranging from 16 to 43. The sex ratio was very close: thirteen males to twelve females. Thirteen of the sample were single and twelve were married; seven women were married and five were single.

As to occupation, six males were skilled and unskilled workers, five were students, and two were professional men. Seven females were housewives, four were employed as office workers and nurses, and one was a student.

TABLE 9-6
MONTHLY DISTRIBUTION OF ATTEMPTED SUICIDES,
EMERGENCY WARD, JINNAH POSTGRADUATE
MEDICAL CENTER, KARACHI, 1976−1978

| Month | Number | | | Percentage |
| | Male | Female | Total | |
|---|---|---|---|---|
| January | 13 | 17 | 30 | 8.31 |
| February | 22 | 15 | 37 | 10.20 |
| March | 22 | 23 | 45 | 12.50 |
| April | 19 | 28 | 47 | 13.00 |
| May | 17 | 14 | 31 | 8.60 |
| June | 10 | 20 | 30 | 8.31 |
| July | 15 | 12 | 27 | 7.50 |
| August | 8 | 8 | 16 | 4.40 |
| September | 10 | 12 | 22 | 6.10 |
| October | 12 | 11 | 23 | 6.40 |
| November | 12 | 8 | 20 | 5.50 |
| December | 17 | 16 | 33 | 9.14 |
| Total | 177 | 184 | 361 | |

Fourteen of the attempters took tablets, four took insecticides, and seven took poison, including kerosene, acid, rat killers, and tinctures.

The families of the twenty-five attempters revealed that twenty-two came from urban areas and three from rural areas. Fourteen of them lived in nuclear families and eleven with extended families. The families were large, as the average number of siblings was 5.8. In ten families the patient was the eldest child; in seven, the second oldest; in two, the youngest. The remaining cases had mixed rankings. As to financial status, the attempters ranged from the lowest to a high professional income, with the average at the middle income level.

The reasons given for the suicide attempts paralleled earlier findings. Family friction, the most frequent cause, accounted for ten cases: six had conflict with spouse; three, with parents; and one, with grandparents. Seven of this group were females. Failure in love affairs was responsible for four attempts, three of them by males. Five attempts were precipitated by chronic illness. One attempter suffered from a grief reaction after losing both parents in one week; another was perhaps a victim of shock after doctors told her she could never have children. Financial and employment problems caused only three attempts.

Most of the twenty-five individuals in the case study made their attempts in familiar surroundings: nineteen at home, one at the office, one at a neighbor's house. Three were at neutral areas: a hotel, a hostel, and an army mess. Consequently, the majority of the victims were brought to the hospital by the immediate family (seventeen) or by relatives (three). Five were brought by outsiders. The spread of time of discovery of the attempts was 20 minutes to 10 hours after the event; the average time was 2.5 hours. In most cases the family took prompt action, bringing the patient to emergency within 1.5 hours. Of the twenty-five, only six were conscious; the rest were unconscious or semiconscious.

The family reaction to the attempts was primarily worry and concern, shown in eighteen cases. Two families revealed an attitude of rejection and anger. In one case the stepfather and the grandparents were angry because the patient had refused an unwanted marriage to a deaf and dumb man; in the other the father was angry because the patient had jeopardized the marriageability of the sisters.

Upon regaining consciousness, eleven of the patients were depressed or anxious and six were hysterical. In less than half the cases the attempters had given prior indications of impending trouble—depression, unusual quietness, restlessness—which the families had ignored. Four had conspicuously taken tablets belonging to a family member. Three either had attempted suicide before or had threatened to do so. Among the latter was the girl affianced to the deaf and dumb man; she told the grandparents that if they forced her to marry him she would kill herself. Evidently the grandparents and the stepfather did not care about the girl; they were adamant about the marriage, for they rejected her after her suicide attempt. Only one attempter, a schizophrenic, was mentally ill. Twenty-three of the twenty-five were Muslims and two were Christians. Nineteen were migrants from India or from outside Karachi.

## SUMMARY

The statistical data and the case study are consistent in showing that suicides and suicide attempters are under 30 years of age, with the largest number in the 15−24 category. The male-female ratio in the JPMC cases shows that slightly more females than males—between 55 and 60 percent more—killed themselves or tried to. On the contrary, Ashraf, in his study (1), found a large preponderance of men. He had surveyed a total of 291 cases, over a five-year period, whereas the JPMC study covered 894 cases, more than three times as many, in three and a quarter years. This comparison indicates the considerable underreporting of suicides and attempted suicides owing to legal prosecutions and sociocultural attitudes. Even the 894 cases reported here come from only one of three centers to which suicides could be taken. The only figure that can be given for comparison with those in other countries is the 1978 attempted suicide rate of 8.45 per 100,000 population.

Methods used in completed and attempted suicides were primarily tablets, insecticides, and poisons of various kinds.

The major reason for the self-destructive act, as shown in the three sources of data, was family problems and frictions, chiefly marital discord, parent-child conflict, or troubles with extended family members. Two other important causes were disappointments in love and financial difficulties. Females were more apt to attempt suicide because of family problems than were men.

As this study clearly reveals, the true dimensions of the suicide problem in Pakistan are unknown, owing to various reasons for concealment. Only the general outlines of the problem can be seen from this report, which indicates that young people are most affected and that interpersonal and interfamilial problems are the outstanding factors contributing to suicide.

## BIBLIOGRAPHY

1. Ashraf, Muhammad. The problem of suicide in Karachi. *Pakistan Armed Forces Med. J.*, 14 (1964):156−167.
2. Jamil, Hamida, Asadullah Khan, Shameem Akhtar, and Nasreen Sultana. Patients with acute poisoning seen in the Department of Intensive Care, Jinnah Postgraduate Medical Centre, Karachi, *J. Pakistan Med. Assoc.* (July 1977).

# 10    KUWAIT

*Editor's Note*

Kuwait is a society in rapid change, representative of Middle East traditions yet more open to Westernization and development than many countries in the surrounding area. Mechanization and industrial projects are helping to make the country prosperous, but a current of traditionalism appears in most transactions.

Kuwaitis continue their clan cohesion. No foreigner is allowed to own land or to establish a business unless a Kuwaiti owns 51 percent of it. The new affluence has created family difficulties because men have tended to marry additional wives. Elsewhere the practice of having four wives has declined because of the expense.

Kuwait's oil is expected to last another twenty years. By the time the rich wells are exhausted Kuwait hopes to have created other sources of income and to have educated its young people so that their technical and professional skills will enable the country to progress and prosper. The contrast between today's wealth and conditions in the future may, however, be extreme.

This study represents the only attempt ever made to collect information on suicide in Kuwait. In spite of its wealth, Kuwait is not up to date in some respects. All the records had to be gone through by hand, read carefully, and evaluated—a very time-consuming process. The senior researcher, Dr. Dorry Ezzat, obtained the assistance of three other psychiatrists and physicians in data collection: Dr. Abdel Kareem Hozaien, Dr. Moustafa Mahmoud, and Dr. Maher El Gabaly. As a result of setting up a procedure for collecting suicide information in the official government files, they were able to gather 1981 figures to add to the original 1978 statistics.

Dr. Ezzat, an Egyptian, is a graduate in psychiatry of Cairo University Medical School. He had further training in Europe and England, and he has specialized in psychiatry and neurology since 1962; a member of the Royal College of Psychiatrists in England since 1970; and a senior consultant in psychiatry since 1972. He is head of a unit in Kuwait Psychological Medicine Hospital and secretary of the Technical Council of the hospital. He has been a member of the permanent senior hospital staff for over twenty years and was elected Fellow of the Royal College of Psychiatrists in England in 1982. Dr. Ezzat has traveled widely in Europe and America visiting psychiatric centers and thus is familiar with theories and practices elsewhere. He is, of course, an authority on Kuwait's situation.

# DORRY H. EZZAT[1]

Kuwait is now one of the richest countries in the world, with a national income per person of more than $19,000 U.S. dollars a year. On the basis of expenditures for the public it may also be the leading welfare state in the world. The wealth comes from vast reserves of oil—a fifth of the world's resources—and large amounts of natural gas. Within the past thirty years Kuwait's wealth has skyrocketed to billions of dollars, in a small country (90 miles long and 95 miles wide).

Members of the Arab Anaiza tribe settled at Kuwait Bay about 1710, built a port, and engaged in fishing, boat making, and pearling. This tribal state, bordered by Iraq, Saudi Arabia, and the Persian Gulf, is gravelly desert with no rivers or lakes and no more than five inches of rain a year. As Kuwait obviously cannot sustain agriculture, most of the food for the growing population has to be imported. Kuwait was an autonomous state until the British established a protectorate in 1899; the protectorate ended in 1961. Oil drilling concessions were granted to the British in 1934, but full oil production did not begin until after World War II.

Early in its history the Anaiza tribe chose the el Sabah family as rulers, and the family continues today to head the emirate of Kuwait, a constitutional monarchy. All literate adult males may vote for members of the national assembly, but women are not permitted to do so as yet. The constitution provides for a democratic way of life and ensures racial, religious, and linguistic equality. The government is paternalistic, devoting large sums to improvement of housing, business, and employment opportunities. Education is free from the earliest grades through the university, and there are special schools for the blind and the handicapped and for older adults who had not previously obtained an education. Medical care is free; today, in contrast with 1949 when there were only four doctors in the whole country, there is one doctor for every 580 persons. Housing is being built rapidly, not only for Kuwaitis, but for foreign workers in industrialization projects. The city of Al-Ahmadi had a population of 232,167 in 1980. Built by the Kuwait Oil Company, it has many American, British, and other foreign residents.

With water reclamation projects increasing the formerly scarce water supply, efforts are being made to irrigate land for agriculture. Hydroponics offers the hope of supplying the food needs of the country. Other developing industries, in building materials, chemicals, furniture making, salt, and marble mining, give the promise of diversifying products and providing employment. The government is also planning recreation centers, such as

[1] I appreciate the helpful cooperation of Dr. Abdel Kareem Hozaien, Dr. Moustafa Mahmoud, and Dr. Maher El Gabaly.

an artificial lake, boating facilities in the harbor of Al-Kuwait, the capital, and resorts on the outskirts of the city.

The population of Kuwait is primarily Arab, although there are almost 800,000 foreigners who are temporarily employed in industries that are playing a role in the country's development. Until Kuwaitis are trained to take technical and administrative positions, it is likely that the transient population of Egyptians, Pakistanis, Iraqis, Palestinians, and other nationals will remain sizable. Kuwaiti men are encouraged to obtain graduate training in other countries. Women constitute more than half the university population, specializing among other subjects in science, education, and medicine. Women have more freedom than in some of the neighboring states, but they are still bound by Islamic law in matters of divorce, marriage, concubinage, property, and the like.

## RELIGION AND SUICIDE

Kuwaitis are of the Sunnah sect of Islam. Their attitude toward an individual who has taken his own life accords with the Islamic prohibition of suicide: he is considered to have brought disgrace and dishonor upon the family. His family, and society in general, regard him as an infidel and an unbeliever who has turned away from his religion. He has not complied with the divine order of God: "Do not kill yourselves, for God is merciful to you." He may be denied burial in a Muslim cemetery, although such denial very rarely occurs. The attitude is quite different—indeed, it becomes an understanding one—if the victim has been sick, especially mentally ill. Islam says, *Lysa ala almareedi harag* ("The diseased is not to be blamed"). The family of an individual who committed suicide is not criticized or censured for his act. If he was the family provider, all social benefits are still given to the family, just as if the death had been a natural one.

Attitudes toward a suicide attempter are tolerant and sympathetic. The individual is understood to be in a state of crisis, needing help and support. Usually he receives this kind of understanding treatment from family, friends, and neighbors or from appropriate agencies. After he has been medically assisted, his physician usually refers him to the psychiatric clinic for assessment and treatment.

## METHODS OF DATA COLLECTION

Data collection is difficult in Kuwait because people are usually suspicious of questions and they do not understand the importance of statistics.

In each of the general hospitals there is an investigator representing the district police station who inquires into injuries caused by accidents, cases of poisoning, attempts at suicide, and so forth. He refers samples of gastric lavage, blood, and the like to the Department of Criminal Evidence and Forensic Medicine for analysis. The department issues a report on the material ingested and lists the death as natural, accidental, or suicidal. After receiving the forensic report, the investigator decides whether or not to prosecute the case.

In Kuwait, as in most Arab countries, suicide is considered a crime. A person who attempts suicide but does not die may theoretically (but rarely in practice) be prosecuted according to the present law. For this reason hospital investigators usually rule that attempted suicide by tablet overdose is simply a mistake, that the tablets, for example, were taken for dieting purposes. A humanitarian wish to save patients and their kin from further pain leads officials to find innocent reasons for the incident and to ignore the suicidal intent.

For these reasons my associates and I turned to the Department of Criminal Evidence and Forensic Medicine, where case facts are clearly registered. At the same time we realized that there were victims of suicidal attempts who had been revived at home or rescued at a private clinic. In clinical practice one hears from patients that they think about driving very fast and crashing their cars as a way of settling crises in their lives. Others talk of jumping in front of oncoming cars. The number of injuries in car accidents in 1977 was 327.8 per 100,000 population; the number of deaths was 28.4 per 100,000. No one knows how many attempted or completed suicides might be found in these statistics, but the comments of patients suggest that the number may be substantial.

My colleagues, physicians and psychiatrists from the staff of the Kuwait Psychological Medicine Hospital, went through the files for the years 1978 and 1981. These files are not organized to report suicides, nor are diagnoses supplied. It was necessary for us to read each case thoroughly to sort out whatever information was pertinent and to make a diagnostic assessment. In view of the varied contents of the files, not all the desired information could be obtained. This effort was the first attempt made in Kuwait to assess the suicide problem. Because of the difficulties we encountered, we suggested that in the future the Department of Criminal Evidence and Forensic Medicine develop a form to be used in recording suicide data. Our report must therefore be considered an initial venture in this field, but it does supply information about the general outlines of the suicide problem.

## CULTURE AND FAMILY

The family organization in Kuwait is undergoing continuous change. The head of the family is no longer a patriarchal despot whose word must be obeyed without question. The spread of education and the influence of the mass media have brought democracy and enlightenment. Larger numbers of women are being emancipated. Until the late 1950s no woman or girl could appear in public unless completely covered by and hidden under an aba, a thick, heavy black garment. Such restrictions disappeared in the early 1960s. Traditional roles with cousin marriages, sometimes frustrating to females, are still to be seen among Bedouins and tribal people. For example, a girl can be bound by unwritten law to her cousin until he marries her, allows her to marry another, or does not allow her to marry at all. This practice is not observed by urban Arabs.

Extended families are found among the Bedouins and the lower socio-economic classes. Among the middle and higher classes, the extended family is giving way to the nuclear family. Elders are still kept in the family, whose younger members care for them, instead of being put in institutions. Usually the eldest son takes the responsibility for the care of older parents, although this tradition may be changing at the present time, as everything is in the process of change in this country. Homes for the care of the elderly may be needed in the future, as geriatric problems become an issue that will require planning.

## COMPLETED SUICIDE

Of the total of thirty-seven suicides in 1978, twenty-nine were males and eight were females. The largest number, twenty-eight, was found in the 20–39 age group, constituting 75.6 percent of the suicides. In 1981 there were fifty-nine suicides, thirty-nine of them in the 20–39 age group, or 66.6 percent of the deaths. There were eight suicides by females in 1978 and twenty-four in 1981.

The rate per 100,000 for the total population was 3.1 in 1978; in 1981 it was 4.35. Rates for the male population were 4.43 in 1978, 4.5 in 1981;

TABLE 10-1
SUICIDES IN KUWAIT, BY AGE GROUP AND SEX, 1978 AND 1981

| Age group | Male 1978 | Male 1981 | Female 1978 | Female 1981 | Percentages 1981 |
|---|---|---|---|---|---|
| Under 20 | 2 | 4 | 1 | 3 | 11.8 |
| 20–29 | | 10 | | 8 | 30.5 |
| 30–39 | 24 | 10 | 4 | 11 | 35.5 |
| 40–49 | 1 | 7 | 1 | 1 | 13.5 |
| 50–59 | 1 | 4 | 1 | 0 | 6.7 |
| 60 and over | 1 | 0 | 1 | 1 | 1.7 |
| Total | 29 | 35 | 8 | 24 | 99.7 |

SOURCE: Department of Criminal Evidence and Forensic Medicine.

TABLE 10-2
METHODS OF COMMITTING SUICIDE, KUWAIT, 1978 AND 1981

| Method | Number 1978 | Percent 1978 | Percent 1981 |
|---|---|---|---|
| Drugs and poisons | 17 | | |
| Psychotropic drugs | 12 | 32.4 | 20.0 |
| Analgesics | 4 | | |
| Benzine | 1 | | |
| Hanging | 9 | 24.3 | 10.0 |
| Jumping | 6 | 21.6 | 22.0 |
| Shooting | 2 | | |
| Drowning | 1 | | |
| Burning | 1 | 2.7 | 27.0 |
| Gas | 1 | | |

SOURCE: Department of Criminal Evidence and Forensic Medicine.

female rates were 1.49 in 1978 and 4.1 in 1981. The increase in female suicides may be related to the larger number of women who have joined the labor ranks and may be encountering stress from work.

In 1981 there were thirteen Kuwaiti suicides and forty-six non-Kuwaiti. Indians lead the list of non-Kuwaiti suicides with twelve cases; Palestinians six; Iranians, Egyptians, and Jordanians with four cases each; and the remainder with two to three cases each from the following countries: Pakistan, Europe, Iraq, Sri Lanka, Oman, Lebanon, and one unknown. Kuwait population figures for 1980 show 562,000 Kuwaitis and 794,000 non-Kuwaitis. (Ministry of Planning, Central Statistical Office, State of Kuwait 1982). In 1981, suicides of Kuwaitis decreased from those of 1978, particularly for female Kuwaitis. Migrant laborers have generally shown higher suicide rates, in the experience of other countries.

The practice of Kuwaiti men taking additional wives may be a source of frustration, unhappiness, and reactive depression for their wives. Such reactions, however, are usually transient and not strong enough to lead to suicide. The first wife is normally more experienced in maneuvering family situations, and she is also the mother of the children. Her position works as an ego support and a status enforcer, helping her to adapt to this particular adversity and to adopt a hopeful outlook for the future.

The methods most frequently used to commit suicide in 1978 were drugs and poisons, followed by hanging (table 10-2). Drugs were a lesser cause in 1981 because new laws restricting the availability of psychotropics have been passed. Increased cases of self-burning, almost double those of 1978, may be related to immigrants from countries which use that method.

Reasons for committing suicide were primarily mental illness and stress, especially family problems (table 10-3). The latter reason showed an increase in the 1981 statistics.

## ATTEMPTED SUICIDES

In 1978 there were 215 suicide attempts, 85 made by males and 130 by females. In 1981 the attempts were fewer, 152; males made 46 attempts and females 106 attempts. As to age, 43.7 percent of the cases were under twenty in 1978, and 20 percent in 1981. Those cases over 20 years of age were 56.1 percent in 1978 and 79 percent in 1981. The 1981 statistics show a more detailed breakdown of ages, as follows:

20—30 years of age, 54 percent of attempts: 24 males, 58 females
31—40 years of age, 21 percent                 9 males, 24 females
41—50 years of age,  4 percent                 4 males,  2 females

Of the 152 cases, 70 were Kuwaitis and 82 non-Kuwaitis. Female non-Kuwaitis attempted suicide three times as often as males, while female Kuwaitis made almost twice as many attempts as males. The fewer cases of attempted suicide may be due to increased alertness to potential suicides, establishment of three more mental health centers offering help to those suffering stress, and to a resurgence of religious feeling from the neo-Islamic movement.

Another possible contributant to the lower attempt figures is the creation by the government of new recreational centers and facilities, something badly needed in Kuwait. Such facilities are marine sporting clubs, skating clubs, special clubs for women, and promotion of cheap collective airline clubs for tourism abroad.

The means used for suicide attempts were primarily analgesics and drugs in both 1978 and 1981. With the restrictions on drug prescriptions, how-

TABLE 10-3
REASONS FOR COMMITTING SUICIDE,
KUWAIT, 1978 AND 1981

|                              | Number |      |
| ---------------------------- | ------ | ---- |
| Reason                       | 1978   | 1981 |
| Mental illness and depression | 27     | 30   |
| Stress, family problems      | 5      | 27   |
| Unknown                      | 5      |      |

SOURCE: Department of Criminal Evidence and Forensic Medicine.

ever, there is a shift to usage of caustics such as insecticides and kerosene. Analgesics were used in 56.2 percent of the cases in both time periods. Psychotropics were used by 29.7 percent in 1978 and 23.7 percent in 1981, caustics by 8.5 percent.

As to nationality, there were 70 Kuwaiti attempted suicides and 82 non-Kuwaitis. Egyptians were second in number, 36 cases. Egyptians constitute 6.1 percent of Kuwait's population and their rate of attempted suicide is the highest, being 42.9/100,000. A number of young female Egyptians work as domestic help in the lower socio-economic strata of society. Palestinians followed with a number of 16 cases and Indians 9 cases. The remaining nationalities had from 1 to 3 suicide attempts each.

We found, in our survey of the 215 suicide attempts in 1978, that the two main reasons were depression (80) and stress (122, or 56.7 percent), as shown in table 10-6. Stress was also the leading cause in 1981. Stress

TABLE 10-4
AGE GROUP OF SUICIDE ATTEMPTERS,
KUWAIT, 1978 AND 1981

| Age group | Number 1978 | | Percentages | |
|---|---|---|---|---|
| | Males | Females | 1978 | 1981 |
| 14 and under | 0 | 1 | | |
| 15 – 19 | 30 | 64 | 43.7 | 20.0 |
| 20 and over | 55 | 65 | 56.1 | 79.0 |

SOURCE: Department of Criminal Evidence and Forensic Medicine.

TABLE 10-5
METHODS OF ATTEMPTING SUICIDE,
KUWAIT, 1978

| Method | Number |
|---|---|
| Analgesics | 121 |
| Minor tranquilizers | 23 |
| Major tranquilizers | 22 |
| Hypnotics | 13 |
| Antidepressants | 6 |
| Antiepilepsy drugs | 6 |
| Miscellaneous[a] | 24 |

SOURCE: Department of Criminal Evidence and Forensic Medicine.
[a]Kerosene, DDT, and others.

included frustration in love; a coercive attitude on the part of parents toward love affairs; sex relationships, especially for girls; rebellious behavior by young people; and contradictory advice from parents or relatives on moral matters or issues of vital importance to adolescents, such as education or the choice of a career. Failure in examinations also led to suicide attempts in an effort to avoid possible blame. Other causes were professional failure, loss of a job, financial losses, and strained interpersonal relationships among family members. Among the latter was parental denial of personal freedom to teenage children, especially females. Table 10-7 compares various aspects of completed and attempted suicides in Kuwait in 1978 and 1981.

Seasonal Incidence

The statistics of 1981 permit a comparison of the seasonal occurrence of suicides and attempted suicides. Suicides peaked during the summer

TABLE 10-6
REASONS FOR ATTEMPTING SUICIDE,
KUWAIT, 1978

| Reason | | Number |
|--------|---|--------|
| Depression | | 80 |
| Endogenous | 45 | |
| Reactive | 35 | |
| Adversity, stress, etc. | | 122 |
| Schizophrenia | | 11 |
| Unknown | | 2 |

SOURCE: Department of Criminal Evidence and Forensic Medicine.

TABLE 10-7
COMPARISON OF ATTEMPTED AND COMPLETED SUICIDES,
KUWAIT, 1978

| Aspect | Attempted suicides | Completed suicides |
|--------|--------------------|--------------------|
| Female to male ratio | 1.6:1 | 1:3.6 |
| Age: under 19 | 43.7 percent | 8.1 percent |
| Cause | | |
| Stress | 56.7 percent | 13.5 percent |
| Mental illness | 26.0 percent | 72.9 percent |
| Method most frequently used | | |
| Analgesics | 56.2 percent | — |
| Psychotropic drugs | 29.7 percent | 32.4 percent |
| Hanging | — | 24.3 percent |

SOURCE: Department of Criminal Evidence and Forensic Medicine.

TABLE 10-8
SUICIDES IN KUWAIT BY RATE PER TOTAL POPULATION,
MALES, FEMALES, AND MALE-FEMALE RATIOS 1978 AND 1981

| Rate/100,000 population | 1978 | 1981 |
|---|---|---|
| Total population | 3.1 | 4.35 |
| Male population | 4.43 | 4.5 |
| Female population | 1.47 | 4.1 |
| Female to Male ratio F:M | 1:3.6 | 1:1.5 |

SOURCE: Department of Criminal Evidence and Forensic Medicine.

months at 39 percent, winter and spring had the same percentages, 22, and autumn had the lowest number at 17 percent. A possible reason for the July-August peak is the extreme heat which sometimes reaches 122 degrees, as well as high humidity and sandstorms.

Attempted suicides showed two peaks with 42.7 percent in winter and 36 percent in summer. Spring and autumn showed about the same incidence with 11.9 percent for spring and 9.2 percent for autumn. Winter is the time of return from vacations abroad to reenter school and summer is the time of school examinations as well as the hottest season of the year.

## CASE HISTORIES OF COMPLETED SUICIDE

### Case A

A 35-year-old well-educated man was a sports commentator. His first marriage brought him only misery, as his wife proved to be an alcoholic with a disordered personality. Life between them was nothing but quarrels, disputes, and beatings. The marriage did not last long and the man soon remarried. Although this match appeared to be suitable, it was not a success. As the husband was strongly affected by his experiences with his first wife, his relations with the new one were strained. Marital dishar-mony, tensions, and disagreements were exacerbated by intervention on the part of friends who hoped to improve the marital relationship. When all efforts to sustain the marriage failed, it ended in divorce. Shortly afterward, the man shot himself in the head, dying instantly. The response of family, friends, and society was compounded of sympathy, sorrow, and awe.

### Case B

A 40-year-old European man, married and with children, had worked in Kuwait for over a year. His job was full of stress and he had strained relations with his colleagues, so he sought psychiatric help for a short period. Aboard a plane taking him back to his country, he suddenly rushed

TABLE 10-9
ATTEMPTED SUICIDES IN KUWAIT BY RATE PER 100,000
POPULATION, MALES, FEMALES, AND MALE-FEMALE RATIOS
1978 AND 1981

| Rate/100,000 population | 1978 | 1981 |
|---|---|---|
| Total population | 17.9 | 11.2 |
| Rate of female population | 23.9 | 18.2 |
| Rate of male population | 12.9 | 5.8 |
| Number of cases | 215 | 152 |
| Female: male ratio | 1.6:1 | 2.3:1 |

SOURCE: Department of Criminal Evidence and Forensic Medicine.

to the door before the plane took off and jumped out of the door. He died from the fall immediately.

## CASE HISTORIES OF ATTEMPTED SUICIDE

### Case A

A 17-year-old unmarried female was a student in a secondary school. She was the second eldest of seven siblings whose parents were at the middle socioeconomic level. She failed in her final examinations in her third year at the school, which she had expected to pass. Her younger siblings started to annoy her and utter unkind comments. They pointed at her as a failure, shouting *al sakta* ("The one who failed"). The girl expected support from her mother, but the mother only blamed and rejected her. The girl, unable to stand all the abuse and the humiliation of failure, decided to take her life. She swallowed thirty aspirin tablets and afterward complained of stomach pains and sweating; she became pale and vomited. The family, alarmed, took her to a general hospital where she was kept for five days. Upon her discharge she was referred to a psychiatrist for assessment and follow-up treatment. The attitude of the family then changed to a more understanding and protective one.

### Case B

A 20-year-old single female with a medium education was a telephone operator. Her parents, who were at a middle socioeconomic level, were both living. The girl had for some time been in love with a man about 25 years old who worked as a clerk in a government ministry. They decided to get married, but she needed the consent and blessing of her parents. On the assumption that they had a much higher social standing than the young

TABLE 10-10
ATTEMPTED SUICIDES IN KUWAIT BY RATE PER 100,000
OF KUWAITI AND NON-KUWAITI POPULATION,
MALE AND FEMALE IN 1981

| Rate/100,000 | Kuwaiti | non-Kuwaiti |
|---|---|---|
| Total | 12.5 | 10.3 |
| Male | 9.0 | 4.2 |
| Female | 15.8 | 20.5 |

SOURCE: Department of Criminal Evidence and Forensic Medicine.

man's family, her parents denied her permission to marry. Despite efforts by mediators to resolve the differences, the girl's family remained adamant. Seeing no way out of her dilemma, the girl decided to commit suicide. To that end she took twenty-five tablets of amitriptyline, a tricyclic antidepressant which was available at home as her mother was using it therapeutically. The girl was rescued and later was seen by a psychiatrist who undertook therapy with all family members concerned. The girl, unable to secure her family's consent, did not marry her suitor.

## SUMMARY

It is noteworthy that a majority of those who committed or attempted suicide were Arabs. It might have been supposed that foreign workers would constitute a larger portion of the suicides since some of them came from countries where depressed conditions exist, and some of the Westerners were single or divorced men, who are supposed to be the most vulnerable to suicide. Non-Kuwaitis represent more than fifty nationalities. Although the nationalities of the cases surveyed were not always recorded in the forensic medicine files, non-Arabs were easily recognized by their names.

Little attention has been paid to suicide as a cause of death in Kuwait and therefore there are no suicide prevention activities. It is noteworthy that accidents—poisonings and acts of violence—were the third major cause of death, according to the annual statistical abstract for 1975, put out by the Central Statistical Office of Kuwait. The primary cause of death was infectious and parasitic diseases; the second, diseases of the circulatory system. It is possible that some of the recorded poisonings were suicidal acts, according to comments of patients in our clinical practice. This study will be of greater usefulness if it stimulates further inquiries into the suicide pattern in Kuwait.

# 11                                              IRAQ

*Editor's Note*

Iraq, considered an "iron curtain" country, is a socialist state in which the ruling political group is the army-dominated Ba'ath party. A recent purge of officers in the state indicates strong control by its leaders. Visitors to the country are closely screened, and most of those who are admitted are connected in some way with the oil industry. Oil is the major source of income for Iraq, although agricultural products, chiefly dates, are also exported. The industries are nationalized, but the degree of industrialization is not high. Unlike most of its Arab neighbors, Iraq has a good supply of arable land and water. The development of farming has been assisted by the government with new strains of seeds, cooperatives, and the like, but primitive methods are still used in some areas.

Iraq's neighbors are Iran, Kuwait, Saudi Arabia, Jordan, Turkey, and Syria, with which Iraq has frequent disagreements. The Kurds in northern Iraq have carried on stubborn fighting for years with the Iraqi government, demanding self-rule. The truces and agreements that are reached inevitably break down. Iraq has a diverse group of people from its long history of conquerors. There are non-Muslim minorities of 200,000 Christians—Catholic, Greek, Syrian, Eastern Orthodox, and Nestorian or Assyrian—and 5,000 Jews. These groups seem to be well amalgamated with the majority Arab population.

Iraq may be compared with Kuwait in the government's attempts to pull an impoverished nation, living in ancient traditional ways, into the mainstream of modern life. The efforts of only twenty to forty years, however, have not been enough to change old ways of thinking and behaving.

The strict government control of Iraqi life and institutions made it difficult to obtain material on suicide in that country and largely restricted the researcher to official reports. Government hospital physicians were reluctant to give information because of the military government and its unexpected arrests and executions. Communications are difficult and the country seems always in a state of crisis. Since nothing is known about Iraqi suicides, this chapter is at least a beginning.

Mrs. Al-Kassir was among the first women in Iraq to obtain a higher education and to work with men in a professional capacity. Previously, women who attained degrees were permitted to teach only in women's colleges. She obtained her LL.B. degree from Baghdad University in 1948 and was appointed director of the Law Library, the first woman to hold office in the law school. Subsequently she won a bachelor of arts degree in political science at the University of California, Berkeley. She had to repeat her undergraduate work because her Baghdad University work could not be credited in the United States at that time. When she returned to Baghdad the government of Iraq would not permit her to teach in the university unless she had a degree in education; she therefore returned to the University of California and earned a second bachelor's degree in educational psychology. After some time she decided that her main interest was in sociology, particularly in the role of the family in developing countries. Her third degree from the University of California, a master of arts in sociology, was granted in 1956. Mrs. Al-Kassir has been teaching family and social institutions in the Sociology Department of Baghdad University since that time.

She became interested in the subject of suicide because it has a bearing on the developing role of the woman and the family in the changing Middle East. Iraq has a more liberal attitude toward women than many surrounding Arab countries. Considerable government funds are available for the training of women and for their inclusion in the country's development. Consequently, many more women are working at jobs in Iraq than in other Arab countries.

# MALIHA AWNI AL-KASSIR

Iraq is one of the most ancient countries in the world. Its civilization began as early as 4000 B.C. with the Chaldean culture of Ur. Succeeding empires held sway until the thirteenth century A.D., when Iraq became part of the Islamic empire. It reached its peak in the Rashiden, Umayyad, and Abbasid cultures. The demise of these empires came with the invasions of the Tatars, who devastated many of the cities and captured the country's riches. Between 1512 and 1917 Iraq, under the control of the Ottoman Empire, made no headway in social, political, economic, or educational development.

In the late nineteenth century Iraq slowly came into contact with the outside world because of its strategic importance as a connecting point between East and West and the discovery of its oil deposits. Britain and Germany were the countries most interested in Iraq, and after World War I it came under the rule of Britain. In the revolutions of 1920 Iraq emerged as a state under the mandate of Britain. In 1921 King Feisal I acceded to the throne, and in 1927 Iraq became an independent kingdom. In 1958, through the revolution of July 14, the kingdom became the Republic of Iraq.

## SOCIAL STRUCTURE

The rate of population growth in Iraq is fairly low (table 11-1), and the population is more urban than rural (table 11-2). By 1975, in contrast with 1965, a much larger proportion of the population had become urban; it was

TABLE 11-1
POPULATION OF IRAQ, 1965, 1970, AND 1975

| Year | Male | Population Female | Total |
|------|------|-------------------|-------|
| 1965 | 4,132,162 | 3.769,663 | 8,097,825 |
| 1970 | 4,785,250 | 4,713,112 | 9,498,362 |
| 1975 | 5,603,000 | 5,521,000 | 11,124,000 |

SOURCE: Ministry of Planning, Baghdad.

estimated that the urban population would more than double in the period 1965–1982.

Of the population, 83 percent Arab and 17 percent Kurdish, 95 percent are Muslims, 4 percent are Christians, 1 percent adhere to other religions.

Rural Population

*The nomads.*—Arab and Kurdish tribes usually occupy land that has no agricultural value. They are found on the mountain slopes and in the hilly areas in the north, and in the rising steppe land to the northwest of Saudi Arabia. Their life is simple and very hard; their occupation of raising livestock is vital to the economy of the country. Kinship and family ties remain strong and group and collective attitudes are predominant. According to the 1947 census they numbered 250,000, or 5.2 percent of the population.

*Settled and semisettled tribes.*—These people live mainly in the middle Euphrates area and along the banks of the Tigris and Euphrates rivers. In 1947 they numbered 2,941,938, or 60.1 percent of the population. In 1975 it was estimated that their number had increased to 4,094,000. The tendency toward settlement is very strong among these tribes, and they pass through a variety of intermediate stages of social and economic life, from pure nomadism to settlement as cultivators. At any time every stage of tribal development can be observed.

The rural population in general consists of the Marsh tribes in the south; the Bedouin tribes, nomadic herders of camels, sheep, and horses; cultivator tribes near the rivers; the semisettled and seminomadic tribes; and the settled tribes and villages. The way of life of all these groups depends upon the climate. Few of the peasants have not gained by transition from the desert to the small towns. Communal living, until recently, has been almost the same as it was a thousand years ago, and collective interest supersedes the welfare of the individual. The administration of justice along lines of tribal customs is gradually being restricted, and government regulation is increasing.

TABLE 11-2
URBAN-RURAL DISTRIBUTION OF POPULATION
IN IRAQ, 1965, 1975, AND 1982

| Year | Population | |
| | Urban | Rural |
| --- | --- | --- |
| 1965 | 4,162,106 | 3,935,124 |
| 1975 | 7,084,000 | 4,040,000 |
| 1982[a] | 9,120,000 | 4,094,000 |

SOURCE: Ministry of Planning, Baghdad.
[a]Figures for 1982 are estimates.

## Urban Population

There has been a large and rapid concentration of population in big cities, especially Baghdad. The migration into urban centers is owing in part to the poor living conditions suffered by the farmer, his meager income, and the insecurity of his title to the land. The instability of his position makes attractive the better living conditions in the cities, with good opportunities and pay, and the fascinating new way of life. The migration has led to the thinning down of the country's agricultural labor supply and to erosion of the vitality and wealth of rural areas.

Baghdad, according to 1974 statistics, had a population of 2,816,000 out of a total urban population of 6,736,000. Basra, with 652,000, was then second in size, and Mosul, with 527,000, was third. In two decades the urban-rural ratio changed dramatically. In 1956 city dwellers represented a little more than a fourth of the total population; in 1975 there were 7,084,000 urbanites and the rural population was 4,040,000.

In order to reach a balance between rural and industrial development, the Land Reform Law of 1958 was passed in an attempt to break down the tribal and feudal system, encourage small farm ownership, and stimulate the development of colonization schemes on new land with favorable conditions for small cultivators. The law did not succeed in reaching the anticipated goals. Recently the government tried to revitalize the Land Reform Law by instituting reforms on land tenure and labor conditions. The objectives included better living conditions, cooperative associations with technical facilities, and encouragement of reverse migration from towns to the country.

It is generally acknowledged that Iraq's gravest difficulty is finding a workable solution to the country's agricultural problem. It will be necessary to bring about changes in every aspect of rural life: reshaping social, kinship, and family ties; improving the standard of living and sanitation methods; creating facilities for better education; opening up economic and recreational opportunities; and strengthening the desire of the people for self-improvement in all facets of daily life.

## CULTURAL FACTORS

The patterns of Iraqi society have been influenced by the different civilizations that have flourished in Iraq, affecting its way of life and its institutions. Among those civilizations are the ancient Sumerian, Assyrian, Arkadian, and Babylonian. Today, however, the main influence on Iraqi society is Islam, which plays a major role in the life of the individual. Although Islam as a religion has lost none of its force, the question that arises now is whether it can preserve its omnipotent position as the arbiter of social life.

The emergence of Iraq as a state and the revolution that followed affected changes in the society. For example, there was a transition from allegiance to tribe and kinship group to an abstract loyalty to the nation. As a result, extended family ties and kinship relations were weakened. The small, stable primary groups of the family unit and kinsmen had been regarded by the majority of the people as the building blocks of the society, and the activities of the individual were closely tied to family obedience. Customs, tradition, and collective attitudes were the predominant values. But the way of life began to change when political and economic development and the discovery of oil increased physical mobility and industrial projects brought people from the country to the cities. Urbanization altered the character of social institutions, especially the family structure and the family's importance as the functional unit. It also created the problem of how to find the necessary security in the seminuclear, independent family of the modern city.

With greatly increased educational facilities, life-styles and values were modernized, becoming more complicated and more competitive. Individualistic versus collective values affected family relations and the development of individual personality. Religion can no longer completely dominate society, but it will not lose its authority as a strong controlling force.

The predominant feature of this transition is the steady development of new ideas in the realm of human relations. The individual began to believe that he could improve his social and economic position through his own ability rather than through the influence of his relationships with family and kinsmen. This kind of thinking contributed to the breakdown of rigid kinship and family traditional ties and influence. It also laid a heavy burden on the individual. Life became more demanding, with a resultant increase in social disorganization.

These cultural changes are taking place through the middle and upper strata of society, especially among the educated. Dissemination of knowledge, and imitation of the upper classes by the lower classes, have facilitated the process.

## FAMILY PATTERNS

Iraq has extremes of modern and traditional family patterns. The law gives a woman rights equal to those of a man in inheritance; owning and selling property in her own name; earning and spending her salary as she likes; free choice of her mate when age 18 or older; the right to equal education and university training; the right to divorce, alimony, and child custody and to live independently if she chooses. Polygamy exists but is severely restricted and the husband must obtain the consent of his first wife before taking a second wife. Women are graduating from medical schools in increasing numbers and entering scientific professions such as engineering and architecture; and there are now more female than male teachers. In 1972 women made up 12 percent of all government workers.

Enjoyment of these rights depends on the educational and economic status and geographical situation of the family. The traditional cohabiting extended family is characterized by male superiority, the husband putting his duty to paternal relatives before that to his wife; women are inferior in status and demeaned. In such families the woman has none of the above rights, not even a husband's open demonstration of affection toward his wife, for the traditional husband considers this a weakness. The husband may divorce the wife at will for trivial reasons. In the more rural and remote areas, girls and women are killed on mere suspicion of flirting or infidelity to save the father's or husband's "honor." There are seldom any murder charges filed because the girl's underage brother stabs her to death and he escapes penalty because he is a juvenile.

The modern nuclear family, found mostly in the cities and towns and among the educated, follows a more democratic, self-sufficient pattern, and personal free choice of life-style prevails. Kinship relations do not rule and spouse and children live in a more healthy psychological environment.

There are intermediate states of family organization between these two extremes, but the trend is toward nuclear families. A strong force for change in this direction is the government's endeavors to eliminate illiteracy, especially among women, through adult education, and to offer equal economic and educational opportunities to women and youth.

## ATTITUDES TOWARD SUICIDE

Altruistic suicides were known and respected in ancient Iraq and in early times in Arabia. The subject is mentioned in early writings and in the works of famous poets, such as abu-al-Atahiyah and Al-Muari. These poems consider suicide a virtue when committed for collective or national honor and welfare. To preserve national or group dignity, prestige, and honor, suicide not only became a virtue, respected and honored, but it was sometimes demanded. Aside from altruistic deaths, however, suicide is deemed worthy only of criticism, condemnation, and ostracism by society. This attitude may explain the rarity of reported suicides in Iraq, both in the past and at present.

### Religious Attitudes

Islam clearly and definitely prohibits suicide, considering it sinful and against God's will. The Koran states: "Do not kill yourself. God was merciful to you. Do not kill yourself, that God forbids." The prophet Muhammad held that those who kill themselves will go to Hell and remain there forever, receiving no mercy or forgiveness from God. Muslims therefore regard suicide as sinful, a view that may be influential in Iraq because religion is still considered a strong force controlling the behavior of the individual as well as of the group.

### Legal Attitudes

In Iraq, according to Article 22, paragraph 2, of the Baghdad Criminal Law of 1969, "A person who encourages or helps another person to commit suicide, and the latter succeeds and dies, is considered a criminal to be punished by imprisonment for not more than seven years with hard labor." For the attempter himself, there is no punishment. The legal explanation for such discrimination is that punishment is intended to make redress, and that attempted suicide is so severe and painful a punishment that further penalties serve no purpose. Iraq is becoming a socialist state, and in socialism, too, individual welfare is relative to the welfare of the group and of society.

## SOURCES OF DATA

In gathering material for this report, I consulted the Holy Books, especially the Koran; Iraqi criminal laws; reports of the Ministry of Social Affairs; the annual abstract of statistics put out by the Ministry of Planning; census reports; reports and files of the Institute of Forensic Medicine; Office of Crime Prevention reports; and reports of the Office for Criminal Investigation. Further data were obtained from interviews with a number of suicide attempters and their families, as well as with the families of those who succeeded in committing suicide.

It was very difficult to get data from official sources because they do not compile statistical data in general or suicide data in particular. The same questions about accuracy of the data obtain in Iraq as in every other country, but here they are probably more pertinent because of religious prohibitions.

The staff and the files of Alwia Emergency Hospital in Baghdad were consulted for data on attempted suicides in 1978.

## COMPLETED SUICIDES

In the period 1934–1975, the largest number of reported suicides was 35 in 1934; the second highest was 25 in 1948, and the third highest was 23, in 1953 and again in 1972 (table 11-3). From 1961 to 1975, suicides tended to cluster around 10 to 18 a year, even though the population had increased significantly. The data suggest that a fairly steady, if small, number of suicides are reported, or perhaps cannot be concealed, yearly.

TABLE 11-3
SUICIDES IN IRAQ, 1934–1975

| Year | Number of suicides | Year | Number of suicides |
|------|-------------------|------|-------------------|
| 1934 | 35 | 1955 | 10 |
| 1935 | 14 | 1956 | 10 |
| 1936 | 13 | 1957 | 12 |
| 1937 | 16 | 1958 | 9 |
| 1938 | 9 | 1959 | 11 |
| 1939 | 11 | 1960 | 13 |
| 1940 | 1 | 1961 | 10 |
| 1941 | 7 | 1962 | 4 |
| 1942 | 10 | 1963 | 9 |
| 1943 | 4 | 1964 | 5 |
| 1944 | 2 | 1965 | 13 |
| 1945 | 0 | 1966 | 2 |
| 1946 | 5 | 1967 | 1 |
| 1947 | 14 | 1968 | 16 |
| 1948 | 25 | 1969 | 18 |
| 1949 | 18 | 1970 | 13 |
| 1950 | 15 | 1971 | 11 |
| 1951 | 17 | 1972 | 23 |
| 1952 | 13 | 1973 | 14 |
| 1953 | 23 | 1974 | 9 |
| 1954 | 16 | 1975 | 12 |

SOURCES: Statistical reports of Ministry of Planning, Baghdad, 1960–1972; reports of Institute of Forensic Medicine, Baghdad, 1970–1975.

## Age

No data were available to correlate suicides directly with age group. Government sources say that the largest number of completed suicides are committed by persons below the age of 30 or above the age of 80.[1] No suicides below the age of 15 were reported. An investigation of the 1975 cases indicated that eight of the twelve completed suicides were committed by persons in the 18−30 age group; one suicide was 50 years old and three were in their 40s.

## Sex Ratio

There are no statistical breakdowns as to the sex of persons who committed suicide, though government reports state that females are much less likely to take their own lives than males. Of the fourteen cases of attempted suicide in 1974 and 1975 which I investigated, the percentage of females was small. In 1974 only two of nine attempters were females; they were in the 20−29 age group. In 1975 all the suicide attempts were made by males. It was extremely difficult to find cases of attempted suicide, as they are almost always reported as accidents. The low incidence of reported completed and attempted suicides by females may be owing to the social attitude that regards suicide as an act bringing shame to the family name and honor, particularly when committed by a female.

## Urban and Rural Incidence

All the reported suicides were committed in urban areas, especially Baghdad. In 1975 ten cases of suicide were registered in Baghdad, one in Mosul, and one in Basra. Files of the Institute of Forensic Medicine in Baghdad indicated that not a single completed suicide had been reported from rural areas since 1934.

Any suicide or attempted suicide that occurs in the countryside is listed as an accident. Social condemnation is stronger in rural areas and families are not willing to be identified as having a member who committed or attempted suicide. An additional reason for the difference from cities may be that life in rural areas is more simple and is not as subject to the strains of modern versus traditional views and standards. Family ties have probably remained intact, and individuals have a strong sense of belonging; they can count on the family to help them cope with life's problems.

## Educational Level

Accurate statistics permitting the determination of the educational level of suicides are not available for past years. In 1975, of the twelve persons

[1]Reports of the Institute of Forensic Medicine, 1936−1975.

who committed suicide, two had higher education, eight had primary or secondary education, and two were illiterate.

Methods

The most frequently used methods of suicide in the period 1934–1975 are shown in table 11-4. The Ministry of Planning has no data giving male and female statistics for each of these methods, but it does report that males most commonly shot themselves and that females seldom used this method. In 1975 nine men of the total of twelve suicides used guns to kill themselves. According to reports, only one woman shot herself to death in 1972. Usually a suicidal person shoots himself in the head, but sometimes through the heart.

Most self-stabbings were in the neck and the second-highest number were in the heart area; very few slashed the arteries in their arms. Men and women are reported to use this method equally.

Self-burning is used by both sexes but primarily by women.

Hanging is employed by both sexes and by all ages.

Poisoning is used more by women than by men. One method is the inhalation of carbon monoxide. Common poisons used are rubbing alcohol, iodine, Firiol, sleeping pills, and tranquilizers.

Drowning is used primarily by men as a suicide method.

Electrocution by household current occurs, but it is rare.

In summary, the methods most frequently used for suicide were gunshot (40 percent), poison (14 percent), and self-burning (14 percent). Together these three methods accounted for 68 percent of suicides. Self-stabbing and

TABLE 11-4
METHODS USED TO COMMIT SUICIDE
IN IRAQ, 1934–1975

| Method | Number |
|--------|--------|
| Gunshot | 198 |
| Poison | 70 |
| Self-burning | 69 |
| Self-stabbing | 49 |
| Hanging | 49 |
| Drowning | 37 |
| Self-strangulation | 10 |
| Gas inhalation | 8 |
| Electrocution | 5 |
| Total | 495 |

SOURCE: Ministry of Planning, Baghdad.

hanging accounted for 9.8 percent each, or together for 19.6 percent, which, added to the 68 percent for the first three methods, makes a total of 87.6 percent. These five methods, therefore, were used by a large majority of suicides: gunshot, poison, self-burning, self-stabbing, and hanging.

Males most frequently killed themselves by gunshot and by drowning. Women were more apt to use the methods of poisoning and self-burning. Self-stabbing and hanging seem to have been used equally by the two sexes.

### Causes

No statistical breakdown of the precipitating causes of suicide is available, but records of the Institute of Forensic Medicine (1934—1975) detail the following cases, which may indicate causes.

A 35-year-old man killed himself because of a failed love affair. He loved an 18-year-old man in a homosexual relationship, spending all his money to support the young man in comfort. Subsequently he began to suspect infidelity. The young man was in fact not faithful, and he refused to respond to the older man's pleas. The older man killed himself, saying he had lost faith in human beings.

A young girl of 19 fell in love with a young man who promised marriage but who then lost interest after an intimate relationship had been established. She begged him to save her name and honor. When he would not listen to her pleas, she killed herself by drinking iodine, in order to escape condemnation and disgrace.

In 1974 a student in his final year of medical school in Baghdad drowned himself in the Tigris River after failing in two previous suicide attempts. His teachers and friends said that although he was very brilliant he was also emotionally unstable and very moody. His family had insisted that he study medicine despite the fact that he had no interest whatsoever in that field. Throughout the two years he spent in medical school he felt miserable. He believed that only death would bring him release and peace of mind, as well as make his family happier.

A well-known wealthy businessman killed himself after becoming bankrupt. In a letter to his family he said that the situation left him no choice but to escape the unbearable. He had to save his honor and his name.

A young wife killed herself after her husband died suddenly of a heart attack. She had no children. In her suicide note she said she had lost all connection with life. Her husband had been her whole life, and she wanted to join him in the otherworld.

These cases reveal interpersonal reasons for suicide which are found in every culture. They might be considered cases of excessive individuation. Those who committed suicide had put their personality, feelings, and values above all other considerations. Social control was temporarily lost; the individual was in a state of mind in which no alternatives or adjustments seemed possible.

## ATTEMPTED SUICIDES

It is extremely difficult to obtain data on attempted suicides. All Iraqi hospitals are government institutions, which means that the researcher is referred to the files of the Institute of Forensic Medicine for official records. The medical staff and the files of Alwia Hospital in Baghdad did, however, supply information on its cases of burns, cuts, wounds, and poisoning in 1978. Of the 1,209 cases in that year, 582 were burn cases and, according to the staff, 116 of those, or 20 percent, were attempted suicides.[2] The determination of attempted suicide was made on the basis of statements from patients. A typical remark would be: "If I had known that burning would be so painful, I would not have done it to myself." Most people apparently believe that burning themselves is an infallible way of committing suicide. Most of the attempters were females over the age of twenty. The reasons for attempting suicide were marital or family frictions.

For 1978 the official files of the Institute of Forensic Medicine in Baghdad showed seventeen completed suicides between the ages of 16 and 30 and two over 40. A third of the suicides were female.

It is evident from this report that numerous suicide cases are concealed, for the discrepancy between 19 and 116 cases is considerable. As there are many cases of food poisoning in Iraq, suicides by taking insecticides or other pills and poisons could readily be concealed as accidents or fatal illnesses. The conditions that presently prevail in Iraq make it unlikely that more accurate data will be obtainable.

## SUMMARY

Accurate statistics on suicide in Iraq are not obtainable at this time. Official reports for the forty-two-year period 1934–1975 show completed suicides ranging from 0 to 35, with the usual number being 10 to 18. No pattern is distinguishable from these reports. A 1978 report on attempted suicides in one hospital in Baghdad shows 116 attempts by self-burning, mostly by females.

Completed suicides tend to be male, between the ages of 15 and 30, with very few cases among older persons. The chief methods were gunshot, poison, and self-burning. Stabbing, hanging, and drowning came next, in descending order. Women tended to use poisoning and self-burning, whereas men used gunshot wounds and drowning. The causes of suicidal attempts were not delineated in official reports, but case records indicate that the most frequent were disappointments in love and family problems. Most suicides had some education, usually primary and secondary.

[2]Based on this figure and the estimate of 3 million as Baghdad's population, the attempted suicide rate for burn cases alone was 3.83 per 100,000 in Baghdad in 1978.

# 12       SYRIA

*Editor's Note*

Syria is a socialist state which has been independent since 1946. The dominant political force is the Ba'ath party. Numerous changes in government have taken place since World War II in attempts to balance Pan-Arabic and national feelings. The socialist movement has grown in strength since the period 1958–1961, when Syria withdrew from the Egypt-Syria United Arab Republic. A continuous struggle goes on between moderate and leftist factions and the military.

Syria has been militarily active in Jordan in support of the Palestinians and has served as a peacekeeping force in the Lebanese civil war. Within its borders the demand of the Kurds for self-rule is a continuing problem. As a result Syria seems always to be mobilized for war, a situation clearly evident to the visitor. These considerations make compulsory military service necessary and affect economic policies. A goodly number of Palestinians and Lebanese are refugees in Syria.

The government is attempting to industrialize the country and to improve agriculture. The project to dam the Euphrates, for example, should greatly improve Syria's productivity. Large sums have been loaned to Syria by the Soviet bloc and by other Arab states to further these objectives. Although education is free, it was estimated in 1976 that 50 percent of the population was illiterate. Medical care is improving, but in 1975 life expectancy was only 58 years for females and 54 for males. Urban Syrians, particularly trained and professional personnel, present a sharp contrast to rural and traditional agricultural and nomadic groups.

It seemed unlikely in my several trips to Syria that I would be able to find anyone interested in the subject of suicide. All the individuals I consulted at government and university levels assured me that suicides did not occur in Syria. Then I found, fortunately, that a psychologist, Khaldoun Al-Hakim, had been gathering information on the subject for some six years and had submitted his material to the Sorbonne for his Ph.D. degree in social psychology. Before receiving his Sorbonne degree he had been an assistant professor at Damascus University with degrees in education and psychology. He had also served as a director and program manager for Syrian television.

Dr. Al-Hakim's interest in suicide was stimulated when he read several books on the subject. Upon inquiring into Syria's suicide statistics and reports from other Islamic countries, he found that no research had been done on this vitally important issue. His study of suicide in Syria was not met with enthusiasm. Many people felt that he should not be "digging out old skeletons long since buried" and that his research was improper because suicide was a shame and a sin. Checking police records to find cases of suicide was an arduous task, particularly because Dr. Al-Hakim had no assistance and modern technical aids were lacking. It is a tribute to his persistence that he was able to obtain the material included in this chapter.

This chapter contains the only material ever collected on suicide in Syria, as far as I can determine. There is no bibliography because, seemingly, no writing has been done on the subject. Dr. Al-Hakim remains in France, continuing to do research at the Sorbonne.

This chapter was translated and condensed from the French language, by the editor of this volume.

# KHALDOUN AL-HAKIM

Syria, a transportation link between Jordan and Lebanon, has its own ports on the Mediterranean. Its neighboring countries are Turkey, Iraq, Jordan, Israel, and Lebanon.

Many ancient civilizations have flourished in this land, which is particularly fertile around the Euphrates. The country is a vast plateau with 7 million inhabitants; the most prosperous and populous areas are the coastal plains and the valleys. The chief products are barley, cotton, fruit, wool, sugar beets, textiles, cement, leather, and asphalt. Oil has been discovered in the northeast, and Syria also derives an income from fees for the Iraqi pipelines that carry oil across the country to shipping ports. Farming is primitive, and sharp contrasts exist between urban areas and the traditional rural areas. Syria is 53 percent rural and 47 percent urban.

## CULTURE

Many ancient customs continue to this day in Syria. The extended family prevails, and lineage remains important. A strong sense of pride and clan cohesion animates the Syrians, especially the various tribes. Each tribe considers itself the most noble and the most important. Each knows its family tree very well and seeks to preserve the purity of the line. A tribal specialist knows by heart all the descendants of the tribe and can place them in the proper order. Family lines are important to the pride of the group, but also because they impose certain rights and responsibilities on family members. Each member must know his predecessors in the line and must know its branches for proper social interaction. Even in the cities one may ask a new acquaintance about his ancestral line; confidence or the lack of it shown in the reply reflects the relative importance and the reputation of the family line.

Poets and orators of a tribe enumerate and glorify clan exploits, accomplishments, and good deeds. Such orations, which take place at tribal gatherings, are educational; they repeat tribal legends in order to create a spirit of common purpose and dignity. Although this practice does stimulate the pride of consanguinity, it also creates divisions between tribes.

Tribes are classified according to their lineage, social position, and power, in descending importance. Two illustrations may clarify the importance of tribal feeling. The son of a sheikh of an important tribe told how his father, after hearing of a poet who wrote a poem about the exploits of his tribe, spent several months searching the desert for the poet so he could ask him for the poem. In another instance a septuagenarian in Damascus had refused to marry for years unless he could find a woman who had seven recognized famous ancestors or who were part of his own family tree. As he had been unsuccessful, in old age he reduced the number of such ancestors to six.

The tribal background is important in the cultural life of Syria. Males are the dominant persons in the family. Marriages are arranged according to family lineage and family status. The father makes the decision after the mother has searched through a suitable group of prospects. She considers such matters as beauty, age, family, personality, and character. If the young person is a girl she has little to say about the choice. In general, the groom, who has to finance the heavy costs of marriage, is eight or more years older than the bride. Men sometimes wait until they are 35 or 40 years old before marrying. Those who live in urban areas also delay marriage because of the high cost of city living. Men often emigrate to Kuwait, Libya, or Algeria, where they can live more economically and can earn enough to return home and get married. Another obstacle to early marriage is the required military service of thirty months. A wide discrepancy therefore may exist between a late adolescent girl's maturity and that of an older man. Even a university man, however, may marry a high school graduate so as to keep control and have the last word. Because Arab men try to maintain their superiority over their wives, family relationships are often discordant and conjugal disputes are frequent.

Marriage for a girl takes place after menstruation begins, the age varying from 15 to 20. Consummation of the marriage is usually proved by blood on a handkerchief, showing rupture of the hymen. If the marriage is not consummated the wife may demand return of the dowry. She has no other role in life than that of wife and mother under the strict control of her husband. As her husband may divorce her for infertility, for lack of sons, or for other reasons, a woman's financial and social security is not guaranteed. If her husband divorces her or dies, the second and smaller part of the dowry is supposed to revert to her for her support, and she may be taken back into her family. If she is divorced, her children are taken from her between the ages of 3 and 9 to live with their father. It is extremely difficult for a woman to remarry. She has few rights, and her word as a witness is legally half as valuable as that of a man. She is expected to be submissive and obedient and to keep to her household duties. In general, her life is demeaning; there are even many common sayings that disparage females. Girls inherit less than their brothers do.

The primary virtues in Syria are virginity for women and honor for men. The emphasis on virginity reflects tribal inheritance systems and the need to keep the blood line pure. In the country provinces, unmarried loss of virginity is regarded by the family as a collective dishonor, but only the woman is punished. Traditionally her brother or her uncle stabs her to death, but the law is not strict in such matters. Even if a woman alleges rape, it may not be taken into account. The prophet Muhammad spoke of the husband's responsibility to take care of his wife, thus inferentially establishing a relationship in which the male is the independent partner and the female is the dependent one. The woman generally defers to her husband in decisions concerning the family. In this rigid system, where women's views and feelings are subjugated to those of males and elders, the result seems to be internalized aggression. Some tension may be expressed by hysterical behavior and somatic disorders, but it evidently finds an outlet in suicidal acts as well.

## RELIGION

Syria is almost totally Muslim. This aspect of the society is discussed later in the section on religion and suicide.

## LEGAL ATTITUDE TOWARD SUICIDE

In Syria, as in all Muslim countries, the religion forbids suicide, but suicides or suicide attempts are not punishable under Syrian law. Those who incite and aid such an action, however, may be punished by ten years in prison if the person dies; if the suicide attempt fails, anyone who has assisted may serve three months to two years in prison, depending upon the extent of damage.

## METHODS OF DATA COLLECTION

To find suicide cases for this study it was necessary to consult police and medical reports filed with the justice department in each province, as there is no central reporting of suicide cases in Syria. In the provincial records cases are filed as "noncriminal," a category including a wide variety of cases. Lacking assistance for this project, and having no time to go through all the provincial files, I decided to search the records in selected provinces for a two- to four-month period and base my conclusions on the data thus gathered. I encountered a practical difficulty in the shortage of electricity caused by the 1973 Arab-Israeli war, which meant that I had to look through masses of dusty files by candlelight. The period under investigation was 1969 through 1972. My basic sample of 475 suicides and attempted suicides was sometimes cut to 340 by eliminating cases on which I had insufficient information.

I selected eight of the thirteen provinces in Syria. They are the most representative of the society and the most populous; they have 75.9 percent of Syria's total population. Damascus and Aleppo are the most heavily populated of the provinces and have many urban residents. Homs, the next largest province, was not chosen because it is very like Damascus. Latakia, a coastal and semirural province, was selected, as was Der'a, a poor province near the Syrian-Israeli border. Idlib in the north was chosen because it represents a rural and very religious area, with many Kurdish tribesmen. Although Deir Ez Zor is similar to Idlib, I added it to my list because I had personal contacts with the Bedouins who are the original inhabitants. Ar Raqqah was included because it is the site of a dam being built on the Euphrates; its population is therefore a mixture of rural Bedouins and newcomers—engineers, technicians, and their families. Haseke in the northeast, my final choice, is populated by semisettled Bedouins and Assyrian Christians; it is the chief producer of cereal grains and cotton in Syria.

Cases found were listed as attempted or completed suicides by age, sex, marital status, living conditions, methods used, nationality, religion, and so on. An estimate of the annual number of suicides in each province was computed on the basis of the number of cases found in a certain number of days. For example, in Damascus 43 cases were found in 62 days, so that one might expect to find 253 cases in 365 days, which yields an annual rate of 4.79 per 100,000 population. Table 12-1 shows the annual rate of suicidal

TABLE 12-1

ESTIMATED ANNUAL RATE PER 100,000 POPULATION OF SUICIDES AND ATTEMPTED
SUICIDES IN EIGHT PROVINCES OF SYRIA, 1969–1972

| Year | Rate |
| --- | --- |
| 1969 | 4.87 |
| 1970 | 3.70 |
| 1971 | 7.20 |
| 1972 | 3.84 |

SOURCE: Justice departments in eight provinces of Syria.

TABLE 12-2

NUMBER OF AND RATE PER 100,000 POPULATION OF
SUICIDES AND ATTEMPTED SUICIDES IN SAMPLE OF 475 CASES IN EIGHT
PROVINCES OF SYRIA, BY SEX, 1969–1972

| Province | Number of attempts | | Number of suicides | | Total | Rate |
|---|---|---|---|---|---|---|
| | Male | Female | Male | Female | | |
| Damascus | 67 | 109 | 26 | 20 | 222 | 4.79 |
| Aleppo | 27 | 46 | 9 | 12 | 94 | 3.44 |
| Latakia | 2 | 14 | 7 | 6 | 29 | 2.80 |
| Der'a | 9 | 17 | 9 | 12 | 47 | 2.25 |
| Idlib | 5 | 5 | 7 | 5 | 22 | 2.15 |
| Deir Ez Zor | 6 | 6 | 7 | 3 | 22 | 2.40 |
| Ar Raqqah | 4 | 1 | 3 | 3 | 11 | 1.63 |
| Haseke | 5 | 7 | 6 | 10 | 28 | 1.67 |
| Total | 125 | 205 | 74 | 71 | 475 | |

SOURCE: Justice departments in eight provinces of Syria.

acts in each of the four years, calculated on this basis. In the basic sample of 475 cases there were more attempts than completed suicides. Although this fact reflects the usual preponderance of attempts over completed acts, it should not be taken too seriously in Syria, where completed suicides are concealed by families whenever possible so as to avoid dishonor and social criticism. It is true, of course, that attempted suicides are also concealed, but more strenuous efforts are made, with the help of sympathetic doctors or friends, to camouflage completed suicides. In any event, suicidal acts are undoubtedly underreported.

More suicidal acts were reported in large urban centers like Damascus than in rural provinces. The difference is attributable not only to the concentration of population in the cities, but also to the lesser degree of concealment in areas where religious and traditional forces are weaker.

## SUICIDE BY SEX

In three of the eight provinces chosen, men committed fewer suicides than women (table 12-2). In two of the provinces that had more male than female suicides and attempted suicides, prisons are located. Although women are generally more likely to attempt suicide than men, particularly in Western countries, I found that in Syria females outnumbered males in attempts by only 61 percent. The ratio is 1 male to 1.62 women in five of the provinces. When the figures are compiled on an annual rather than a provincial basis (table 12-3), male and female suicides were fairly close in number, whereas in every one of the four years females outnumbered males in suicide

TABLE 12-3
SUICIDES AND SUICIDE ATTEMPTS IN SAMPLE
OF 475 CASES IN EIGHT PROVINCES OF SYRIA, BY SEX, 1969–1972

| Year | Attempts | | Suicides | | |
| | Male | Female | Male | Female | Total |
|------|------|--------|------|--------|-------|
| 1969 | 29 | 46 | 15 | 18 | 108 |
| 1970 | 26 | 34 | 17 | 18 | 95 |
| 1971 | 35 | 54 | 21 | 17 | 127 |
| 1972 | 35 | 71 | 21 | 18 | 145 |
| Total | 125 | 205 | 74 | 71 | 475 |

SOURCE: Justice departments in eight provinces of Syria.

attempts. A possible explanation of the high female incidence in attempts is the restrictive atmosphere created by the sociocultural attitude toward women, who have fewer alternatives within the society than men.

## AGE DISTRIBUTION

By far the largest number of suicidal acts in the smaller sample of 340 cases occurred before the age of 25, with 53.35 percent in the age group 15–24 and 8.46 percent in the 8–14 group (table 12-4), or a total of 61.8 percent. From age 25 on the number decreased rapidly. If the data are broken down by sex (table 12-5), it is clear that more females (66 percent) than males (34 percent) attempted suicide and that in completed suicides the sexes were almost equal. For all age groups, the sample of attempted and completed suicides was 39.7 percent male and 60.3 percent female.

TABLE 12-4
AGE DISTRIBUTION OF SUICIDES AND ATTEMPTED SUICIDES IN SAMPLE OF 340
CASES IN EIGHT PROVINCES OF SYRIA,
1969–1972

| Age group | Suicides | |
| | Number[a] | Percentage |
|-----------|----------|------------|
| 8–14 | 29 | 8.46 |
| 15–24 | 183 | 53.35 |
| 25–39 | 80 | 23.32 |
| 40–59 | 33 | 9.62 |
| 60–89 | 18 | 5.25 |

SOURCE: Justice departments in eight provinces of Syria.
[a]The total number here is 343 because there were three double suicides.

The largest number of females who attempted suicide were in the 15−24 age group, with a substantial number in the 8−14 group (table 12-5). The 15−24 group represents the period of engagement and marriage, when disagreements with family about the choice of a husband are likely to be at a maximum. It is also the period of adjustment following marriage. The highest number of male attempts was also in the 15−24 group, presumably because they are in the process of adjusting to work and marriage. The small number of attempts by persons aged 40 and over seems to reflect the security of the established older person. The highest peak for completed suicides was also in the 15−24 age group—34 females and 22 males. It is noteworthy that males far exceeded females among persons aged 60 and over. (See table 12-5.)

## RELIGION AND SUICIDE

The strength of religious groups in Syria as percentages of the total population is shown in table 12-6. It is noteworthy that the Sunnites, with 76 percent of the population, were responsible, according to the files of the justice departments in the eight Syrian provinces selected for this survey, for 90 percent of the suicidal acts committed in those provinces in 1969−1972. The Christians, altogether composing 7.30 percent of the population, committed only 5.29 percent of the suicidal acts in the same years. One reason for the disparity may be that most Sunnites live in large cities where suicide rates are higher. Another is that Christians in Syria show marked social cohesion. Since they constitute a peaceable and well-ordered group, they do not attract negative attention. They share with their Muslim neighbors many of the same values, such as the preservation by females of

TABLE 12-5

SUICIDES AND ATTEMPTED SUICIDES IN SAMPLE OF 340 CASES
IN EIGHT PROVINCES OF SYRIA, BY AGE AND SEX, 1969−1972

| | Attempts | | | | Suicides | | | |
| | Male | | Female | | Male | | Female | |
| Age group | Number | Per-centage | Number | Per-centage | Number | Per-centage | Number | Per-centage |
|---|---|---|---|---|---|---|---|---|
| 8−14 | 5 | 22.7 | 17 | 77.3 | 4 | 57.0 | 3 | 43.0 |
| 15−24 | 46 | 35.7 | 81 | 64.3 | 22 | 39.2 | 34 | 60.7 |
| 25−39 | 16 | 34.0 | 31 | 66.0 | 18 | 54.5 | 15 | 45.5 |
| 40−59 | 6 | 35.2 | 11 | 64.8 | 8 | 50.0 | 8 | 50.0 |
| 60 and over | 1 | 20.0 | 4 | 80.0 | 10 | 77.0 | 3 | 23.0 |

SOURCE: Justice departments in eight provinces of Syria.
NOTE: The total number here is 343 because there were three double suicides.

TABLE 12-6
STRENGTH OF RELIGIOUS GROUPS IN SYRIA

| Religious group | | Percentage of population |
|---|---|---|
| Muslims | | 92.7 |
| Sunnites | 76.0 | |
| Alaouites | 12.0 | |
| Druzes | 3.3 | |
| Ismailis | 0.9 | |
| Shiites | 0.5 | |
| Christians | | 7.30 |
| Orthodox | 6.22 | |
| Catholics | 0.95 | |
| Protestants | 0.13 | |

SOURCE: Syrian Arab Republic, Population Census, 1970, I:14.

their virginity. A more detailed picture of the incidence of suicide, both attempted and completed, among religious groups in Syria is shown in Table 12-7.

## METHODS

Writers on suicide hold widely varying views on the significance of the methods used. Those of the psychoanalytic school feel that the choice of means for the suicidal act shows trends and symbolism related to unconscious factors. Nonpsychoanalytic researchers are inclined to the opinion that the availability of a suicidal means is the most important factor, although there may also be significance in the person's life-style. Here I am concerned with availability of means, the general use of such means, and the significance of the choice of means.

Poisons were used in a third of the cases in the 1969–1972 sample and pills and medicines, in another third. As previously noted, suicide attempts were more frequent in more highly urbanized settings, and the figures indicate that use of pills, medications, and poisons also increases in such locales. In Damascus, pills were used in 40.8 percent of the cases, yet in the city of Aleppo, insecticides and farm poisons represented 62 percent of all the methods used. In Aleppo, whose population is homogeneous and closely knit, imitation is also a factor.

Suicides by fire were most numerous in Deir Ez Zor, accounting for 35 percent of all cases in that province; burning was also the method used most frequently in the past. In the city itself this method is currently used, especially by young girls whose families oblige them to marry men whom they do not like.

TABLE 12-7
SUICIDES AND ATTEMPTED SUICIDES IN SAMPLE OF
340 CASES IN EIGHT PROVINCES OF SYRIA,
BY RELIGIOUS GROUP AND SEX, 1969–1972

| Religious group | Attempts | | | Suicides | | |
|---|---|---|---|---|---|---|
| | Male | Female | Total | Male | Female | Total |
| Sunnites | 67 | 130 | 197 | 54 | 55 | 109 |
| Shiites | 0 | 1 | 1 | 1 | 0 | 1 |
| Alaouites | 1 | 3 | 4 | 3 | 3 | 6 |
| Ismailis | 1 | 0 | 1 | 0 | 0 | 0 |
| Druzes | 0 | 0 | 0 | 2 | 1 | 3 |
| Total | 69 | 134 | 203 | 60 | 59 | 119 |
| Christians | 4 | 8 | 12 | 2 | 4 | 6 |
| Grand total | 73 | 142 | 215 | 62 | 63 | 125 |

SOURCE: Justice departments in eight provinces of Syria.

The geographical character of a region favors the selection of methods. For example, in desert areas there are no deaths by drowning. Jumping from high buildings, as in Aleppo, is not possible in the one-story buildings in the rural areas of Der'a, Deir Ez Zor, Ar Raqqah, and Haseke. Gas was not used in the cases I surveyed, possibly because its fatal effects were not understood.

Prisoners must perforce utilize the means at their disposal for suicidal acts. In general, they cut blood vessels, stomach, or neck with a piece of glass, razor blades "found" in the prison courtyard, or nails. They also collected tablets prescribed by the doctor until they had a lethal dose, or they burned themselves.

The choice of method is a reflection not only of the individual personality but also of how a certain act appears to society or fits in with the values of society. In some cases, for example, an accusation of thievery seemingly forced an individual to attempt suicide by cutting his veins, perhaps because the Islamic code decrees that the hand of the robber should be cut off. The slashing of wrists may symbolically wipe out the accusation. Similarly, cutting the throat has an Islamic significance. Since the neck is considered as the joining of reason (the head) and emotions (the body), to cut one's throat may mean to a Muslim that one offers strong proof of innocence.

Fire has a purification value in some cases, related to purification of natural elements by fire, and to the fires of Hell. For example, a 19-year-old single girl had a sociable, happy disposition, which her family criticized as too overt. She had had a romantic attachment to a medical student for two years and had become pregnant. When he deserted her she asked her family's help in persuading the man to marry her. The family, ignorant of the pregnancy, thought her too young. She then threw herself on the stove. Her family broke down the locked door to rescue her, but she died four days later in the hospital. Although her choice of means may have been for purification, as virginity is a prime value in Islamic women, it may also have expressed aggressiveness toward her former lover and her family as well.

Some psychiatrists have held that suicides of alcoholics are usually accomplished by drowning or hanging. Among the seven alcoholics whose cases were included in this study, four died of acute delirium, two by drowning, and one by poisoning. One may add that of four males who committed suicide, allegedly because of the real or fancied infidelity of their wives, three were found nude.

### Sexual Differences

Poisons and pills were used by 80.3 percent of the females and by 47.7 percent of the males surveyed. Harsh methods of suicide were used mainly by men, and firearms were used only by them. A possible reason for the female preference for pills and poisons may lie in Syrian values and customs. A beautiful appearance is particularly cherished by women, as it may lead to a good marriage. Marriage, the highest good for a woman, may depend solely upon physical attractiveness. Consequently, women are likely to choose suicidal methods that will not mutilate the body and may preserve femininity and beauty. An Islamic custom may reinforce this idea. It is customary for the corpse to be unclothed and washed in the family home, either in the kitchen or in the bathroom. All persons of consanguinity, such as brothers, sisters, children, parents, nieces, and nephews of the deceased, may be present and assist in this part of the mourning process. The appearance in death may be quite important to the woman as her final impression upon the family.

### Age Groups

Persons under 15 years of age accounted for 8.5 percent of the sample; those in the 15–24 bracket, for 53.8 percent. Of those under 15, 86 percent used pills or poisoning agents; 75.0 percent of the 15–24 group used these same methods.

Suicidal acts using more lethal means seem to increase with age; those who used firearms in our sample were usually older persons (table 12-8). A similar distribution is found with other seriously lethal methods, such as hanging and stabbing.

Suicide attempts are more numerous among the young in age than among older persons. Completed suicides seem to increase with age.

In summary, the choice of methods for suicidal acts may be dictated by availability and the style of suicides in a locality, by the impact of suicide

TABLE 12-8
USE OF FIREARMS TO COMMIT SUICIDE IN
EIGHT PROVINCES OF SYRIA, BY
AGE GROUP, 1969–1972

| Age group | Number |
|-----------|--------|
| Under 15 | 1 |
| 15–24 | 4 |
| 25–39 | 6 |
| 40–54 | 3 |
| 55 and over | 3 |

SOURCE: Justice departments in eight provinces of Syria.

upon persons at whom the hostility is directed, and by values and customs of the country.

## TIME OF SUICIDES

### Monthly Incidence

Of the 475 suicidal cases in the basic sample, the largest number 28, came in both May and July; January was second with 22 and September, with 21, was third (table 12-9). The rate then declined sharply through December. Certain factors may cause these monthly differences.

Secondary school examinations are held in May and university examinations, in June and July. The period May – July is also sees the heaviest influx of peasants to the city as they look for jobs. In late July and August temperatures are high and the excessive heat enervates people. So these factors may have a possible bearing on the higher rate in those months. Religious festival days seem to correlate with the periods of lower incidence: October–December and February. Observance of the holy month of Ramadan, which features daytime fasting and prayers, varies from year to year because it is determined by the lunar year. In the period 1969–1972, its beginning varied from November 9 to October 8. Ramadan could therefore end any time from November 5 to December 7. Al-Fitre is another religious holiday that takes place in November and December and Al-Adha, "the day of sacrifice," comes in February.

### Daily Incidence

The patterns of suicidal behavior seem to differ between urban and rural groups. Urban suicidal acts occurred in the following daily sequence, from most frequent to least frequent: Saturday, Tuesday, Monday, Thursday, Wednesday, Friday, Sunday. Friday, the Islamic holy day, corresponds to

TABLE 12-9
MONTHLY INCIDENCE OF COMPLETED SUICIDES IN
BASIC SAMPLE OF 475 CASES IN EIGHT
PROVINCES OF SYRIA, 1969—1972

| Month | Suicides | |
| --- | --- | --- |
| | Number | Percentage |
| January | 22 | 10.52 |
| February | 13 | 6.25 |
| March | 9 | 4.33 |
| April | 19 | 9.13 |
| May | 28 | 13.46 |
| June | 15 | 7.21 |
| July | 28 | 13.46 |
| August | 10 | 4.80 |
| September | 21 | 10.10 |
| October | 18 | 8.66 |
| November | 14 | 6.73 |
| December | 11 | 5.30 |

SOURCE: Justice departments in eight provinces of Syria.

the Christian Sunday; Saturday therefore corresponds to the Christian Monday. In rural areas the comparable order was as follows: Friday, Saturday, and Thursday, with equal incidence, followed by Wednesday, Monday, Sunday, Tuesday.

The most interesting aspect of the study is that almost 30 percent of the suicidal acts occurred on Saturday and Sunday (table 12-10). Saturday is the high point of the week for social activity, which diminishes on Sunday. A tentative explanation for the first ranking of Friday, the Sabbath or holy day, in rural areas is that on that day the whole family is gathered together and that therefore the greatest impact can be made by an appeal for help or, conversely, by a hostile gesture. The true Muslim also wants his death to take place on Friday, his sacred day. Because the rural Muslim is more religious and traditional than his urban counterpart he may tend to choose Friday for his suicidal act, even though suicide is forbidden by his religion. It may also be pointed out that on Friday the man is the central figure, the dominating person, in the household. His act, if perpetrated on that day, would therefore be more dramatic and have the greatest possible impact.

Hourly Incidence

In Western countries suicides generally take place in daytime. Before I present my findings on Syria, several comments on the Syrian view of time may be of interest.

TABLE 12-10
DAILY INCIDENCE OF SUICIDES AND ATTEMPTED
SUICIDES IN EIGHT PROVINCES OF
SYRIA, 1969—1972

| Day | Percentage of total | Percentage | |
| --- | --- | --- | --- |
| | | Male | Female |
| Saturday | 18.53 | 35 | 65 |
| Sunday | 10.60 | 42 | 58 |
| Monday | 14.12 | 42 | 58 |
| Tuesday | 12.64 | 40 | 60 |
| Wednesday | 13.82 | 45 | 55 |
| Thursday | 14.20 | 34 | 66 |
| Friday | 15.58 | 48 | 52 |

SOURCE: Justice departments in eight provinces of Syria.

The value of time is minimal in Syria in contrast with the manner of life of the Westerner. The daily rhythm of life for Islamic believers is attuned to the hours of prayer, which is required five times a day. These hours are set by a general relationship to the cycles of the sun and the moon. Morning prayer takes place before the sun rises; the second prayer comes at noon; the afternoon prayer is technically 220 minutes after the noon prayer; the fourth is the evening or sunset prayer; and the night prayer is approximately 90 minutes later. The religiously devout offer a midnight prayer to reassure themselves of the mercy of God and of his blessings for the future. Times of relaxation follow the evening prayer; widely observed customs are gossiping, singing, listening to music, and playing card games.

For the Eastern mind, passive, almost complete resignation to the will of God plays a large role in making the Syrian indifferent to time. In contrast, the Westerner is conscious of each moment of the day. Time in the Syrian mind is fluid and vague, with semifixed limits. The morning extends from 6 A.M. to 12 noon; the afternoon, from noon to 3 P.M.; the evening, from 3 P.M. to 7 P.M.; the night, from 7 P.M. to 2 A.M.; and the dawn, from 2 A.M. to 6 A.M. These divisions are used in table 12-11, which shows the hourly incidence of the suicidal acts covered in this survey. As the table shows, 49.1 percent of the suicidal acts took place between 6 A.M. and 3 P.M. and 46.5 percent, between 3 P.M. and 2 A.M. About 72 percent occurred in the most socially active hours of morning, afternoon, and evening. This finding agrees with Emile Durkheim's opinion that the suicides favor the time when social interaction is at a maximum. According to the sample used for this survey, hostile and retaliatory suicide acts took place at night, when the setting was primarily familial.

TABLE 12-11
TIME OF DAY OF SUICIDAL ACTS IN 340 CASES
IN EIGHT PROVINCES OF SYRIA, 1969—1972

| Time of day | Number | Percentage |
|---|---|---|
| Morning | 101 | 29.7 |
| Afternoon | 66 | 19.4 |
| Evening | 78 | 23.0 |
| Night | 80 | 23.5 |
| Dawn | 15 | 4.4 |
| Total | 340 | 100.0 |

SOURCE: Justice departments in eight provinces of Syria.

Male suicidal acts were most frequent from 7 P.M. to 6 A.M., whereas females preferred the hours between 6 A.M. and 7 P.M. for suicidal acts. In fact, female suicidal acts in the daytime were twice those of males. Completed male suicides were more numerous during nighttime hours, suggesting either that males thus express their depression or their hostility toward family members or that, on the contrary, there is less chance of intercession at night.

Attempted suicides, both male and female, were most frequent during the afternoon and night, corresponding to lunch and dinner hours when the whole family would have gathered together. Young people—53.35 percent of the 15—24 age group—chose these time periods in which to reveal their despair.

Completed suicides by highly lethal means took place between 2 A.M and 6 A.M. In my sample there were four shootings, two jumpings, two drownings, three poisonings, one hanging, one stabbing, and two medication ingestions in these dawn hours. Medical and psychiatric opinions on these 15 cases held that the individuals showed depression, dementia, mental confusion, and psychosis. The data indicate that nine of these suicides had been contemplated and planned for some time. The choice of dawn hours would probably ensure the absence of interference by family members.

## NATIONALITY AND SUICIDE

Table 12-12 shows the size of the nationalities living in Syria in 1970, the percentage of each nationality to the total population, the number of each nationality living in the selected provinces, and the percentage of the latter to the total population of that nationality. For example, the 155,725 Palestinians living in Syria constituted 2.47 percent of Syria's total population; the 144,351 Palestinians living in the selected provinces constituted

TABLE 12-12
NATIONALITIES LIVING IN SYRIA, 1970

| Nationality | Total population Number | Total population Percentage | Population in selected provinces Number | Population in selected provinces Percentage |
|---|---|---|---|---|
| Syrians | 6,074,389 | 96.68 | 4,596,685 | 75.42 |
| Palestinians | 155,725 | 2.47 | 144,351 | 92.70 |
| Arabs[a] | 44,369 | 0.70 | 35,101 | 79.10 |
| Foreigners | 8,652 | 0.13 | 8,006 | 92.50 |

SOURCE: Syrian Arab Republic, Population Census, 1970, I:14–15.
[a]This category includes Egyptians, Lebanese, and Iraqis.

92.7 percent of all Palestinians in Syria. Many Palestinians, forced out of their homes by the Arab-Israeli wars, have immigrated to Syria in search of jobs or simply to live in camps for displaced persons. Similarly, many Lebanese fled their homeland because of continuing warfare there and moved to Syria, where they are found largely in the cities or wherever work is available. Syrians are therefore slightly underrepresented in this sample.

Of the 340 cases in the sample, 41 (table 12-13), or 12.05 percent, were attributable to non-Syrians: Palestinians, 8.52 percent; Arabs, 3.23 percent; foreigners, 0.29 percent. The non-Syrian cases were concentrated in three provinces: Damascus had 30, Aleppo had 2, and Der'a had 1. They were particularly numerous in the city of Damascus, capital of the country. The four Egyptians who attempted suicide were seeking attention and aid in returning home. Egyptians, who are very attached to their country, have a saying: "An Egyptian is like a fish; if he leaves the water he dies."

The rate of attempted and completed suicides by Palestinians was 10 per 100,000 population, or three times the rate of 3.3 shown by the general population represented in the basic sample. The high rate is a reflection of the desperate situation of the Palestinians, who suffer psychologically, sociologically, and economically as they are crowded into refugee camps and shantytowns. Their plight in Syria is serious, but it is just as bad in the surrounding countries to which they have had to flee. They are like orphans, poor, homeless, and miserable.

The Syrians who committed suicidal acts were primarily from Damascus, Aleppo, Latakia and Deir Ez Zor, possibly because of their large populations and their particular features. Aleppo is the commercial center of the north, and Latakia is the largest and most important port in Syria. Deir Ez Zor is the principal connecting point between the semisettled Bedouins and the nomad Bedouins of the desert. Damascus, the largest city, is the center of national affairs. It has grown so rapidly that the 1977 census takers did not know whether the population had increased by 1 or 2 million since the

TABLE 12-13
SUICIDES AND SUICIDE ATTEMPTS IN SAMPLE OF 340
CASES IN EIGHT PROVINCES OF SYRIA, BY
NATIONALITY AND SEX, 1969–1972

| Nationality | Attempts | | | Suicides | | | Total | | |
|---|---|---|---|---|---|---|---|---|---|
| | Male | Female | Total | Male | Female | Total | Male | Female | Total |
| Syrians | 67 | 123 | 190 | 53 | 56 | 109 | 120 | 179 | 299 |
| Palestinians | 5 | 9 | 14 | 8 | 7 | 15 | 13 | 16 | 29 |
| Arabs | 1 | 9 | 10 | 1 | 0 | 1 | 2 | 9 | 11 |
| Foreigners | 0 | 1 | 1 | 0 | 0 | 0 | 0 | 1 | 1 |
| Total | 73 | 142 | 215 | 62 | 63 | 125 | 135 | 205 | 340 |

SOURCE: Justice departments in eight provinces of Syria.

preceding census. Peasants migrate to the city and, although their situation is not good there, they prefer to live in misery rather than return to the country. Most of the suicides were committed by persons in the lowest economic classes, always living in unsettled conditions.

In Der'a there are peasants and traders and the camps of Palestinians. The suicide rate there is low, perhaps because the city itself is on the Syria-Israel border and always in danger of attack. In the face of a common peril, one tends not to focus on personal misfortunes. Der'a is also near the Syria-Jordan frontier in the south and not far from the Lebanese border. Thus it trades with three countries. In addition to the war danger, well-armed customs officers are a potential hazard. The city is poor but very religious.

## LIVING CONDITIONS

Of the suicide cases in the survey, 68 percent lived independently in their own apartments. The next largest percentage shared a room in an apartment. The data indicate that the living arrangements of persons who attempted or completed suicide were seldom an important factor in suicidal behavior but that the sharing of a residence with poor family relations was likely to be the most disturbing element. Of all the persons surveyed, 90.9 percent lived with their families or with other people and only 6.8 percent lived alone; these figures reflect the customary life-style in Syria. Those who did live alone were mostly widowed or divorced individuals without family. Communal relationships may be negative forces if quarters are poor and crowded and may lead to additional strain. For example, a young wife attempted suicide because her husband falsely accused her of infidelity with a roomer in their apartment.

Living alone may be a problem in the West, but it is not so serious in Syria, where family relationships, including those with cousins, uncles, and so on, remain strong. Muhammad specifically recommended close relations with cousins and other extended family members. Elderly persons sometimes live alone, but they are visited daily by some family member and are included in all social events. Case histories of those who were living alone and attempted or committed suicide usually showed a combination of economic, familial, and psychological difficulties, as well as physical impairments. A divorced woman of 46, a tailor by occupation, developed a paralysis of the limbs. She said she wanted to die because she was sick, she had no money, and there was no one to care for her.

## EDUCATIONAL LEVEL

The general level of education is low in Syria. The 1970 census reported that 54.17 of the population were illiterate, 25.38 percent could read and write, 12.91 percent had attended primary school, 6.28 percent had attended secondary school, and only 0.7 percent had achieved higher education. Only 0.55 percent were technically qualified. The suicide pattern reflects a similar distribution: 35.59 percent of the suicidal cases were illiterate, 26.47 percent could read and write, 21.4 percent had attended primary school, 1.76 percent were high school graduates, and only 0.88 percent had earned degrees.

Education has become an important prestige symbol in Syria, but it is also a route to a better economic future. Writers, poets, and cultured persons have held a high place in the esteem of Muslims for centuries. It is important to obtain a school certificate so that one may become an employee in business or a professional and not have to do manual labor; it is particularly important to Bedouins, who disdain manual labor and who in the past had their own slaves.

Student failures may understandably result in suicidal behavior. In my sample, however, the number of suicidal acts resulting from this factor was not large, only fifteen. Thirteen of these were attempted suicides, almost equally divided between males and females. Two males who had failed to secure a secondary school certificate of graduation committed suicide. Such certification is necessary to enter the university, technical schools, or officer candidate schools run by the army and to obtain government employment. This factor is more important to a man who, when married, will have to support a family and, if necessary, his parents and other relatives. The two males who committed suicide were adolescents who used fire and firearms as soon as they learned they had not passed their examinations. Most of the attempts may have been made to elicit sympathy, as well as to inflict self-punishment, for failing in school tests. It is noteworthy that they occurred during the morning or afternoon and in the presence of the family.

## WORK AND PROFESSION

The percentage of unemployed among suicide cases was higher than in the general population. Of the men in the sample, 59.3 percent were in the working years, 15 to 59. The percentage of working women in the sample was double that in the general population, but figures for the latter are misleading. For reasons of status men deny that their wives are working, although it is clearly the pattern in farming.

Those in the sample who had no profession or technical proficiency ranked highest in suicidal behavior; mothers of families were second, students were third, and more or less skilled workers came fourth. The sample contained almost no professional people. Unemployment was an important factor because, besides creating economic problems, it meant a lack of prestige for men.

## MARITAL STATUS

Single persons, including those who were affianced, committed 58 percent of the suicidal acts. This figure is close to the large percentage of those in the 15 – 24 age group of suicidal persons. Married persons, including some who had remarried, accounted for 31.16 percent of the suicidal acts; divorced persons, for 4.71 percent; widowed, for 3.5 percent; widowed and divorced, for 0.58 percent; and abandoned, for 0.58 percent.

In Syria 6 percent of all marriages end in divorce. Islam takes the view that divorce is the last resort, and the two parental families attempt to act as intermediaries to avoid such an outcome. A man has much more freedom than a woman to demand divorce, and he usually does so without serious difficulty in traditional settings. Twelve of the thirteen divorced women who attempted suicide were without family connections.

Among married persons in the sample, 11 males and 46 females attempted suicide. The numbers of married males and females who completed suicide were almost equal, 21 and 23, respectively. Even though most of the married persons had children—three to five, on the average—that did not seem to deter them from suicidal behavior.

The average age of widowers and widows in the sample was 56. Their attempts tended to serious lethality: three by fire, one each by firearms and stabbing, and three by jumping from windows. Characteristic reasons were depression over loss of spouse, increasing age, and illness.

## ILLNESS AND SUICIDAL BEHAVIOR

In the sample there were 38 cases of physical illness, ranging from serious to mild. The total sample included 22 persons who made very serious attempts that failed to result in death, or a percentage of 6.5. The 8 such

TABLE 12-14
PHYSICAL ILLNESS AS A CAUSE OF SUICIDAL BEHAVIOR IN
EIGHT PROVINCES OF SYRIA, 1969–1972

| Sex | Attempts | Suicides | Total |
|---|---|---|---|
| Male | 5 | 10 | 15 |
| Female | 14 | 9 | 23 |
| Total | 19 | 19 | 38 |

SOURCE: Justice departments in eight provinces of Syria.

failures among the 38 cases of illness, or 21 percent, suggests that illness is a serious factor contributing to suicidal behavior. Females with physical ailments were more inclined to suicidal attempts than males; in completed suicides the sexes were almost equal (table 12-14).

The data indicate that the primary reason for suicidal behavior among ill persons was loss of hope of recovery. A secondary cause was the common view of death as salvation. The attempts seemed to be aimed at obtaining medical aid when financial resources were exhausted. For example, a retired police officer suffering from gangrene had had both legs amputated. When the illness spread to a hand he attempted to kill himself by taking drugs; his action was a protest against the indifference of the minister of the interior and an effort to obtain from him the necessary care.

Medical care in Syria, especially in provincial areas, is insufficient. Peasants, in their poverty and ignorance, instead of consulting a doctor go to sheikhs who care for them according to verses of the Koran or verses written by ancient saints. Nomads are particularly prone to treat themselves by "Arab medicine." Negligence and the lack of understanding of illness aggravate the situation, often leading to premature deaths. Many of those who suffer serious illness are poor and have no social security.

In Syria, the attitude toward the invalid or the sick person remains charged with moral significance arising more or less from religion. An illiterate religious man may consider illness to be a divine chastisement or a test. Such a man will therefore fear to do the slightest harm to those who are already ill. He looks at a sick person and says, "May God restore you." If the illness grows worse parents and relatives, especially older women, pray to God for divine assistance, particularly at midnight and dawn. If the sick person recovers, the family sacrifices a lamb (usually) and distributes the meat to the poor. The prayers and offerings often have a positive effect on the person who is ill; in any event, he receives close attention and warm family support. Nevertheless, the chronically ill sometimes make statements before a suicide or after an unsuccessful attempt that hopelessness and depression caused them to seek to end their lives. In some instances

TABLE 12-15
SUICIDAL METHODS USED BY THE CHRONICALLY
ILL IN SAMPLE FROM EIGHT PROVINCES
OF SYRIA, 1969—1972

| Method | Number of times used | Percentage of times used |
|---|---|---|
| Poison | 8 | 21.0 |
| Overdose of medicine | 10 | 26.3 |
| Fire | 5 | 13.2 |
| Firearms | 5 | 13.2 |
| Jumping | 3 | 7.9 |
| Stabbing | 3 | 7.9 |
| Cutting | 2 | 5.3 |
| Drowning | 1 | 2.6 |
| Hanging | 1 | 2.6 |
| Total | 38 | 100.0 |

SOURCE: Justice departments in eight provinces of Syria.

they also wanted to free their families or spouses of care and expense. It is noteworthy, however, that overdoses of medicine were the suicidal method used in only 26.3 percent of the cases surveyed (table 12-15).

Among those with psychological disorders, seven had senile dementia. Persons so afflicted are regarded in a kindly way by Syrians and the problems thereby engendered are overlooked. Three were alcoholics, and as alcoholism is specifically condemned by the Koran the normal result is alienation from the family.

It was difficult to determine the number of psychiatric cases. Those who had been in mental institutions or had received psychiatric care as out-patients could definitely be so listed; there were fourteen such cases. Families who do not take patients in for psychiatric care may rely on treatment by sheikhs, which usually is nothing more than writing verses of the Koran several times on a piece of paper and tying the paper around the person's neck. The police in Idlib asked the husband of a young wife who had committed suicide because of mental illness whether he had sought treatment for her. He replied that of course he had done so: he had tied verses around her neck five times or more.

## RECIDIVISM

Twenty-six persons in the sample had attempted suicide more than once: sixteen had made a second attempt; six, a third attempt; two, a fourth attempt; and two, a fifth attempt. In twelve cases there was evidence of earlier suicidal acts by someone else in the family.

## SUICIDE AMONG PRISONERS

No research studies have been made on prisoners in Syria. They number between 3,500 and 4,000, or 0.06 percent of the population. I had the opportunity to visit several prisons during the course of this study. I found the conditions very bad. The amount allotted for the care of prisoners is about one franc per day. They are given only one mediocre meal a day and must supply their own mattresses and blankets. No matter how serious or minor their offenses, they all receive the same treatment. Health care is deplorable. The only prisons that have hospitals or dispensaries are in Damascus and Aleppo, and these facilities are limited and insufficient. Most prisoners receive no medical reviews or examinations, and there is no kind of social assistance. No activities are provided for prisoners; no apprenticeship systems are developed. The few female prisoners have been incarcerated for prostitution and given a maximum sentence of two years. Most males are thieves and pickpockets. Homosexuality is frequently practiced by prisoners.

Two of the sixteen prisoners who had attempted suicide were females. Aged 20 and 26, respectively, they were both divorced, had no children, were illiterate, and lacked work skills. Their acts seemed to be an appeal for help and a protest against the injustice of society. One of them said, "I was suddenly abandoned and I had nothing. I attempted suicide to get rid of myself." The other woman said she had hoped to end a life of misery.

Fourteen male prisoners attempted suicide in protest against others who accused them of cheating at cards, or as appeals for help from their families or the prison authorities. Most of them were young: one was 14 years old; thirteen were between 16 and 22; and four were between 28 and 35. Only one male was elderly; he was 70. Eleven of them were serving sentences for thievery, two for swindling, two for murder, and one for battery. Most of the males were illiterate; five could read and write, and only three had some primary school education. Almost all were unskilled.

In all, nineteen prisoners committed suicidal acts. Four of them used fire and three died as a result. The latter were under arrest but had not yet been sentenced, for the method of fire may have been difficult to implement in prison. Fear of prison may have been the impelling force. The other prisoners, already sentenced, knew the approximate time of their release. Eight of the nineteen chose Friday, the holy day and also the visiting day, for their acts. In these cases the expected family visit did not occur.

The factors leading to suicidal behavior by prisoners are probably a poor life situation before committing offenses against the law and a much worse situation in prison. Under these circumstances their acts were probably an appeal for help and simultaneously an expression of hopelessness that their lot would ever be improved.

## SOCIAL FACTORS IN SUICIDE

### Parental Absence

The absence of parents was a factor in forty cases in the sample (table 12-16). Death, divorce, or abandonment of the mother seemed to affect daughters adversely, partly because a daughter identifies with her mother and partly because a mother acts as protectress of her daughter. As females are treated as inferiors, such championing by the mother before and after marriage is particularly important to a daughter. It is customary for daughters and mothers to visit each other daily if they live in the same town or to telephone daily. It seems clear from table 12-16 that a boy's loss of his father is also traumatic, even though he has more power in society. A case example: "My father married again after my mother's death. One day my stepmother wore my mother's clothes. I asked for some as a souvenir and she refused. I felt great anguish and attempted suicide."

### Honor and Virginity

In Syria the woman is the victim of the Arab concept of honor, centering on virginity. Of the thirty-four persons in the sample affected by this value, three were males and thirty-one were females. In nineteen cases the individuals were between 13 and 19 years of age, and in twelve cases they were in the 20–24 age group. The toll was heavy among young girls.

TABLE 12-16
PARENTAL ABSENCE AS A FACTOR CONTRIBUTING
TO SUICIDAL BEHAVIOR IN FORTY CASES
IN SAMPLE FROM EIGHT PROVINCES OF
SYRIA, 1969–1972

| Reason for absence | Number of suicides | Number of attempts | Total | Sex |
|---|---|---|---|---|
| Father deceased | 5 | 7 | 12 | 10 males, 2 females |
| Mother deceased | 1 | 4 | 5 | All females |
| Both parents deceased | 0 | 2 | 2 | Both female |
| Parents divorced | 3 | 8 | 11 | 2 males, 9 females |
| Mother abandoned | 2 | 1 | 3 | 1 male, 2 females |
| Father absent | 0 | 2 | 2 | Both male |
| Both parents absent | 0 | 5 | 5 | 2 males, 3 females |

SOURCE: Justice departments in eight provinces of Syria.

The ideas of honor and virginity are so strict that small occurrences—a girl being seen on a balcony, in the courtyard, or even going to a cousin's house—may give rise to accusations of misbehavior threatening the family's honor. For example, a girl of 22 went to visit her cousin. When she was a little late in returning her mother reproached her with the comment: "Even prostitutes are more honorable than you." The girl thereupon attempted suicide. A Syrian man, on the contrary, is often obsessed with the idea of sexual conquest outside his marriage. Should he succeed, he then feels guilty and offers prayers, believing that a merciful God will show indulgence toward him. Meanwhile he is suspiciously guarding his wife to see that she does not stray.

City attitudes are less stringent about the loss of virginity than those in rural areas, and it would be rare for a brother to kill his sister for this reason. As country attitudes continue to be very strict, a girl who has been violated may try to escape from her village and go to the city, where at least she may kill herself by her own hands. The sample had five cases of loss of virginity, one in Damascus, one near Damascus, and three in the primitive provinces. One of the latter, according to medicolegal reports based on the evidence, was a case of rape, but the girl killed herself because she had no hope that her family would have mercy.

Married women would never risk extramarital relations, for such conduct would bring on threats of divorce. If actual threats are made, the woman may attempt suicide in order to alert her family and ask for help. A single girl may be accused of having sexual relations on the slightest pretext and may not be believed when she gives her account of a simple visit. With such frustration and hostility toward critical and unbelieving parents, a girl's best resource is to marry and leave to set up her own home.

### Adolescent Love Affairs

Fourteen cases in the sample, thirteen of them female, involved romantic love. Eight of them were completed suicides. In most instances the family had intervened or the man had abandoned the girl. These completed and attempted suicides took place in Damascus and Aleppo, where young people can go to the movies and can more easily see persons outside the family circle. Syrians do not believe that marriages should be contracted on the basis of love; some of them, especially the traditional natives, feel that love is almost synonymous with illicit sex and dishonor. In the villages strict control is maintained over a girl's actions, and romantic love affairs are unlikely to develop. The victims of this traditional outlook are usually single adolescents.

### Insults

Insulting remarks may be a factor in causing suicide in Syria. Depreciatory statements, ranging from light to serious criticism, are common. It may be that the weak sense of democracy in the country has encouraged derogatory behavior, which is founded in autocratic traditions and a wish to exercise authority. Parents exercise complete control over their children, teachers are autocratic, and work supervisors are quick to point out faults. In twenty-nine cases in the sample, seven male and twenty-two female, insults were a factor contributing to suicidal acts. The young are especially vulnerable to insults owing to the superior positions of older persons and authorities. A single woman 30 years old, who lived in the desert at Ar Raqqah, killed herself by fire when her father's family was disdainful of her because her mother had developed an albino condition, which is despised by Bedouins. Two girls committed suicide by poisoning themselves as a result of an Arab custom called *choucheh bi choucheh* (two brothers are married to two sisters). The point of this custom is to avoid the dowry. Each father exchanges a like amount of money, coming out in effect with no cost. One's fortunes are therefore tied up inextricably with the behavior of the other three persons, and there is no security.

## SUMMARY

In the pattern of Syrian suicides as seen in this study, the largest number of suicidal acts took place before age 25, particularly between 15 and 24. Attempted suicides were 66 percent female. Up to the age of 55 completed suicides were almost equal between males and females; in later life more men killed themselves than women. The estimated rate per 100,000 for the four years 1969–1972 varied from 3.7 to 7.2 for all suicidal acts. The large majority of individuals covered by the survey were Muslims of the Sunnite sect. Approximately a third of those who committed or attempted suicide took pills and medicines; another third used poisons. Females tended to use poison and pills. Female suicidal acts seemed to be related to their inferior position in the society and their limited ability to protect themselves or to alter their circumstances. Young persons were more vulnerable to stress than older persons in this rigidly hierarchical society.

# JORDAN

# 13

*Editor's Note*

This chapter records the results of the first research undertaken in Jordan on the subject of suicide. It was a monumental job, requiring a great deal of patience and determination. Jordan, a tribal, unwesternized country, is undeveloped and poor. Even its university is quite new. Jordan is one of the Middle East countries particularly affected by the Palestinian problem.

Dr. Mohammed Issa Barhoum is associate professor of sociology at the University of Jordan, in Amman. He is deeply respected by his colleagues in the Middle East, and he is frequently requested to speak or to serve on policy committees. He has done research at Princeton University and at Georgetown University, and in Tokyo.

## MOHAMMED ISSA BARHOUM

## INTRODUCTION

Jordan is a developing country situated between Africa and Asia. It is bounded by Syria on the north, by Iraq on the northeast, by Saudi Arabia on the south and east, and by Israel and the occupied West Bank on the west. Jordan covers an area of approximately 37,500 square miles, mostly east of the river Jordan. A small part of its territory, about 2,350 square miles, lies west of the river.

Between the two world wars the area was mandated to Great Britain by the League of Nations as Palestine and Trans-Jordan. Jordan became known as the Hashemite Kingdom of Jordan under the rule of the late King Abdullah ibn Husein, who was crowned in 1946; the present ruler, Hussein, grandson of Abdullah, was proclaimed king in 1952. According to its constitution, the country is an independent sovereign state and the people form part of the Arab nation. The form of government is parliamentary with a hereditary monarchy.

This study is of an exploratory nature; its main aim is to provide the reader interested in suicide with some information about the etiology of the phenomenon in Jordan. As in other developing countries, information about suicide in Jordan is notable by its absence. Moreover, until now no research has been done on this subject in Jordan. Studies of this kind are needed, both in Asia and in the Middle East, for scientific comparison with information available in Western societies.

As the large majority of the people in Jordan are Muslims (88 percent), it is to be expected that most of the prevailing social values are Islamic in origin. The value structure affects the social attitudes of the people toward suicide, which are reflected in the comparatively low rate of suicide in Jordan. The people are strongly influenced by the strict religious proscription of suicide, particularly evident in the statistics on suicidal attempts. For example, 84.6 percent of those who attempted suicide confessed that they were unbelievers who did not adhere to Islamic teachings. The Koran clearly says that God prohibits suicide. In different sections of the holy book God reminds people that since he has created the sacred soul it must under no circumstances be destroyed and that the prohibition against slaying a human being also forbids suicide. The same attitude toward suicide was expressed by the Prophet, who warned Muslims not to kill themselves:

> He who kills himself with an iron [any sharp weapon], then his iron shall be in his hand, with which he pierces his abdomen, in the fire of Hell [on the day of judgment] and shall live there everlasting and eternally; and he who kills himself by a poison, then this poison shall be in his hand from which he shall sip in the fire of Hell, everlasting and eternally; and he who jumps from a mountain [or high place] to kill himself shall be falling into the fire of Hell, everlasting and eternally.

## SOCIOCULTURAL VALUES

Jordan continues its traditional ways, particularly in villages and among nomad tribes. The extended family is the predominant social unit and Islam is the chief consolidating force. Elders are respected and men are dominant. Women are to be chaste, modest, and submissive. Cousin marriages are largely practiced in rural areas, supposedly as a means of reducing family frictions. The husband's loyalty, however, is first to his family; if the family does not like his wife he may be forced to divorce her, even against his will. When inhabitants of small villages were queried about cousin marriages, it was found that 58 percent of the heads of households were married to cousins or relatives.

Marriages are usually arranged on the presumption that families rather than individuals are marrying each other. Girls generally marry by the age of 20, and husbands may be five to ten years older or more. Parents choose marriage partners; frequently the young people have met through relatives, though the girl may not even have seen her prospective husband until the engagement party. She may also be forced to marry someone whom she does not like. The marriage process is in three steps: the engagement, the

signing of the marriage contract with the dowry, and the marriage ceremony. Engagement may last for six months before the second step, and it is
possible for either party to secure a divorce at this stage. A deferred dowry
is paid to the wife should there be a divorce. Alimony is paid to the divorced
wife for only three months unless she has children living with her. In that
event the husband has to pay alimony as long as the wife is keeping the
children. Usually a divorced woman returns to her family as she cannot live
on either the deferred dowry or the alimony.

The wife's responsibility is to bear children and to take care of the home.
Sons are preferred. Divorce may take place if there are no children or if no
sons are born. In my study of divorce (2) I found that two-thirds of the
women in a research sample who were divorced had no children but that the
divorce had often taken place within three years of marriage. Of the
divorced women, 30 percent were in the 20–24 age group; as the men were
over 35, the customary age discrepancy was obvious.

Men easily obtain divorces in Jordan. Women may request divorce on
various grounds, but in actual practice, as my study revealed, wives that did
so seldom received the portion of deferred dowry owing them. In other
cases men who wanted a divorce withheld the dowry portion until the wife
had agreed to the divorce. Divorced women are looked down upon and find
it difficult to marry again. Those who have technical or professional training find opportunities for work, but illiterate women are usually blocked
from returning even to their former occupations. As girls are much less
likely to have schooling and training than boys, untrained women who get
divorced must return to the protection of their families. In 1973 the divorce
rate in Jordan was 171 per 1,000 marriages; by 1979 it had increased to more
than 200. No sexual instruction is given to girls and boys, a lack that, along
with differences in maturity owing to the age gap, contributes to marital
difficulties and divorce.

For both men and women in Jordan, success and a good family repute are
important. Conformity to and agreement with the will of elders are generally required. Older people are under less stress than their juniors, and
females have fewer options than males.

## METHODS OF DATA COLLECTION

This study is divided into two parts: the first one is statistical, based on data
collected from the coroner's files in Amman for the years 1968 and 1971–
1978.[1] The second part is a case study of eighty suicide attempters who

[1]Data for 1969 and 1970 were not available. Data for 1979–1981 are included but have not
been compared with those for other years.

were interviewed at length. The case study illustrates and rounds out the information gleaned from the coroner's files. The interviews were designed to give a clear picture of the main reasons motivating suicidal behavior.

Although some people, like Stengel (18), argue that suicide attempts do not tell much about completed suicide because the latter is distinctly different, I believe that much can be learned from information provided by the individuals who have tried, but failed, to commit suicide. Worth mentioning, too, is the fact that it often proved difficult, if not impossible, to meet or interview members of the family of the suicide victim. Their reluctance may be owing in large part to sociocultural factors that keep most Jordanese from confessing that a death in the family was actually a suicide. This attitude in itself suggests that a sound investigation of suicidal actions in sociological terms is necessary.

The social meaning of suicide is made clearer if it is studied in its sociopsychological perspective. In this study, both techniques—statistical and case study—are employed to explore this social meaning. Statistical data on suicide in Jordan are, however, not very reliable for many reasons, social and otherwise. The unreliability is emphasized in general terms by Gregory Zilborg (6:18):

> Statistical data on suicide as they are compiled today deserve little if any credence; it has been repeatedly pointed out by scientific students of the problem that suicide cannot be subject to statistical evaluation, since all too many suicides are not reported.

The use of these two techniques in this study helps to support Douglas's theory of explaining suicide in social terms (5:258):

> We propose to study human actions and their [meaning] from the bottom . . . upward, at least in some good part. . . . The ideal of this approach is to go from what people say and do in the real world situations upward toward an analysis of the patterns that can be found in their actions and the meaning of their statements and behaviour; then only when the problems of these levels of investigations have been solved, to proceed to develop theories of the social meaning.

## RESEARCH FINDINGS

### Suicide Rate

In spite of the rapid social and environmental changes in Jordan, the suicide rate was comparatively low in the years covered by the survey (table 13-1). The analysis of 232 completed suicides and 935 attempted suicides in the same years revealed a noticeable increase in suicidal incidents as a percentage of the total for those years. Completed suicides rose from 8.2 percent of the cases reported in the coroner's files in 1968 to 15.5 percent in

1978. Attempted suicides also escalated, increasing from 3.9 percent in 1968 to 17.4 percent a decade later. (See table 13-2.)

Sex Ratio

The percentage of males who committed suicide in the years surveyed was higher than that of females, whereas more females than males at-

TABLE 13-1
SUICIDE RATE PER 100,000 POPULATION
IN JORDAN, 1968, 1971–1981

| Year | Rate |
|------|------|
| 1968 | 1.1 |
| 1971 | 1.4 |
| 1972 | 1.0 |
| 1973 | 1.2 |
| 1974 | 1.3 |
| 1975 | 1.6 |
| 1976 | 1.7 |
| 1977 | 1.8 |
| 1978 | 1.8 |
| 1979 | 2.5 |
| 1980 | 2.7 |
| 1981 | 3.1 |

SOURCE: Coroner's office, Amman.

TABLE 13-2
PERCENTAGE DISTRIBUTION OF SUICIDES
AND SUICIDE ATTEMPTS IN JORDAN,
1968, 1971–1978

| Year | Suicides | Attempts |
|------|----------|----------|
| 1968 | 8.2 | 3.9 |
| 1971 | 10.8 | 5.2 |
| 1972 | 7.3 | 7.1 |
| 1973 | 9.1 | 7.7 |
| 1974 | 9.9 | 13.4 |
| 1975 | 12.1 | 13.9 |
| 1976 | 12.9 | 15.1 |
| 1977 | 14.2 | 16.3 |
| 1978 | 15.5 | 17.4 |

SOURCE: Coroner's office, Amman.

tempted suicide (table 13-3). The difference between the sexes in attempts is, however, minimal.

## Suicide and Age

The majority of suicidal persons covered in the survey were less than 30 years old, in respect to both completed and attempted suicides (table 13-4). The reason may be that young people are under more sociopsychological strain than any other age group.

## Marital Status

The majority of those who completed suicide in 1968 and 1971–1978 were married, whereas most of those who attempted suicide were single (table 13-5). These high rankings are also explainable in terms of sociopsychological strain. The strain is particularly felt by married persons because most marriages in Jordan are arranged (3). When a marriage does not work as well as expected, or when harmony cannot easily be achieved, or when the husband and wife face serious problems, suicide may be chosen as the only way out of the difficulties.

TABLE 13-3

PERCENTAGE DISTRIBUTION OF SUICIDES AND SUICIDE
ATTEMPTS IN JORDAN, BY SEX, 1968, 1971–1978

| Sex | Suicides | Attempts |
|---|---|---|
| Male | 57.8 | 47.6 |
| Female | 42.2 | 52.4 |

SOURCE: Coroner's office, Amman.

TABLE 13-4

PERCENTAGE DISTRIBUTION OF SUICIDES AND SUICIDE
ATTEMPTS IN JORDAN, BY AGE GROUP,
1968, 1971–1978

| Age group | Suicides | Attempts |
|---|---|---|
| 10–19 | 39.6 | 50.4 |
| 20–29 | 40.5 | 39.4 |
| 30–39 | 9.9 | 6.3 |
| 40–49 | 7.8 | 2.2 |
| 50–59 | 1.7 | 1.4 |
| 60 and over | 0.9 | 0.3 |

SOURCE: Coroner's office, Amman.

## Religion and Suicide

Data on religion show that suicide among Muslims was high in the period surveyed when compared with Christians, who make up 12 percent of Jordan's population but who accounted for only 9.9 percent of the completed suicides (table 13-6).

## Methods

Poisoning was by far the most commonly used method both in committing and attempting suicide (41.4 and 67.4 percent, respectively) by the individuals covered in the survey (table 13-7). Shooting came next in completed suicides (20.7 percent), burning third, and insecticides fourth. In attempted suicides, insecticides came second and stabbing third.

It is noteworthy that more violent methods were used by those who succeeded in killing themselves than by those who attempted to. Violent methods, which reflect to a great extent the psychological state of the person before committing suicide, ensure almost instantaneous death; they indicate that hope has ended for people choosing them. In attempting suicide, however, about 84 percent of the subjects surveyed used either poison or insecticides, presumably hoping for rescue before dying.

TABLE 13-5

PERCENTAGE DISTRIBUTION OF SUICIDES AND
SUICIDE ATTEMPTS IN JORDAN, BY
MARITAL STATUS, 1968, 1971—1978

| Marital status | Suicides | Attempts |
|---|---|---|
| Single | 36.6 | 63.2 |
| Widowed | 1.7 | 0.6 |
| Married | 58.6 | 34.9 |
| Divorced | 3.1 | 1.3 |

SOURCE: Coroner's office, Amman.

TABLE 13-6

PERCENTAGE DISTRIBUTION OF SUICIDES AND SUICIDE
ATTEMPTS IN JORDAN, BY RELIGIOUS
AFFILIATION, 1968, 1971—1978

| Religion | Suicides | Attempts |
|---|---|---|
| Muslim | 90.1 | 93.1 |
| Christian | 9.9 | 6.9 |

SOURCE: Coroner's office, Amman.

TABLE 13-7
PERCENTAGE DISTRIBUTION OF SUICIDES AND
SUICIDE ATTEMPTS IN JORDAN, BY
METHOD USED, 1968, 1971–1978

| Method | Suicides | Attempts |
|--------|----------|----------|
| Hanging | 7.8 | 1.0 |
| Shooting | 20.7 | 2.6 |
| Jumping | 0.4 | 0.6 |
| Insecticides | 9.5 | 16.8 |
| Drowning | 0.4 | – |
| Burning | 15.5 | 4.9 |
| Poisoning | 41.4 | 67.4 |
| Stabbing | 4.3 | 6.7 |

SOURCE: Coroner's office, Amman.

## Occupational Status

In the cases of suicidal acts surveyed, housewives accounted for the highest percentage of both completed and attempted suicides (31.5 and 33.7, respectively). Unemployed persons had the second highest rate (25 percent) in the completed suicide category, followed by workers (16.8 percent), students (12.9 percent), civil servants (7.3 percent), and soldiers (6.5 percent). Among suicide attempters, students ranked second to housewives with 21.6 percent, followed by the unemployed with 18.7 percent, workers with 11.6 percent, civil servants with 8.7 percent, and soldiers with 5.7 percent. (See table 13-8.)

## Precipitating Causes

Family and marital disputes showed the highest percentage among all precipitating causes of both completed and attempted suicides (43.6 and 53.2 percent, respectively), in the sample surveyed (table 13-9). Financial problems occupied second place in completed suicides and physical illness came third; sex and love affairs followed closely in fourth place. In attempted suicides, however, sex and love affairs ranked second and financial problems third. Failure in examinations was a strong reason for completed as well as attempted suicide (8.6 and 9.4 percent, respectively).

## Suicide in Rural and Urban Areas

Of the persons surveyed, 72.8 percent of those who completed suicide and 84.8 percent of those who attempted suicide lived in urban sectors of Jordan. These high percentages suggest two possible contributing factors. Either social solidarity in rural areas, owing to the still existing tribal structure, is strong enough to discourage suicide, or the coroner's files are not reliable enough to make a correct correlation. Of course, both factors may have been operating. The percentages in rural areas were 27.2 for completed suicides and 15.2 for attempts.

## INTERVIEWS WITH SUICIDE ATTEMPTERS

Eighty persons who attempted suicide were interviewed in an effort to obtain information about sociocultural problems related to suicide, as well as about the etiology of the act. A question might be raised here: Why were those who attempted suicide interviewed rather than the families of those who completed suicide? The answer is simply that all efforts to meet with such families failed. The only option left was to meet with persons who had

TABLE 13-8

PERCENTAGE DISTRIBUTION OF SUICIDES AND
ATTEMPTED SUICIDES IN JORDAN, BY
OCCUPATION, 1968, 1971–1978

| Occupation | Suicides | Attempts |
|------------|----------|----------|
| Student | 12.9 | 21.6 |
| Housewife | 31.5 | 33.7 |
| Soldier | 6.5 | 5.7 |
| Civil servant | 7.3 | 8.7 |
| Unemployed | 25.0 | 18.7 |
| Worker | 16.8 | 11.6 |

SOURCE: Coroner's office, Amman.

TABLE 13-9

PERCENTAGE DISTRIBUTION OF SUICIDES AND
ATTEMPTED SUICIDES IN JORDAN, BY
PRECIPITATING CAUSE, 1968, 1971–1978

| Cause | Suicides | Attempts |
|-------|----------|----------|
| Physical illness | 14.6 | 8.2 |
| Family and marital disputes | 43.6 | 53.2 |
| Financial problems | 16.8 | 10.7 |
| Old age and senility | 0.4 | 0.7 |
| Sex and love affairs | 14.3 | 14.9 |
| Failure in examinations | 8.6 | 9.4 |
| Forced marriages | 1.7 | 2.9 |

SOURCE: Coroner's office, Amman.

recently attempted suicide. Those persons, chosen on a random basis from the capital city of Amman, were interviewed by a female research assistant who visited them immediately after the act. We are grateful to the Police Department for providing us with the necessary information.

Of the 80 persons, 48 (60 percent) were males and 32 (40 percent) were females. The median age of the males was 25; of the females, 22. A large majority of the 80 subjects were Muslims (76); the remaining 4 were Christians. Of the sample, 72 were single, 6 were married, and 2 were divorced.

The most common methods were poisoning and the use of insecticides; these two methods together were used by 81 percent of the subjects, most of them females. Seventy-six of the subjects attempted suicide at home, apparently with the hope of being rescued.

Ninety percent of the attempters were in the 15–29 age group; they most often cited interpersonal problems with spouse or family as the reason. Those females who attempted suicide did so in order to attract their parents' attention by expressing their dissatisfaction and distress. Of the female subjects in the case study, 36.5 percent attempted suicide because they were forced by their parents to marry a spouse whom they either had not seen or did not want to marry. Failure in examinations was a major reason for those under 20 years of age to attempt suicide, showing the high value placed upon success by this society.

It is known that religious beliefs play an important role in the social control process, particularly in traditional societies. More than 84.6 percent of our subjects did not practice religion in any form, and the majority did not believe in religion. Fifty-nine percent of the subjects suffered from psychological distress, a factor perhaps contributing to the suicide attempt.

Sexual education is taboo in Jordan. A family is not supposed to give any information of this sort to sons or daughters. As a result, the young people turn to other sources that are sometimes, if not most of the time, unable to assist those seeking help and knowledge. Thus the door is left open to conflicting as well as distorted ideas about sex. Such ideas, along with other factors, may increase tension in the personality structure, and when that tension reaches its limit it may blow up. Of the subjects in the sample, 83 percent obtained their sexual knowledge from sources other than the family.

We found that 82 percent of the subjects had had poor relations with their teachers and peers in school. More than 86 percent of those subjects were rated below average in their classes, and they had no friends. All of them more or less had faced family troubles; they were not on good terms with their parents, a fact that probably contributed to their psychological stress. Of the entire sample, 67.4 percent came from large families (more than six members) in which understanding and social control were lacking. More than 40 percent of the respondents had very low income, a fact mentioned by more than half of the subjects when asked about early childhood. They expressed unhappiness and dissatisfaction with the kind of socialization they had experienced as young children.

## CONCLUSIONS

Suicide rates are low in Jordan as compared with other countries, presumably because Jordanian society is still largely traditional. The extended family, still in existence on a large scale, constitutes an important feature of Jordanian society. Economically speaking, the importance of the extended family stems from the fact that the individual is dependent for a good many years of his life on various family members. Thus is created a social obligation to the family which results in social solidarity in the family. All members of the family feel obliged to help one another. This relationship is another facet of the tribalism that persists in the rural areas of Jordan. The low suicide rates in rural areas, in comparison with urban areas, may be explained by this close relationship. Thus relationships in Jordan still depend heavily upon a very strong sense of belonging to a family, a sense that serves as an effective social control.

The fact that more than two-thirds of the subjects in the sample came from relatively large families with limited resources and authoritarian fathers was a significant finding of the survey. Another important finding was that 71 percent of the subjects lived in almost complete isolation and had no friends, and 82 percent of the subjects had had poor relations with their peers as well as their teachers.

## SUMMARY

Suicide is more prevalent among married subjects; suicide attempts were made more frequently by single subjects. The first finding may be attributable to family troubles that occur in marriage. On the other hand, failure in a love affair and forcing a female to get married to a disliked person seemed to be cogent reasons for attempting suicide.

Insecticides and poisoning were found to be the most common methods used in committing suicide in both the statistical and the case studies sections of our survey.

The highest percentage among completed suicides were in the 20−29 age group. Persons under 20 had the highest rate of attempted suicide, in both the statistical report and the case studies.

Since suicide is still considered by official standards not to be a major problem in Jordan, no emphasis is placed on preventive measures. In my opinion, however, the need for further research into both the nature of suicide and its prevention is obvious.

# BIBLIOGRAPHY

1. Barhoum, M. The application of time series to the study of suicide. Unpublished Ph.D. thesis, University of Birmingham, 1971.
2. Barhoum, M. The marriage system in a Jordanian village. *Jabir: The Social National Journal* (1977). Published by the Social and Criminological Centre, Cairo.
3. Barhoum, M. The marriage system in a Jordanian village. *El-Majallah El-Ijtimaiyya El-Qawmiyya* (Cairo), no. 1 (1978).
4. Bond, H. Suicide from the sociological aspect. *Brit. Med. J.* (1931):234–238.
5. Douglas, J. *The Social Meanings of Suicide*. Princeton: Princeton University Press, 1967.
6. Durkheim, E. *Suicide* (1897). London: Routledge and Kegan Paul, 1966.
7. Fedden, H. *Suicide: A Social and Historical Study*. London: Peter Davies, 1938.
8. Henry, A., and J. Short. *Suicide and Homicide*. London: Collier-Macmillan, 1964.
9. Hurlburt, C. Prosperity, depression and the suicide rate. *Amer. J. Sociol.*, 37 (1931):714–719.
10. Lewis, A. Statistical aspects of suicide. *Canad. Med. Assoc. J.*, 74 (1956):99–104.
11. Lunden, A. Suicides in France, 1910–1943. *J. Social Sciences*, 52 (1947): 321–334.
12. Rose, L. A modern review of the suicide problem. *Med. Practice*, 227 (1952): 40–43.
13. Sainsbury, P. *Suicide in London*. London: Chapman and Hill, 1955.
14. Schmid, G., and V. Arsdol. Completed and attempted suicides: A comparative analysis. *Amer. Sociol. Rev.*, 20 (1955):273–283.
15. Shneidman, E. S., and N. Farberow. *Clues to Suicide*. New York: McGraw-Hill, 1957.
16. Simpson, G. Methodological problems in determining the etiology of suicide. *Amer. Sociol. Rev.*, 15 (1950):658–663.
17. Stengel, E. Recent research into suicide and attempted suicide. *Amer. J. Psychiatry*, 118 (1962):725–727.
18. Stengel, E. *Suicide and Attempted Suicide*. Harmondsworth: Penguin Books, 1969.
19. Wright, M. B. Sociological factors which influence the suicide rate. *Psyche*, 12 (1931):52–61.

# EGYPT

14

*Editor's Note*

The world is familiar with Egypt's famous monuments, the heritage of its pharaohs, and its twenty-five hundred years of cultural accomplishments. In more modern times, Egypt has been occupied by Romans, Arabs, Turks, Tunisians, Fatimids, Saladin's dynasty, and the French and British. Since 1950 it has been the Arab Republic of Egypt with a constitutional government, the first popular government after an unbroken history of kings. Egyptians live on the borders of the Nile and the Suez Canal, which are the only habitable areas. The country is 46 percent urban and 54 percent rural; its total population in 1976 was 38.5 million. The chief products, besides agricultural produce, are chemicals, fertilizers, paper, textiles, and steel. Oil is found in the Sinai area.

Egypt has been Muslim since A.D. 639, although before then the population was largely Christian Copts. Arabic is the national language, but non-Semitic languages, such as Nubian and Berber, are spoken in some areas.

Egypt had been the political center of the Arabs before its peace negotiations with Israel. At present strained relations exist between Egypt and other Arab countries, whose leaders feel that Egypt, in acting unilaterally, ignored their interests. It may prove economically disastrous for Egypt if the Arab oil states totally withdraw their financial input.

Poverty is omnipresent in the country, and the millions of illiterate peasants have difficulty in making an adequate living. Egypt's poverty and overpopulation are its most notable features; the lack of technically skilled persons hinders its progress toward industrialization. Religious leaders oppose government attempts at birth control, and the population grows at an alarming rate in view of the country's resources and land space.

Dr. Ahmed Okasha is head of the Psychiatry Department of Ain Shams Medical School. He has received postgraduate training in Edinburgh and London, and he serves on the boards of the Egyptian Psychological Association and the Mental Health Society. He is a consultant for the Egyptian army and is an adviser to the World Health Organization in the eastern Mediterranean area. Dr. Okasha, editor-in-chief of the *Egyptian Journal of Psychiatry*, has published fifty-five articles in national and international journals and has edited six books. His chief interests are transcultural and biological psychiatry and suicide.

Dr. Farouk Lotaief is a senior psychiatrist on Dr. Okasha's staff at the University Hospital and is assistant professor in the Psychiatry Department, Ain Shams Medical School.

The two authors are to be congratulated for gathering the data for this chapter, as conditions in Egypt are not conducive to the kind of research they were doing.

# AHMED OKASHA AND FAROUK LOTAIEF

Suicide has not previously been studied in Egypt except for Samaan's 1963 report (15) and two forthcoming works we have prepared (13, 14). A possible reason is the widespread belief held by laymen and scientific researchers alike that the Muslim religion deters people from killing themselves. The relationship between suicide and religion has been stressed repeatedly in the literature. Durkheim, Stengel (17), and others have claimed that religion promotes the integration of the individual into the social environment, gives meaning to life, and alleviates feelings of isolation or alienation. Some view religion as a magic defense against the fear of death. No doubt religion is a factor contributing to social cohesiveness, which is considered helpful in preventing suicides.

Another reason that Egypt has received little attention from suicidologists is that suicide has not been looked upon as a problem of any importance; although it does occur, there is a wish to deny its existence. This attitude may be explained partly by the fact that Egyptians from the dawn of their history have worshipped life. Rather than accepting death as an end to life, they consider it as the beginning of a new life. As Egyptians always think of themselves as being owned by God, neither the beginning nor the ending of life has been regarded as the individual's to command. To end one's own life has always been deemed an act against the will of God and therefore subject to punishment in the new life after death. Suicide thus would not end a person's misery.

## RELIGION

Ancient Egyptian religions have played an important part in the formulation of the Egyptian's concepts of life and death. As a living being one belongs to God. God and his deputies, the pharaohs, were the only beings empowered to give or to end life. These ideas, accepted and respected by the people, led to a strong conviction of the need to preserve life for the very powers that had determined one's destination.

References to suicide are extremely rare in ancient Egyptian sources; the subject has been dealt with only marginally in the literature of Egyptology. Suicide has never been treated as a subject on its own, but there are some direct allusions to it. Ipou-wer, an Egyptian sage, witnessed a period of common peril and disaster during the first and second intermediate dynasties, when kingship, once the strongest guarantee for a well-functioning

Egyptian world, broke down. He is quoted in the literature as saying, "Crocodiles sink down because of what they have carried off, for men go to them of their own accord."[1]

Another reference to suicide is in one of the most interesting as well as the most difficult texts, "The Dialogue of a Man with His Soul," which probably dates from the same period and recalls the same disastrous condition of Egyptian society. It poses suicide as the central question. The "man" argues with his soul that he would be much better off to commit suicide and get rid of his corpse than to continue being under unbearable conditions. In the course of the eloquent and beautifully written arguments, the soul succeeds in convincing the man that suicide—particularly the burning of the corpse—would bring disaster to both of them. By the destruction of the body instead of having it embalmed according to tradition and nourished by offerings, as had been the practice ever since Egyptians came into existence, the soul (which stands for the ego, the everlasting divine essence) would lose its "house." According to Egyptian belief, the soul must return every night to its "house" in order to be renewed and reborn the following morning at sunrise—that is, to live eternally.

Here is the very essence of the Egyptian creed and the intriguing question of Egyptian ethics. From one point of view, the soul's argument sounds egoistic and opportunistic. On the other hand the Egyptians feel that not only the *ba* (soul) but the whole body and its organs, such as heart, liver, and kidneys, are God's responsibility. The body is the dwelling place of the divine powers to the extent that eating and drinking become virtually a duty of man toward those powers. At this point individual welfare and cosmic divine existence no longer contradict each other. The question whether suicide is sinful and thus subject to eternal condemnation becomes irrelevant; if the mere preserving of the corpse by embalming it and supplying it with offerings suffices to keep the soul alive, it apparently no longer matters if man dies by committing suicide or by awaiting death deliberately—just so long as the corpse itself is not destroyed by fire or drowning. The accent no longer lies on accepting and humbly bearing the sufferings inflicted by God. Thus it is easier to understand the Graeco-Roman approach toward suicide as expressed in a Ramesside document dealing with the consequences of royal murder following a harem revolt: "While the criminals of lower rank are sentenced to death and eventually killed, the noblemen involved are politely asked to meet the inevitable consequences for themselves: They took their own lives; no penalty was carried out on them."[2]

At the end of the glorious years of the ancient Egyptian kingdom, the country was occupied by numerous foreign peoples. People were so passive and so miserable that they even lost the will to kill themselves. There were

[1]John A. Wilson, *The Burden of Egypt*, p. 109.
[2]Wilson, *Burden of Egypt*, p. 269.

no references to suicide after Cleopatra's death until the present time.

The Muslim religion condemns suicide as an act of murder. According to the Koran, killing one person is the same as killing all people, and this dictate is applicable to suicide. The word "suicide" is not mentioned directly, but the relevant verses refer to the killing of oneself. This idea is present in many chapters of the Koran, two of them giving data about the Jews. No punishments are prescribed in the Koran for the families of suicides. The Islamic Sharia (sacred law) condemns suicide but permits its victims to be given religious burial ceremonies.

## CULTURAL ATTITUDES

Egyptian culture is full of contradictions, a situation to be expected in a country with a wide variety of civilizations, a country that has been occupied by many invaders bringing with them their different cultures and religions. Romans, Arabs, and Europeans have left their mark on the Egyptian outlook on life. Yet in spite of all these influences, the original religious concepts and attitudes to life and death form a predominant theme that still exists in the minds of the Egyptian people. For Egyptians, it is not pleasant to speak about or refer to suicide. When suicide occurs, the victim's family denies it, not only at the family level but also at the official level.

The coming of Islam has brought many of the cultural features of that religion, particularly male dominance and female submission. Christian ideas are intermingled with Islamic ones, and the differences between the two create frictions. The upper classes are becoming more westernized in outlook. The influence of radio, movies, and television, among other factors, brings peasants to the large cities hoping for work and a better future. This migration has increased the already serious overcrowding and has lowered the economic status of many persons. Housing crises, worsening every day, affect family life and the ability of young people to marry and be on their own. Egypt's economic situation and its uncertain prospects contribute to depression and thoughts of suicide.

The country is 89 percent Muslim and 11 percent Christian (Copts). The family is still the most important force in determining and directing an individual's life. Females are expected to be submissive and dependent and to accept the aggressiveness of males and the authority of elders. In an earlier study (11) I found that men have not adjusted to the fact that women now have more freedom. Even if a man allows his wife to work outside the home, he expects her to maintain the same obligations and duties on his behalf as before. He expects her to function as a housewife, teacher, cook, servant, and hostess while obeying his instructions—and in addition go out to work. Such painful and distressing situations may lead to depression, despair, and suicide. Overpopulation and the bearing of too many children continue in spite of family planning centers, which have largely failed because Muslim religious leaders oppose family planning. The average age of marriage is now 25 or 26 because of economic and housing difficulties. A professional person may decide not to marry until he is 30 years old; before marriage a male professional student may remain at home.

## METHODS OF DATA COLLECTION

According to official statistics, the incidence of suicide in Egypt was 0.2 per 100,000 (19), the lowest among the twenty-six countries surveyed by the World Health Organization.

Epidemiological and psychological studies of suicide and attempted suicide in Arab countries are scarce. Dabbagh (4) reports the official rates per 100,000 population obtained from various Arab countries as follows: Iraq, 0.1−0.2; Syria, 0.38−0.45; Jordan, 0.23; and Lebanon, 1.8. The only available research on this problem in Egypt is Samaan's (15). For his study of suicide in Cairo, he used the official rates determined by the Ministry of Interior for 1959: for suicides, 3.6 per 100,000; for attempted suicides, 2.8 per 100,000.

It is generally agreed that current statistics on the incidence of suicide are grossly inadequate and that their comparisons based on the figures available are at best inaccurate and often misleading (16). Dublin (5) held the opinion that actual suicides in the United States were 30 percent above the officially reported numbers. In a report on Edinburgh, Kessel (9) estimated that official figures counted only about 50 percent of the suicides in the city. Barraclough (2) reported that if deaths due to undetermined causes are for the most part concealed suicides, the official suicide rate estimated for England may be as much as 22 percent too low.

The fact that only clear-cut cases are reported as suicides in Egypt largely explains the low incidence of suicide in official reports. Under Egyptian law suicide is considered as an act of violence and the perpetrator as liable to prosecution. Official records in the Egyptian Ministry of Interior show 103 suicides in the whole country in 1971, 88 in 1972, and 81 in 1973, and 43, 40, and 40 attempts, respectively, in the same years. It is because these official suicide figures are questionable that we have undertaken to provide more information about the nature and extent of suicide attempts in Egypt.

Psychiatric studies of suicide were not attempted in Egypt before early 1972. Since then two studies have been completed: a survey of the general characteristics of patients who attempted suicide (12), and a retrospective study of the general behavior of a group of people who successfully committed suicide (14). The aim of the latter was to collect data so as to identify the factors that may have played a part in the act of self-destruction. The study includes psychiatric histories of nineteen Egyptian suicides personally attended in clinical practice by the authors, prior to the suicides. The findings of both studies are included here.

Ain Shams University Hospital is located east of Cairo (present population approximately 8 million). Serving a population of about 3 million, it is the major portal of entry for suicide attempters, and its patients cover the full range of social classes and racial groups. We surveyed 200 of the 1,155 persons who, after attempting suicide, were admitted to the hospital's casualty department in 1975. The first 16 or 17 cases admitted in each month were selected for review. Interviews were based on Ain Shams case report forms and on a questionnaire specially designed for this study. It is possible that not all attempted suicides were seen by a psychiatrist; some may have been referred to other physicians or other hospitals. For this reason our data may underreport the true situation. Our definition of suicidal attempts is that set forth by Wexler et al. (18): a suicidal attempt is any intentionally self-inflicted injury unless there is strong evidence, both in circumstances and in the patient's statements, that there was not the slightest ambiguity about the self-destructive intent. Lack of intent was not assumed simply on the basis of the patient's denial, or on the absence of serious risk to life, or on added manipulative elements. Cases of accidental self-injury in which self-destructive intent was only suspected were excluded because the injury was not intentional.

In 1975 the Ain Shams casualty department received a total of 75,931 patients, of whom 1,155 had attempted suicide. The magnitude of the work of this hospital is seen in the fact that its outpatient clinics served 199,507 patients in different medical specialties in the same year. Of these patients, 3,827 came directly to the psychiatric outpatient clinic, excluding those referred from other outpatient clinics for psychiatric consultation.

## ATTEMPTED SUICIDES

As noted above, in an area with about 3 million population there were 1,155 suicide attempts, yielding a crude rate for Cairo of 38.5 per 100,000. It is generally agreed that suicide attempts are roughly eight to ten times as numerous as suicides, so the completed suicide rate in Cairo may be estimated as 3.80 or 3.85 per 100,000.

### Sex

Of the 200 suicide attempters covered by our survey, 123 or 61.5 percent were males and 77 or 38.5 percent were females. Attempts by females may be underreported because in Egypt a suicide or suicidal attempt is considered a stigma that may lower the prospects of marriage for a single girl or bring shame to the husband if she is married. The husband would regard the attempt as a direct insult to his honor and an affront to his ability to protect his wife. Female attempts are therefore more often concealed than male attempts.

Age

We found the highest incident of attempted suicide (60.0 percent) in the 15−24 age group and the second highest (25.5 percent) in the 25−34 bracket (table 14-1). These figures are in accord with the tendency for suicide attempts to be made more often by young people.

Religion

Our survey revealed that 20 percent of the 200 who attempted suicide were Christians, mainly Coptics, in an almost exact correlation with their actual distribution in the population. The only difference was the very low incidence of attempted suicides by female Coptics under the age of 25. The rest of the cases in our sample were Muslims.

Marital Status

Single persons showed the highest rate among our cases (53.0 percent) followed by married persons with 34.0 percent (table 14-2). Widowed persons made the fewest attempts to commit suicide. Married males made more attempts than married females, whereas widows were more likely to attempt suicide than widowers. The 15−24 age group, claiming more than half of those who attempted suicide, is composed mainly of unmarried persons.

Employment and Education

Our survey of 200 cases revealed that students ranked highest with 40.0 percent and that professional people ranked lowest with 6.0 percent (table

TABLE 14-1
AGE DISTRIBUTION IN SAMPLE OF 200 CASES OF
ATTEMPTED SUICIDE, 1975

|            | Suicide attempts | |
| Age group  | Number | Percentage |
|------------|--------|------------|
| 15−24      | 120    | 60.0       |
| 25−34      | 51     | 25.5       |
| 35−44      | 0      | 0.0        |
| 45−65      | 29     | 14.5       |
| Total      | 200    | 100.0      |

SOURCE: Ain Shams University Hospital, Cairo.

14-3). Suicide attempts were made most frequently by those who had a secondary school education and least often by university or technical school graduates (table 14-4).

## Social Class

All social classes were represented in the sample of attempted suicides, but most of the victims came from the middle and lower socioeconomic classes.

## Methods

In 160 of the 200 cases of attempted suicide in Cairo in 1975, or 80 percent, the method chosen was an overdose of drugs, such as tranquilizers, hypnotics, analgesics, and antipyretics. It was the commonest method for both sexes. Poisonous materials, including disinfectants, were used by 10

TABLE 14-2
MARITAL STATUS AND SEX IN SAMPLE OF
200 CASES OF ATTEMPTED SUICIDE, 1975

| Marital status | Suicide attempts | | | |
|---|---|---|---|---|
| | Male | Female | Total | Percentage of total cases |
| Single | 72 | 34 | 106 | 53.0 |
| Married | 35 | 33 | 68 | 34.0 |
| Widowed | 2 | 6 | 8 | 4.0 |
| Divorced | 14 | 4 | 18 | 9.0 |

SOURCE: Ain Shams University Hospital, Cairo.

TABLE 14-3
EMPLOYMENT STATUS IN SAMPLE OF 200 CASES OF
ATTEMPTED SUICIDE, 1975

| Employment status | Suicide attempts | |
|---|---|---|
| | Number | Percentage |
| Student | 80 | 40.0 |
| Housewife | 33 | 16.5 |
| Unskilled worker | 29 | 14.5 |
| Skilled worker | 23 | 11.5 |
| Professional person | 12 | 6.0 |
| Unemployed | 23 | 11.5 |

SOURCE: Ain Shams University Hospital, Cairo.

percent of the patients. Seventeen of the twenty who chose this method were females. The poisons used were mainly phosphorus compounds. The third most common method, overdose of opium and other addictive drugs, was used only by six males (3.0 percent). Other methods—gas, burning, strangulation—were employed in fourteen cases (7.0 percent). (See table 14-5.)

Diagnosis

Depressive illnesses were diagnosed in 126 (63 percent) of the 200 cases (table 14-6). Males were overrepresented (83 cases) owing to their higher ratio in the original sample. Endogenous depression was more frequent in males, whereas reactive depression afflicted more females. Depressive illnesses as a whole were more common among single persons than among married or widowed persons. The majority of cases showed mixed symptoms of depression. Hypochondriacal symptoms were evident in the major-

TABLE 14-4

EDUCATIONAL LEVEL IN SAMPLE OF 200 CASES OF
ATTEMPTED SUICIDE, 1975

|  | Suicide attempts | |
| --- | --- | --- |
| Educational level | Number | Percentage |
| University graduate | 20 | 10.0 |
| Secondary school graduate | 70 | 35.0 |
| Primary school graduate | 37 | 18.5 |
| Technical school graduate | 20 | 10.0 |
| Just literate | 21 | 10.5 |
| Illiterate | 32 | 16.0 |

SOURCE: Ain Shams University Hospital, Cairo.

TABLE 14-5

METHODS USED IN 200 CASES OF ATTEMPTED
SUICIDE IN CAIRO, 1975

|  | Suicide attempts | | | |
| --- | --- | --- | --- | --- |
| Method | Male | Female | Total | Percentage |
| Overdose of drugs | 98 | 62 | 160 | 80.0 |
| Poisonous materials | 3 | 17 | 20 | 10.0 |
| Opium and other addictive drugs | 6 | 0 | 6 | 3.0 |
| Other | 14 | 0 | 14 | 7.0 |

SOURCE: Ain Shams University Hospital, Cairo.

TABLE 14-6
PSYCHIATRIC DIAGNOSIS IN 200 CASES OF ATTEMPTED
SUICIDE IN CAIRO, 1975

| Diagnosis | Suicide attempts | | | |
|---|---|---|---|---|
| | Male | Female | Total | Percentage |
| Depressive illness | 83 | 43 | 126 | 63.0 |
| Hysterical reaction | 6 | 20 | 26 | 13.0 |
| Schizophrenia | 15 | 1 | 16 | 8.0 |
| Personality disorder | 5 | 5 | 10 | 5.0 |
| Drug addiction and alcoholism | 5 | 0 | 5 | 2.5 |
| Situational disorder | 9 | 8 | 17 | 8.5 |

SOURCE: Ain Shams University Hospital, Cairo.

ity of cases; thought and perceptual disorders were infrequent. Ideas of poverty and sin were not uncommon, however, as noticed in depressive cases in Egypt (12). The duration of the spell of illness preceding the attempt was less than four months in 75 percent of the cases and less than eight months in the others.

Hysterical reaction was diagnosed in twenty-six cases (13 percent). Females showed this state more frequently than males and mainly in the age group 15−24. Among those who attempted suicide dissociative symptoms were seen more frequently than conversion reactions. Schizophrenia occurred in sixteen cases: five schizo-affective, four paranoids, two catatonics, two hebephrenics, and three of the simple type. All patients had had their symptoms for more than six months, and nine of the sixteen were not under psychiatric treatment. Personality disorders were diagnosed in ten patients, six of them of the inadequate type with an oversolicitous mother or wife.

Repeated Attempts

Of the 200 patients, 87 percent had made no previous attempt to commit suicide; 5 percent had tried once before, 7 percent, twice, and 1 percent, three times. Only 5 percent of the cases had received psychiatric treatment prior to the attempt. The family history of those who attempted suicide was positive in 17 percent of the cases.

Causes

Attempted suicides were caused either by lack of attention to the person's needs or by loss of the source of dependency through death, divorce, or desertion. Seventeen patients had situational disorders stemming from acute or chronic marital problems. The commonest family problems were friction between husband and wife, infidelity of either or both partners, or stress from financial difficulties. Failure in examinations, unemployment, and job dissatisfactions were other reasons for attempting suicide.

Monthly Incidence

The largest number of the attempted suicides in 1975 came to Ain Shams casualty department in April, May, June, and July. May had the highest number and July the second highest. Total referrals to the casualty wards did not show the same pattern, as they were high from April to December (table 14-7).

There were more males than females in our survey; more suicide attempters were in the age groups 15–24 and 25–45 than in other groups. The majority of patients were under 45 years, probably because this part of an individual's life is particularly subject to stress. Political unrest, overcrowding, housing problems, lack of social support from school, work, and community, and financial difficulties may play an important role. The lack of attempts among the elderly is owing to the respect paid by the younger generation to their elders, who often live with their married children, to family cohesion, and to religious teachings urging the care and the welfare of the elderly. In contrast, the youth are subjected to the stresses of

TABLE 14-7
MONTHLY INCIDENCE OF SUICIDE ATTEMPTERS REFERRED TO
CASUALTY DEPARTMENT IN CAIRO IN 1975,
COMPARED WITH TOTAL REFERRALS AND TOTAL
NUMBER OF PSYCHIATRIC OUTPATIENTS

| Month | Suicide attempters | Total referrals | Psychiatric outpatients |
|---|---|---|---|
| January | 65 | 4,556 | 306 |
| February | 75 | 5,083 | 287 |
| March | 93 | 5,894 | 346 |
| April | 101 | 6,381 | 294 |
| May | 144 | 6,670 | 338 |
| June | 113 | 7,390 | 344 |
| July | 134 | 7,369 | 297 |
| August | 99 | 7,265 | 308 |
| September | 63 | 6,912 | 264 |
| October | 90 | 6,804 | 341 |
| November | 97 | 5,897 | 416 |
| December | 81 | 5,710 | 486 |
| Total | 1,155 | 75,931 | 4,027 |

SOURCE: Ain Shams University Hospital, Cairo.

traditions, adaptation, industrialization, frustrated aspirations, and limited expectations (11).

These conclusions are borne out by other researchers (3, 8), who also found that suicide rates were high among teenagers, reached a peak in young adults, and declined with advancing age. Another team of investigators (10) showed similar results, with a tendency toward an older age in females. They also found a higher rate of suicide attempts among married females, although we found that married males were more likely to try suicide than married females.

Although religion is thought to help prevent suicide, 72 percent of the suicide attempters in our survey were fulfilling their religious duties.

## COMPLETED SUICIDES

Our study of completed suicides from our clinical files covered nineteen cases. Eleven of the victims were female. The suicides were more frequent among younger people, especially females aged 20−39 and males aged 30−39 (table 14-8). Six males and five females were single, but married females, numbering six, were seemingly just as vulnerable. Seventeen victims were Muslims and two were Christian Copts (table 14-9). As twelve of the Muslims were deeply religious, their beliefs did not act as a deterrent. In fact, one of the Muslims considered death as a way of reuniting with God. The Coptic females were also religious.

### Social Class

Seventeen of the suicides in our survey were from the middle class and two were from the upper class.

TABLE 14-8
AGE DISTRIBUTION IN SAMPLE OF NINETEEN CASES
OF SUICIDE IN CAIRO, 1975

| Age group | Males | Females | Total |
|-----------|-------|---------|-------|
| Under 20  | 2     | 1       | 3     |
| 20−29     | 0     | 5       | 5     |
| 30−39     | 3     | 5       | 8     |
| 40−49     | 1     | 0       | 1     |
| 50−59     | 2     | 0       | 2     |
| Total     | 8     | 11      | 19    |

SOURCE: Clinical files of Okasha and Lotaief, Ain Shams University Hospital.

TABLE 14-9
RELIGION OF NINETEEN SUICIDE VICTIMS
IN CAIRO, 1975

| Religion | Males | Females | Total |
|----------|-------|---------|-------|
| Muslim | 8 | 9 | 17 |
| Christian | 0 | 2 | 2 |
| Total | 8 | 11 | 19 |

SOURCE: Clinical files of Okasha and Lotaief, Ain Shams University Hospital, Cairo.

TABLE 14-10
EDUCATIONAL LEVEL OF NINETEEN SUICIDE VICTIMS
IN CAIRO, 1975

| Educational level | Males | Females | Total |
|-------------------|-------|---------|-------|
| Primary school graduate | 1 | 2 | 3 |
| Secondary school graduate | 0 | 4 | 4 |
| University undergraduate | 3 | 0 | 3 |
| University graduate | 4 | 5 | 9 |
| Total | 8 | 11 | 19 |

SOURCE: Clinical files of Okasha and Lotaief, Ain Shams University Hospital, Cairo.

## Education

The majority of the females in our survey had received some schooling, and five of them were university graduates (table 14-10).

## Repeated Attempts

Of the nineteen suicides on whom we had clinical records, nine had made no previous attempt to commit suicide, four had made one attempt, five had made two attempts, and one had made four earlier attempts.

## Methods

The method most often used by those in our sample was an overdose of drugs (used by 7); second was shooting (used by 5). Falling from a height, burning, and drowning each claimed two victims; swallowing a caustic substance was the method chosen by one suicide. (See table 14-11.)

## Diagnosis and Family History

In five of the nineteen cases of suicide (3 females and 2 males) we found a positive family history of psychiatric morbidity, mainly depression and

TABLE 14-11
METHOD OF SUICIDE IN NINETEEN CASES
IN CAIRO, 1975

| Method | Males | Females | Total |
|---|---|---|---|
| Falling from a height | 0 | 2 | 2 |
| Burning | 0 | 2 | 2 |
| Drug overdose | 2 | 5 | 7 |
| Swallowing caustic substance | 0 | 1 | 1 |
| Drowning | 2 | 0 | 2 |
| Shooting | 4 | 1 | 5 |
| Total | 8 | 11 | 19 |

SOURCE: Clinical files of Okasha and Lotaief, Ain Shams University Hospital, Cairo.

schizophrenia. Fourteen victims were diagnosed and treated as having a primary psychiatric illness: ten suffered from depressive illness, two of them from the endogenous type; two, from hysterical reaction; and two, from schizophrenia. Five individuals were depressed because of social and family problems: two had trouble with parents and three with spouses.

Males were fewer than females; the younger age groups had more suicides than older people; most of the victims were married and living with their families; most of them were employed or were going to school. Although this brief survey covers only a small number of persons who succeeded in killing themselves, it points to the necessity of further studies of broader range to obtain knowledge of the characteristics of people who commit suicide.

### Suicide Prevention

Because of lack of interest and a desire not to focus on suicide, no suicide prevention activities have developed in Egypt.

## CASE STUDIES

### Case A

A 36-year-old female graduate of Cairo University, a strictly religious Christian who engaged in all religious activities, came from a family of moderate income. She was happy and contented with her life, though she was not considered a great beauty. At the age of 25 she met a handsome Muslim from a rich family. They fell in love and established a relationship sponsored by her family but rejected by his. She adapted herself to the new situation and gave financial support to her family. As time passed her brothers grew up, obtained good jobs, and bettered their financial situation. They began to object to her relationship with the young man, demanding that she separate from him and accusing her of all sorts of misdeeds, especially of being unfaithful to her religion. Unable to leave each other, she and her friend decided to get married. Her family rejected this step, condemned the marriage as being against religion, and complained more and more of her disregard of her religious beliefs. Thus with no support from her family, she felt cornered and alone; she began to feel depressed and unhappy and to have feelings of sin and guilt. This state of mind led her to isolate herself. The family greeted this behavior happily, thinking that the problem would be solved in their favor. Her husband kept an astonished silence, thinking that he had lost her love. Feeling worse and worse, she finally sacrificed herself by burning herself to death.

### Case B

A nineteen-year-old single man, a student at the university, was the eldest of the children, with a six-year difference between him and the second-oldest child. He liked to be alone, preferring not to mix with other people. He was polite; he was successful in his studies, and his parents had no problems with him. A year before his death he started to feel difficulties in respiration, especially during bathing. He consulted several physicians, but they found no organic pathology to explain his trouble. Four months before his death, when he started to feel depressed, with frequent attacks of feeling morbid and suicidal, he was referred to a psychiatrist. The young man developed an interest in religion, which gradually came to preoccupy him. He was advised to enter psychotherapy, supplemented by antidepressants.

During the course of his treatment he expressed his feelings freely and complained that his father had ill-treated him in his childhood, an allegation that proved to be true. He also expressed discontent that he received less than his brothers did from the family, especially his father, in the way of affection and financial support. Family therapy then began, with father, mother, and younger brothers included. The young man rapidly improved, but not to the extent that treatment could be terminated. As the father sensed his son's improvement, however, he prematurely ordered that treatment be stopped. The patient returned to the psychiatrist in two weeks, severely depressed and unhappy, and was advised to resume treatment. The father wanted to send him to a hospital, but the patient refused. He was reassured, and the treatment using tablets and psychotherapy resumed, with some improvement resulting. Soon afterward the young man drowned himself. The father, who thanked the psychiatrist for his help and expressed grief at his son's death, was clearly relieved that he no longer had to deal with a problem he did not understand.

## CONCLUSION AND SUMMARY

Of 1,155 patients who attempted suicide in 1975 and were admitted to Ain Shams University Hospital in Cairo, from an area populated by approximately 3 million people, 200 were the subject of this study. The crude rate of suicide attempts in Cairo was estimated at 38.5 per 100,000 population, and the rate of completed suicides, at 3.80 to 3.85. The highest incidence was between 15 and 24 years of age (60 percent) and the second highest, between 25 and 44 (25.5 percent). There was only a slight preponderance of males in the sample, possibly reflecting the more urgent need in the culture for females to conceal suicidal attempts. Single patients accounted for 53 percent of the total; students showed the highest risk (40 percent). Depressive illnesses, hysterical reactions, and situational disorders were the main causes of attempts, in that order of frequency. Overdose by tablet ingestion was the most common method used (80 percent).

The larger number of attempts in youth may be owing to the severe stress they encountered in adapting traditional ways to a period of industrialization and in finding their aspirations frustrated even though their expectations were limited. The elderly are respected and protected in Egypt's culture. As most attempters were deeply religious Muslims, religion did not seem to be a deterrent to suicidal behavior.

Official reports on both attempted and completed suicides are misleading. The records of the Ministry of Interior in 1971, 1972, and 1973 listed 103, 88, and 81 cases of suicide, respectively, and 43, 40, and 40 cases of attempted suicide. Thus the official annual report for the whole of Egypt lists fewer attempted suicides than were admitted in one month to Ain Shams University Hospital.

## BIBLIOGRAPHY

1. Bagley, C. Causes and prevention of repeated attempted suicide. *Social and Economic Administration*, 4 (1970):322−330.
2. Barraclough, B. M. Poisoning cases: Suicide or accident? *Brit. J. Psychiatry*, 124 (1974):526−530.
3. Burke, A. W. Clinical aspects of attempted suicide among women in Trinidad and Tobago. *Brit. J. Psychiatry*, 125 (1974):175−176.
4. Dabbagh, F. *Death: A Choice*. Beirut, 1968.
5. Dublin, L. I. *Suicide: A Sociological and Statistical Study*. New York: Ronald Press, 1963.
6. Egypt. *Social Security Reports* (1970, 1971, 1972).
7. Fox, R. Consultant psychiatrist report. In *Annual Report of the Samaritans, 1969−1970*. London, 1970.
8. Kennedy, P., N. Kreitman, and I. Overstone. The prevalence of suicide and parasuicide in Edinburgh. *Brit. J. Psychiatry*, 124 (1974):36−41.
9. Kessel, N. Self-poisoning. *Brit. Med. J.* (1965):1265−1270, 1336−1340.

10. Kreitman, N., P. Smith, and E. Tan. Attempted suicides as a language: An empirical study. *Brit. J. Psychiatry*, 116 (1970):465—473.
11. Okasha, A. Trials and turmoils of youth in developing countries. Paper read at 6th World Congress of Psychiatry, Honolulu, 1977.
12. Okasha, A., M. Kamel, and A. Hassan. Preliminary psychiatric observations in Egypt. *Brit. J. Psychiatry*, 114 (1978):949—955.
13. Okasha, A., and F. Lotaief. Attempted suicide in Egypt. *Acta Psychiatr. Scand.* In press.
14. Okasha, A., and F. Lotaief. *A Retrospective Study of Suicide in Egypt.* Forthcoming.
15. Samaan, M. *Suicidal Behaviour in Cairo: A Psycho-social Study.* Cairo: Dar el Maaref, 1963.
16. Schneidman, E. S. Current overview of suicide. In *Suicidology: Contemporary Development*, ed. E. S. Schneidman. New York: Grune and Stratton, 1976.
17. Stengel, E. *Suicide and Attempted Suicide.* Harmondsworth: Penguin Books, 1969.
18. Wexler, L., M. Weissman, and S. Kasl. *Suicide Attempts, 1970—1975: Updating a United States Study and Comparisons with International Trends.* 1978.
19. World Health Organization. *W.H.O. Statistical Report 21.* No. 6. 1968.

# CONCLUSION

In summary, the suicide profile in Asia is the opposite of the Western profile in that in most countries the largest number of suicides occur in youth and that the number decreases with age. Females account for a higher proportion of suicides and attempted suicides than in Western countries.

In all the countries covered in this report, the number of completed suicides is consistently high among young people below the age of 30. The age group most frequently showing suicidal behavior is 15–24, followed by the 20–29 group. In some countries there is a sizable proportion of suicides in the age range 10–19: Jordan, 39.6 percent; India, 15.3 percent; Sri Lanka, approximately 30.0 percent; Japan, 18.4 percent; Taiwan; and Thailand.

In Asian countries, in contrast with Western countries, the incidence of suicide declines with age, especially after 30–35. There are a few exceptions, countries with a U-curve such as Japan's, or a modified version thereof. In Japan the curve reaches a very high peak over the age of 60, particularly among females. In Thailand, with a modified U-curve, suicides increase in an irregular pattern at age 55–60, then decline, and rise again at age 74. The latter rise does not reach a number equal to that for the 20–25 age group; it may be a third less. The Sri Lanka curve is more like Japan's in that it lacks the intervening peaks of Thailand's curve and begins to descend at age 30 and to rise at age 60. At age 70 it equals the youthful peak and then surpasses it at age 80 for males. Female rates in Taiwan approximate a U-curve.

It has been suggested the high incidence of suicide among Japan's aged people is owing to sociocultural changes in that country. As the nuclear family has become increasingly common, the protection given to elders by the extended family has diminished. In addition, traditional modes of life have changed, with the result that elderly persons may feel displaced and alienated. These explanations do not serve for Thailand, where older persons continue to enjoy the respect of and protection from their families and kin; moreover, they often have a valued place in the house as caretaker for children whose parents have to go to work. Another benefit for elders is that Thailand is not as deeply committed to Westernization and industrialization as is Japan, although those living in urban areas may find less security because of urbanization and the trend toward Western styles. In Sri Lanka the extended family system is still strong and elderly persons have an honored place. Suicides among the elderly are therefore not attributable to displacement and alienation. An investigation of a small number of aged Sri Lankans who committed suicide revealed no particular pattern. Organic disease, grief reaction, alcoholism, and economic problems were approximately equal as causes of suicide. Unfortunately, the data presently available do not fully answer the questions about suicidal behavior in Sri Lanka.

There is no significant difference in the age pattern of attempted suicides and completed suicides. Young persons aged 10−29 have the greatest risk of attempts, and the age range is likely to be lower than for completed suicides. In Jordan 50.4 percent of the attempted suicides were 10−19 years old; in Kuwait, 43.7 percent were in the 15−19 group in 1978; in Taiwan, 19.0 percent were in the 15−19 range; in Japan, 11.1 percent were in the same range; in Pakistan, 40.9 percent were between the ages of 11 and 20; 91 of 198 attempted suicides in India were between 10 and 19 years of age; about 30 percent of the attempted suicides surveyed in Iran were in the 10−19 age group; in Syria about 10 percent of those who attempted suicide were under 15 years of age, and about three-fourths of them were females. An interesting feature of Syrian attempted suicides was that about 10 percent were over 40, with males and females equally divided.

It is likely that the high suicide rates among young people are related to the rigidity of the cultural systems in countries where older persons are in a dominant position and where vital decisions—choosing a marital partner, finding employment, selecting a domicile, for example—may be made against the wishes of the young. In most Asian countries young people are expected to meet a specific cultural norm, and those who do not are subjected to hostility and criticism. For most young people the age span 15−24 is the period in which to assert their own individuality, to achieve recognition as a separate identity, and to carve out a respected place within family and community.

The normal surge of self-assertion and rebelliousness of the teenager or young adult is likely to be in full tide at these ages and, if identity and self-esteem are submerged in favor of other persons, aggressiveness develops and needs to find expression. The aggression may be self-directed if all other avenues of possible adjustment are closed and thus may lead to suicide attempts in an effort to punish and threaten the authority figures. It is noteworthy that attitudes toward attempted suicide and completed suicide are significantly different in most of these countries. The family regards a consummated suicide as bringing shame, disgrace, and dishonor upon the surviving members. On the other hand, when a suicide is attempted, the family is frequently supportive, concerned, understanding, and conciliatory. Attempted suicide may be the court of last resort for youth. The serious attempter who dies may fantasize his coming death as a means of ultimately obtaining sympathy and acceptance.

Concern about attempted suicides of young people has been increasing in the United States. In Western countries, where experimentation and self-expression are more prevalent and where a much wider range of expression of ego needs is possible, the problem seems to be more one of confusion of goals and standards than of opposition to authority. The 1960s demonstrated that youth is willing and able in Western countries to defy authority and its views. The problem then becomes one of asserting other goals, standards, and life-styles to supplant those recently attacked. It is obvious from the cultural descriptions and psychological autopsies presented here that youth in Asian countries face an entirely different situation, that rebellion and self-assertiveness are not feasible.

## SEX RATIOS

In Western countries the proportion of male suicides is higher than that of females. Although the gap in other Western countries may not be so wide as in the United States (between 3 and 4 males to 1 female), in general females are less prone to suicide. Asian statistics show that the differences in rates between males and females are much smaller; in fact, the rates are practically equal in a number of countries. In Egypt, Pakistan, Syria, Japan, and Singapore the overall male and female deaths are approximately the same. In Jordan male suicides accounted for 58 percent of the total; in India, for 62 percent. In Thailand, male rates range between 4 and 5 per 100,000 population, while in 1975 the female rate was 4.8 per 100,000, showing a significant and steady increase in female suicides. The Iraqi government statistics show that more males than females committed suicide; the Taiwan male:female ratio was 1.5:1. Two countries reported a higher ratio of males to females: 2.6:1 in Sri Lanka and 3.6:1 in Kuwait. In a number of Middle East countries, however, female suicides were likely to be concealed more than male suicides and therefore to be underreported to government bureaus. The reason for the disparity is that the family status is damaged more by female suicides than by male suicides.

In Western countries there are more attempted suicides by females than by males. This Western pattern is followed by Taiwan and Japan, where female attempts are three times those of males, but in other Asian countries the male:female ratio is much less disproportionate. Thailand has 2 females to 1 male in nonserious attempts, but as the lethality of the attempt increases the ratio lessens until it is approximately 1:1. Iran and Kuwait show ratios of approximately 1 male to 1.5 females; Iran, 1:1.5; Kuwait, 1:1.6. The ratio is 1:1 in India and Pakistan.

Three Arabic countries show a preponderance of females but not to a large degree. In Syria, 62 percent of attempts were by females, and in

Jordan, 52 percent; in Iraq more attempts were by females than by males. The exceptions to the rule are Sri Lanka and Egypt, where males exceeded females in attempts. Sri Lanka reported a male:female ratio of 1.9:1, and in Egypt 61.5 percent of the attempters were male. The latter figure is probably inaccurate, however, and in reality the female proportion is substantially higher.

There can be little doubt that the preponderance of female over male suicides is related to the status of women in Asian countries, most of whom have less freedom—legally, socially, and culturally—than do men. The major problems encountered by women, as described in these reports, center on marriage and divorce, marital friction, in-law problems, infertility which in Arab nations is related to divorce, and disappointments in love. Marriages are usually arranged by parents on an economic basis rather than on personal choice. The options for women to refuse marriages they do not want, for support should they be divorced, and for status in the society other than as wife and mother are limited. Japan and Singapore may be moving in the direction of greater freedom of choice for a woman, but countries in central Asia and in the Middle East maintain the strict traditional roles of women as inferior and submissive beings.

According to Durkheim, marriage is an institution that favors men and disadvantages women, a view that must have been considered revolutionary in his time. "Conjugal society, so disadvantageous for women, must even in the absence of children, be admitted to be advantageous to men. . . . It (marriage) is supposed to have been originated for the wife to protect her weakness against masculine caprice: actually whatever historical causes may have made him accept this restriction [monogamy] he benefits more by it." Durkheim's point is that marriage itself is not a preservative factor against suicide but that children and the family are the preservative, from which primarily males benefit. As he says, "In itself conjugal society is harmful to the woman and aggravates her tendency to suicide. . . . In general, the wife profits less from family life than the husband."[1]

Durkheim, by contrasting countries in which divorce is permitted with those in which it is prohibited came to the conclusion that female suicides lessen as divorces increase and vice versa: "In France where until recently marriage was not weakened by divorce, the inflexible rule it imposed on women was a very heavy, profitless yoke for them." And again, "From the standpoint of suicide, marriage is more favorable to the wife the more widely practised divorce is and vice versa"; "Turning to peoples among

[1]E. Durkheim, *Suicide* (Glencoe: Free Press, 1951), pp. 275, 188.

whom the institution of divorce is widespread, woman gains by marriage and man loses."[2]

The data in Asian countries seem to support Durkheim's views. Many attempted and completed suicides are women's protests against unwanted marriages. In Arabic countries such a protest is often manifested by a woman's burning herself to death, a method that is certainly forceful and dramatic. Such suicides have occurred in India, Syria, Iraq, and Jordan. A large number of female self-poisonings are based on marital problems: infidelity of the husband, abuse, quarrels over interference from the extended family, the mother-in-law's criticism, and the like. The age discrepancy between a young wife and an older husband often leads to marital difficulties.

Divorces may be obtained by women in Arabic countries, but most commonly women are divorced by their husbands. Although divorced women find themselves in an unenviable position, both socially and financially, many of them, especially in Jordan, prefer to remain in that status rather than remarry. No doubt a large proportion of Muslim women are deterred from divorce not only by law but also by lack of alternatives for the future. Another significant reason is a woman's certainty that she will lose her children to their father. Muslim religious law is a compelling disadvantageous factor for women who are unhappy in marriage, often leading them to attempt suicide.

Divorces in Southeast Asia and central Asia are difficult for women, who face serious financial problems, especially if they are allowed to keep the children. Divorced women are also socially disadvantaged, as they have been in Western societies until very recently. In the West, women's situation has improved largely because more economic opportunities are open to them and because public attitudes have changed. Asian women who choose not to incur the disadvantages of divorce or who feel unable to leave a painful conjugal situation may see suicide as the only avenue of escape.

Durkheim, almost inferentially, mentions a type of suicide which comes close to the condition of Asian youth and females: "There is a type of suicide the opposite of anomic. It is the suicide deriving from excessive regulation, that of persons with futures pitilessly blocked and passions violently choked by oppressive discipline. . . . Do not the suicides of slaves, which are said to be frequent under certain conditions, belong to this type, or all suicides attributable to excessive physical or moral despotism—a rule against which there is no appeal. We might call it fatalistic suicide."

Asian women may be under constant domination and have restricted opportunities for self-determination, but this condition exists for young

[2]Ibid., pp. 189, 274, 269.

males as well. In patriarchal systems and in very rigid cultures, the man is often severely limited in his actions by his elders and others in positions of authority. In Japan, for example, a young man must meet strict standards of performance; he is not allowed to show a spirit of rebellion or to try an individualistic approach to a situation. In many Asian cultures a young man may not challenge an elder in the important areas of choice of career, marriage, place of residence, or opinions on family and economic matters. The expectations for performance and for success are higher for a young man than for his sister, although in different facets of life, and failure is keenly felt.

Many a young man has had to give up his plans for study or a career in order to take over family responsibilities when his father dies, and he may have to assume the burden not only of his immediate family but also of relatives. An eldest son is expected to be willing and ready to assume some responsibility for his siblings even before the father's death. Disappointments in a marriage choice or in hopes for a desired career, and strong demands for success to please others, are not easy to tolerate. Males in patriarchal cultures are allowed the outlets of sexual alliances and drinking, to some extent, but these panaceas may not be an effective relief for thwarted self-assertion. The frequency of suicide attempts by young Asian men is at once a measure of the conflicts that exist within the social systems in Eastern countries and an argument for increased self-determination.

Durkheim based his differentiation of suicidal types on sociological data of large societal conditions. At the time when his book was published, Freud's ideas about psychological functioning were not generally accepted. The Asian suicides described in this volume do not appear to fit Durkheim's types. In my opinion a more accurate description would be a psychological one that includes the sociological setting.

Psychologically, the most basic human need is the establishment of a personal identity that is respected and recognized both by the individual and by others, particularly close family members. Equally vital is a sense of control over one's life and destiny. Societies with hierarchical systems which are based on unalterable factors such as sex and age and give minimal allowance for individuation exert strong pressure on those not automatically selected for the elite. In Asia these categories are the young, females, and the poor. Family frictions therefore frequently provide the stimulus for suicides and suicide attempts, since in this area young people and females are least able to assert their egos and determine their own futures. The stricter and the more rigid the authoritative controlling system, the more suicide attempts will be made and, in all likelihood, the higher the incidence of psychosomatic illnesses. Suicide attempts may not be only self-directed aggression; they may express as well aggressiveness toward the controlling power. If prevention of suicides is to be effective, societal changes are necessary in order to provide alternatives for youths and females in the area of self-determination.

## SUICIDE RATES

It comes as no surprise that official government figures on suicide in Asian countries are found to be inaccurate and to understate the actual incidence. Suicide statistics in all countries are believed to be inaccurate, as Dublin, Sainsbury, Stengel, Farberow, and others have pointed out. In Asian statistics, however, the size of the discrepancy is noteworthy. In India government statistics showed a suicide rate of 6 to 8 per 100,000 population, yet coroner's autopsy figures yielded an annual rate of 33 to 43 for Madurai alone in the years 1958–1962. The death certificates surveyed by Bussaratid revealed a suicide rate of 15 per 100,000 in Thailand, whereas the official rate was 4.9. In Iran the number of suicide deaths in one small city in ten months was half the number officially reported for a year in a city ten times its size. The number of attempted suicides by poisoning alone in a three-year period in Tehran was from 70 to 108 times as large as the average number of suicide deaths officially reported for the same period. The number of suicide cases treated at Ain Shams Hospital in Cairo in one month was higher than the total of suicidal deaths reported for all Egypt in a year.

No doubt differences in ways of reporting deaths, in budgets assigned to statistical departments, and in official views of the value of demographic statistics, combined with other bureaucratic problems, have contributed to the inaccuracy of official reports. It is more likely, however, that the inaccuracy stems from the attitudes within a country toward suicide. As several researchers have pointed out, people in Arabic countries prefer not to think about suicide; they wish it were nonexistent so as to accord with cultural norms and expectations. If suicide is supposed not to be a problem, it is as well not to pursue data too energetically.

The biggest problem, however, seems to be concealment of suicides, chiefly for economic and psychological rather than religious reasons. As family prestige ultimately depends on power and wealth, Muslims and other Asians conceal suicides in order to maintain the family's repute, which affects marriageability of the children and social ranking within the community. Psychologically and economically, suicides may hurt the family. Burial practices in which direct religious prohibitions may be involved do not seem to be a significant problem even if the dead person committed suicide. In countries where laws against suicide are actively prosecuted by the police, as in Pakistan, it is important to conceal attempts or suicides to protect the family from interrogation and prevent threats from the authorities. The low rates cited for Muslim suicides reflect these family needs for concealment. Medical men find reasons to list a suicide as an accident in order to spare a grieving and distraught family from further harassment by authorities.

## METHODS

The chief methods of suicide in Asian countries are seemingly drug overdoses and poisoning, especially by insecticides and agricultural pesticides. Poisons and pills are used by 51 percent of suicides in Taiwan; in Thailand the primary methods are pills and poisons. Hanging is a popular method in Japan, however, as are also gas and drowning. In Singapore the most frequently used method is jumping from high buildings; next come hanging, poisoning, and drowning, in that order. Hanging is frequently used in Taiwan (18 percent), Thailand, and Singapore. Drowning is employed in Japan, Taiwan, and Singapore. Firearms are used in Thailand but not in the other Southeast Asian countries.

In central Asia—Sri Lanka, India, Iran, and Pakistan—suicides use drugs and poisons. Sri Lanka's second most frequent method is hanging; India's is drowning. Self-burning occurs in Sri Lanka, Pakistan, and India.

Suicides in the Middle East are primarily by pills and poisons, as in Egypt, Syria, Jordan, and Kuwait. This method ranks second in Iraq. In Jordan and Iraq, suicides frequently use firearms, and self-burning— usually by women—is found in Jordan, Syria, and Iraq.

A medication overdose may be a possible resort when drugs can be obtained without difficulty, as they can in Japan and Singapore. It is difficult to account for the prevalence of deaths by jumping in Singapore, for residents there could just as easily die less violently by using pills, which are not hard to obtain. The same is true of hanging in Japan, where drug overdoses are also possible. The theory that a method is chosen because of its availability therefore does not explain these suicides in Japan and Singapore.

People who take agricultural poisons may have few other methods to choose from, except for hanging and drowning. Insecticides and pesticides may mean a painful death, a fact of which suicides may not be aware.

There is some evidence that women who burned themselves to death were not aware of the possibility of pain. The method is generally used by illiterate and lower-class women who feel it is certain to accomplish the desired end, and in fact few do survive. A traditional element seems to be present in such suicidal actions, but its exact meaning is not clear. I have questioned a number of professional persons in burn centers about this phenomenon and its meaning, but I have not obtained answers that seem definitive or helpful. One problem in this kind of investigation is that few such suicides survive to speak for themselves.

As firearms seem no more readily available in Iraq or Jordan than in similar countries in the Middle East, the reason for the choice of this method is unclear. Firearms are employed by men almost exclusively, for women tend to use less violent means of killing themselves. Choice of method on the basis of availability is not demonstrable from the Asian data gathered by contributors to this volume.

Drug overdoses and poison ingestion are apparently the preferred methods in attempted suicides. Poisons include agricultural, household, and industrial varieties. Suicide attempters are able to estimate roughly the lethality of these means, but unsophisticated persons may easily underestimate the damage potential. In Japan and Thailand a number of attempts were made by stabbing. In general, suicide attempters use less lethal means and are apt to make their attempts in situations where they are likely to be discovered in time.

## REASONS FOR SUICIDES AND SUICIDE ATTEMPTS

The most common precipitating cause for suicidal acts is interpersonal problems. Among them, family problems, a category including marital friction, child-parent disagreements, extended family disputes, and in-law troubles, stand first. The second-largest category is disappointments in love, a cause found in all countries, especially among young people. In several countries, however, unhappy love affairs motivated older people as well.

Failure in examinations is generally listed separately as a cause, but data here reported indicate that such a failure is either a blow to interfamilial relations or a loss of economic and financial advantage. Probably the latter also raises problems in familial relationships.

Poverty and economic failure constitute a significant factor in suicidal behavior. Data from Japan suggest a high rate of suicide among the economically disadvantaged and the unemployed. Similar findings are reported for India, Singapore, Jordan, and Syria. As Dr. Rao observes, the Asiatic does not cling to life in spite of extreme poverty but frequently suicides because of it.

Psychiatrists tend to list causes for suicide in medical-psychiatric terms such as psychosis, neurosis, depression, and the like. This practice is understandable as it is consonant with their training and usual diagnostic procedures, but it does not clarify the personal reasons for suicide. Nor does it lend itself to suicide prevention activities, which obviously cannot be directed toward the elimination of psychosis, for example. The question whether mental disorders are organically or environmentally based is a complex one, and every researcher sees the circumstances of a suicide in his particular frame of reference. For a wider perspective, it is useful to view the suicide as a person responding to idiosyncratic personal factors, including constitutional makeup, interpersonal and interfamilial relationships, and wider socioeconomic and cultural influences. These elements combine to determine whether or not an individual can find a viable solution to his or her dilemma. A number of the contributors to this volume have delineated factors that a community or a society might seek to change in order to decrease suicides among their members.

Family problems rank high among the precipitating factors for female suicides and attempted suicides. This response is in conformity with the position of Asian women in the family and in the culture, which is quite different from that of Western women. Even in countries where women are in the work force in significant numbers, as in Japan, Taiwan, Singapore, and Iraq, family difficulties rank as a prominent cause of suicide. Such frictions occur in all societies, but the dominant factor in Asia seems to be the inflexibility of the social systems, which offer few alternatives for alleviation of distress. Family problems were also high in the statistics on male suicidal acts, suggesting that the same strictures seriously affect them.

Unhappy love affairs may attract more attention than their numbers warrant, and in the last analysis many of the frictions attributed to love affairs may be parent-child and family problems, except for cases of abandonment and rejection. Suicides and attempts related to unwanted arranged marriages seem to differ little from those related to love affairs, so that the underlying problem is the ability or inability to choose one's own destiny.

Failure in examinations is a serious problem affecting suicidal behavior in Japan, but again it seems to hark back to family relationships, especially with the mother. Student failures are more important in Japan than elsewhere, for, although they are among the causes of suicide in India, Syria, and Egypt, for example, they rank lower there than in Japan.

Poverty is a prevalent cause of suicide in Asia. Unemployment, marginal employment, and low-paying jobs are behind a significant number of suicides, especially in Japan, India, Taiwan, Singapore, and Jordan. Poverty is often the cause of multiple suicides in Japan and in India. Iran reportedly also has multiple suicides for this reason, but it was impossible to obtain an accurate account from the coroner's office.

Education

Another indication of the significance of financial factors is the educational level of those who commit suicide. In general, there are few suicides by professionals and highly skilled persons or by those in managerial positions. Most suicides have had primary and possibly secondary education, but substantial numbers are illiterate. It may be argued that the families of those in a comfortable financial position are better able to conceal suicides and suicide attempts. This possibility suggests that data about educational levels should be viewed with some caution.

### Urban Versus Rural Residence

The area of residence could not be consistently surveyed because nationwide statistics were not always obtainable. A number of reports concern larger cities, such as Karachi, Tehran, and Cairo, because detailed information could be gathered only where organizations and facilities existed for a study of suicide. Some data are available for Japan and Sri Lanka, where completed suicides in rural areas were more common than in urban areas. For the other countries the data are inconclusive. In some of them it would be almost impossible to determine the rural incidence of suicide because of reporting problems owing back to the bureaucratic situation and to more serious efforts at concealment in the countryside.

### Marital Status

Since the largest number of suicides and attempts were by persons in the 15—24 age group, the comparison of married with single persons is almost meaningless, for normally people under 20 are apt to be unmarried in many of these societies. There is a widely held misconception that marriages in Asia take place at very early ages, and that may have been true several generations ago. Now, however, the marriage age is rising, particularly in urban areas where there are more possibilities to obtain an education or technical training. Older people who commit suicide are likely to be widowed or divorced, but few fall into this age category. The majority of those aged 25 and over are married, and yet there is a noteworthy incidence of suicidal behavior between the ages of 25 and 40. According to Durkheim, the presence of children rather than the conjugal state was the preservative factor. Most married individuals in the 25—40 age group have children, yet this is not always a deterrent. Dr. Sathyavathi's study of multiple suicides in India show that married couples commit suicide in spite of children and Dr. Al-Hakim found that most married persons who committed suicide had three to five children.

In Western countries single status usually implies a degree of isolation. As various reports in this study have demonstrated, single status in Asian countries where the extended family remains a force does not mean cessation of family contacts or lack of integration into the social fabric of the extended family. Single persons may live at home or may have separate habitations, but visiting and social intercourse continue among both close and extended family members.

## RELIGION

The data presented in these reports are not conclusive evidence that religion is a preservative against suicide. Part of the problem, of course, is the different interpretations of religion in different countries, the mixture of religious and ethical systems as in Singapore and Taiwan, and the varying emphases on beliefs. Even more important is the degree of religiosity, which is difficult to evaluate for a country as a whole. An accurate estimation is hardly possible. The Japanese, for example, inherit Buddhist and Shintoist beliefs, but the varieties of Buddhist doctrine there range from the strict and severe Zen Buddhism, for example, to Amida Buddhism, which alleges that simply calling on Amida's name assures salvation or entrance into a better world. Islam appears to be more homogeneous in its attitude toward suicide.

Near Eastern Muslim countries that have a Christian population should theoretically have a high rate of Christian suicides, as do Western Christian countries, such as Catholic Austria. Attempted suicides in Egypt, however, were 80 percent Muslim and 20 percent Christian, the same as the proportion of Christians in the population. Of the Muslims, 72 percent were fulfilling their religious duties. Christians accounted for about 10 percent of the completed suicides; the Muslims making up the remaining 90 percent were religious and observant. Syrian Christians committed suicide less often than their proportion in the total population of Syria would suggest. In Jordan, Muslims were responsible for 90.3 percent of the completed suicides and Christians, for 9.7 percent, a figure only slightly above their proportion (7.5 percent) in the population. Of attempted suicides in Jordan, 93 percent were Muslim and 7 percent were Christian. In Kuwait most suicidal acts were perpetrated by Arabs, by inference Muslims; 4 percent were attributable to non-Arabs.

These reports show that Muslim suicides in the Middle East ranged from 1.1 per 100,000 (1968) to 1.6 (1975) in Jordan and from 3.85 to 4.80 in Egypt (1978); they stood at 3.08 in Kuwait (1978) and at 5.60 in Iran (1972). Attempted suicides ranged from 146 per 100,000 (Iran) to 17.93 per 100,000 (Kuwait). A difficulty with these figures is that all researchers point out the high rate of concealment of suicidal acts, for various reasons. In Southeast Asia, Singapore reported 1.7 per 100,000 for Muslim Malay males and 1.0 for females (1968–1971).

## CHINESE ETHNIC GROUPS

Similar ethnic groups that may be compared are the Chinese in Taiwan, Singapore, and Hong Kong. It is noteworthy that although many of the suicidal death patterns are comparable as to age and sex factors, the overall patterns are quite dissimilar. The present Hong Kong suicide profile is also unlike that reported by Yap for 1953—1954. Perhaps the clearest way of showing the variations among these three countries is by a tabular arrangement.

|  | Singapore | Hong Kong | Taiwan |
|---|---|---|---|
| Overall rate per 100,000 population | 7—16 | 11—14 | 9—16 |
| Age group With highest rate | 20—30 | 60 and over | 20—24 |
| With low rate | 30—45 | 30—45 | 30—50 |
| With high rate | 60—70 | 20—30 | 60—65 |
| Sex ratio | Males predominate; more females in 15—24 age group; more males 35 and over | More male deaths; more females in 10—19 age group; more males 40 and over | More male deaths; females high in 20—24 age group; more males in 60—70 age group |

It is unfortunate that no information could be obtained from mainland China, although I attempted to do so on my visits there. Yap reported that in 1917 a survey of Peking found the rate in that city to be 15.5 per 100,000 population.[3] The present People's Republic of China undoubtedly has more urgent matters at hand than the compilation of suicide statistics. My discussions in various parts of China elicited two themes from my informants: (1) frequent suicides resulted from harassment and humiliation during the Cultural Revolution; (2) suicides and attempted suicides occur among lovers who are opposed or thwarted by their families.

The suicide prevention centers in Singapore, Hong Kong, and Taiwan have found that the major stressful concerns of their clients are unhappy interpersonal relationships with family or spouses and boy-girl love affairs. Wives in Hong Kong and Singapore are upset about concubines and husbands who gamble. The second most significant percentage comprises people concerned about economic problems.

[3]S. A. Gamble and J. S. Burgess, *Peking: A Social Survey* (New York, 1921), pp. 116, 117, 416.

## SUICIDE PREVENTION

Statistics from the Samaritans and other suicide prevention centers reveal that many persons suffer from severe emotional stresses, usually caused by interpersonal frictions but also by financial and job-related problems. These depressed people are often young persons in the 15−29 age group, and a major proportion of them are female. It is useful to observe that the kinds of desperate people served by these centers correspond to the suicide attempters seen at treatment centers, for the comparison defines the target population that must be reached if the suicide toll is to be decreased. In general, middle-aged persons are not a high-risk group, and in some countries neither are the elderly. In rapidly changing societies, as in Japan, however, older people are a suicide risk when traditional resources are no longer available.

I believe that suicide prevention centers and crisis centers in medical and nonmedical settings would provide more succinct and helpful information if their statistical tabulations were standardized by mutual consent. In collating raw data given to me I found that many descriptive entries could have been put together under general headings of family problems, marital discord, parental difficulties, unhappy love affairs, financial hardships, and so on. Ages were bracketed in different groupings, such as 20−29, 20−24, 25−34, and even in wider ranges. Standardizing ages in five- or ten-year intervals—20−24, 35−39, or 20−29, 40−49—would yield a more accurate picture of the critical age of persons who attempt and commit suicide. By providing a format that personnel could check in columns, centers and agencies would get more comprehensive and incisive results and would certainly be more efficient.

Efforts to diminish suicides and attempts should therefore be directed mainly at the young and those related to them. In view of the research findings, preventive measures should begin in primary and secondary schools and continue through the university. To change attitudes toward suicide probably means that one must learn how to cope constructively with conflict situations, a process that involves parents and authorities in schools and other agencies. Many social attitudes are culturally determined and change very slowly without intercession by both governmental and popular movements.

Centers for brief psychotherapy treatments and longer-term counseling centers need to be established for suicidal individuals and their families. Their efficacy would depend partly on the individuals' willingness to accept trained assistance, an attitude that can be created by government and by community effort. Precisely because the causes of suicidal behavior are rooted in the family, problems are often not constructively dealt with there but must be tackled by trained volunteers or professionals. As Asia has few such centers, a vigorous training program is needed to train personnel to staff counseling agencies. Voluntary groups patterned on family service agencies could be established, and it is evident that a nucleus exists for that kind of community effort. In the United States voluntary agencies have often paved the way for social services later provided by government, by showing what could be done and by creating a model counseling service.

A fairly recent development in the United States, especially in the Western states, has considerable potential. The Parental Stress hot lines are designed to offer parents a means of ventilating the emotional stress they typically experience in raising children; the volunteers manning the lines offer emotional support and suggestions for coping with the problems. Primary and secondary schools have instituted psychological counseling services for students obviously depressed or disturbed by family problems. Parents are included in a three-way effort to resolve difficulties. Marital counseling is increasingly sought to improve the ability of spouses to cooperate and be constructive in their attitudes and behavior. Established health or educational centers would be a logical starting point for similar services in Asia.

Another service offers temporary refuge to physically abused women and children in a community-supported center. Activity and drop-in centers for elderly persons provide opportunities for meeting with other older persons, facilities such as a game room and a reading room, and simple but nourishing meals. Transportation is often arranged by volunteers so that single or widowed older persons can participate as they wish. Religious organizations sometimes sponsor these centers for the psychologically and physically needy; others are supported by a community or by voluntary service groups.

Since the suicide potential is highest among the least privileged—the young, the poor, and females—governmental action seems essential for remedial services. In particular, the plight of the poor, especially the aged poor, is largely the province of government. Unhappy and deprived persons threaten the stability of government and affect the productivity of the nation as a whole. Authorities in power have to take the responsibility for passing laws to prevent injustices to certain groups and to equalize, insofar as possible, the opportunities available to youth and to women.

Suicide prevention centers have made a significant contribution to the welfare of their communities. Although it may not be demonstrable that these centers affect the suicide rate, yet everyone must know from his own experience how much benefit is derived from a respectful, caring, and helpful person when one is either psychologically or practically in trouble. Contact with a volunteer serving in such a center may prevent a suicide or a psychosomatic disturbance or may alleviate the misery of a continuing depression.

The information in this volume, obviously gathered with extreme difficulty, gives only the general outlines of suicidal behavior in Asian countries. I hope that the many gaps in the data will stimulate future researchers to work in the field and thus contribute to a wider understanding, in these countries and elsewhere, of the serious problem of suicide and its prevention.

# Index

Designer: UC Press Staff
Compositor: Trend Western
Printer: Thomson-Shore
Binder: Thomson-Shore
Text: 10/12 Janson
Display: Bodoni

★ Moscow

★ Bucharest

*Black Sea*

*Caspian Sea*

JLGARIA

thens

★ Ankara

TURKEY

Nicosia

SYRI

CYPRUS

Crete
(Gr.)

Beirut

Damascus ★

IRAQ

Baghdad ★

LEBANON

ISRAEL

★ Amman

Cairo ★

JORDAN

EGYPT

Kabul

AFGHANISTAN

Islāmābād ★

Chinese line
of control

Indian
claim

IRAN

PAKISTAN

New Delhi
★

NI

Kat

KUWAIT
★ Kuwait

Iraq–Saudi Arabia
Neutral Zone

BAHRAIN

Manama ★

QATAR
★ Doha

OMAN

Abu Dhabi
★

Riyadh
★

UNITED ARAB
EMIRATES

★ Muscat

SAUDI ARABIA

OMAN

INDIA

*Red Sea*

no defined boundary

Khartoum
★

Sanaa
★

YEMEN
(ADEN)

*Arabian Sea*

*Socotra
(Yemen-A)*

Lakshadweep
(India)

SUDAN

YEMEN
(SANAA)

Djibouti ★ DJIBOUTI

★ Aden

ETHIOPIA

★
Addis Ababa

SRI LAN

Colombo ★

SOMALIA

★ Male

MALDIVES

UGANDA

Kampala
★

KENYA

★ Mogadishu

*Equator*

RWANDA ★ Kigali

BURUNDI ★ Bujumbura

★ Nairobi

★ Victoria

British Indian
Ocean Territory
(U.K.)

TANZANIA

★ Dar es Salaam

SEYCHELLES

*INDIAN*

MALAWI

Lilongwe ★

Moroni
★

Glorioso Islands
(Fr.)

ZAMBIA

Lusaka ★

COMOROS

*OCEAN*

Salisbury ★

Juan de Nova
Island
(Fr.)

Tromelin Island
(Fr.)

ZIMBABWE

MOZAMBIQUE

Bassas
da India
(Fr.)

Antananarivo
★

Saint-
Denis
★

MAURITIUS
★ Port Louis

ANA

Pretoria ★

★ Maputo

Europa Island
(Fr.)

MADAGASCAR

Reunion
(Fr.)